Marilyn Monroe Unveiled: A Family History

Marilyn Monroe Unveiled: A Family History

Jason Edward Kennedy

Jennifer Jean Miller

J.J. Avenue Productions

New Jersey, 2016

Marilyn Monroe Unveiled: A Family History

Copyright © 2016 Jason Edward Kennedy and Jennifer Jean Miller

First Edition – February 11, 2016

All rights reserved. No part of this book may be used or reproduced by any means, graphic, electronic, or mechanical, including photocopying, recording, taping or by any information storage retrieval system without the written permission of the authors.

Cover illustration by Jason Edward Kennedy and Jennifer Jean Miller, inspired by 1953 Ben Ross Marilyn Monroe Photo.

All images within this book are public domain, are fair use, or are used with appropriate permissions and are credited to their respective owners.

First Edition - ISBN: 978-0-9914291-5-8

In Memory of Norma Jeane and Family.

Marilyn Monroe Unveiled | A Family History

TABLE OF CONTENTS

ACKNOWLEDGEMENTS	PAGE 1
FOREWORD	PAGE 2
CHAPTER ONE	PAGE 3
CHAPTER TWO	PAGE 17
CHAPTER THREE	PAGE 27
CHAPTER FOUR	PAGE 39
CHAPTER FIVE	PAGE 43
CHAPTER SIX	PAGE 51
CHAPTER SEVEN	PAGE 67
CHAPTER EIGHT	PAGE 89
CHAPTER NINE	PAGE 93
CHAPTER TEN	PAGE 99
MARILYN MONROE'S FAMILY	PAGE 145
CHAPTER ELEVEN	PAGE 155
CHAPTER TWELVE	PAGE 179
CHAPTER THIRTEEN	PAGE 185
CHAPTER FOURTEEN	PAGE 199
CHAPTER FIFTEEN	PAGE 209
CHAPTER SIXTEEN	PAGE 213
CHAPTER SEVENTEEN	PAGE 243
CHAPTER EIGHTEEN	PAGE 261
CHAPTER NINETEEN	PAGE 283
CALIFORNIA RELATIVES	PAGE 303
CHAPTER TWENTY	PAGE 347
CHAPTER TWENTY-ONE	PAGE 351
CONCLUSION	PAGE 367
PHOTO SOURCES AND ACKNOWLEDGMENTS	PAGE 371
AUTHOR BIOGRAPHIES	PAGE 373

Acknowledgements

Grateful acknowledgements to God above for connecting the two of us and giving us "God winks" that led us in the right direction to bring the truths to the surface that share the real life story of Marilyn Monroe.

To our children, thank you for your love and for sharing our enthusiasm about Marilyn. Jadin Edward-Su, Su Jing Kai, Chris and Amanda.

To Ted Stampfer, we thank you for your friendship and for generously sharing precious image relics from your collection.

Thank you to Roy Turner for your insights.

To family members who contributed, thank you so much: Karen, Rebecca, Helen, Velma Lu, Tera, Norman and Debbie, Tara, Joel, Scott, TY, Kim, and Helen. To family for your support: George, Aleta, Katie, Amber.

Research Insights: Grant Pinnix, Diamonds Delight, Sandra Freshner, Logan Lynn.

To Marilyn friends and friends and family overall, thank you for your support! Laura and John DeYoung, Diane Ratcliffe, April Lynne, William (Bill) Turner, Billy White, lisa Renee, Darin Scines, Russell Schultz, Robin Nickolson, Ted Stampfer, Jorg Grewe, David Leatherwood, Christine Krogull, Ian Ayres, Kelly Heart, Peter Gonzalez, Eric Woodard, Tina Faye Ayres, John DeYoung III, Kristie Wong, Joel Aronson, Jennifer Fratangelo, Vangie Rochelle, Barbara Gugluizza, Vita Thompson, Wolf RV Blender, William Bostock, Mary Belzunce, Mark Gelis, Andrea Pryke, Merja Pohjola, Caterina Piredda, Christina Goray, Ayesha Jay, Trisha Cavosi, Ken Burger, Andreea Pittei, Heidi Freeman, Stephanie Steck, Phyllis Marino, Jennifer Pena, Cristina Norcross, Glen Mordecai, Erica Cooper, Tara Tate, David Fernandez, David Solono, Kari Flowers, Maria Venidis, David Fernandez, Helen Tatsios, Debra Hull, Ann Marano, Lauren Demody, Peter Schnug, Vanlee Garba, Joseph Ayala, Mauro Laina, and our many friends in the Official Marilyn Monroe Family Group, so numerous to mention.

Foreword

This is the book that is going to overturn the way you view the life story of Marilyn Monroe. That is because the authors have taken great care to reveal facts about her life that have remained buried in archives, and left aside by biographers who did not wish to disturb the narrative.

That narrative has been of the ignored orphan child, abandoned by family and shifted around to about a dozen foster homes. To the contrary, though Marilyn Monroe's mother was hospitalized, and her father's identity was suppressed, she was not born illegitimate, nor was she without a mother. In fact, prior to Gladys's hospitalization, she was a working mother who was doting on her daughter Norma Jeane, and who was in her life during Norma Jeane's early adulthood, and transformation to Marilyn Monroe.

As Marilyn, she cast aside the legacy of Norma Jeane to appear like the Cinderella who everyone wished to rescue and shoe with the one glass slipper. However, Marilyn Monroe did not grow up without as often has been portrayed. She zigzagged from her own beginnings to push the narrative that would sell her star. And in the process, she made herself vulnerable to the worst wolves of Hollywood. They cocooned her with euphemisms, rhetoric, Freudianism, alcohol and drugs, pretending to be her advocates, while reaching their hands into her back pockets to fish out Marilyn's money and later her legacy.

These people were the death of Marilyn Monroe, and these sociopaths were a part of the informal cult that recruited Marilyn Monroe, and created a new fiction that added on to the Hollywood Cinderella story that Marilyn and family friend Grace Goddard had innocently dreamt up. These people further stole Marilyn away from those who could have been her true supporters.

In other words, Marilyn's family cringed as they watched their relative move deeper and deeper into the abyss, but when they attempted to reach her, they were brushed off and slandered. So were the people of her past who were like family, including her mother's best friend, Grace and the first woman who helped to care for her, Ida Bolender.

And then there was Marilyn's network of cousins throughout the country, relatives who the narrators that hijacked her story and estate erased then and still try to erase today. As readers will learn in this book, however, while Marilyn's relatives were often defamed as "no good," many of them were some of the most influential people of their communities, including some living in Los Angeles.

The authors of this book, who are also Marilyn's relatives strive to chip away at the myths that have suffocated the legacy of Norma Jeane Mortensen aka Marilyn Monroe since prior to her death in August of 1962. It is our hope that this book will help to restore Marilyn Monroe history in the way that it should have always been written. Readers, in turn, will become better acquainted with the authentic life story of Marilyn Monroe and Marilyn herself than they ever have, with the opportunity to truly learn about her family history.

Jason Edward Kennedy and Jennifer Jean Miller

CHAPTER ONE

MARILYN MONROE'S FAMILY history has always been assumed to be known by the general public. Fan magazine writers, reputed respected biographers, and even well known printed "news" publications communicated her story (plus *My Story,* generated later by Milton Greene) to the masses with melodramatic prose; the May 14, 1956 cover story for *TIME* magazine[1] emitted:

"Sin, sin, sin. Morning and night, that was all they talked about in the little frame house in the California poor-town where Norma Jeane Baker lived in the early years of the Depression."

"'You're wicked, Norma Jeane," the old woman used to shrill at the little girl. "You better be careful, or you know where you'll go.'"

This…is how the world became acquainted with the "new" Marilyn Monroe.

"The poor little waif has become a big business," the *TIME* article enthusiastically broadcasted.

For *TIME* magazine, it was not the facts that were important, but what they wrote about you that was most memorable. When readers picked up their copies of *TIME*, they expected what they were reading to be factual — but here it was far from.

What was written about cousin Marilyn Monroe was nothing more than a ploy to sell an entertainment myth and a legend to the public. It was, after all, Hollywood and New York, the epicenters of make-believe; movies and theater.

Certain details of Marilyn Monroe's life became the creative launching pad to elaborate and exaggerate on an already elusive past. And what a story was told; she came from a family with a history of mental illness. She was born illegitimate and neglected. She was poor, orphaned and an abused little girl fashioned after "Oliver Twist" and "Orphan Annie" who grew up to be the "Golden Girl" that Hollywood dreams are made of. She was the Atom Blonde that just wanted to be loved. *TIME* stated, "In Hollywood's pagan pantheon, Marilyn Monroe is the Goddess of Love."

Marilyn's natural and sophisticated beauty contrasted with her childlike innocence was a prescription for Hollywood success. Marilyn was "Cinderella" personified. Her story and image captured a gawking public; the agenda was clear and Marilyn Monroe was elevated to the pinnacle of 1950s Hollywood royalty.

At moments, the fragments of detail that Marilyn herself exposed to the public throughout her career seemingly supported what biographers gleaned from public records and other scattered hearsay. However, in most other cases, conflicting details were at odds with her manufactured public image that began during the reign of the fan magazines of the late 1940s.

In 1981 the newspapers unveiled a family secret — that *"Marilyn Monroe Was Legitimate Baby After All."* Her legally named father had been living and working in California her entire life.

Published reports asserted that Martin Edward Mortensen, 85, died while behind the wheel of his car from a heart attack on February 10, 1981.[2]

Hollywood publicist Jet Fore confessed that Marilyn told him to write in her first studio biography that her father was deceased. Fore said a story surfaced later that her mother Gladys had been abandoned by Marilyn's father.[3]

Marilyn Monroe Unveiled | A Family History

A Cinderella Story

MARKETING MARILYN MONROE

"Teach Me to Love You!"

Marilyn Monroe Unveiled | A Family History

That was one of the many family secrets that would be exposed over the years concerning Marilyn Monroe.

Friends of Mortensen's aired following his death that he was hurt and upset by the tales that he had abandoned Gladys and Norma Jeane. He stated that his wife and mother-in-law would not let him see his child. Yellowed newspaper clippings of the star, her birth certificate and his marriage and divorce documents were among his important papers.[4]

Marilyn used the last name of Mortenson consistently up to her marriage with Joe DiMaggio on legal documents. It is evident, in spite of speaking of the man who looked like Clark Gable, Charles Stanley Gifford and stating he was her father, that she knew otherwise. She put Martin Edward Mortensen down as her father on marriage applications for both Jim Dougherty and Joe DiMaggio. Gladys spelled the name on the birth certificate "Mortenson" instead of "Mortensen."

In her well-researched book, Sarah Churchwell[5] recognized that there was indeed inconsistency in what is now called "Marilyn's orphan stories." Churchwell stated, "As soon as one begins reading about Marilyn Monroe, one encounters immediately the idea that 'Marilyn' was a persona so artificial, so manufactured and packaged, that it eradicated the person." Churchwell continued, "The desire to view, or construct Monroe as an innocent, a creature of natural, almost helpless sexuality is such a crucial part of the story that the magazines' editors were not interested in hearing anything else."[6]

Certainly, driving Marilyn's success was a powerful media machine that contrived a simple strategy: use Marilyn's ostensibly meager beginnings, personality and sexuality to drive her character to the top of Hollywood stardom. Any contradictions discovered by astute researchers in Marilyn's story were quickly suppressed by the incestuous relationship between the fan magazines, news magazines, and the entertainment industry insiders of the 1950s; a relationship that was driven by a multimillion dollar business.[7]

And behind-the-scenes, unmistakably, the business of producing "Cinderellas" in Hollywood was literally advancing. It all began in the 1922. The Western Association of Motion Picture Advertisers (or otherwise known as WAMPAS) was actively searching for studio signed hopefuls to become the next "baby stars." This particular campaign lasted until 1934 when studio politics fractured WAMPAS and caused the organization to be dissolved. However, WAMPAS was so successful in recognizing such big stars as Clara Bow, Joan Blondell, Patsy Ruth Miller, Joan Crawford, and others, that the studio publicists unofficially took up the campaign in subsequent years.

From 1941 to 1945, which were considered the "years of war," the publicist promoted what was coined the "cheesecake" GI pin-ups. It was said, looking at pin-ups was "better than eating cheesecake!" And as happened previously, the cream of the crop "baby star" models flourished into mega movie stars — Rita Hayworth, Jane Russell, and of course, Betty Grable.

Then, by 1947 the pin-ups were losing momentum. The post war public wanted to get back to normality. A producer of calendars stated that pin-ups would be second to nature.[8] The public wanted more nature scenery instead of photographs of women.

Thus, the trend of "baby stars" had switched course. But like all successful themes, a downturn will always yield an upturn. One newspaper in 1931 reported, "No wonder Cinderella is the favorite heroine of all scenario writers. Cinderella stories happen in real life often in Hollywood. An extra girl is taken from the crowd and given a leading role. A newcomer wins over all the veterans of the screen. Every girl or boy in the country, suffering from that virulent disease, movie-struck-itis, takes new heart and buys a ticket to Hollywood. What has happened can happen again, even if the percentage is one thousand to one."[9]

And indeed, that is exactly what occurred; it did happen again.

A May 12, 1951 article by *Associated Press* reporter Bob Thomas stated that the Army needed more pin-ups. He said that the factories in Hollywood are working hard to build new Cinderellas!

And what better Cinderella than one who was a ward of the State of California for 18 years of her youth! As early as November 20, 1948 newspapers such as *The Bakersfield Californian* headlined, "Monroe, United's Newest, Hits Cinderella Highway."

Marilyn Monroe's mother married Martin Edward Mortensen (aka Edward Mortensen). Her mother Gladys wrote that Edward was Marilyn's father on her birth certificate. Marilyn continued to document that Edward Mortensen was her father on her marriage documents to Dougherty and DiMaggio, by writing "Norma Jeane Mortenson."

Marilyn Monroe Unveiled | A Family History

M-635	1822	26-036580	M-560 7791

California State Board of Health
BUREAU OF VITAL STATISTICS
STANDARD CERTIFICATE OF BIRTH

PLACE OF BIRTH: Dist. No. _____
County of _____
City or Town of _____ (No. Gen. Hospital St.; _____ Ward)
or Rural Registration District _____
Local Registered No. _____
[If birth occurred in a hospital or institution, give its NAME instead of street and number.]

FULL NAME OF CHILD Baby Norma Jeane Mortensen
[If child is not yet named, make supplemental report as directed.]

PERSONAL AND STATISTICAL PARTICULARS

SEX OF CHILD	Twin, Triplet, or Other	Number in Order of Birth	DATE OF BIRTH
Female			June 1, 1926

FATHER		MOTHER	
FULL NAME	Edward Mortensen	FULL MAIDEN NAME	Gladys Monroe
RESIDENCE	Unknown	RESIDENCE	5454 W. Blvd. Hwd. Calif
COLOR OR RACE	Cauc	COLOR OR RACE	Cauc
AGE AT LAST BIRTHDAY	29	AGE AT LAST BIRTHDAY	24
BIRTHPLACE	Calif	BIRTHPLACE	Mex
OCCUPATION	Baker	OCCUPATION	Motion Picture Indu.

Number of children born to this mother, including present birth: 3
Number of children of this mother now living: 1

CERTIFICATE OF ATTENDING PHYSICIAN OR MIDWIFE

I hereby certify that I attended the birth of this child, who was Born alive at 9:30 A.M. on the date above stated.

(Signature) A. M. Leeman M.D.
Dated 6-1 1926 Phys
Address 1100 Mission Road, LA
Filed JUN-5 '26 19__

Given name added from a supplemental report _____ 19__

8

STATE OF CALIFORNIA
DEPARTMENT OF PUBLIC HEALTH
VITAL STATISTICS

STANDARD CERTIFICATE OF MARRIAGE
PERSONAL AND STATISTICAL PARTICULARS

Place of Marriage: County of LOS ANGELES
Local Registered No. 12654

GROOM
- Full Name: James Edward Dougherty
- Residence: 14747 Archwood, L.A.
- Color or Race: white
- Age at Last Birthday: 21 (4/12/21)
- Single
- Number of Marriage: First
- Birthplace: Los Angeles
- Occupation: Shaper operator
- Industry: Lockheed A.C.
- Name of Father: Edward Dougherty
- Birthplace of Father: Colorado
- Maiden Name of Mother: Ethel Beatty
- Birthplace of Mother: Colorado

BRIDE
- Full Name: Norma Jeane Mortensen
- Residence: 11348 Nebraska Ave
- Color or Race: white
- Age at Last Birthday: 16 (6/1/26)
- Single
- Number of Marriage: first
- Birthplace: Los Angeles Calif.
- Occupation: none
- Industry: none
- Name of Father: E. Mortensen
- Birthplace of Father: unknown
- Maiden Name of Mother: none
- Birthplace of Mother: unknown

WE, the groom and bride named in this Certificate, hereby certify that the information given therein is correct, to the best of our knowledge and belief.

James E. Dougherty — Groom
Norma Jeane Mortensen — Bride

CERTIFICATE OF PERSON PERFORMING CEREMONY

I hereby certify that James Edward Dougherty and Norma Jeane Mortensen were joined in marriage by me in accordance with the laws of the State of California, at Westwood this 19th day of June 1942.

Signature of Witness to the Marriage: Marian E. Dougherty
Signature of Person Performing the Ceremony: B.H. Lingenfelder
Official position: Minister of Gospel
Residence: 2319 Purdue L.A.

FILED JUN 22 1942

Marilyn Monroe Unveiled | A Family History

CERTIFICATE OF REGISTRY OF MARRIAGE — No. 268
BOOK 1074 PAGE 195

Field	Groom
Name	Joseph Paul Di Maggio
Age	39
Usual Residence	2150 Beach, San Francisco, S.F.
Color or Race	White
Marital Status	Divorced
Number of Previous Marriages	1
Birthplace	Calif.
Father of Groom	Joseph Di Maggio — Italy
Maiden Name of Mother	Rosalie Mercurio — Italy

Field	Bride
Name	Norma Jeane Dougherty
Age	25
Usual Residence	882 No. Doheny Dr., Los Angeles, L.A.
Color or Race	White
Marital Status	Divorced
Number of Previous Marriages	1
Birthplace	Calif.
Father of Bride	Edward Mortenson — unknown
Maiden Name of Mother	Gladys Monroe — Mexico
Maiden Name of Bride if Previously Married	Norma Jean Mortenson

Bride's signature: Norma Jeane Mortenson
Groom's signature: Joseph P. DiMaggio

County Clerk: Martin Mongan
County of Issue of License: San Francisco
Date License Issued: JAN 14 1954
License Number: 8595

I hereby certify that the above named bride and groom were joined by me in marriage in accordance with the laws of the State of California on January 14, 1954, San Francisco, California.

Signature of Witness: Tom DiMaggio
Address of Witness: 3789 Fillmore St., San Francisco, Calif.

Signature of Person Performing Ceremony: Charles Peery
Official Title: Municipal Judge
Address: San Francisco, Calif.

Date Received by Local Registrar: JAN 15 1954
Local Registrar: Thomas A. Toomey, San Francisco County

If the claim was nine months or 18 years, it made little difference to the accuracy of Marilyn Monroe's orphan story. This bold exaggeration set Norma Jeane in motion and there was no turning back destiny on Hollywood's Cinderella treadmill.

The 1951 headlines made no mistake about it.[10]

"Hollywood Will Bring Back to Life Cheesecake---

The Birth of New Cinderellas"

And leading the pack was none other than Marilyn Monroe. In fact, she was named "Miss Cheesecake" by the G.I. Editors of *Stars and Stripes* in Germany for 1951. Reporter Bob Thomas of the Associated Press remarked that Marilyn had moves reminiscent of Jean Harlow and called her "well qualified" for the title.[11]

While Marilyn Monroe stole the "Cheesecake" fanfare, there was also another family secret hidden in full public view. In fact, that "secret" even accused Marilyn of using some of *her* stories to exaggerate Marilyn's orphan story further. The 1950s public was not privy to those details because Marilyn Monroe herself, the studio publicist and the media at large distorted and covered up those facts. Marilyn was the prime focus for the studios and certainly, the public did not need to be distracted with yet another "Orphan Annie" screen siren while they were concurrently promoting Marilyn.

The studios had laid their bets firmly on Marilyn Monroe; she had the right story, at the right "baby star" moment, and the camera ready physical beauty to sell Hollywood tickets. That is certainly where the word "business" in the term *show business* comes from.

It was never about truth or truth in reporting, it was about marketing and promotion. And according to an explanation by a fan magazine publisher, the type of stories that best suited Marilyn Monroe were crafted to generate public sympathy. He stated, "Liz [Elizabeth Taylor] is a stronger woman, more independent, and doesn't need public sympathy. Marilyn was too sensitive, too human."[12] In other words, the studios had a plan to hyper-promote Marilyn.

In 1956 *TIME* magazine sent out Ezra Goodman, its Hollywood correspondent of four years. His task — to research Marilyn Monroe for the cover of *TIME*.

The Terre Haute Tribune. Tuesday, January 8, 1957.

... Ezra Goodman (of Time mag's H'wood branch) has a new romance, Dory Langden, songwriter ...

Goodman stated, "I interviewed more than a hundred of Monroe's friends and enemies, spent a good deal of time with her and then transmitted my thoroughly documented findings — running to almost book length — to New York via the magazine's private teletype system."

He continued, "This material was then put into the editorial meat grinder and came out the other end, as it invariably did, couched in *TIME*'s portentous and stentorian gobbledygook and without much resemblance to what had been fed it."

"[They] turned non-fiction into fiction," he lambasted.

Marilyn Monroe Unveiled | A Family History

Hollywood was literally creating Cinderellas. As early as 1948, newspapers were already promoting Marilyn Monroe as an orphan: "Making Miss Monroe's film fortune even more spectacular is her youthful years, 18 of which she passed as a ward of the state of California."

4 Saturday, November 20, 1948 — The Bakersfield Californian

Monroe, United's Newest, Hits Cinderella Highway

Hollywood's newest Cinderella story stars a beautiful, 20-year-old Los Angeles girl, Marilyn Monroe, who was signed to a long-term contract by Producer Lester Cowan, it was announced today.

A young Bergman-like person, Miss Monroe's road to stardom starts in Producer Cowan's forthcoming Marx Brothers-Ilona Massey-Vera Ellen-Marion Hutton film-comedy, "Love Happy," which will be released early next year by United Artists. She makes her bow in the Groucho Marx sequences, which were just completed in Hollywood.

Making Miss Monroe's film fortune even more spectacular is her youthful years, 18 of which she passed as a ward of the state of California.

Immediate plans for her next screen appearance have been concluded by Mr. Cowan. She will be cast for an important supporting role in his next production "The Customer's Always Right."

Marilyn Monroe Unveiled | A Family History

Oxnard Press-Courier
SERVING VENTURA COUNTY

Marilyn Monroe Unveiled

OXNARD, CALIFORNIA, FRIDAY, FEBRUARY 10, 1956

Marilyn Monroe Unveiled | A Family History

About his research, Goodman emphasized, "Monroe's version of things, of course was only one version. And at different times, she has given out varying versions."

He stated that those who were involved with her upbringing had their own stories and that their stories were corroborated better than Marilyn's.

What was significant for the public about the *TIME* cover story misrepresenting the facts about Marilyn Monroe's family history? Nothing. Goodman recalled in 1961, "as one relieved Twentieth Century-Fox press agent, who had been concerned about the *TIME* cover said to me when it was all over: "Well, it's just another version of the same old thing Little Orphan Annie in Hollywood.' He offered his condolences for the effort that had needlessly gone into the story."

TIME correspondent Ezra Goodman demonstrated keen insight, he understood exactly what had happened. "A Hollywood story at *TIME* is of no cosmic significance in a world that is concerned with more important problems than getting a few glimmers of fact about a movie blonde."

Thus, the entertainment value of Marilyn Monroe was just that — entertainment and nothing more of paramount importance.

Beyond the fanfare of the 1956 *TIME* cover story and Marilyn's veil, there were many relatives and they did care about the direction her career was taking her.

While Marilyn Monroe was a young model and beginning to forge her climb to fame during the middle to late 1940s and moving into 1950, the weight, power, and influence of the media, which consisted of her publicists, fan magazines, news magazines, and Marilyn Monroe herself, pressured those family members who knew the actual version of the truth to stay publicly quiet.

The pattern of silence would remain for the relatives of Marilyn Monroe until the writing of *My Sister Marilyn* by Berniece and Mona Miracle, *Marilyn Monroe & Joe DiMaggio - Love In Japan, Korea & Beyond* by Jennifer Jean Miller, and finally this book; *Marilyn Monroe Unveiled: A Family History* by Jason Edward Kennedy (Marilyn's second cousin) and Jennifer Jean Miller.

As the *TIME* cover story broke in 1956 many of Marilyn Monroe's relatives (including those non-relatives who directly cared for Marilyn as a child) had already passed away some three to seven years earlier during the early 1950s and late 1940s. The relatives that passed on included: Grace McKee Goddard (Marilyn's legal guardian), Edith Ana Atchinson (Grace McKee's aunt Ana Lower), Ida Martin (the mother of Olive Brunings – Olive was married to Gladys Monroe's brother Marion Otis Monroe) and most of Gladys Monroe's aunts and uncles, bar one. Indeed, the public at large did not know about Gladys Monroe's Hogan and Monroe relatives. The Hogans and the Monroes were another hidden family secret beneath Marilyn's veil.

What remained of Marilyn Monroe's relatives after the late 1940s were many of Gladys Monroe's first cousins (children of her Hogan aunts and uncles and descendants of theirs), other Hogan and Monroe relatives and Marilyn's first cousins (and descendants of theirs), the son and daughters of Marion Otis Monroe – namely Jack Monroe, Ida Mae Monroe, Elizabeth Monroe, and their mother Olive Monroe.

Many first cousins and extended cousins gradually had less interaction and contact with each other on the different family lines after the 1960s.

Those first cousins and extended cousins that knew about and followed Marilyn's career were amazed and excited at her rapid seizure of Hollywood fame. Her death on August 4, 1962, however,

---

Las Vegas Daily Optic

Thursday, March 1, 1956

Try And Stop Me
By BENNETT CERF

Ezra Goodman, magazine representative in Hollywood movie circles, asked Producer Sam Goldwyn if he planned ever to write his memoirs. "I will never write my autobiography," asserted Mr. Goldwyn, "as long as I live."

When Goodman is interviewing a victim, thorough is the word for him. Victim Humphrey Bogart, for example, opines, "Goodman is the kind of guy who sits right across the table from you, looks you square in the eyes and ask you what color your eyes are."

caught them by grim surprise; they were shocked, saddened, and depressed by it. And many knew something went horribly wrong with cousin Norma Jeane behind-the-scenes. In fact, it is known that one of Gladys Monroe's Hogan first cousins wanted to hire an investigator because she was very suspicious of Marilyn's death, but it is not known to what extent it was pursued, if any.

While most relatives who knew what was going on felt some sort of foul play had taken Marilyn's life, many were reluctant to become involved. Firstly, evidence contrary to suicide was difficult to prove at the time, especially because of the high profile names of those individuals involved. Secondly, the intimidation factor, after all, it was being reported that a United States President might have been involved in her death.

As a result, Marilyn's tragic demise was taken at face value, whether by acceptance of the situation or frustration in not being able to do anything about it.

As time progressed, Marilyn's relatives certainly had less interaction and contact with each other. Descendants of each Hogan line and those who were more directly involved on the Monroe side of the family inevitably lost contact with each other.

While the public has taken for granted that Marilyn and her mother Gladys had little to no relatives growing up, factually the opposite was true. And, in fact, many of their relatives were living right in Los Angeles, California.

Marilyn did not bring some of her relatives into the media frenzy until she was confronted that her mother was still living. All along, another family secret until 1952, Marilyn had been leading the public to believe that she was an orphan; that both of her parents were dead. A January 5, 1951 story asserted that Marilyn's parents were both deceased shortly after her birth 22 years prior (another fabrication since Marilyn was nearly 25). One detail erred that her father was killed in a car wreck and the other that her mother could not care for her due to illness, and she perished soon after.[13]

When Marilyn decided to bring family members into the light with her stories to the press, the tall tales were unfavorable. That is why those cousins more directly involved on the Monroe family side chose (and still choose) to remain isolated from the media, feeling powerless to change the public's perceptions and frustrated with their interaction with previous so-called biographers who twisted their words and their family history to fit the "Little Orphan Annie in Hollywood" story.

Consequently, the 1956 *TIME* cover story went forward unchallenged. Undeniably, the relatives of Marilyn Monroe never had the "media might" to conquer what amounted to a highly sophisticated, well-funded and calculated marketing scheme to promote the "new" Marilyn Monroe to the public. Norma Jeane and the people who promoted her screen personality literally molded her into the Cinderella-like character of Marilyn Monroe regardless of her family facts.

CHAPTER ONE Supporting Resources

[1] *TIME* magazine – Monday, May 14, 1956. Cover story on Marilyn Monroe.
[2] *Authorities believe Mira Loma man was Marilyn Monroe's dad* – The San Bernardino County Sun, February 12, 1981.
[3] *Marilyn Monroe Was Legitimate Baby After All* – Santa Cruz Sentinel, Santa Cruz, California. February 12, 1981.
[4] *Marilyn Monroe Was Legitimate Baby After All* – Santa Cruz Sentinel, Santa Cruz, California. February 12, 1981.
[5] *The Many Lives of Marilyn Monroe* – Sarah Churchwell.
[6] *The Many Lives of Marilyn Monroe* – Sarah Churchwell.
[7] Anthony Slide-*Inside the Hollywood Fan Magazine: A History of Star Makers, Fabricators, and Gossip Mongers* – University Press of Mississippi, Feb 26, 2010
[8] *Pin-up Girls Lose Out in '47 Calendars* – The Mason City Globe-Gazette, Mason City, Iowa. December 18, 1946.
[9] *Frances Dee A Cinderella* – The Lewiston Daily Sun, September 12, 1931.
[10] *Hollywood Revives Cheesecake -- New Cinderellas Are Born* – Southern Illinoisan, Carbondale, Illinois, May 12, 1951.
[11] *Marilyn Monroe Gaining Fame as Pin-up Favorite* – The Paris News, 5 Jan 1951, Fri, Page 6
[12] Anthony Slide-*Inside the Hollywood Fan Magazine: A History of Star Makers, Fabricators, and Gossip Mongers* – University Press of Mississippi, Feb 26, 2010
[13] *First New Pin-Up Queen Of War Would Rather Read Than Pose* – The Plain Speaker, Hazleton, PA., January 5, 1951.

CHAPTER TWO

WHILE THE "OLD" Marilyn innocently forged a Hollywood career (from pinup to film) with the help of studio publicist at United Artists, Twentieth Century-Fox Film Corporation and the influence of her legal guardian Grace McKee Goddard. The promotion of the "new" Marilyn was much different.

As early as January 1955, the releasing of multiple newspaper articles across the country began promoting the "new" Marilyn Monroe. The release was on par with a professional propaganda campaign to literally win the hearts and minds of the public. At its core, it was designed to manipulate the public's perceptions of what the press coined "Marilyn's new friends." However, rather than the manipulation occurring on a television or a screen in a theater or on stage, it was played out in real-time across America, and no doubt, the world.

"Their" ability to manipulate through mass communication was executed for effect. A serial article by Jim Cook (*New York Post* and Mirror Enterprises Company) began making its rounds by July 11, 1956 promoting Marilyn as a hotshot entrepreneur and business woman, Cook compared her split from Hollywood and her move to New York to a military style campaign with her headquarters located in the Waldorf Astoria Hotel. He stated that she wanted to start her own company Marilyn Monroe Productions and learn how to be a better actress.

What was advertised as Marilyn Monroe's break from Hollywood was in reality a hostile takeover by Marilyn's "new" friends. They used a "carrot and stick tactic" to motivate her to come to New York. In the beginning, these seemingly unrelated individuals were privately working to drive the "new Marilyn" theme. The explanation was that Marilyn wanted to better herself through her acting. The illusion was simply that they wanted to help her to better herself. While they conspired to unite together, one was the odd man out. The clear leader would continue to do everything in his power to control Marilyn Monroe over the course of seven years; from 1955 to 1962. He had the allies, the resources, and the psychological reach to pursue his exploitive agenda, essentially without restraint, and they used a false orphan story to cocoon Marilyn Monroe.

Negative and damaging rumors quickly began to jeopardize the criminal intent of Marilyn's "new" friends beginning early in 1955. While some media professionals caught on to the unethical problems brewing behind the cameras, her "new" friends were unfortunately able to divert the attention of her surviving relatives, the public, and subsequently the police through their abuse and control over mass media. Marilyn Monroe was indeed under siege and her "new" friends literally got away with financial extortion and her murder for over fifty years — until now.

The media influence of a *TIME* Magazine cover story held control over how Marilyn Monroe's family history was presented to the world. Marilyn's relatives were powerless to change it especially since many of her older and more well-informed relatives had already passed away before 1954. Ezra Goodman, even with his reputation and no-nonsense journalistic acumen, could not influence the outcome of how the public would perceive the *TIME* article. However, his research, some of which was formally released in his aptly titled 1961 book *The Fifty Year Decline and Fall of Hollywood* was one of the first to document a fabricated "Little Orphan Annie in Hollywood" story that would turn against Marilyn Monroe and eventually be used a tool of her destruction.

Marilyn Monroe Unveiled | A Family History

What Ezra Goodman found reveals the extent that *TIME* magazine, media professionals, and Marilyn's "new friends" would go to promote and exaggerate the false orphan story. *TIME* focused on two people who they claimed were an overly devoted religious family that foster cared Marilyn between her birth in 1926 until she was eight in 1934. Ida Bolender and husband Albert were described as a "lowly" couple who bordered children. Future biographers would claim that her mother Gladys abandoned Marilyn during that period and was in mental institutions the entire duration, which of course is another falsehood. The 1956 *TIME* article boldly stated, "When Norma Jeane was twelve days old, she was put to board (for $25 a month) with a family of religious zealots who lived in a sort of 'semi-rural semi-slum' on the outskirts of Los Angeles." However, factually, Ida Bolender and her husband Albert W. Bolender (he had a stable job as a letter carrier — a postman) legally adopted two children, Lester and Nancy, and provided childcare for a single mother, watching Marilyn while Gladys

Albert Bolender had a stable job as a a mailman as documented in newspaper directories.

worked nights in Hollywood. Ida, who was essentially a nanny-for-hire, told Ezra Goodman, "Most of the time …Mrs. Baker was with me. She stayed in Hollywood when working nights, as a negative cutter, and stayed with me while working days." The 1930 Census report verifies that Gladys was indeed a boarder at Bolender home, along with Marilyn (aka Norma Jeane).

Ida Bolender was never previously accused or charged with abusing Marilyn, yet she ended up being directly slandered by *TIME*.

While Goodman's research into the Bolenders was summarily rejected, *TIME* went forward with what he described as their policy to "divert its readers and the contents be damned."

Ida Bolender was painted as a mean-spirited religious foster mother who severely chastised a young Marilyn. *TIME* quoted Ida as saying, "You're wicked, Norma Jeane. You better be careful, or you know where you'll go."

Goodman knew exactly why the Bolenders never publicly came forward to challenge the *TIME* article. He revealed, "The Bolenders, who were wrongfully described as 'a family of religious zealots' living in a 'semi-rural semi-slum' on the outskirts of Los Angeles, were mollified by *TIME* with a cash payment."

Both Gladys Baker and Norma Jeane are listed as boarders in the 1930 Census.

Marilyn Monroe Unveiled | A Family History

While external pressures suppressed the truth about Marilyn's family history to promote the Cinderella story, there were internal pressures as well to hide the truth and "protect" Marilyn's movie star career. Marilyn's half-sister Berniece Miracle stated, "and so often [Marilyn] would repeat to me as we said goodbye, 'Please promise me you won't give out stories about me.' And I would always say, 'I promise.' I had vowed to myself that I would never be a troublesome relative." The point was clear, and both the media and Marilyn continued to kept the fantasy alive; none of Marilyn's family wanted to be that troublesome relative.

Behind-the-scenes, Marilyn Monroe's relatives did care about the family defamation that was being reported in the media. While the public accepted the false stories as fact, some of Marilyn's relatives and her nanny Ida gossiped among themselves. In a sort of hypocritical fashion, Ida Bolender, who accepted a cash payment from *TIME* magazine some seven years earlier, wrote a letter to Marilyn's half-sister Berniece Miracle in 1962. She stated, "It has almost broken my heart to read the terrible stories that have been written about her early childhood, when I know personally they are so untrue."[1] Ida Bolender emphasized to Ezra Goodman in 1956, "She was never neglected and always nicely dressed."

Marilyn's half-sister Berniece Baker Miracle and niece Mona Rae Miracle publicly documented the reason why Marilyn fabricated the conditions of her childhood. They revealed in their 1994 book, *My Sister Marilyn*, that the stories about Marilyn's childhood were made up by Grace McKee Goddard (Marilyn's legal guardian) and Marilyn herself for a biographical story that the studios required. Berniece and Mona wrote:

> Grace takes the phone and excitedly tells Berniece about the story that she and Marilyn have just invented. 'We had to have a biographical story and we had to have one fast! We hadn't dreamed that we would need one, and suddenly things were happening too fast. We made up a story about Marilyn having no parents and being in a lot of foster homes and spending time in an orphanage and Marilyn signed it as being the truth.' Their breathless fantasy seems unrestrained by the fact that Gladys is often at Marilyn's side. They know the public loves a rags-to-riches drama. That story was Grace's idea. She built it around the fact that Marilyn had spent time in an orphanage. Other than that, it wasn't true, but the story served its publicity purpose. And it kept reporters away from Mamita.[2]

Using Marilyn's attendance in the orphanage as a means of self-promotion to get what they wanted was not a unique occurrence. Grace McKee Goddard used the same tactic to gain sympathy years earlier when Marilyn married her first husband James Dougherty on June 19, 1942. Dougherty, who was initially hesitant about the marriage, stated in a 1964 interview, "Doc[i] and Grace were moving to Huntington West Virginia where Doc was being transferred and Norma Jeane was going to have to go back to the orphanage. Grace told this to my mother."[3] As a result, James was persuaded to marry Norma Jeane.

Grace McKee Goddard was the early driving force in Marilyn's career. Her exaggerations about Marilyn became a means of manipulating others for whatever perceived advantage it could afford her or Marilyn. They both used the tactic to manipulate situations in their favor and to help drive Marilyn's early career from pin-up model to movie star.

Recall that in 1981 Jet Fore (Twentieth Century-Fox) stated that the details of her very first studio biography were fabricated because that is what Marilyn wanted.[4]

These independent quotes, which were documented years apart by Marilyn's half-sister Berniece, publicist Jet Fore who wrote that first studio biography, and James Dougherty all help to verify the exaggerations of Marilyn's early life.

---

[i] Ervin Silliman "Doc" Goddard married Grace McKee Goddard August 10, 1935 in Las Vegas, Nevada. He had three children from a previous marriage: Eleanor "Bebe"(born December 17, 1926), John (born June 4, 1928), and Josephine (born October 19,1930).

Marilyn Monroe Unveiled | A Family History

Nonetheless, even as Marilyn's half-sister Berniece unveiled Marilyn in 1994, the legend and propaganda was still too strong to be derailed, as the myth and legend persisted. It is continually perpetuated today by the media and by those who hijacked Marilyn's estate, her image, her voice, and indeed her soul.

The fabricated biographical story that Grace, Marilyn, and the studios promoted took its toll on Marilyn's half-sister Berniece. Mona Miracle speaking about Berniece and a collection of fan magazines wrote, "articles that perpetuate the orphan story, adding on more foster homes each year, upset her and are flung into the trash can." In fact, Berniece even tried to insulate her mother Gladys from the false stories. Mona explained, "A story appears in the media saying that Marilyn was raped as a child. Berniece shudders to think of Gladys's reaction if she should chance upon it. She is grateful that Gladys restricts her reading to Christian Science literature. Berniece explains to an old friend that the stories in the movie magazines never tell the truth about Marilyn's personal life."

By unapologetically supporting the continued fabrication of her past, Marilyn Monroe inadvertently began to isolate herself from some relatives.

What started out as an innocent and exaggerated biographical story to separate herself in the media from other movie hopefuls, the "Little Orphan Annie in Hollywood" story became instrumental in forming a set of circumstances around Marilyn that would exacerbate her situation drastically — a perfect storm.

Descendants of Della Mae Hogan[i] (through her son Marion Monroe) reported that the more famous Marilyn became the less they saw of her as they felt their relationship with her was diminishing over time. In fact, a descendant of Jack Monroe (Marilyn's first cousin) even stated that the name "Marilyn Monroe" was persona non grata in their household while growing up, apparently because Jack was so disillusioned and disgusted with the negative fanfare and Marilyn's death. Nonetheless, while Marilyn was alive, Jack Monroe still continued to keep in contact with his cousin Marilyn. On November 8, 1954 she received a typed phone message to call him while she was in Cedars of Lebanon Hospital for her surgery (November 7 through November 12, 1954) which addressed her female reproductive issues from painful endometriosis. She was still using the legal name of "DiMaggio," although divorced from Joe. Jack Monroe and Marilyn would continue to stay in touch through her life and was later found listed in her personal 1961 phone directory even while some biographers would later slanderously claim that he molested Marilyn when they were both young teens.

In another case, after Marilyn became famous, a descendant of Ida Mae Monroe wanted to meet Marilyn when she was a child, but unfortunately that never happened because Marilyn kept putting off the invitation. And again, Ida Bolender, with whom Gladys and Marilyn stayed with from 1926 to 1934 also had her invitations to see Marilyn ignored. Ida told Goodman, "I talked to Norma Jeane on the phone about two years ago [approximately 1954 or 1955] when her mother was staying with me between times in the hospitals. On the phone I said, 'Norma Jeane, why don't you come to see me?' She said 'I always thought because I'm in the movies you might not like me any more.' 'Because you're in the movies don't make any difference,' I said. 'You come to see me.' 'But she didn't.'"

Astute followers of Marilyn Monroe may interpret her response, "I always thought because I'm in the movies you might not like me any more" as some sort of "proof" that Ida Bolender chastised Marilyn with religious fervor as a child for watching movies. However, this orphan story interpretation is challenged when the reader considers that Marilyn's early orphan stories were defaming Ida and her husband Albert and they knew it! Of course their names were never used directly in the fan magazines, however, Ida Bolender, who was never interviewed prior to Ezra Goodman in 1956, told him that she always wanted to contact "someone" because she knew Marilyn was never abused as a child and she certainly was never an orphan. Ida Bolender wanted to defend herself and Marilyn's childhood from the claims of abuse.

TIME magazine, disregarding Ezra Goodman's research, used Ida's statement that she was a churchgoer and not a moviegoer and used it as exaggerated fodder to support the "Little Orphan Annie

---
[i] Della Mae Hogan was Marilyn Monroe's grandmother. She passed away in 1927.

Marilyn Monroe Unveiled | A Family History

Marilyn's first cousin Jack Monroe sent her a telegram in 1954.

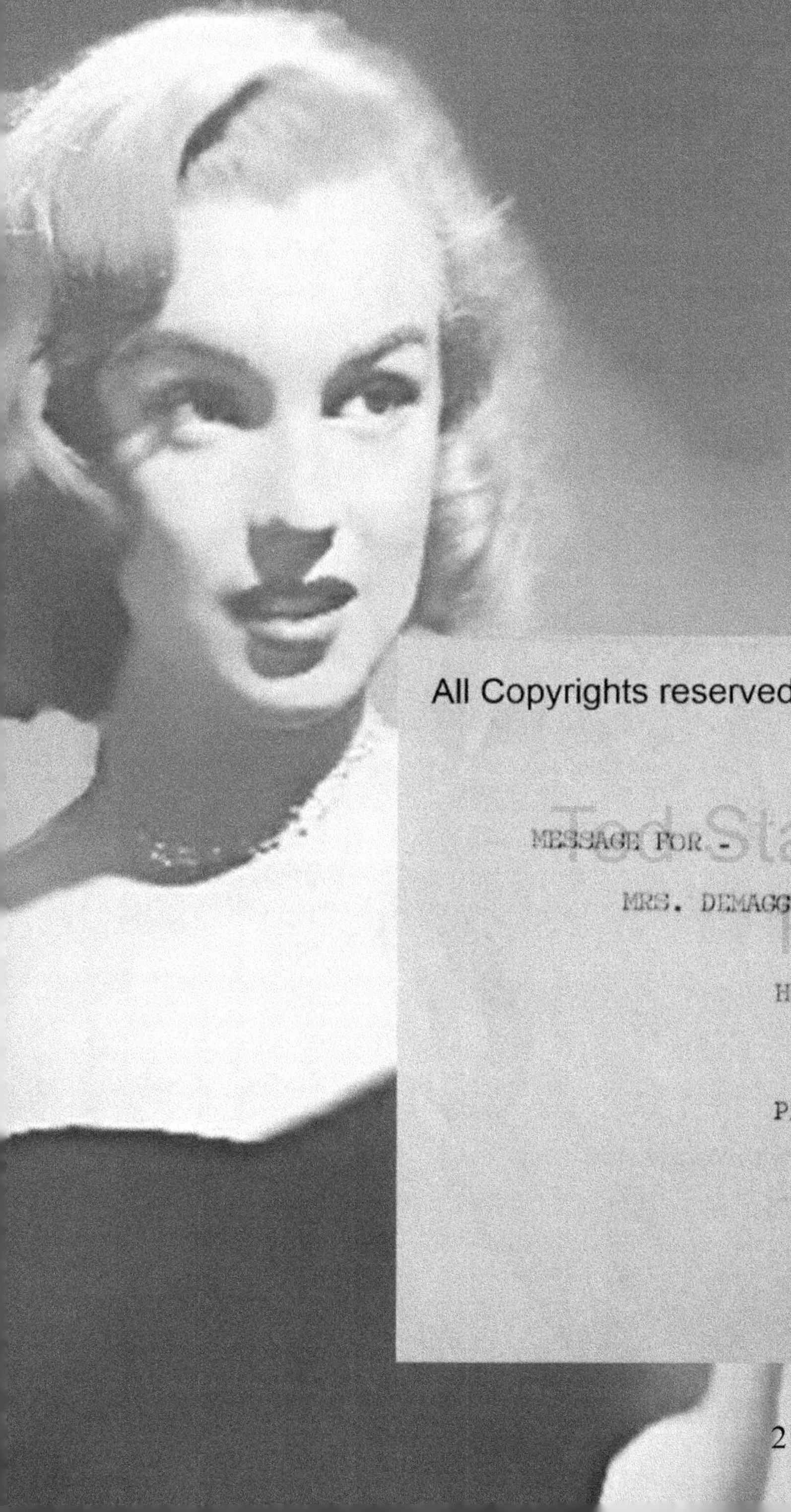

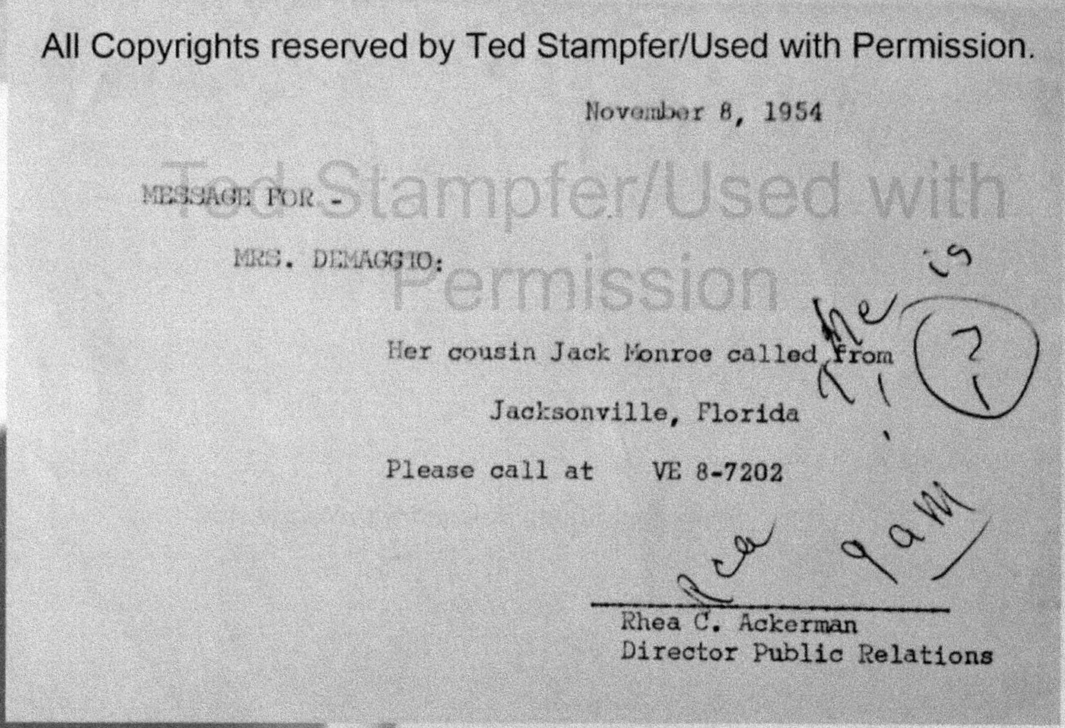

All Copyrights reserved by Ted Stampfer/Used with Permission.

November 8, 1954

MESSAGE FOR -

MRS. DEMAGGIO:

Her cousin Jack Monroe called from

Jacksonville, Florida

Please call at   VE 8-7202

Rhea C. Ackerman
Director Public Relations

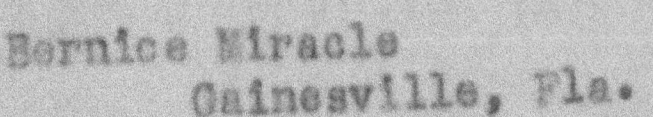

Jack Monroe listed in Marilyn's personal 1962 phone directory.

```
Bernice Miracle                                    Franklin
        Gainesville, Fla.
                                                   2-0594


Harold Mirisch (Lottie)                            CR 5-3000
        1545 Lexington Ave.
                                                   CR 6-2301
                                   Studio:         HO 9-6161


                                                   EL 5-
MM
        444 East 57th Street
        New York 22                                2385
                 12305 - 5th Helena Drive          476-1890
                 Los Angeles 49
                 Studio Office Private             CR 6-6000


                                                   MA 8-
Jack Monroe
                                                   1465
```

All Copyrights reserved by Ted Stampfer/Used with Permission.

in Hollywood" story. Ezra Goodman stated, "The 'religious family' [in the *TIME* cover story on Marilyn] who were supposed to have abused her as a child were presumably Mr. And Mrs. Albert Bolender of Hawthorne, a small suburb of Los Angeles."

While Ida may have had some aversion to actresses and Hollywood in general (no evidence exist as of this writing except that she stated she was a churchgoer and not a moviegoer), she told Marilyn, "because you're in the movies don't make any difference. You come to see me."

Clearly, Ida Bolender still wanted to have a relationship with Marilyn in 1954 and 1955 regardless if she was an actress or not and even though Marilyn was publicly slandering her and her husband.

Some personal insight into Ida Bolender's personality was documented when Ezra Goodman interviewed her in 1956. He noticed a magazine prominently displayed on her living room coffee table containing the works of poet and playwright Edna St. Vincent Millay. Millay's husband was the painter and actor Charles Frederick Ellis, yet she was known as being openly bisexual and publicly explored the issues of female sexuality and feminism as early as 1920. Ida Bolender at least had some interest in the arts and possibly followed the issues of feminism, which is counter to the "lowly" and religious fanatic that *TIME* accused of chastising puritan beliefs down Norma Jeane's throat.

TIME magazine's agenda, nor Marilyn's, was never intended to slander the Bolenders specifically for past transgressions. *TIME* 's agenda was to sell the new Marilyn Monroe and her new friends to the public. And certainly, to sell a rags-to-riches Cinderella story. That is why the Bolenders received a payoff directly from *TIME*. Both *TIME* magazine and Marilyn justified that agenda on the fact that Marilyn — was in the movies! And movies, of course, are make-believe just like the stories Marilyn told the public about her childhood.

If Marilyn did realize how her orphan stories hurt relatives, she overlooked the severity of it because it was not real life. Cinderella was the role she played — in Hollywood.

Marilyn's statement, "I always thought because I'm in the movies you might not like me any more" may have been a thinly veiled attempt to acknowledge that the Bolenders were upset with her because she was publicly lying about them to support her movie career; she justified it because she was working "in the movies."

Ezra Goodman stated in 1961 about his early research into Marilyn:

> It is understandable, then, that putting together any sort of remotely searching story about Marilyn Monroe takes on all the aspects of a pathological detective story, a blend of bertha the Sewing Machine Girl and Raymond Chandler, with maybe a dash of Tennessee Williams. The difficulties in the way of ascertaining the facts about Monroe are many. For one thing, she herself is not very accessible now. She is sick (or maybe just scared at having to prove that she is an actress in *Bus Stop*) and, at this writing, is incommunicado in St. Vincent's hospital with what is described as bronchitis while Joshua Logan is desperately trying to find scenes to shoot around her. (Monroe like to hide out in hospitals — and in ladies rooms.) And, when you get to Monroe, if you are lucky, she is disarmingly vague and uninformative. The people around her only complicate matters. There is a conspiracy of silence around her, perhaps because of the high publicity value of anything involving her and also because of the sensitive nature of much of her past (Monroe is reported as being scared to death about what *TIME* Magazine will unearth about her).

Marilyn was clearly in an awkward position with relatives and the press. She certainly understood Hollywood movies were fantasy and also understood her role in the self-promotion of her character. She was pressured to be notoriously vague about her relatives for fear of it having a negative impact on her career and had to ride that fine line between the press and her secret family relationships.

When Ida Bolender spoke to Marilyn on the phone sometime in 1954 or 1955, Ida was still boardering Marilyn's mother Gladys in between her stays in the hospital. Recall that she stated to Ezra Goodman in 1956, "I talked to Norma Jeane on the phone about two years ago when her mother

Marilyn Monroe Unveiled | A Family History

Gladys Monroe and her best friend Grace McKee Goddard probably met sometime in 1923 or earlier. By 1924 they were living together at 1211 Hyperion Avenue in Los Angeles, California.

Los Angeles City Precinct No. 528
LOS ANGELES COUNTY, CALIFORNIA, 1924

164 Musch, Ed H, sht mtl wrkr, 4206 Ellie st, DS

Mc

165 McAulay, Mrs Juanita, hswf, 4227 Virginia av, DS
166 McAulay, Jr, Oscar M, hlth offr, 4227 Virginia av, R
334 McAulay, William B, svryr, 4227 Virginia av, R
335 McAuliffe, Mrs Amelia, at hm, 4206 Lexington av, DS
167 McAuliffe, Edward S, slsmn, 4206 Lexington av, R
168 McBride, Miss Rose M, clrk, 1122 Sanborn av, R
169 McCarty, Mrs Anna M, hswf, 1254 Hyperion av, D
336 McCloskey, Miss Anna S, mscn, 1138 Manzanita st, R
549 McCullough, Charles W, rtrd, 1751 Childs av, P
172 McKee, Bertis J, insrnce, 4175 Lexington av, R
173 McKee, Mrs Grace, flm cuttr, 1211 Hyperion av, R
174 McLean, Mrs Murray T, hswf, 4337 Sunset blvd, R
175 McLean, Norman E, rl est, 4337 Sunset blvd, R
176 McPherson, Dean, clrk, 1205 Myra st, R

was staying with me between times in hospitals." Her statement is accurate at face value because Gladys Monroe was staying at the Rockhaven Sanatorium at 2713 Honolulu Avenue, Verdugo City in California which was about 30 miles from Ida's home in Hawthorne California.

In 1964 the Bolenders were once again interviewed for the next main Marilyn documentary after the TIME cover story and her death — *The Legend of Marilyn Monroe*. Would the Bolenders voluntarily subject themselves to more slander after the TIME cover story fiasco in 1956? Would they again accept monies to have their story twisted a second time?

Whatever was captured by the interviewer documenting the Bolenders defending Marilyn's childhood, no question, ended up on the cutting room floor. The content of the interview never addressed anything that resembled what the Bolenders told Ezra Goodman, except that "[Marilyn] was a well-behaved child." In fact, what ended up in the final cut was a small segment with Ida describing how she could not always get the children she watched to Sunday School, which did not make her sound like a religious zealot.

Whereas the TIME article defamed Ida Bolender and her husband Albert after disregarding their interview with Ezra Goodman, the 1964 documentary *The Legend of Marilyn Monroe* used them to defame Marilyn's grandmother Della Mae Monroe. Without much in context (it is suspected that Della was suffering the effects of Malaria. She died shortly after this event), Ida explained that Marilyn's Grandmother came over one day and broke a glass window near their door. Ida, attempting to remember, glanced back to her husband Albert to verify if they did call the police in response or not. Nonetheless, the director of *The Legend of Marilyn Monroe* used that segment to claim that Della was crazy just like her daughter Gladys. John Huston the narrator, sensationally and pointedly emphasizes that "Della Monroe went berserk!" And again the documentary followed the "Little Orphan Annie in Hollywood" story and the Bolenders had their interview twisted, if not ignored, a second time.

In fact, the documentary offers no evidence to support multiple foster homes that Marilyn is claimed to have experienced, but instead states that 13 "foster" brothers and sisters came and went, referring to other children that Bolenders watched in their home. In the interview Ida only numbered about four or five children she may have watched at any given time. These children were not foster children to Ida, but other children she was babysitting for other mothers just like Gladys Monroe. Of course these children would come and go; this was clearly another attempt to falsely exaggerate Marilyn's family story in favor of what Marilyn's new friends were trying to sell to the public.

Nonetheless, the negative stories promoted over the years about relatives in the press came at grievous price; instead of encouraging family engagement, Marilyn herself was discouraging it with most relatives.

However, Marilyn did continue to keep in contact with her half-sister Berniece Miracle and niece Mona Rae and certainly her mother Gladys. But even those relationships were seriously impeded by Marilyn's "new friends." A manipulative theme that hampered Marilyn's relationship with all of her relatives was that these "new friends" were her only family — ever. That they were the only people who ever loved Marilyn. Berniece Miracle stated, "Some things that have been published about Marilyn's life are such fabrications that further comment would be less than worthy. But of all the distortions that have circulated since her death, I have always wanted most keenly to erase the myth that Marilyn had no family to love her."

Marilyn Monroe had family that loved her when she was a child, she had family that loved her while she was a teen, and she had family that loved her while she was an adult. And she still has family today that care about what happened to her and are sickened by those still profiting off of an illegally seized estate and legacy that was obtained through massive undue and coercive influence and her murder!

While the family issues were a discouragement for relatives, the sinister agenda by Marilyn's "new friends" festered beneath both Marilyn's veil and the public's.

It all started about 14 months prior to the TIME release of its cover story on Marilyn in January of 1955. However, the fabricated orphan stories that were used to lay the foundation of their public deception began many years before, going all the way back to 1935 and was the result of a longtime friendship between Marilyn's mother Gladys and Grace McKee Goddard.

CHAPTER TWO Supporting Resources

[1] Letter to Berniece Miracle to Ida Bolender. Dated August 8, 1962.
[2] *My Sister Marilyn* – Berniece Baker Miracle and Mona Rae Miracle; 1994, 2003; Published by iUniverse,Inc.
[3] *The Legend of Marilyn Monroe* – Directed by Terry Sanders, and narrated by John Huston, 1964
[4] *Marilyn Monroe Was Legitimate Baby After All* – Santa Cruz Sentinel, Santa Cruz, California. February 12, 1981.

CHAPTER THREE

IN AN ALMOST prophetic way, Marilyn discussed wolves in a letter to her guardian Grace McKee Goddard on June 15, 1944. Marilyn stated, "I was all set to get a Civil Service job with the Army, she wrote. "All my papers filled out and everything set to go, and then I found out I would be working with all Army fellows." She continued, "I was over there one day. There are just too many wolves to be working with, there are enough of those at Radioplane Co. without a whole Army full of them."

With that one statement Marilyn would choose a path where the wolves were much more cunning and not so obvious. The sparkling road to Hollywood gave these wolves cover. It started out as dream career, her introduction to photography at a munitions factory in Van Nuys, California. Army photographer David Conover was taking pictures for *Yank* magazine. He was sent there by his commanding officer who was none other than Ronald Reagan; a small world indeed. Nonetheless, the wolves in Hollywood and New York were not camouflaged with clearly distinguishable army fatigues. They blended in and took refuge among the lights and festivity of the theater and movie productions. These are the most dangerous types of wolves as the story of *Little Red Riding Hood* can attest to. The wolves who disguise themselves and dress up like harmless acting coaches, photographers, playwrights, and poets. Behind these individuals came the advisors to the wolves; their lawyers, their psychotherapists, and their assistants. They now became her "family" and then they had the story; her story — *My Story*.

The "new" Marilyn Monroe had no one in her corner, not because none of her family cared, but because these wolves hoodwinked everyone; Marilyn, the public, her surviving family (half-sister Berniece Miracle and niece Mona Miracle) and extended family, Joe DiMaggio, and without question the Los Angeles Police Department. They seduced Marilyn with their charm and their offerings of success. Their esoteric careers made them experts in mass media manipulations.

What else is a movie or a theater, but a manipulation of human behavior. They craft imaginary scenes that, for an hour or two can cause the observer to cry, to be angry, to feel sadness, to feel excitement, and a variety of other emotions. In fact, could they also cause a person to feel guilt and an unhealthy attachment to certain individuals?

The authority of their professions also buffered their motives and aided in deflecting criticism concerning their relationship with Marilyn Monroe. Of course, they were chosen by Marilyn to "help" her — to fix her. And when she died a suspicious death they would say that some problems just could not be fixed. It was always her problem. It was her orphaned and abused childhood. It was her inherited mental problems. It was her being late. It was her suicidal tendencies. It was always her and her fault. That is what they communicated to the public and certainly to Marilyn herself. They absolved themselves of all responsibility. They controlled how the public perceived her and her family history. If it was at all possible, they wanted to completely erase Marilyn Monroe's family and history! And they wanted the public to always know it was her fault — of course, her suicide, her accident, or maybe the Kennedys murdered her.

It was all a ruse to muddy the waters with false or exaggerated "facts." They wielded their great power over the epicenters of theater and movies and mass communication. Norma Jeane was in far too deep. The *TIME* cover story demonstrated the power they had over their cult and the extent with which they would continue to propagate the myth and legend of the "Little Orphan Annie in Hollywood" story.

The seduction of their cult was instantaneous; components of the "perfect storm" coming together in full force. The first sign of love-bombing is what is termed "cult cocoonment." All at once the wolves presented themselves as Marilyn's instant community, her instant friends, her instant family and in that, she had instant purpose. Marilyn wanted to become a better actress and make more money and they could offer her that in addition to the keys to New York theater. The devil was now Hollywood. Her savior was now New York and her "new" friends.

Strangely, they also had the tools to pry open her childhood memories and the technology to dig deep into her mind. And who dug it the best? None other than Marilyn Monroe! The reader should, while reading this book, also explore and examine the lyrics and song for the television series SMASH — "dig deep."[1] The reader will soon understand how "nuts" the Method[i] actors were over Sigmund Freud.

There is no question that Marilyn did have some childhood difficulties during the circumstances of her youth. When her mother Gladys became ill, Grace McKee Goddard, her best friend since at least 1923, petitioned the court to become Marilyn's legal guardian. Marilyn's relatives had no say in the matter. It was what Gladys wanted and it is what Grace wanted. During this period Marilyn was required by California State law to stay in the Los Angeles Orphans' Home (later named Hollygrove) while Grace petitioned the court. The transition from living with her mother Gladys and Ida Bolender to the orphans' home would assuredly be traumatic and scary for any nine-year-old.

> SAN BERNARDINO DAILY SUN, WEDNESDAY, NOVEMBER 30, 1932
>
> Mrs. D. G. Stephens dean of clubwomen in Southern California, celebrated her 94th birthday Monday. More than 500 women gathered to honor her at the Santa Monica Bay Woman's club, which she founded, this being but one of her many activities in club and philanthropic work. She founded the Santa Monica Industrial center, social welfare, service, Los Angeles Orphans' home, and the Ventura school for girls. Guest speakers at the celebration were Governor Rolph and Rabbi Magnin who paid high tribute to her. The governor made the trip south by airplane especially for the meeting.

The high profile status of the Los Angeles Orphans' Home in 1932 was well known.

However, contrary to what has been reported Marilyn's stay in the orphanage was buffered by the fact that she always had a solid family support system during her childhood and young adulthood; she had a lot of relatives living nearby in Los Angeles.

Grace was not a stranger to Marilyn as a child, but her mother's best friend since at least 1923, which was years before Marilyn's birth.

In fact, Marilyn's problem as a child (which really was not a problem at all) was not one of neglect; everyone wanted to take care of Marilyn as passed down by relatives.[ii]

> Since its founding in 1880 by a few public spirited women, headed by Mrs. D. G. Stephens, the Orphans' home has grown with the general advance of Los Angeles until a broader scheme of buildings and grounds is a necessity in its progress. Plans contemplated for the new home provide for an administrative building and groups of cottages, with an industrial building and extensive athletic grounds. In addition the new site will be utilized to the best advantage in giving the children every benefit of California outdoor life, including instruction in the rudiments of farming and gardening.

Los Angeles Orphans' Home founded in 1880.

---

[i] Method Acting refers to an assemblage of techniques that actors utilize in creating characters. The teachings originated in the ideas of Constantin Stanislavski which were later basterdized by acting theorist Lee Strasberg. Followers of Lee Strasberg refer to themselves as "Method" actors.

[ii] Gladys Monroe's first cousin Rebecca (Becky Fritz) Hogan reported that her father and mother (William Marion Hogan and Clara Slough) tried to have Marilyn stay with them as a child. However Gladys, his niece, stated that he had too many children at that time to watch Marilyn well. Additionally, Rebecca also stated that other relatives also offered to help. Proof that William and Clara were willing and able to take on a new child? In 1937, William and Clara adopted a young girl named Carol Ann.

Marilyn Monroe Unveiled | A Family History

Official court documents prove that Marilyn legally resided with only three people from 1936 through 1940; her legal guardian, the aunt of her legal guardian, and her aunt's (by marriage) mother.

1	Guardian is entitled to Credits as follows:	
2		
3	Care of Minor Child and Incompetent	
4	To Guardian - board and room of minor from October, 1936 to November, 1937,	
5	inclusive - 14 Months @ $20.00 per month	280.00
6	To Ida Martin - board and room of minor from December, 1937 to August, 1938	
7	inclusive - 9 months @ $30.00 per month	270.00
8	To E. Ana Lower - board and room of minor from September, 1938 to February, 1940	
9	inclusive - 18 months @ $30.00 per month	540.00

10	Dec. 5, 1936	to Guardian - clothes for minor	15.00
11	16	" May Company - coat	11.22
12	Jan. 19 1937	to Guardian - Misc. for minor	10.00
13	Feb. 14 1938	Ida Martin for minor child	5.00
14	Mar. 15	" " " " "	5.00
15	Apr. 30	" " " " "	15.00
16	Jul 14	" " " " "	5.00
17	Sep. 14	" Guardian - clothes for minor	15.00
18	Oct. 26		10.00
19	Dec. 1		5.00
20	Jan. 30, 1939	E. Ana Lower for minor child	10.00

Marilyn Monroe's Childhood Timeline

-based on official court documents.

- June 1, 1926, Los Angeles, California | Marilyn Monroe was born. As soon as her mother came home from the hospital after delivery, Ida Bolender was providing child care for Marilyn Monroe so Gladys, her mother, could work.

- Circa 1933 | Marilyn Monroe left Ida Bolender's home after residing there with her mother Gladys since birth. Then Marilyn lived exclusively with her mother until Gladys had a nervous breakdown and was hospitalized.

- April 4, 1935 | Grace McKee appointed guardian of the Estate of Gladys Baker.

- September 13, 1935 | Marilyn Monroe went into orphanage.

- December 6, 1935 | Marilyn Monroe was in the orphanage.

- January 15 1935 | Gladys Monroe judged insane.

- March 6, 1936 | payment to orphanage.

- March 27, 1936 | Letters of Guardianship for Grace McKee are signed.

- April 22, 1936 | payment to orphanage.

- May 27, 1936 | payment to orphanage.

- June, 21, 1936 | payment to orphanage.

- Documents from the courts by Grace show no further payments to the orphanage after June of 1936.

- July 1936 to September 1936 (approximately 2.5 months) are unaccounted for. Court documents show no further payments to orphanage.

- Marilyn Monroe stays in the orphanage approximately 9 to 11 months.

- October 1936 to November 1937 the court allocates from Gladys Monroe's estate to Grace McKee monies for room and board.

- December 1937 to August 1938 the court allocates from Gladys Monroe's estate to Ida Martin monies for room and board.

- September 1938 to February 1940 the court allocates from Gladys Monroe's estate to E. Ana Lower for room and board.

- April 4, 1940 the U.S. Federal Census was taken and Norma Jeane (spelled Norma Jean Baker) was listed as a ward in the household of Ervin and Grace Goddard at 11336 Nebraska Avenue, Los Angeles.

- By June 19, 1942 Norma Jeane marries Jim Dougherty.

Nonetheless, despite any possible emotional impact to a young Marilyn, the legal process to guardianship was a formality that laid the foundation of Grace's and Marilyn's "Little Orphan Annie in Hollywood" story. All future exaggerations of abuse and neglect were based on it. And it was the cornerstone of propaganda to cover and hide those who were after her estate; namely her money, her name, her signature, her image, and her legacy at all costs (as early as 1955).

Marilyn was required by the State of California to stay in an approved foster home or orphanage while waiting for the legal process of guardianship to be finalized. The mandatory requirements consisted of an investigation into the suitability of Grace, and other legal procedures. The fabricated stories of Marilyn's attendance at the orphanage required the reader to suspend logic; the fact that the State of California not only had a robust legal system since the founding of the Los Angeles Orphans' Home in 1880, but also its high profile status was an important part of the Los Angeles community. Any scandal of abused or overworked children would have quickly made headlines; there were none.

INFLATED RUBBER CARICATURES capture the imagination of these kiddies in a large exhibition staged in Gilmore circus for Los Angeles Orphan's Home benefit.

Judith Nelson, President and Chief Executive Officer of Hollygrove stated, "There are probably 40 books that talk about her time here, and each has a different story. One book says she cleaned 100 toilets here. Of course, there have never been 100 toilets here to clean."[2]

The *TIME* cover story beguiled, "[Marilyn] hated the orphanage. As one of the older children, Norma Jeane was assigned to wash the dishes: 100 plates, 100 cups, 100 knives, forks, spoons. 'I did it three times a day, seven days a week,' says Marilyn. 'But it wasn't so bad. It was worse to scrub out the toilets.'"

This harsh but colorful claim demonstrated the classic Cinderella Story.

Ezra Goodman stated, "She told me that she was admitted to the Los Angeles Orphans' Home Society when she was nine. There, she said, she was forced to do all sorts of dirty work, like washing hundreds of dishes. (This too, turned out to be an exaggeration.)"

News articles about the Los Angeles Orphans' Home in the 1920s and 1930s unveiled an orphanage involved with the community and a Hollywood that was involved with the children. "Unused box lunches are sent to the Los Angeles Orphans' Home when rain storms drive [film] companies off location. They say the kiddies are getting to be experts in sky reading — and if that isn't a touch of pathos in between smiles, what is?"[3]

The orphanage was a repository for charity and a variety of interesting activities for many children who suffered the loss of parents or otherwise, however, what better location to share in unfortunate circumstances than

THE BILLINGS GAZETTE
Sunday, June 27, 1926.
ORPHAN GIRLS PERFORM.

Two hundred little girls from the Los Angeles Orphans' home had the thrill of their lives recently when they appeared in a scene in "The Fire Brigade," the spectacular fire-prevention picture which Hunt Stromberg is producing for the Metro-Goldwyn-Mayer studios. The children came to the studio at 9 o'clock with 20 teachers sent from the city schools, and they studied until noon, when they were given lunch. From 1 to 4 p. m. they worked in "The Fire Brigade" and were then taken back to their home.

SAN BERNARDINO DAILY SUN, TUESDAY, DECEMBER 6, 1938
Women of Golden West Plan Children's Party

Many clubs shorten their schedules this month because of the personal pressure of the holiday season upon their members. But the California Women of the Golden West in Los Angeles, are completely putting aside all their regular programs and are giving their entire time as well as their financial contributions, to preparing for a big Christmas party at which 400 little children will be their guests.

The party will be given in the Ambassador theater on Saturday afternoon, Dec. 17, and for every youngster there will be a gift, as well as fruit and candy, distributed by a white bearded Santa Claus.

The children will come from the Kiddie Home, the Los Angeles Orphans Home and the Salvation Army.

that of a Hollywood California orphanage? Extracurricular activities at the orphanage allowed children to attend circuses, Christmas parties, and even perform in film productions such as with Metro-Goldwyn-Mayer studios.

The Los Angeles Orphans' Home was a very important part of the local Los Angeles community and the activities and functions were not characteristic of the institution that the studios and Grace McKee Goddard and Marilyn created with their "Little Orphan Annie in Hollywood" story.

In 1956 Ezra Goodman attempted to access Marilyn's records with the Bureau of Public Assistance of the Los Angeles Department of Charities. He stated, Marilyn was "secretive about her parents" and "also vague about her foster parent." And that the official records "were exceptionally rigidly classified and completely inaccessible (partially, the report went, through Monroe's intervention.)"

"Fox's publicity boss, Harry Brand, with whom Monroe was always at odds, complimented [Marilyn Monroe] with, 'She's the biggest thing we've had at the studio since Shirley Temple and Betty Grable. With Temple, we had twenty rumors a year that she was kidnapped. With Grable, we had twenty rumors a years that she was raped. With Monroe, we have twenty rumors a year that she has been raped and kidnapped.'"[4]

Grace McKee Goddard, as Marilyn's legal guardian, had to follow very strict protocol.

> *The Guardian and Ward* (1935),
> Under the law, the courts have a two-fold function in guardianship. The first is a judicial one. It entails the determination of the child's need for guardianship and, when there is need, the appointment of a suitable guardian over his person, estate, or both. The second is an administrative one. It entails the maintenance of a proper record of the child's wardship and continuing superintendence over the guardian to make sure that he serves the child's interest and welfare at all times.

Grace could not just abandon Marilyn. She could not just move away or out of state. She could not just drop Marilyn off at a stranger's house for extended periods without properly informing the court. There was a legal process that Grace was held accountable to. And the court needed to approve monies from Gladys Monroe's estate to pay for room and board and other necessities. Again, *The Guardian and Ward* from 1935 stated, "Whenever a guardian fails, neglects or refuses to furnish suitable and necessary maintenance, support or education for his ward, the court may order him to do so, and enforce such order by proper process."[5]

Marilyn Monroe, as a child, was <u>never</u> going to be adopted or sent back to the orphanage — ever. A fact that will become clear as the reader learns how many relatives Marilyn Monroe had in Los Angeles and other parts of the United States. Her mother Gladys <u>never</u> wanted or intended to give up her parental rights. An adoption is a complete severance of the parent/child relationship. Moreover, it would have been a complete severance to any family ties Marilyn Monroe had as a child, including all of her relatives residing in Los Angeles, Portland Oregon, and elsewhere.

> In *The Guardian and Ward* (1935),
> A guardianship is not an adoption. In an adoption, you are assuming the legal equivalent of a parent/child relationship, as if the minor was your natural child. A guardianship is not as permanent a relationship. However, by obtaining a guardianship, you will have the responsibility of caring for all of the minor's needs including: food, shelter, health care, education, and emotional and physical well-being.

Based on the facts of Marilyn's case, it would have been absurd for her mother Gladys to give up her parental rights completely!

Marilyn Monroe Unveiled | A Family History

To become Marilyn's legal guardian Grace had to take an oath that she was not committing perjury, stating that no other relatives lived in the State of California, as the reader shall see was far from the truth.

Gladys Monroe could have had Marilyn stay with her aunts and uncles or her cousins just as easily as she, herself, stayed with her aunt Dora Graham (Dora Hogan/Andros/Bruce/Schulties/Graham) in 1945.

Dora Graham was living in Portland Oregon and took Gladys into her home after helping her out of the Agnews State Hospital in San Jose, California.

Who also visited that same year while on a photography road trip? Photographer Andre de Dienes, and Marilyn (at that time she went by Norma Jeane). In fact, that same year in Portland Oregon, Gladys's first cousin Rebecca Esther Hogan (Becky Fritz) gave birth to her first child on March 13, 1945. Rebecca herself was born in the very same Los Angeles County Hospital as Marilyn less than seven months after.

It can be logically surmised that if Marilyn Monroe knew about her mother's aunt Dora Hogan in 1945, then she indeed knew about all of her relatives, especially all the relatives living in Los Angeles and Oregon.

Dora Hogan was well aware of her father Tilford Marion Hogan and all of her aunts and uncles (brothers and sisters of Tilford) and cousins, which included relatives that lived close by in Los Angeles, California while Marilyn was a child and while Marilyn was becoming famous.

Marilyn Monroe's mother Gladys rebuffed offered assistance from relatives to help with long term care of Marilyn when she was a child. When Gladys became ill in January of 1935 she relied instead on her best friend, Grace McKee Goddard. Grace enlisted the help of two other people who legally received monies from Gladys's estate for room and board and care of Marilyn. Ida Martin (the mother of Olive Brunings — Olive was married to Gladys Monroe's brother Marion Otis Monroe), and the other person was Edith Ana Lower (Atchinson) who was Grace's aunt. The actual court document prove that Marilyn only stayed with these three individuals from October 1936 to February of 1940. In addition, it is verified by clothes purchased for Marilyn during the stated dates. Any other unverified and unofficial information fails as a result of this single document. The erroneous gossip that Marilyn Monroe was bounced from foster home to foster home is not only a gross exaggeration, it is completely and utterly false. Grace McKee Goddard was Marilyn's only legal guardian. Ida Bolender in 1956 told Ezra Goodman "After the orphan home, Norma Jeane stayed with Aunt Ana and with Grace McKee Goddard until she got married. We went to see her lots of times. I don't know where those stories come from about her staying in twelve foster homes." Ida Bolender's statement to Ezra fits logically and accurately with the actual court documents.

Marilyn was in the orphanage only about nine months — from September 13, 1935 to June of 1936. Biographers from Donald Spoto and J. Randy Taraborrelli have stated that Marilyn Monroe left the orphanage in 1937.

Spoto wrote, "She left the Los Angeles Orphans Home and arrived at the Goddard's bungalow in Van Nuys on June 7, 1937 — a week after her eleventh birthday. Just as she was climbing into Grace's car that evening, radio bulletins announced the death of Jean Harlow, who died suddenly of uremic poisoning at twenty-six."[6]

Taraborrelli wrote, "Finally, on June 26, 1937, Norma Jeane left the Los Angeles Orphans' Home to live once again with Grace and Doc Goddard. A month earlier, the young actress whom Grace had hoped to fashion Norma Jeane after — Jean Harlow — had died at just twenty-six. With typical flair for the dramatic, Marilyn Monroe recalled many years later that she had a 'strange feeling I was being set free into a world in which Jean Harlow no longer lived.'"

It is assumed by the authors of this book that a June 26, 1937 date for Marilyn Monroe leaving the orphanage originated from an October 2, 1955 article written by Maurice Zolotow which is written in the style of earlier fan magazines and supporting the "Little Orphan Annie in Hollywood" story as reported by Ezra Goodman and the May 14, 1956 Marilyn Monroe cover story for *TIME* magazine. Through indirect evidence these articles are believed to have been funded by Marilyn's "new" friends.

Marilyn Monroe Unveiled | A Family History

It certainly makes a much more sensational story to say that Marilyn Monroe left the orphanage the same day Jean Harlow died or to quote something "dramatic" about Marilyn's life and Jean Harlow. The actual court documents provide a more accurate and truthful story.

Marilyn Monroe's family was not the abusive or uncaring individuals that the public has been conditioned to believe. On the contrary, they all had robust families that still carry on today beneath the public veil as the reader shall see in the following chapters.

Much of the actual stories of Marilyn Monroe's everyday life while growing up in Southern California will remain hidden somewhere in the darkness of time because, as a matter of fact, most of it just was not written down. Far too many so-called biographers have taken creative liberty, creating fully written and elaborate stories off of sparse documentation and hearsay, crafting their stories from already flawed fan magazine stories which were based on Grace and Marilyn's exaggerated biographical story.

Many so called "witnesses" have corrupted the story even further; most certainly they wanted to become a part of the Marilyn Monroe legend. Creative additions to hearsay becoming more elaborate as rumor seeded with the "Little Orphan Annie in Hollywood" story continued to grow. Exaggerations were passed from one person to the next, every writer trying to make any details "fit" a horrible orphan story.

It is important for the reader to understand that the events of Marilyn Monroe's childhood occurred in the 1920s and 1930s; some 20 to 30 years after Marilyn Monroe became famous. Most of those relatives who knew most about Marilyn's childhood passed away well before 1954. Yet, biographers have gone so far as in describing actual conversations as if they were there with a notepad and pen listening in on private moments of the lives of people they never knew many years after the fact.

|Gladys Baker (Monroe) and Norma Jeane lived with Ida Bolender.

|Milton Stores Andros, Gladys Monroe's first cousin, worked as a plaster artist in the Hollywood motion picture industry.

Geographically, how close were some of the Marilyn's relatives when she was a child? In 1930 one of Gladys Monroe's first cousins lived in Los Angeles beginning around Marilyn's birth until his death in Woodland Hills, California in 1973. He lived with his family about 11 miles away from Gladys and Norma Jeane when they lived at Ida Bolender's house. He resided at 1736 Hauser Blvd, Los Angeles, California and Gladys and Norma Jeane lived at 459 Rhode Island Ave, Los Angeles which has since been renumbered 4201 W. 134th Street.

Milton Stores Andros previously lived in Portland Oregon in 1920 where his mother Dora Graham lived. He eventually worked for the old Warner Brother Studios at 5800 Sunset Boulevard in Hollywood as a set and prop designer.

Rebecca Esther Hogan (Becky Fritz)-

Gladys Monroe's first cousin and Marilyn Monroe's first cousin once removed.

The January 1, 1927 Birth Certificate for Rebecca Esther Hogan. She was born at the Los Angeles County General Hospital less than seven months after Marilyn. Her name was listed as "Baby Nance" after her grandmother Charlotte (Jennie) Virginia Nance. She also went by the name Becky Fritz. William Marion Hogan was her father and Clara May Slough was her mother. Relatives had family ties to Portland, Oregon. Becky is Gladys Monroe's first cousin, and the author's (Jason Edward Kennedy) grandmother.

Marilyn Monroe Unveiled | A Family History

Relatives remember that he was involved with the making of the original *King Kong* as well as other films during his career.

These are the kind of family details that Marilyn could have certainly shared with the public, but it was all suppressed because it countered her career as the "Cinderella in Hollywood." The sensationalism of a poor and neglected Norma Jeane washing 100 toilets captured the public's attention much more than her mother's first cousin being involved in his own Hollywood career.

As the stories of family mental illness, abuse and neglect became part and parcel the legend of Marilyn Monroe, Ezra Goodman concluded his research stating, "Most of the highly publicized Marilyn Monroe legend about her family background and upbringing has been revealed as begin nothing more than a legend."

Marilyn Monroe Unveiled | A Family History

CHAPTER THREE Supporting Resources

[1] *SMASH "dig deep"* – Writers: Marc Shaiman, Scott Wittman. Producer: Marc Shaiman, Columbia 2012.

[2] *A Haven for Children in L.A. – Closes After 125 Years*
Hollygrove home, where Marilyn Monroe once lived, is a casualty of changing views on treating abused and at-risk youngsters. December 20, 2005|Bob Pool | TIME's Staff Writer
http://articles.latimes.com/2005/dec/20/local/me-hollygrove20

[3] The Winnipeg Tribune (Winnipeg, Manitoba, Canada); May 6, 1933; Page 10.

[4] *The fifty-year decline and fall of Hollywood* – Ezra Goodman, MacFadden Books, 1962.

[5] *Guardian and Ward-* University of Chicago Press – 1935; Hasseltine, Byrd, Taylor.

[6] *Marilyn Monroe: The Biography* – By Donald Spoto; Page 49.

CHAPTER FOUR

W̲HILE MARILYN MONROE never challenged the myths she helped to create, Elizabeth Taylor did challenge fabrications in the media. In a case against fan magazine deception, Taylor charged that her image and family were damaged from a "flagrant disregard of the truth." In a scathing 1960 lawsuit, Taylor challenged seven fan magazines.

The lawsuit read:

> Defendants acted maliciously, irresponsibly and wickedly, for the crass commercial purpose of stimulating circulation of motion picture fan magazines, in flagrant disregard of the truth and of resulting injury and distress inflicted on the plaintiffs and their infant children. Among devices used by defendants to accomplish their objective was lurid display of front cover teaser headlines, leading the public to believe that articles in said magazines would reveal scandalous conduct on the part of the plaintiffs, thereby exciting prurient curiosity of the public and inciting it to purchase the magazines---whereas the articles themselves in no way substantiated those headlines and often belied them. By such sensational, yellow journalism--- in subversion of every standard of honest, responsible reporting--- the defendants acted in furtherance of continuing campaign calculated to exploit for profit and popularity the prominence of the plaintiffs and other motion picture and performing artists, to the grave impairment of their professional and family lives.[1]

This well formulated legal charge could have been wielded in defense of Marilyn and her family. In 1960, Joe Hyams *(Herald Tribune Service)* wrote in his article "Once Popular Film Fan Magazines Fading Out" that magazines were spinning out of control, literally, until Elizabeth Taylor and Eddie Fisher derailed them with lawsuits.

Even Jacqueline Kennedy Onassis was subjected to the fan magazine assaults, however she chose to ignore them. A press secretary commented, "She feels that people who buy them realize they aren't news magazines." [2]

Unfortunately, Marilyn Monroe had a different relationship with the fan magazines and the media than Elizabeth Taylor or Jacqueline Kennedy Onassis. Due to the biographical story that Marilyn and Grace McKee Goddard fabricated early on, Marilyn was intimately tied to that dynamic and to that story; her career depended on it from the beginning, or so it seemed.

Marilyn made no effort to unveil herself to the public. Certainly, the powers behind Marilyn, those who were helping to drive the "new Marilyn Monroe" theme would never let the "Little Orphan Annie in Hollywood" story fade from the public's conscience. It added a layer of misinformation that over time became a valuable asset while they manipulated her for their own benefit and to cover up their crime.

While the 1956 *TIME* cover story acted just like a fan magazine and fabricated and promoted the "Little Orphan Annie in Hollywood" story about Marilyn's childhood, it also captured some very important critical facts. Ezra Goodman quoted American screenwriter and producer Jerry Wald in his book: "It was typical in most ways of the average Hollywood glamour-girl story. 'It's the same story with different names. First they say, 'If only I could get a part.' After they get the part, it's 'Gee, they like me! I wonder if I'm gonna get another part?' Then comes phase three: 'I should be getting bigger and more important parts.' After that: 'How can I get more money?' At this stage they start to become surrounded by sycophants and suckerfish who feed on the whale, who massage their ego."

And who were the sycophants and suckerfish surrounding Marilyn Monroe in the beginning of 1955? And who wanted to help Marilyn get bigger and better parts and to help her obtain more money?

The *TIME* cover story revealed exactly who most of those sycophants and suckerfish were — they were more devious and cunning than the wolves Norma Jeane wrote about on June 15, 1944. They could not help but to have their names attached to hers. Unquestionably they had their "own names" in the world of theater, playwriting, poetry and photography. In spite of that, they had their own needs and motives as well and Marilyn Monroe was bigger than them all. Was it just a coincidence that those "friends" were on her payroll or otherwise? Was it just a coincidence that those "friends" just wanted to help her get bigger and more important roles and to obtain more money?

The sycophants and suckerfish dazzled Marilyn with what they could offer her in New York. With the hook set, they now needed a devil. And specific to Marilyn and the public, the devil came in the form of a fabricated orphan story to sell to the public and defame her family line. If they could continue to defame Marilyn's relatives and separate her from them, then they could completely own Marilyn Monroe. And that is exactly what they did...

They even had the technology and tools to unleash the devil: Lee Strasberg's Method Acting and Anna Freud's child psychotherapy were BOTH focusing on childhood trauma, specifically, Marilyn Monroe's childhood trauma!

What appeared to the public as a promotion of the "new" Marilyn Monroe and an innocent business deal among "friends" was even more insidious than anyone could ever imagine. The *TIME* cover story represented nothing more than a propaganda piece that was written for effect — "they" wanted to let the world know who Marilyn Monroe belonged to. And they would not give her up at any cost. Aptly called "her friends," their names stood out as a calling card for extortion and then finally murder by 1962 when they began to lose what they worked so hard to keep.

They all were documented in Marilyn's *TIME* cover story: Lee Strasberg, Paula Strasberg (the Strasbergs were her acting theorists), photographer Milton Greene (her then business partner), Arthur Miller (playwright and later her third husband), and finally Norman and Hedda Rosten (he was a poet and novelist, she conveniently would go on to work as a part of Marilyn's office staff and both were longtime college friends of none other than Arthur Miller at the University of Michigan).

Their obsession with Marilyn Monroe demanded that they have their names attached to hers and they all made the cover of *TIME* magazine, right along with Marilyn.

The sychophants that were not specifically named in the *TIME* article had critical roles behind-the-scenes and were affiliated in one way or another with Lee Strasberg and/or Milton Greene. They were psychotherapist Dr. Margaret Hohenberg, Dr. Marianne Kris, Dr. Ralph Greenson, and none other than Anna Freud, who connected herself through her own surrogate underlings.

Through the fan magazine flagrant disregard for the truth, the practice of sensationalizing stories allowed these individuals to continue to perpetuate Marilyn's orphan myth unhindered. Unfortunately Marilyn was a participant in helping these individuals cover their assault against her.

CHAPTER FOUR Supporting Resources

[1] Anthony Slide-*Inside the Hollywood Fan Magazine: A History of Star Makers, Fabricators, and Gossip Mongers* – University Press of Mississippi, Feb 26, 2010

[2] Anthony Slide-*Inside the Hollywood Fan Magazine: A History of Star Makers, Fabricators, and Gossip Mongers* – University Press of Mississippi, Feb 26, 2010

CHAPTER FIVE

THE PATTERN OF deceit started in January 1955. It is no coincidence that Marilyn essentially met[i] and became professionally involved (or otherwise) with these specific individuals during the early parts of January.

Milton Greene was the initial mastermind of this group as reported in newspapers across the United States. The headlines for 1955 made no mistake about it: Milton Greene was going to profit from his idea of a "new" Marilyn![1] He offered Marilyn Monroe the carrot to come to New York City. It was the promise of being a business woman. It was the promise of bigger and better roles. It was the promise of making more money. And it was the promise of becoming a more serious actress. Milton Greene introduced Marilyn Monroe to the Actors' Studio which was ran by none other than Lee Strasberg.

In 2013, the following quote appeared on the website owned by Joshua Greene (Milton Greene's son):

> It was Milton who physically brought Marilyn Monroe to Lee Strasberg's Actors' Studio and the reason being, his friend Marion was a member. It was that friendship that got Milton's wife Amy involved as the Chairman for the Actors' Studio and her first day was to sell tables for the *Rose Tattoo* benefit to be held in December, 1955.[ii]

Marilyn started "acting training" with Lee Strasberg. Lee Strasberg was actively using psychotherapy as a requirement with his acting students. Innocently, he required them to attend psychotherapy sessions.

Susan Strasberg, his daughter bragged, "He sent numerous actors to psychiatrists, and many doctors sent their patients to class because they felt his work helped theirs in analysis."[2] Strasberg and the Freudian therapist were working hand-in-hand.

In 2012 the Method actors bragged, "And we're just nuts about Sigmund Freud."[3]

Why was psychotherapy so important for Lee Strasberg's "Method Acting?" Strasberg was literally "digging up childhood trauma." That was his basis for reliving emotions on stage; emotional memory and/or sense memory it was coined. In fact, Strasberg and the psychotherapist were attempting to dig up "repressed memories." Memories that the American Psychological Association today states, "it is not possible to distinguish repressed memories from false ones without corroborating evidence."

In July of 2000, Nadya Wynd, an actress and also a licensed therapist herself stated, "The Method is all about using your past, your own emotional experiences, your own demons, if you will," Wynd said. "It is psychotherapy really. Because there is not really a therapist there, it's sort of dangerous psychotherapy, because some people might go off of the deep end."[4]

If Lee Strasberg and Marilyn's psychotherapist were overly focusing on her childhood trauma

---

[i] Brief and sporadic encounters did happen previous to January 1955, however no extensive business relationship developed as a result of those encounters until January of 1955 with the exception of Milton Greene, whose work-for-hire photography landed him working with Marilyn as early as 1953 for Look magazine.

[ii] Joshua Greene is the owner of http://archiveimages.com/

for the purposes of "acting," it would not be unreasonable to surmise that Strasberg and the psychotherapist had complete control of Marilyn Monroe's childhood recollections and narrative. What better way to convince someone to defame their own family?

Is this why Marilyn Monroe tended to have less contact with relatives after 1955? Did they play off of Marilyn's and Grace's fabricated orphan story and convince Marilyn to actually believe that her childhood was horrible and abusive?

Was Lee Strasberg using the techniques of Method Acting to regress Marilyn to a child-like state?

Ezra Goodman wrote in 1961, "Monroe was quoted as saying she remembered someone trying to smother her with a pillow when she was two years old. Psychiatrists will tell you that clear memories at that age are rare and often distorted."

There is no question, what started out as a simple and innocent biographical story (that the studios required), Lee Strasberg and the Freudian psychotherapist commandeered and intensified it. Certainly, Marilyn may have bought into and believed their "professional" rhetoric.

Contemporary acting academics are fully cognizant of the extent Lee Strasberg was manipulating students with what has been called the breakdown to obtain a breakthrough method. In fact, it has been a major source of contention, not only with Lee Strasberg, but the "acting coach" profession in general.

Theater critic Richard Hornby[5] pointed out, "The teacher or director interrogates the actor about his emotional life, often in the most intimate and or uncontrolled weeping as a triumphant 'breakthrough.'"

Hornby argued, "That such experiences do not transfer to the stage, and may even damage the person's ability to act..."

American Director, Elia Kazan, close colleague and friend of Lee Strasberg and Arthur Miller wrote, "Even before the Group Theatre existed, Lee had noticed that actors would humble themselves before his rhetoric and the intensity of his emotion. The more naive and self-doubting the actors, the more total was Lee's power over them."[6]

Lee Strasberg intimately knew how to "overawe" his students in order to make them do what he wanted.

> Elia Kazan described, "Two young actresses, apprentices as I was, did a scene. When they were through, they looked to [Strasberg] for judgment. He said nothing. They waited. He stared at them. His face gave no hint of what he thought, but it was forbidding. The two actresses began to come apart; everyone could see they were on the verge of tears.
>
> Silence is the cruelest weapon when someone loves you, and Lee knew it. Finally one of them, in a voice that quavered, asked, 'Lee, what did you think?' He turned his face away.... No one dared comment for fear of saying the wrong thing and having Lee turn on them. Finally, speaking quietly, he asked the stricken actress, 'Are you nervous and uncertain now?' 'Yes, yes,' one actress said."

Elia Kazan's description of Strasberg's method of coercive persuasion is verified by Lee's own "training" transcripts. In his book, *Strasberg: At the Actors' Studio — Tape-recorded Sessions*, Lee demonstrates his power to "break" actors into fits of tearful weeping.

It is a fact that Marilyn was subjected to this type of manipulative interrogation by Lee Strasberg on a continual basis.

In January of 1955, Marilyn began seeing Dr. Margaret Hohenberg (a medical doctor and Freudian psychotherapist) who also happened to be none other than Milton Greene's therapist, the person with whom Marilyn was a business partner with (Milton referred Hohenberg to Marilyn conveniently, at the same time that Lee Strasberg required her to have a psychotherapist for acting). This relationship was clearly unethical at the outset.

Marilyn Monroe Unveiled | A Family History

Dr. Margaret Hohenberg was also an "old friend" of none other than Anna Freud going back to the Viennese Society of Psychoanalysis.

On January 7, 1955 the formation of Marilyn Monroe Productions, Inc. was announced in partnership with Milton Greene.

On Wednesday, June 1, 1955 Marilyn Monroe met Mrs. Hedda Rosten for the very first time according to the *The Evening Standard* of Uniontown Pennsylvania. Within nine months, her daughter Patricia would be on Marilyn's first will; for all of her education and more if Marilyn died. Marilyn's own niece, Mona Miracle, who was 16 years old in 1956 was bequested nothing for her education or anything else.

Between June 2 and September 1955, Marilyn wrote a letter[i] while staying at the Waldorf Astoria Hotel in New York City stating that, while under duress[ii], Lee Strasberg wanted a theater and that Dr. Margeret Hohenberg wanted "a permanent psychiatric cure." With criminal intent they conveyed their hopes and dreams to her. Additionally, and still under duress, she was told that Arthur Miller was "disappointed." Lee Strasberg, Milton Greene, Arthur Miller, Dr. Margaret Hohenberg, and Norman and Hedda Rosten are all named in the letter as knowing and/or participating in and subjecting Marilyn to a coercive psychologically invasive medical procedure. This letter verifies that the above named individuals were intending to financially extort Marilyn Monroe using the full force of 1950s illegal behavioral modification technology.

This letter also verified that these individuals were actively working to coerce Marilyn as a TEAM and not as independent and unrelated players beginning in 1955. It is the very first documented evidence that was eventually backed-up by a highly public move that would again prove that Milton Greene, Arthur Miller, and Lee Strasberg were all actively collaboratoring against Marilyn together.

Is it absurd to think that Lee Strasberg would use coersive behavioral modification techniques for acting and/or to manipulate a students mind? Absolutely not! "Indeed, 'Method actors' and behavioral psychologist have a common intention: they are both in the business of controlling [human] behavior."[7]

And the science of Method Acting was at the core of how these individuals were actively manipulating Marilyn.

Lee Strasberg and Dr. Margaret Hohenberg took behavioral modification to the next level of coercion.

Marilyn's letter will be explored further and in more sufficient depth in the next book from www.MarilynMonroeFamily.com: *Surgeon Story: Means, Motive, Murder* by Marilyn Monroe's second cousin Jason Edward Kennedy.

In January of 1956 Arthur Miller announced that he was divorcing his wife Mary Grace Slattery.

Within five to eight months after being subjected to an illegal behavioral modification procedure that intended to make Marilyn Monroe feel guilty over Lee Strasberg not having his theater and Dr. Margaret Hohenberg not having a permanent psychiatric cure, Marilyn's very first will was written in February 1956 to help Strasberg and Hohenberg to fulfill their hopes and dreams.

There was $100,000 (a buying power of $876,161.76 in 2015 dollars) earmarked for Arthur Miller (Marilyn was not even married to Arthur yet, and he was still married to Mary Grace Slattery); $25,000 to Lee and Paula Strasberg for his theater; $20,000 to Dr. Margaret Hohenberg, for "a permanent psychiatric cure;" $10,000 to the Actors' Studio (Lee Strasberg managed the Actors' Studio which is a theater, and in essence, was slated to inherit $35,000 total); and $10,000 to the education of Patricia Rosten, the daughter of Norman and Hedda Rosten (close friends of Arthur Miller and Mary Grace Slattery since attending the University of Michigan in the 1930s).

Marilyn's own mother Gladys was set up to receive $25,000. That was less than Lee Strasberg. Lee and Paula would have been bequeathed $25,000 plus an additional $10,000 for the

---

[i] See *Fragments: Poems, Intimate Notes, Letters* by Marilyn Monroe. – SURGEON STORY.
[ii] Psychic Driving, Dissociative Anesthetic Drugs, and Sensory Deprivation.

Actors' Studio, the theater, which Strasberg managed.

It is not known if provisions were set in place on the first will for the company Marilyn Monroe Productions or otherwise. However, Milton Greene already owned 49.6 percent of Marilyn Monroe Productions and would eventually own 100 percent of Marilyn's photographs while taken under its umbrella.

On Thursday February 23, 1956 Marilyn was interviewed in her New York apartment by Olga Curtis (a Pulitzer Prize nominated journalist who interviewed other celebrities such as Grace Kelly and Robert Redford). Marilyn stated publicly, "I have no plans. No romance. I haven't even been dating."

However, it is well-known that Miller and Marilyn were indeed pursuing a relationship as early as 1955, while Miller was still married to his wife Mary Grace Slattery.

On Monday, May 14, 1956 *TIME* magazine released its mostly fictional cover story on Marilyn Monroe. Lee Strasberg, Paula Strasberg, Milton Greene, Arthur Miller and Norman and Hedda Rosten are described in the *TIME* article as Marilyn Monroe's "new friends," arguably to match the "new" Marilyn theme. It would have been too conspicuous to quote in *TIME* magazine that they all became so close as "friends" in nine to 14 months that most of them (except Milton Greene) were listed as beneficiaries on Marilyn's very first will, which was signed — more or less — three months prior.

As a matter of fact, the will was signed at none other than Milton Greene's home (Fanton Hill Road, Weston, Connecticut) by none other than Milton Greene's attorney Irving Stein in February 1956.

Why was Milton Greene's own attorney acting as Marilyn's counsel? Why would these specific individuals, who quickly entered into a business relationship with Marilyn within months of meeting her, be the major benificiaries of Marilyn Monroe's Estate — within one year? Were they planning on her dying?

Irving Stein would become a board member for Marilyn Monroe Productions as well, clearly not representing Marilyn, but Milton Greene.

There were clear signs that something was wrong with Marilyn's business situation early on.

Arthur Miller was still not completely divorced from his wife Mary Grace Slattery at the signing of this will. What potential legal implications did that insinuate? If Marilyn died before she married Arthur, would Mary Grace Slattery have had legal access to Arthur Miller's bequest of $100,000 dollars?

Some more interesting questions: was Marilyn Monroe a beneficiary on any of *their* wills in 1956 or any another time? Why were Marilyn's own half-sister Berniece Miracle or her niece Mona Miracle not on the first will as beneficiaries? Why would Norman and Hedda's daughter have a bequest for $10,000 for her education, but Marilyn's own niece Mona was slated to receive nothing? Tuition for a Harvard and/or Yale education from 1956 to 1964 ranged from $1,000 to $1,700 per year.

Why would Lee Strasberg get the same amount of money as Marilyn's mother of $25,000 (adjusted for inflation that would be $197,561.26) plus an additional $10,000 (adjusted for inflation that would be an additional $75,758.10) for the Actors' Studio which he headed? If one is going to promote an orphan story why was not the Los Angeles Orphans' Home a beneficiary? What about any friends or family who were not on Marilyn's payroll?

The circle of New York "new friends" who were promoting and profiting off of a "new Marilyn" were all on the very first will, except Milton Greene within nine to 14 months. Milton was her business partner after all and would be receiving 49.6 percent of her earnings on her current and future effort.

When Marilyn Monroe broke her contract with Twentieth Century-Fox, her "new friends" wanted her to move to New York to make more money by forming Marilyn Monroe Productions. In fact, they <u>encouraged</u> her to break her Fox contract. They all were a part of that equation. Marilyn was big business as the *TIME* article stated. Money was the clear agenda and her "new" friends all bragged about that fact on the cover of *TIME*.

Marilyn's move to New York was all about money. How then could she have made more money when she would be giving, what amounted to half her earnings, directly to Milton Greene?! And it would not only be half her earning through motion pictures, but real estate, books, and any investments she entertained while under Marilyn Monroe Productions!

On January 14, 1955 Milton Greene was already planning on releasing a photography book with Marilyn's pictures he had taken.[8] Marilyn was even beginning to sell her name while with Milton Greene. *The Kingsport Times* on May 9, 1955 reported that A. Perlman Company, which was a New York corset manufacturer, would be producing Marilyn Monroe bras.[9] Milton Greene, in effect, would own dead close to half of Marilyn Monroe for the life of the company, including from the sale of her name! Again, that was 49.6 percent. Marilyn's "new friends" certainly knew what Marilyn was worth in 1955. They demonstrated that they were fully aware that Marilyn Monroe could sell her name and image for huge profits. Is this when they first realized that they did not necessarily need Marilyn alive to profit from her directly?

Marilyn's "new friends" were the sycophants and suckerfish that wanted to make money for Marilyn and get her better motion pictures roles for their own benefit, not hers.

The first sign of love-bombing in a cult is what is termed "cult cocoonment." All at once Milton Greene, Lee Strasberg, Arthur Miller, Norman and Hedda Rosten presented themselves as Marilyn's instant community, her instant friends, and her instant family and they had a fabricated orphan story to prove it!

In an October of 2012 interview with Scott Feinberg, Amy Greene (Milton Greene's wife) admitted, "She felt protected. We cocooned her. Whereas no one else had done that before."

Marilyn's and Grace McKee Goddard's exaggerated biographical story became a weapon. The use of the orphan story was used as a cover to publically hide their assault against Marilyn. It was theatrical magic. The use of misdirection — sleight of hand — to focus the publics attention on an "orphaned and abused" little Norma Jeane, and to distract them from the manipulation and extortion of Marilyn Monroe. That is what they were experts in — managing the audience's attention just like they do in theater and film. "The true skill of the magician is in the skill he exhibits in influencing the spectators mind."[10]

If Marilyn was not the strong independent business woman, then she was a childlike and suicidal adult who needed help and protection. This is exactly how they convinced the public and the police to not pursue them when Marilyn died in 1962.

These contrasting personality elements were manipulated for effect.

In the 2011 movie *My Week With Marilyn*, the character of Milton Greene boldly stated, "Larry, she needs her people. We are the only family she's ever had!"

They wanted the public to continue to believe, even in 2011, that they were Marilyn's savior; "the only family she's ever had!" The New York "new friends" surrounded and cocooned Marilyn and still use today the formula of an orphan story tactic to profit financially from her efforts. It was and still is — a deception. It is nothing but the continued extortion of Marilyn Monroe.

Did Marilyn really need a partner? Why was Marilyn Monroe cash poor in 1955? This business deal was hugely in Milton Greene's favor. There is no question that this was a very bad business deal for Marilyn Monroe. In fact, behind-the-scenes, a struggle for control over Marilyn was brewing between her "new" friends and the issue of Marilyn Monroe Productions would become the major contention.

Milton Greene would also go on to own 100 percent of Marilyn Monroe's photographs while taken under the umbrella of Marilyn Monroe Productions. Reasonably, one would think Marilyn Monroe would own the controlling rights to her own photographs; after all she was the star and Marilyn owned a controlling interest (50.4 percent) in what was supposed to be her company. Yet all of the photos Milton Greene took while a participant of Marilyn's company, even after Marilyn fired him, belonged to him; again, all 100 percent!

As reported in 1955, the burlesque legend Evelyn West, who was popular from the 1940s thru the 1960s was receiving $12,500 per photograph in **1955**.[11] Adjusting for inflation that was a whopping $111,154.85 for a single photograph — in 1955!

There was clearly a major problem how Marilyn's career was being managed at the detriment to her own financial success.

Why was Marilyn Monroe at the mercy of this group of New York friends?

Marilyn had the clear ability and asset to be financially successful on her own.

This fact alone should set off bells and whistles for the reader.

These new friends admittedly surrounded her because she was big business as conveyed by their *TIME* cover story.

Yet Marilyn Monroe was essentially broke.

If fact, she was directly at the mercy of Milton Greene who was funding her business startup Marilyn Monroe Productions.

Marilyn Monroe was NOT a cunning business woman.

However, not being astute in business is not a crime. What this proves is that Marilyn was naive in business matters and was open to be taken advantage of.

What monetary amount was Marilyn Monroe receiving for her photographs in 1955? Did Milton Greene pay her anything for her photographs? Or was Marilyn Monroe spending all of her time changing dresses, applying makeup, and doing her hair just so Milton Greene could own 100 percent of her photos on her time?! Does this make any logical sense?

According to an *Associated Press* article, on July 11, 2013, an unidentified collector placed up for auction 3,700 of unpublished negatives and transparencies of Marilyn. The collector obtained them about 10 years prior from the Milton Greene estate. The negatives and transparencies were being sold with copyright. The deal happened with a Polish financial institution that had received the photos in a business transaction. Apparently, Joshua Greene (Milton Greene's son), while dissolving the partnership, unfortunately gave the partner copyright ownership of Marilyn's pictures. Joshua called it "a bad business deal" to lose the copyright.

Likewise, was it also a "bad business deal" for Marilyn Monroe to not own any of her photographs after Milton Greene was fired by Marilyn Monroe in 1958 (a breakup that started in April of 1957)? Was it even a deal? Why would Marilyn knowingly give Milton Greene full 100 percent copyright if it was clear that Marilyn Monroe's photographs were a goldmine as one article written by Alfred Leech stated in 1955?[12] Yes, Marilyn's photos were a goldmine in 1955!

In an attempt at personal communication with Joshua Greene (Milton Greene's son), he would not answer questions one of the authors of this book asked him, inquiring how his father owned 100 percent of Marilyn's photographs while taken under Marilyn's company Marilyn Monroe Productions. He also did not respond to a request for comment about the exact nature of his father and mother's relationship with Lee Strasberg.

Though Marilyn fired Joshua Greene's father Milton Greene, Joshua Greene is still in the Marilyn business today marketing the same pictures of Marilyn his father obtained while under the umbrella of Marilyn's company — Marilyn Monroe Productions. He is working directly with Authentic Brands Group, the company that markets many of the mass marketed Marilyn Monroe images.

Milton Greene also claimed 100 percent ownership of the book, *My Story* which supported the *TIME* cover story "Little Orphan Annie in Hollywood," originally started by Grace McKee Goddard and Marilyn. *My Story* will be explored further in a later chapter in this book.

CHAPTER FIVE Supporting Resources

[1] *Milton Greene Cashes In On His "New" Marilyn Idea* – Hollywood UP article, January 17, 1955.
[2] *Marilyn and Me -- Sisters Rivals Friends* by Susan Strasberg – Warner Books; 1992; Page 31.
[3] *SMASH "dig deep"* – Writers: Marc Shaiman, Scott Wittman. Producer: Marc Shaiman, Columbia 2012.
[4] *Aptos filmmaker's success no Illusion* – Wallace Baine, July 14, 2000, Santa Cruz Sentinel (Santa Cruz, California).
[5] *The End of Acting: A Radical View* – by Richard Hornby, May 1, 2000.
[6] *Elia Kazan, A Life* – New York: Alfred A. Knopf, 1988), Page 539.
[7] *Backstage Behaviorism: How the Method actor uses spiders, puppies, and roast chicken to create character in the theater* – Michael Schulman. Psychology Today, June 1973.
[8] *Lucky Photographer Joins Marilyn Monroe Enterprise* – The Daily Herald, 14 Jan 1955, Fri, Page 9
[9] *Louella Parsons* – Hollywood, Kingsport Times, May 9, 1955.
[10] *Magic by Misdirection* – Dariel Fitzkee, copyright 1975, Page 33.
[11] *Marilyn Monroe Is Gold Mine for Calendar Maker* – by Alfred Leech, Daily News - Miner, Fairbanks Alaska. Tuesday, March 8, 1955.
[12] *Marilyn Monroe Is Gold Mine for Calendar Maker* – by Alfred Leech, Daily News - Miner, Fairbanks Alaska. Tuesday, March 8, 1955.

CHAPTER SIX

As early as July 1, 1955 rumors of "control over Marilyn Monroe" became the talk of the country. What is a major and significant piece evidence, the newspaper reporters began picking up on and reporting on the gossip that leaked from the crews working on Marilyn's movie sets.

People were beginning to notice that something was definately amiss with Marilyn behind-the-scenes. The headlines stated that Lee Strasberg was usurping Milton Greene as Marilyn Monroe's "svengali!"

"Svengali" is a very strong word for an innocent business relationship among Marilyn's "new" friends.

The word is the name of a "musician in George du Maurier's 1894 novel *Trilby* who trains Trilby's voice and controls her stage singing hypnotically." Or in other words, an evil hypnotist. A standard definition is "a person who controls another's mind, usually with sinister intentions."[1] Set crews knew Marilyn was being unduly influenced and taken advantage of by Lee Strasberg and Milton Greene.

Columnist Dorothy Kilgallen reported, "Quote from one chum: 'Marilyn listens to everything Strasberg has to say the way she used to listen to everything Milton has to say. Milton isn't too happy about the situation.'"[2]

Major red flags began to surround Marilyn in 1955. The sychophants were obsessing over Marilyn Monroe to such a degree that it spilled over into the public streets.

Another article dated July 21, 1955, stated that Lee Strasberg was giving Marilyn dramatic lessons at his New York Fire Island home.

On October 5, 1956 Dorothy Kilgallen again, in her *Voice of Broadway* column stated that, "Members of the Marilyn Monroe inner circle are standing by for an explosion between Arthur Miller and Milton Greene." Arthur is "reportedly furious" over Marilyn's contract with Milton.

At this juncture Arthur Miller portrayed himself as protecting Marilyn from an unscrupulous business partner who netted nearly half ownership of her current and future earnings — a contract that was in Milton Greene's favor by any business standard. Arthur finally convinced Marilyn that her contract with Milton Greene was ill-conceived and poorly written; it was not in her best interest. Marilyn had no legal representation during the formation of Marilyn Monroe Productions, instead relying on Milton Greene's attorneys for legal advice as they wrote the contract. She finally publicly argued why should she give Milton Greene half her income when she was the sole company asset. While Arthur Miller intervened to help Marilyn in her business dealings with Milton, he would soon expose his true intentions and loyalty to Marilyn Monroe. In a major shocker he was caught red-handed publicly protecting Milton Greene and Lee Strasberg in a move that was self-incriminating. Arthur Miller's marriage to Marilyn Monroe was a deceitful sham from the beginning — it was a fraudulent marriage.

By the middle of October and early December of 1956 the public rumors were taking their toll on the inner circle. Their financial extortion of Marilyn Monroe was being threatend by public scrutiny.

On December 9, 1956 the rumors broke the camel's back. What is clearly another propaganda article funded by Milton Greene, Arthur Miller, and Lee Strasberg took the newspapers by storm.

Marilyn Monroe Unveiled | A Family History

Maurice Zolotow, a popular expert on the stars, began advertising what was called "his" new article "Who Runs Marilyn Monroe?"

It was to their benefit that Zolotow was an advocate and personal friend to them all, especially none other than Arthur Miller.

This article publicly captured and exposed serious undue influence exerted on Marilyn Monroe.

Undue influence can be defined as, "when one party uses undue influence to persuade another party into entering into a contract or the transfer of property which is disadvantageous to the influenced party."

Marilyn's contract with Milton Greene was, on its surface, exceedingly disadvantageous for Marilyn. The dog and pony show article was an attempt to hide the behind-the-scenes jostling of control over Marilyn's favor and money.

Marilyn's "new" friends were clearly profiting hugely off of Marilyn, yet they wanted to suppress the fact that Marilyn was being unethically controlled by any of them.

The leaked rumors were of grave concern for Lee Strasberg, Milton Greene, and Arthur Miller. The Zolotow article captured, in detail, the damaging threat of their conspiracy against Marilyn. Lee Strasberg and Milton Greene were wrecking the relationship between Marilyn Monroe and Arthur Miller. Lee Strasberg and Milton Greene were unduly influencing and controlling Marilyn. Specifically, Marilyn was not making decisions on her own, but did exactly as the "gang" wanted her to do. Marilyn Monroe was unequivocally under siege in 1955!

The December 16, 1956 *American Weekly* article would not only answer the rumors that Marilyn was being controlled, but it would also put a positive spin on Milton, Arthur, Lee and Paula Strasberg and, of course, all at Marilyn's expense. This article, while it made Hollywood levity of the drama, was defensive by design. The gang wanted the public to continue to believe it was all Marilyn's fault. The Zolotow article exposed the dichotomy between the Marilyn Monroe they wanted to sell the public versus the "Norma Jeane" they were severely manipulating behind-the-scenes. The reader should focus on that distinction because it exposed how the inner circle was manipulating the public as well. Marilyn was either the Cinderella business woman who overcame adversity to become a star, or she was the helpless little girl with mental problems that the inner circle needed to control. When the inner circle wanted to make money, Marilyn was advertised as the first. When the inner circle wanted to hide and justify their obvious inappropriate relationship with her, Marilyn was the latter.

On December 19, 1956 the provoked response to the rumors was released to the public.

One of the major revelations in this article was that Marilyn's seemily unrelated "new" friends, that she innocently happened to meet in 1955 more or less, were all part of Marilyn's entourage.

- Milton Greene- The mastermind and photographer.
- Lee Strasberg - The coach and diagnostician who could fix actor problems.
- Paula Strasberg- The coach and motherly figure.
- Arthur Miller- The odd man out.
- Norman and Hedda Rosten - Arthur Miller's long term college friends who were along for the ride and to make money.

In poker you are to never show your hand. They publicly broke that fundamental strategy. The proverbial hand in the cookie jar with all of their cards laid out for the public to see. Their arrogance fully exposed them and their motives of manipulation and financial extortion. The journalist that reacted to the negative rumors in 1955 and 1956 called them out, and they took the bait.

While their tool of the media profession exposed their manipulative motives, unfortunately, the right people were not paying attention to the obvious unveiled signs. And if they were, they could not penetrate the wall that the New York "new" friends built around Marilyn Monroe.

Ezra Goodman stated, "There is a conspiracy of silence around her...she is now big business, she is surrounded with intrigue and a coterie of advisers headed by Milton Greene who runs interference for her...no one gets to Monroe without first clearing him."

Marilyn Monroe Unveiled | A Family History

Zolotow pointed out that theatrical circles had predicted that there would be personality conflicts between the gang members. Some even said that Marilyn and Arthur would break up soon. However, Zolotow expertly predicted at the end of his article that Arthur and Marilyn would be together forever, thus dispelling the rumor that there was any problems between them at all. In fact, Paula Strasberg entered in as the motherly figure. She was the motherly figure, not for Marilyn, but to massage public sentiments. She propagandized, "What you feel when you're with them is the love and tenderness he has for her and the affection she feels for him." Indeed, an overly sentimental response to smooth over any preceived conflict's that were occuring between Arthur and Marilyn.

If one gets their hand caught in the cookie jar what does one tend to do? Of course, one blames the cookie. And that is exactly what happened.

Zolotow did not describe Marilyn Monroe as a strong independent business woman in control of her situation until near the end of the article.

The image of Marilyn that was conveyed in the earlier May 14, 1956 *TIME* cover story was classic Cinderella. The cruel foster mother berating the young child who just wanted to be loved. She was then sent to an orphanage to toil away in servitude until she had that magical transformation as a savvy Hollywood movie star.

TIME stated, "she began to look suspiciously like a shrewd business woman."

The woman described in the December 16, 1956 Zolotow article was not the same. Recall that this article was defensive by design. It was an article to cover up a crime that was occuring in full public view. They were defending themselves against negative public rumors specifically about their inappropriate relationship with Marilyn behind-the-scenes.

In the article, Marilyn was introduced as having "intricate psychological convolutions." She was described as a woman who had problems that they needed to cater to and that some of those problems needed fixing. Strangely, there was not a mention of her being an orphan specifically. They were not selling the Cinderella version of Marilyn. In fact, Marilyn's childhood problems were not problems anymore. They were an asset to be dug up and explored by Lee Strasberg and the Freudians and advertised as a means to "make" her a better and more "serious actress."

Psychotherapy was not recommended to help Marilyn resolve her childhood trauma, but to advertise the perceived benefits to her theatrical performances. In reality it did nothing but cause Marilyn to be more dependent on Lee Strasberg.

Recall what actress and licensed therapist, Nadya Wynd stated about Lee Strasberg's Method Acting, "The Method is all about using your past, your own emotional experiences, your own demons, if you will. It is psychotherapy really. Because there is not really a therapist there, it's sort of dangerous psychotherapy, because some people might go off of the deep end."

In 2012 the Lee Strasberg's Method Actors chimed in about Marilyn Monroe, "The challenge of the actor is to use sense memory of childhood trauma. Well there ain't no sin to remove your skin. So open up my id for a good clean sweep. We're just nuts about Sigmund Freud."

The Lee Strasberg Method Actors bragged that they were working together with the Freudians. And who could dig her mind better than them all? Of course, Marilyn Monroe. Factually, Marilyn was not digging her own mind, Lee Strasberg and the Freudians were and they were interpreting it!

Lee Strasberg and the Freudians clearly held an ethically sensitive position over Marilyn. Yet, after Marilyn died in 1962 Lee Strasberg obtained 75 percent of her estate for his theater and Anna Freud received 25 percent of her estate for her permanent psychiatric cure (research for the Anna Freud Centre). Lee Strasberg and the Freudians were clearly manipulating Marilyn Monroe together and at the detriment to her physical and mental health and they acted grossly unethical and criminal.

And what were Marilyn's problems that needed to be coddled or fixed in the Zolotow article? And why does Marilyn need her "new" friends?

- She had no money.
- She was dependent on Milton Greene for financial support.
- She was interested only in herself.
- She was a new bride and of course, all new brides have many emotional and physical problems.

- She had to deal with her professional issues.
- She needed to learn to share a bed with Arthur Miller.
- She had to learn to share the boardroom with Arthur Miller who was a playwright.
- She needed to get along with her business partner Milton Greene.
- She was spiritually transforming herself from a dumb blonde to a more serious actress.
- She had to master the art of a creative artist.
- She took it personally when Arthur focused on writing his plays.
- She wanted attention all the time, because when she was married to Joe DiMaggio he would watch TV and would ignore her.
- She had issues with tardiness.

And who could especially fix her problem with being late? None other than Lee Strasberg. In fact, that is what Strasberg did, he claimed to repair problems and he wanted the public to know that he could specifically repair Marilyn Monroe's problems. He bragged about it in the Zolotow article. He promoted that he could diagnose theater problems with actors and fix them. In fact, the implication was that he needed to repair everything for Marilyn Monroe and he had to deal with her childlike behaviors. He was the "Surgeon" with his hand-in-the-cookie-jar who blames the cookie — and he has been unveiled.

In the Zolotow article, Strasberg was not describing an independent woman who is a successful actress, but a needy actress that was dependent on him and the gang and she needed fixing! Lee Strasberg desperately tried to show the public Marilyn Monroe needed him. And certainly that she needed Milton Greene as well for financial support.

If the marketing of the "new" Marilyn was to promote Cinderella, the marketing of the "needy" Marilyn was to cover up the premeditated financial extortion by her associates.

What were all the rumors that the article was trying to eliminate and dirvert suspicions about the gang's activities behind-the-scenes?

- Arthur Miller and Marilyn would be divorcing soon.
- Arthur Miller was trying to get rid of Milton Greene.
- Lee and Paula Strasberg's coaching negatively impacted Marilyn's private life.
- Arthur Miller was in a feud with Lee and Paula Strasberg.
- Milton Greene was Marilyn's Svengali.
- Lee Strasberg was Marilyn's Svengali.
- Arthur Miller was Marilyn's Svengali.

Every point in the Zolotow article was a documented statement of clear undue influence perpetrated against Marilyn Monroe. If fact, it was a statement of confession by Milton Greene, Arthur Miller, Lee and Paula Strasberg!

With a little humor, some phone calls and some cable messages, Zolotow stated that he was going to get to the bottom of all these negative rumors. Surely, Arthur Miller must be concurrently writing a play about these interesting facts, he whimsically wrote.

These "rumors," if they were true, were all damaging -- harmful -- and caused great injury to one person — Marilyn.

And then they even used Marilyn as a witness against herself in their defense.

Suddenly, Marilyn became the astute and strong business women. She stated, "What happens with Monroe Productions is business, strictly business. My feelings about Arthur are personal. I'm in love with him. I don't see why people mix up love and business. I have no idea of asking Arthur to be a director of my company. He has his work to do and I have my work to do."

Milton expressed in the article that he and Arthur were good friends and that there was no problem between them. He said he would never sell his stock in Marilyn Monroe Productions.

Arthur expressed in the article that he is not involved in Marilyn's business. He stated that any rumors about Milton and him having a battle were nothing more than fanciful newspaper space fillers.

Marilyn Monroe Unveiled | A Family History

Marilyn, acting as the final authority against herself, expressed that no one controls her and that no one is her Svengali. She even gave an example. She stated that one newspaper reported she was at the Strasberg home on Fire Island in New York. She was going to pose on the beach, Strasberg told her not to, and she complied. Marilyn said that was not true. Jokingly, she pointed out in the article that maybe people will think Arthur Miller is her Svengali.

Zolotow then says the rumors that Arthur is in a feud with Lee and Paula Strasberg are nothing but imagination.

What was the point of the December 16, 1956 Zolotow article?

There was nothing here to look at — move along — no one was unduly controlling or influencing Marilyn Monroe.

In reality and as a matter of fact, the December 16, 1956 Zolotow article caught Milton Greene, Arthur Miller, and Lee and Paula Strasberg in a massive lie and attempted cover-up.

How do we know? Arthur Miller wrote a letter to Marilyn some six months earlier on Friday, May 25, 1956.

Arthur Miller was — the odd man out.

Arthur Miller penned, in his own words, exactly how they were unduly influencing Marilyn Monroe to give up her authority and power to the gang. They focused on trinkets, her desires to be an actress, her desires to better herself, and worst of all, her desires for a husband's love.

Arthur Miller was an expert in writing plays and manipulating audiences. In his letter he demonstrated, without restraint, that Marilyn was his puppet and indeed he was acting as her svengali.

Arthur Miller stated to Marilyn about Milton Greene, "My sole irritation with him is what yours is — that he seems to have assumed some kind of proprietary function over you in his mind. It seems to me sometimes that he conceives of you as something he almost created himself."

Was Arthur saying that Milton thought he owned Marilyn Monroe? Absolutely — yes! Milton was acting like Marilyn's Svengali and was trying to control the direction of how Marilyn will make money. In other words, how he would make money. In fact, he was trying to control Marilyn by bribing her with diamonds through one of his allies; the promise of more money.

This letter was about making money in business and how best to pursue it and which direction Marilyn is going to choose. However, she did not have a choice. The letter was about Arthur, on one hand, saying he has no problem with Milton Greene, but then aggressively described his problem with Milton. The letter was about Arthur telling Marilyn he loves her, but then threatening to remove his love if she chooses Milton's path to make money. This letter was about manipulation, power and control over Marilyn Monroe and who would lead her. Arthur said, "What is at stake here, my Darling, are two viewpoints about work and life. One is the majority viewpoint, the other is that of the artist."

Arthur clarified, "All this, I think, would make [Milton] feel that you are about to be led out of the circle of glamour and into the circle of what you and I call art..."

Milton Greene masterminded the carrot to attract Marilyn to New York with the dream of making more money. Lee Strasberg bolstered the carrot with the dream of becoming a more serious actress.

Arthur Miller used the carrot of the artist to charm Marilyn to side with his theory of making money. And Arthur Miller wanted it all.

Arthur Miller was acting as Marilyn's Svengali by trying to force her to choose his path against her will. If Marilyn chooses his path then Arthur gained control and ownership over her.

Arthur pointed out that if one pursues the art, then the money would follow.

While that point of view was certainly a noble carrot to pursue in itself, it is pathetic how Arthur coerced Marilyn to accept it.

Arthur Miller was clearly trying to force Marilyn to put Milton Greene, at this point, into a more managerial business role in Marilyn Monroe Productions, instead of a more strategic role.

He stated, "It is possible, I say, that [Milton] can retreat to a managerial position, in which he would deal with business only, and some day come even to enjoy that position. You have done what was necessary to do, and what I tried to intimate to you often in the past you would have to do--which is to define yourself for him in so many words, and to define what his function is to be and what it can no longer be."

Arthur said, "And if I resent him, Darling, it is not because I fear you will fall for him."

Falling for Milton means that Marilyn would choose his path to make money, which is the path of glamour.

Arthur continued, "If you did — (the very thought is impossible) but if you did, why then I should say that I knew nothing about anyone, and more importantly, that it would have been wrong and fated for disaster for us to think of living together for very long."

Arthur Miller was telling Marilyn that it was impossible for her to choose Milton's path! But if she did choose Milton's path to make money, he would be a bad judge of her character and thus their relationship of living together for very long would be "wrong and fated for disaster."

Was Arthur Miller using Marilyn's love for him as a weapon against her if she chose to stay with Milton's way of making money? Absolutely — yes! Arthur Miller was a very manipulative man. This letter proved beyond a reasonable doubt that he did NOT love Marilyn and that he was forcing her to side with him to oust Milton Greene from the picture. He was not acting as Marilyn's soon-to-be husband, but a hustler attempting to swindle her power and money! He was not asking her but was coercing her. Arthur Miller was acting as — her svengali! Their subsequent marriage was a hoax! He was not even married to her when he wrote the letter, but would be in 36 days on June 29, 1956. Lee Strasberg gave away the bride, and Milton Greene was the wedding photographer!

The manipulation continued. He stated that he does not believe she would fall for Milton. Reinforcing that if she did, their relationship would be a disaster. This pressure demonstrated that he did not love her. This was pure, simple, unadulterated emotional manipulation.

Arthur Miller elaborated further, "Milton is tuned-in very sharply to his own advantage and to money-making," and "he is marshalling all his allies in the hope of forcing you back into the cage he found you in."

The cage being the dumb glamour blonde roles she played before she became a "human being;" a more serious artist, according to Arthur.

Arthur continued to feed her the carrot of the artist and to emphasize that she was now a human being since she was with him and certainly since she had been "training" with Lee Strasberg.

Was Marilyn Monroe not *always* a human being?

How could anyone ever say that to a woman who was to be their wife in less than a month? It not only demonstrated his lack of respect for her, but a clear intent to manipulate her.

He then pointed out that Henry, one of Milton's allies, came to offer diamonds to Marilyn as a means to entice Marilyn to side with Milton and his direction to make money.

Arthur responded and manipulated "love" to draw Marilyn back into him. He wrote, "I am being insulted by such a gift to you, for I love you so that what you are reflects upon me."

Was Arthur saying that if she accepted that gift and chose Milton's path to make money then that would reflect poorly on him? Absolutely — yes!

Then Arthur hammered Marilyn with unambiguous matter-of-fact language. He wrote, "And of course, there is always the simplest fact of all-- that I simply have a killing fury against anyone moving in or trying to move in. I hope you made things clear to [Milton] so that he understands. I still believe, of course, that [Milton] is going to be in England unless he knows for sure there is no hope."

Arthur was not asking her, but telling Marilyn to put Milton in his place. Arthur did not want Milton controlling or interfering in the direction of how Marilyn made money; he wanted him out! And he had a "killing fury against anyone moving in or trying to move in." This was all about Arthur Miller controlling Marilyn Monroe.

Arthur then dangled the carrot of the artist again in front her, "You have come an awfuly long way in a year or so, Pusso," acknowledging the work that she has been doing with none other than Lee Strasberg to become "a more serious actress."

Why would Arthur Miller publically lie in the December 16, 1956 Zolotow article when he was clearly trying to stop Marilyn from pursuing Milton's agenda and influence over the direction of making money some six months earlier on Friday May 25, 1956?

Recall that on October 5, 1956 Dorothy Kilgallen reported that Arthur was "furious" over

Marilyn Monroe Unveiled | A Family History

Marilyn's contract with Milton Greene.

Would not a concerned husband continue to protect his wife from an unscrupulous business partner? Why would he participate in the Zolotow article? If Arthur was protecting his wife why would he go public and defend his relationship Milton Greene? Arthur Miller should have never participated in the Zolotow article if he truly was against Milton or anyone exploiting his soon-to-be wife.

A simple analogy to ponder: if your spouse was involved with an unscrupulous business partner, would you ever publically side with that business partner to cover up negative public rumors that this partner and others were conspiring against your wife? Never — unless you were conspiring with those people to extort your own spouse!

More specifically, why would Arthur Miller, Milton Greene, and Lee Strasberg all come to a consensus and lie that there was no conflict between ANY of them in the December 16, 1956 Zolotow article? Remember, they ALL agreed to respond to this article and furthermore Arthur and Zolotow were friends outside of the industry. The only logical deduction is that if they ALL were in cahoots to lie together in the December 16, 1956 Zolotow article, then they must ALL have been conspiring to hide the fact that they were ALL actively trying to unduly control Marilyn and unduly influence her behind-the-scenes! And furthermore, they ALL wanted to divert public scrutiny against any claim that any of them were trying to control Marilyn in an unethical and/or criminal way. Again, if Arthur Miller really loved Marilyn and if he was concerned for her financial well-being, why would he continue to lie? He lied because he was a part of the gang and he was protecting the gang!

Arthur Miller, Milton Greene, and Lee Strasberg are unveiled.

There is no question that Lee Strasberg stepped in for damage control; for a short time he was able convince Arthur Miller that he needed to repair the "negative rumors" which were quickly undermining their criminal agenda against Marilyn! The rumors that these "new" friends were trying to unethically control Marilyn Monroe were absolutely true! The reason the December 16, 1956 Zolotow article was written was to stop the public from thinking there was something very wrong with Marilyn Monroe's situation behind-the-scenes between ALL of them. The December 16, 1956 Zolotow article was the *smoking gun*!

This gang was working together! It was nothing more than damage control to protect the group and their investment and to continue to hide their financial extortion of Marilyn from the public.

Adding more solid evidence for this surreptitious plan, Amy Greene (Milton Greene's wife) stated in a 2012 interview with Scott Feinberg that Milton (speaking about how Arthur Miller was the cause of Marilyn's and Milton's break up of Marilyn Monroe Productions), "knew then that he couldn't handle Arthur and that he [Arthur Miller] would not give her what she needed which was major motion pictures — to me *The Misfits* is a piece of shit! How dare he do this and again she is playing a dumb blonde."

This quote by Amy Greene should give the reader great pause. Not only does Amy Greene verify that there was indeed a conflict between Milton and Arthur about the direction of how Marilyn should make money (i.e. dumb blonde roles, the carrot of glamour verses major motion pictures, the carrot of the more serious artist.), but in the same interview she also inadvertently verified that they were using this as a means of controlling Marilyn Monroe. Amy Greene admitted, "She felt protected. We cocooned her. Whereas no one else had done that before."

Who were they to protect Marilyn Monroe? Why did Marilyn Monroe need protecting? Why did Marilyn need to be "cocooned"?

If they believe they had convinced the public at large that they needed to protect the poor abused orphan girl, then they gave themselves public legitimacy to continue to control the poor abused orphan girl to exploit her for her money — follow the money!

If Norma Jeane Mortenson was not the poor abused orphan girl and if her relatives do not fit that characterization then their game is done. They can no longer continue the criminal charade that has been going on for well over fifty years.

In Arthur Miller's letter to Marilyn dated Friday May 25, 1956, Arthur made the case that Milton Greene was focusing on glamour and not the art to make money using Marilyn, and further, that he wanted to keep Marilyn in the cage that he found her in — which was the dumb blonde roles.

December 9, 1956 - *Who Runs Marilyn Monroe?* by Maurice Zolotow. Actual text of Arthur Miller lying. Why would Miller lie when we know 6 months earlier he was already forcing Marilyn to suppress and counter Milton Greene?

BECAUSE... HE WAS A PART OF THE GANG!

AND HE WAS PROTECTING THE GANG!

> Q: Are you taking an active part in Marilyn Monroe Productions? Are you and Milton Greene in accord? Have you been made an officer of the corporation?
>
> Miller: I have no connection with Marilyn Monroe Productions beyond the fact that its president is my wife. I have no more than the normal family interest in my wife's business affairs and am happy to state this works out fine. Rumors of conflict between myself and Milton Greene are space fillers for unimaginative columnists.

Lee Strasberg

Milton Greene

Arthur Miller

Milton Greene, Lee Strasberg, and Arthur Miller ALL conspired to manipulate Marilyn Monroe together.
They are the GANG!

Furthermore, the 1956 Zolotow article made it a point to brag about Milton's credentials. Milton was "a top-ranking still photographer of what is known in the magazine business as glamour poses."

Zolotow continued, "He had no experience in motion pictures or the theater until his alliance with Miss Monroe and he came to know Marilyn while he was shooting pictures layouts of her for a national magazine."

And notice how Zolotow called Milton's relationship with Marilyn — an alliance. It was clearly an alliance concurrently with Lee Strasberg and Arthur Miller as well.

Why was Amy Greene, in 2012, trying to switch sides?

Recall that she stated, "[Milton] knew then that he couldn't handle Arthur and that he [Arthur Miller] would not give her what she needed which was major motion pictures — to me *The Misfits* is a piece of shit! How dare he do this and again she is playing a dumb blonde."

We know clearly that Arthur and Strasberg were both for the more serious actress — the carrot of the artist and that Milton Greene, who "had no experience in motion pictures or the theater" was for the carrot of glamour. Remember, that they ALL agreed to participate in the December 16, 1956 Zolotow article. The article was written for them and shined a positive light on all of them, thus they certainly ALL agreed with the content of the article.

In 1957, newspapers across the country were reporting that the reason Marilyn fired Milton was not only that Milton Greene was mismanaging Marilyn Monroe Productions, but that both Arthur and Marilyn were upset over how her contract was written, that Marilyn would be giving to Milton Greene essentially half her earnings when she was the sole income provider.

Why then is Amy Greene trying to change history and the facts? Well of course, if she reported the facts, it would then make Milton Greene look like he was acting as Marilyn's svengali! It is long overdue for Amy Greene to come clean about what they all were doing to Marilyn behind-the-scenes, although a confession is not expected.

The Zolotow article stated it exactly — "Who Runs Marilyn Monroe?" Arthur Miller, Norman and Hedda Rosten, Lee Strasberg, Paula Strasberg, and Milton Greene all hid beneath Marilyn's veil, while they were ALL running Marilyn Monroe at her expense. In the Zolotow article, they ALL described a Marilyn who was not independently her own person. They described a Marilyn who they could control and were controlling; they ALL were her svengali and by Amy Greene's own admission, they cocooned her!

Additionally, why should it matter if Marilyn Monroe did more glamour roles rather than dramatic roles anyway? Why was this such a contentious issue between Arthur Miller, Lee Strasberg, and Milton and Amy Greene? Certainly, many actors have led very successful entertainment careers pursuing either or both. Marilyn was at a point in her career where she could have chosen any number of different roles to "prove" her diversity as an actress. It was an issue because they knew how serious Marilyn Monroe believed in it and pursued it. In fact, as early as December 28, 1952 the *Lubbock Avalanche-Journal* reported a Hollywood article that headlined Marilyn's goal and motivation was to become a more competent actress, in addition to the top glamour girl.[3]

Ezra Goodman quoted Director George Sidney, "These girls go through it all not for the money or the purple Jaguar but for the poison, the fire — they want to be an actress and nothing is going to get in the way of it. I say you take a normal person, your aunt Matilda, and put makeup on them and it affects their brain. I say to the makeup man: 'What have you got in that stuff!' When these girls get this ambition and drive, nothing stops them."

Miller, Strasberg, and Greene took advantage of Marilyn's belief in the carrot they could offer her. They offered her the "golden" New York carrot, which really was not even a carrot at all, but a criminal assault to financially extort her. It was a core topic between the gang because they knew they could dangle it in front of Marilyn to manipulate and unduly control her.

What can be concluded is that regardless of what the gang told Marilyn about becoming a more serious actress, the movies *Bus Stop, The Prince and the Showgirl, Some Like It Hot, Let's Make Love, The Misfits*, and *Something's Got to Give*, which she made in the period when Milton Greene, Arthur Miller, and Lee Strasberg controlled her, can arguably all be considered falling into the "dumb blonde" category. They did nothing to help her become that "more serious actress." And Amy Greene admitted to some of that in her interview with Scott Feinberg.

What Marilyn did not realize at the time was that she was already that serious actress. She had already become an "artist" long before her involvement with the gang of "new" New York friends.

On June 21, 1956 Arthur Miller stated in a televised interview while attending the House of Un-American Activities Commitee he had plans to marry Marilyn Monroe as he answered legal questions about his communist political activity. Why would Arthur Miller potentially damage his future wife's reputation and her career by publicly associating her with his legal problems? In fact, the February 19, 1957 *Escanaba Daily Press* in Michigan headlined "Husband of Marilyn Monroe Called Out for Contempt in Communism Case."

Arthur Miller was not Arthur anymore, he was "Marilyn's husband." He was using Marilyn Monroe's name to divert media attention from himself and his communist activities. More damaging was the fact that Marilyn Monroe was now associated with Communism.

On June 29, 1956 Marilyn married Arthur Miller. Who gave away the bride? None other than Lee Strasberg. Milton Greene, of course, was there taking pictures, which he still owns and markets today. Amy Greene, Norman and Hedda Rosten (she was a bridesmaid) and Paula Strasberg were all there as well. None of Marilyn's relatives, including half-sister Berniece, were in attendance, though unlike her somewhat spontaneous marriage to Joe DiMaggio, this was a more planned and elaborate affair.

During the filming of *The Prince and the Showgirl,* sometime between August 7, 1956 and November 17, 1956, Marilyn observed Arthur Miller's diary and some other papers face up, unconcealed and readily visible on a desk. Miller wrote an entry into the diary complaining that he was "disappointed" in her and other disparaging remarks. Marilyn was so emotionally devastated that she found it difficult to work and sleep. She had Dr. Margaret Hohenberg flown in from England to calm her with medication. Did Hohenberg also evaluate Marilyn's psychological response to the phrase, "Arthur is disappointed" which was coerced into her brain using illegal behavioral modification techniques during the middle of 1955?

This disturbing incident was verified in 1994 by Marilyn's half-sister Berniece Miracle. She stated, "her confidence in Arthur is dropped after she discovered a disturbing journal entry critical of her habits."[4]

In 2010, Vanity Fair[5] wrote an article about the incident which again came to light in a collection of Marilyn's diary extracts that were made public. According to Berniece, Marilyn stated, "Things were never the same after I saw Arthur's note about me."

Berniece replied, "You mean the note in the diary?"

"Yes," said Marilyn.

"Marilyn recalls, hashing it over again, the entry in Arthur's journal she read during the filming of the The Prince and the Showgirl," Berniece wrote.

The reader should remember that Lee Strasberg, Dr. Margaret Hohenberg, Milton Greene, Arthur Miller, and Norman and Hedda Rosten were all named in a letter written by Marilyn as knowing about and/or participating in and subjecting Marilyn (while under duress) to an illegal psychological invasive medical procedure where she was told that Arthur Miller was "disappointed" in her.

Was this "operation" designed to induce a future psychologically and emotional response to the word "disappointment" for reason's of manipulating behavior? Were they trying to invoke a negative emotion into the mind of their patient like they invoke emotions for a theater audience?

They used dissociative drugs, sensory deprivation, and psychic driving to implant the feeling of guilt into her mind.

In a video interview on February 6, 1995, Arthur Miller, talking about his 1953 work on his play *The Crucible* eerily states, "You know the suggestability in people's minds is fantastic."

Arthur would know, he had first hand experience with behavioral modification writing *The Crucible* in 1953 and he had practical experience on Marilyn Monroe beginning in 1955. It was no coincidence that Marilyn stumbled across his diary and some papers spread out and clearly visible on a desk with words handpicked to criticize her.

This was a major issue in Marilyn's life. After their marriage Arthur himself even wrote about it in his play *After the Fall*. They all wanted her estate and they used every Freudian mental trick to obtain it. This will be discussed in more depth in the book by Jason Edward Kennedy — *Surgeon Story: Means, Motive, Murder.*

Sometime after Arthur Miller married Marilyn, he reportedly became the sole beneficiary of Marilyn Monroe's estate.[i] The entire gang was removed from Marilyn's will, even Marilyn Monroe's own mother!

Arthur Miller's Svengali influence over Marilyn worked.

As the odd man out, Arthur Miller decided to finally fracture the gang — Milton Greene was out.

Lee Strasberg's attempt to hold the gang's alliance together had failed.

By April 12, 1957 Arthur Miller convinced Marilyn to fire Milton Greene.

On April 17, 1957, the *Albany Democrat-Herald* reported that Marilyn elected a new board of directors. The new directors were documented as Arthur Miller's attorney Robert H. Montgomery Jr., George Levine who was Arthurs friend, and his brother-in-law George Kupchick. They replaced what Marilyn called "Greene's men," his lawyers Irving Stein and Joseph Carr. Marilyn again, had no legal representation of her own. She was at their mercy for her own company.

Arthur Miller cocooned Marilyn for himself.

It is no wonder that Amy Greene stated in the 2012 interview with Scott Feinberg that, "Arthur was a bore…son-of-a-bitch…creep. I saw through him the first time I met him."

The December 16, 1956 Zolotow article predicted that Milton Greene could have profited from his interest in Marilyn Monroe Productions of up to $5 million dollars by 1957. Whatever the realistic amount was, it was a huge monetary loss for Milton and Amy Greene to be pried away from half ownership of Marilyn Monroe.

However, somehow Milton was able to hold 100 percent copyright for every single picture he took of Marilyn while under Marilyn's company. Was that his payoff to keep quiet about the rest of the gangs activities? Did Lee Strasberg negotiate that deal to keep Milton Greene silenced?

Arthur Miller never made any public comment about Milton owning all of Marilyn's photographs while taken under Marilyn Monroe Productions. One would surmise that he and his lawyers would have fought dearly for that after the breakup of Milton and Marilyn, which he orchestrated. Especially since other artist such as Evelyn "$50,000 Treasure Chest" West, the burlesque legend, was selling her photographs in 1955 for thousands of dollars!

That never happened. Marilyn Monroe's photographs, as reported in 1955 were a gold mine! And Milton Greene ran away with owning 100 percent copyright!

On November 11, 1960, Arthur Miller and Marilyn Monroe announced their divorce.

Arthur Miller and Marilyn were not officially divorced until January 20, 1961, however, Marilyn's new will was signed with urgency on January 14, 1961 as purported by the date on the will and Aaron Frosch. However, this date is highly questionable.

On December 4, 1963, in a typed memorandum, Eileen Atkinson wrote to Inez Melson Marilyn's "will was drawn in eighteen minutes and it was just a fluke that it was done when it was."

Most of the gang was immediately all back on the will except for a few changes. Was that a fluke?

It included $10,000 plus an additional $40,000 to May Reis. May Reis was conveniently Arthur Miller's secretary for many years before becoming Marilyn's secretary. Her brother Irving Reis directed the movie version of Arthur Miller's play *All my Sons*. Was May Reis an insider informant for Arthur Miller? Did Arthur Miller eventually receive a payoff from May Reis when she collected from Marilyn's estate after Marilyn's death?

Once again there were monies for Norman and Hedda Rosten and/or Patricia Rosten in the amount of $5,000. The way it was written this time aground put the money right into Norman and

---

[i] The supposed second will leaving Arthur Miller as sole-beneficiary of Marilyn's Estate has never been officially verified, although it was verbally documented as existing by Aaron Frosch, Eileen Atkinson, and Berniece Miracle.

Marilyn Monroe Unveiled | A Family History

Hedda's pocket:

"c) I give and bequeath to NORMAN and HEDDA ROSTEN, or to the survivor of them, or if they should both predecease me, then to their daughter, PATRICIA ROSTEN, the sum of $5,000.00, it being my wish that such sum be used for the education of PATRICIA ROSTEN."

This time, monies were allocated not to Dr. Margaret Hohenberg for a "permanent Freudian psychatric cure," but to Dr. Marianne Kris for a "permanent Freudian psychatric cure;" 25 percent of Marilyn's Estate worth. Dr. Kris was one step away from none other than Anna Freud. Dr. Kris took over Marilyn's psychological manipulation after Dr. Margaret Hohenberg. In previous years, her father was the Sigmund Freud family physician. She also lived with Freud's daughter Anna Freud while a child and was considered an "adopted" daughter of Sigmund Freud. Additionally, Dr. Marianne Kris was a major asset to the Anna Freud Centre. Her office was conveniently in the same building where none other than Lee Strasberg lived — 135 Central Park West, in New York City.

The remaining 75 percent of Marilyn's estate was earmarked for Lee Strasberg. Susan Strasberg, Lee's daughter, wrote in her book, "...three times a week after work he and Marilyn disappeared into the living room. Soon I'd hear laughing or weeping, sometimes an outburst of anger, a diatribe against her studio or someone who'd betrayed her trust. She was very unforgiving during these bouts, it was all black and white for her. People were either for her or against her, there was no middle ground. If she even suspected they were against her and she could be very suspicious, she'd go wild. I don't know if 'those bastards...sons of bitches...,' And so on were ever told off in person, but if they were, I doubt they would have ever gotten away with it. And she didn't stutter once."

Susan Strasberg continued, "[My father] seemed to have a calming effect on her. Her tirade would evaporate and, as if nothing had occurred, they'd be speaking quietly about very personal matters -- men, her mother, her feelings of worthlessness or hopelessness. It was such a stark contrast to the way she behaved with me, I could hardly believe it was the same woman."

Disappearing three times a week in the living room with Lee Strasberg? Was this meeting as innocent as acting training or was it something more sinister such as behavioral modification: a breakdown to obtain a breakthrough!

Was Lee Strasberg telling her how her family was not a family at all? Did Lee Strasberg tell her that her life with her mother Gladys, Ida Bolender and Grace McKee was not a life at all? Was Lee Strasberg telling her that her family must have been abusive that is why she has so many problems? Did Lee Strasberg tell her she could end up crazy and mental just like her mother? Was Lee Strasberg causing Marilyn to be an independent actress or a woman dependent on him?

Was Lee Strasberg inducing in Norma Jeane what psychologists call "transference?" A therapist has the patient recline on a bed or on what is called the Freudian couch. This technique comes from the field of hypnosis and facilitates placing the patient into a trance. Appropriately called the talking treatment, Freud found that as patients began to verbalize their symptoms he could trace their problems back to traumatic childhood experiences. Does this have anything to do with "digging up childhood trauma?" Absolutely, yes!

What Freud found is that patients would "transfer" their passionate feelings of their parents onto him. Or in a general sense, "Transference is the unconscious redirection of feelings from one person to another."

In Freud's case, he found that patients would become sexually attracted to him. The result can be grounds for exploitation by the therapist who can abuse a very normal process that naturally occurs during therapy. One can already surmise the immediate problems with doctor/patient relationships that could arise from this dynamic; from sexual assault — unduly coercing patients to give money to a foundation the therapist is associated with — unduly influencing the signing of wills. The therapist is in a sensitive position where they can exploit the patient's dependence on them.

It is a documented fact that Lee Strasberg, portraying himself as an acting theorist and guru, took on all the roles of an unlicenced therapist and more. He had the tools to manipulate behavior by instilling guilt, shame, and anxiety into his students. Abraham Nievod Ph.D., J.D., in his article, *Undue Influence in Contract and Probate Law*, wrote:

Marilyn Monroe Unveiled | A Family History

Recent litigation has seen the rise of causes of action based on the premise that totalistic groups, both of a religious and nonreligious character, have developed and employed programmatically applied techniques to control and manipulate behavior in a weaker or subservient party in order to induce the weaker party to enter into a contract or execute a will in favor of the group or the charismatic leader of the group. Briefly, such groups used 'coordinated programs of coercion and behavior control' for example, the organization and application of intense guilt, shame, and/or anxiety manipulation, combined with the production of strong emotional arousal in settings designed to produce behavior that furthered the ends of the group or the leader.[6]

Dr. Rosemary Malague, Senior Lecturer in Theatre Arts at the Annenberg Center for Performing Arts pointed out that "the actors' commercial success directly contributes to the reputation and revenues of the institution(s) and/or teacher(s)."[7]

Lee Strasberg had strong motive to cocoon Marilyn Monroe — to extort her name and her image.

In fact, the Actors' Studio saw almost immediate results from her affiliation when she initially began attending the studio in early 1955.

The Abilene Reporter News, January 2, 1957 reported, "The Actors' Studio, which became known to millions of people who had never considered studying for the theater when Marilyn Monroe started sitting in on classes there..."[8]

Marlon Brando, who was intimately familiar with the Actors' Studio politics recognized how manipulative Lee Strasberg was to studio members.

He wrote, "After I had some success, Lee Strasberg tried to take credit for teaching me how to act. He never taught me anything. He would have claimed credit for the sun and the moon if he believed he could get away with it. He was an ambitious, selfish man who exploited the people who attended the Actors' Studio and he tried to project himself as an acting oracle and guru. Some people worshiped him, but I never knew why. To me he was a tasteless and untalented person whome I didn't like very much."[9]

Brando also knew exactly what Lee Strasberg was doing to Marilyn Monroe. He stated that she was "was being exploited by Lee Strasberg."[10]

Lee Strasberg's daughter Susan chillingly wrote about her father, "If they were needy, financially or emotionally, and if they were talented. He said that often the depth of the emotional problem was correspondent to the degree of talent. He was fascinated with the transmutation of antisocial behavior into creative work. Because of this, he was accused of doing therapy. One student and friend remarked, 'Lee, you should have been a therapist.' He shook his head. 'Why, darling? I have more freedom in my work.'"

Recall that Elia Kazan stated about Strasberg, "Silence is the cruelest weapon when someone loves you, and Lee knew it."

Lee Strasberg was not a master at acting, but of coercive persuasion and undue influence.

California Civil Code Section 1575 defines "undue influence,"

1. In the use, by one in whom a confidence is reposed by another, or who holds a real or apparent authority over him, of such confidence or authority for the purpose of obtaining an unfair advantage over him;
2. In taking an unfair advantage of another's weakness of mind; or
3. In taking a grossly oppressive and unfair advantage of another's necessities or distress.

The Lee Strasberg Theatre and Film Institute was founded on the gross manipulation of acting students and there should be no question that Lee Strasberg continually demonstrated his intent to financially extort Marilyn Monroe.

Lee Strasberg's strategy was based on classic cult indoctrination. A cult leader breaks down his targets thought patterns. His role as acting teacher placed Marilyn in emotional vulnerable position. He used the breakdown to obtain a breakthrough method to promote emotional distress in her. He even used the influence of other members of the studio, like Shelley Winters, to soften Marilyn's resolve Shelley was a former roomate and a longtime friend of Marilyn's.

He was then able to convince Marilyn he could solve her problems; that he could "fix" her. This is same sort of techniques used by cult leaders such as David Berg and Charles Manson. Lee Strasberg was performing this in a ritualisic fashion at the Actors' Studio. It is absolutely disgusting that the institution that he created still profits from Marilyn's extortion and murder today.

Lee Strasberg opened his Lee Strasberg Theatre and Film Institute October 27, 1969. They then opened the THE MARILYN MONROE THEATRE to continue to promote Lee Strasberg and his attachment to Marilyn Monroe.

Dr. Rosemary Malague referred to Lee Strasberg as a "Big Daddy."

She asked, "Can Method training lead an actress to a sense of strength as an independent artist? Or is it inevitable that a good Method actress must be a 'good little girl,' acting to please 'Big Daddy?'"

CHAPTER SIX Supporting Resources

[1] Svengali. Dictionary.com. Unabridged. Random House, Inc. http://dictionary.reference.com/browse/svengali (accessed: September 17, 2015).

[2] Voice of Broadway – Dorothy Kilgallen Anderson Daily Bulletin, 1 Jul 1955, Fri, Page

[3] *Marilyn Monroe's Ambition Is To B Competent Actress* – Edith Kermit Roosevelt, December 27, 1952.

[4] *My Sister Marilyn*, Berniece Baker Miracle and Mona Rae Miracle; 1994, 2003; Published by iUniverse, Inc.

[5] Fragments: Poems, Intimate Notes, Letters by Marilyn Monroe – edited by Stanley Buchthal and Bernard Comment, to be published October 12th by Farrar, Straus and Giroux, LLC (US), HarperCollins (Canada and UK); © 2010 by LSAS International, Inc.

[6] *Thought Reform Programs and the Production of Psychiatric Casualties* – by M. T. Singer & R. Ofshe, 20 Psychiatric Annals No. 4, April 1990, Page 188-193. Via *Undue Influence in Contract and Probate Law*, by Abraham Nievod, Ph.D., J.D., San Francisco, California.

[7] *An Actress Prepares: Women and "the Method"* – Rosemary Malague, Taylor & Francis Ltd, March 2, 2012.

[8] *Actors Studio Gives New Start Old Way* – Abilene Reporter News, January 2, 1957.

[9] *Marlon Brando: Songs My Mother Taught Me* – Marlon Brando, Page 44.

[10] *Marlon Brando: Songs My Mother Taught Me* – Marlon Brando, Page 77.

CHAPTER SEVEN

D ID MARILYN MONROE please "Big Daddy" Lee Strasberg by DYING and leaving 75 percent of her estate to him for his theater ambitions?!

Marilyn stated to her half-sister Berniece Miracle, "'They tried to rush me into signing a will just before I went into the hospital,' Marilyn fumes to Berniece. 'They kept insisting.'

'For the surgery?'

'No! When I was going to Payne Whitney. My secretary and my attorney stuck a will in my face to sign as I was going out the door. It was already made.'

'I was furious! I told them I was not going to sign it! I stood and argued.'"[1]

Who was Marilyn's secretary? None other than May Reis. She was listed as a beneficiary ($10,000 plus an additional $40,000) on the will she helped force Marilyn to sign. Who was the attorney? Aaron Frosch, who was Marilyn's business lawyer during her divorce from Arthur Miller.

On June 21, 1961 Marilyn's appointment book, now in the hands of memorabilia collector Ted Stampfer, documented a meeting between Aaron Frosch and none other than Lee Strasberg. Why was Marilyn Monroe's legal counsel for her business affairs meeting with her acting coach? In fact, an August 7, 1961 business letter to Marilyn documents Aaron Frosh actively meeting with Lee Strasberg to discuss her movie business deals. Aaron Frosch wrote, "Dear Marilyn: Before Lee Strasberg left on his trip, he discussed with me his several meetings with Joe Moskowitz. Lee said that Fox would be prepared to acquire the rights and that he thought that Marlon Brando might well want to do the film with you." Strasberg was more that an acting coach to Marilyn and was actively involved in negotiating her movie business contracts!

In 2006, author Lois Banner began investigating a relative of Inez Melson who had obtained two of Marilyn's filing cabinets from Inez when she passed away. Inez was Marilyn's business manager who was referred to Marilyn by Joe DiMaggio. After Marilyn died Inez Melson took the cabinets from Marilyn's home which contained an unprecedented collection of Marilyn's personal documents. They came to light after Lois Banner spearheaded their recovery back to Anna Strasberg[i] after some legal manuvering. In her book (which is really Anna Strasberg's book), *MM-Personal: From the Private Archive of Marilyn Monroe*, Lois Banner verified that indeed, Inez Melson had suspicions that Aaron Frosch and the Strasbergs conspired to commit fraud against Marilyn in the signing of her will.[2]

There is no question that Aaron Frosch and Lee Strasberg were making side deals concerning Marilyn Monroe's estate.

While Marilyn's will reflects being signed on January 14, 1961, Marilyn's appointment book had no appointment scheduled for January 14, 1961, which was a Saturday. There is however, an appointment scheduled with Aaron Frosch on Friday, January 13, 1961.

The apparent discrepancy between Marilyn's appointment book listing an appointment with Aaron Frosch on Friday January 13, 1961 and no appointment on Saturday, January 14, 1961 when

---

[i] Anna Strasberg is third wife of Lee Strasberg. She never met Marilyn and ended up owning Lee Strasberg's share of her estate after Lee Strasberg died. She's no Miracle, Monroe, or Hogan.

> MOORE 172nd day — 193 days follow
>
> Maxine in town
>
> 3PM LDCall
>
> 3:30 Aaron Frosch
> 3 Lee Strasberg
>
> Jack Cole
> Desiree Miller
>
> 11:50 Richard Cole
>
> Max Lerner
>
> Room Yes modern Friday
>
> Joan Copeland

3:30 Appointment with both Aaron Frosch and Lee Strasberg together.

All Copyrights reserved by Ted Stampfer/Used with Permission.

her will was allegedly signed, cannot be overlooked. In fact, on September 6, 1962 Inez Melson, Marilyn's business manager, wrote a letter to Joe DiMaggio. She had major concerns about the will being signed on January 14, 1961. She stated, "On January 14th, 1961, the date on which our baby purportedly executed her will, she had car rental charges as follows:"

4 1/2 hours - 8:45-1:15 (From Paul A. Reilly, Inc.)
2 1/2 hours - 4:45-7-15 (528 E. 73rd Street, N.Y. 21)

Inez wrote:

> I have a reason for wanting to know if the car was used and if so, where did she go but if I write directly, it might create a situation. Do you know anyone who could obtain this information quietly. Those hours appear on the bill and I know the rental agency would have a record of where she went. I know it sounds like a 'Perry Mason' television script but I am (between thee and me) very suspicious about that will and my only interest lies in the protection of future care of Mrs. Eley [Marilyn's mother Gladys]. If you can help me, fine- if not, I will see what I can do elsewhere since I appreciate how you feel.
> I have pretty well constructed what happened on that day and I find it impossible to see why Mr. Frosch had to be a witness along with his secretary.
> I know that you will understand how very discreet I must be about this.

According to Inez Melson's letter to Joe DiMaggio, Marilyn could not have signed her will on January 14, 1961.

However, remember that Marilyn's half-sister Berniece Miracle stated that May Reis and Aaron Frosch literally forced Marilyn to sign it the day Dr. Marianne Kris tricked her into entering Payne Whitney.

Marilyn was placed in a mental security ward of the hospital. Her right to leave of her own free volition was denied. Even writing a letter to Lee and Paula Strasberg failed to convince any of her new "friends" to try to bail her out.

Marilyn stated in that letter sent to the Strasbergs on February 8, 1961:

"Dr. Kris has had me put into the New York Hospital - psychiatric division under the care of two idiot doctors - they both should not be my doctors."

"You haven't heard from me because I'm locked up with all these poor nutty people."

"I'm sure to end up a nut if I stay in this nightmare- please help me Lee, this is the last place I should be - maybe if you called Dr. Kris and assured her of my sensitivity and that I must get back to class..."

Marilyn attempted to bargain with Lee Strasberg, emphazing her sensitivity. Sensitivity was the measuring rod Lee Strasberg used to determine the creative prowess of actors. Lee Strasberg used the carrot of sensitivity to enamor and overinflate Marilyn's ego. If Lee Strasberg praised her sensitivity, then it was obvious that Marilyn attempted to use its perceived value as currency to sway Strasberg to help her in her moment of psychological duress.

Did Marilyn come across as the strong independent business woman and actress in her letter to the Strasbergs? Absolutely not! In fact, Marilyn sounded exactly like the woman described by the gang in the December 16, 1956 Zolotow article. Marilyn's letter to Lee Strasberg proves that Marilyn was unduly influenced by Strasberg's carrot of sensitivity; he was, after all, her svengali.

Again, Marilyn stated, "Maybe if you called Dr. Kris and assured her of my sensitivity and that I must get back to class..."

Marilyn's statement was one of desperation and not one of self-control.

Marilyn Monroe was naive and controlled. Her need to bargain with Lee Strasberg demonstrated a dependent woman who tried to use the only stock she felt she had with Strasberg to try to convince him to get her out of the Payne Whitney Psychiatric Clinic — the security mental ward.

Marilyn Monroe Unveiled | A Family History

Her utter pleas for assistance from her new "friends" were rejected as expected.

Nonetheless, Marilyn was somehow able to phone Joe DiMaggio[i] who arrived to rescue her.

If Marilyn Monroe was so mentally fragile as purported by a "Little Orphan Annie in Hollywood" story and the December 16, 1956 Zolotow article and by her "friends" and therapist, how did Dr. Marianne Kris err in having her enter a mental security ward?

She did not err, she placed Marilyn there with deceitful purpose.

And that purpose would financially benefit none other than Lee Strasberg and Anna Freud.

Both Anna Freud and Dr. Marianne Kris had a long history together. Not only did they live together as part of the Freud family, but they worked together as analysts and colleagues.

The journal, *The Psychoanalytic Study of the Child* was founded in 1945 by Anna Freud, Heinz Hartmann, and Ernst Kris.

Who was Ernst Kris? None other than Dr. Marianne Kris's husband. The journal was the main forum for the Hampstead Clinic which later changed its name to the Anna Freud Centre. When Ernst Kris died on February 27, 1957, Dr. Marianne Kris obtained his position as an editor of the journal. By 1964, both Anna Freud and Dr. Marianne Kris fought to include a child analysis forum under the American Psychoanalysis Association (APsaA). Both lifelong friends and colleagues fighting for *a permanent psychiatric cure* using the Anna Freud Centre!

Was Marilyn's incarceration in the Payne Whitney Psychiatric Clinic an attempt to mentally fracture her and send her over the abyss of mental insanity? Is this why Lee Strasberg never came to her rescue and never contacted Dr. Marianne Kris whose office was in the same building that he resided in?

This event was a criminal ploy by Dr. Marianne Kris and Lee Strasberg to attempt to either push Marilyn Monroe to commit suicide or to stop Marilyn Monroe from ever being legally competent to change her will again. Recall that Lee Strasberg and the psychotherapist were working together. And Method actors bragged that they were nuts about Sigmund Freud! They both obtained Marilyn Monroe's Estate!

Inez Melson chronologically documented the day that Aaron Frosch and his secretary Louise White claimed to have witnessed the signing of Marilyn's will. While there was a Friday January 13, 1961 appointment listed to see Aaron Frosch in Marilyn's appointment book, there was nothing listed on Saturday January 14, 1961.

Melson stated, "I have pretty well constructed what happened on that day and I find it impossible to see why Mr. Frosch had to be a witness along with his secretary."

Marilyn's half-sister Berniece Miracle stated that Marilyn told her that Aaron Frosch and *her* secretary May Reis argued with her to sign the will on the day Dr. Marianne Kris incarcerated her at Payne Whitney Psychiatric Clinic — that was on February 5, 1961.

The evidence in this case, arguably, is more accurate in favor of Berniece Miracle's version of events. Although, it is possible, that if Berniece Miracle is mistaken, which it would not have been a mistake, but a lie about her claim of events, then Aaron Frosch and his secretary both made a mistake of writing the 14th, instead of the 13th as the day the will was signed.

Nonetheless, altering the date that a will was signed is still a crime. However, if the will was signed on February 5, 1961 instead of Saturday January 13, 1961 and if Berniece Miracle and Inez Melson are accurate and truthful in their statements, then Marilyn's incarceration (if she had a mental breakdown) would have easily invalidated Marilyn's will to the detriment of gang. A will signed under psychological duress, especially the very day Marilyn was incarcerated would have immediatly invalidated that will.

In an unrelated event which just happened to involve the Los Angeles Orphans' Home in 1944, a niece challenged the will of her aunt Mrs. Elisa Haeni Stassforth. The niece argued that her aunt was mentally incompetent and therefore could not sign over "gifts of stock and other securities totaling $63,122" to the charity.

This hypothesis follows that Aaron Frosch, working in collusion with Strasberg had to pre-date the will, which they made the mistake of the 14th, rather than Friday January 13, 1961, which was the

---
[i] Baseball legend Joe DiMaggio was Marilyn Monroe's ex-husband.

actual date that Marilyn did have an appointment with Aaron Frosch.

It is surmised that Aaron Frosch and his secretary both lied and predated her will as early as possible. They made the mistake of predating the will on Saturday January 14, 1961 instead of the Friday January 13, 1961, which was the actual date they had a scheduled appointment with Marilyn.

The evidence may also suggest that Marilyn Monroe's will was signed on Sunday February 5, 1961 while Marilyn argued with attorney Aaron Frosch and her secretary May Reis.

Author Lois Banner, who was involved with Anna Strasberg and the recovery of the Marilyn's filing cabinets suggested that Marilyn's car rental charges on January 14, 1961 were innocently the result of Aaron Frosch physically driving Marilyn to New Jersey to sign her will on the 14th.[3] However, the newspaper *Standard-Speaker* of Hazleton, Pennsylvania on Friday, August 10, 1962 reported that both Milton Rudin and Aaron Frosch said the will was signed in New York. Furthermore, the *Pottstown Mercury* in Pottstown, Pennsylvania on Thu, Sep 27, 1962 quoted Frosch stating that Marilyn's will was signed January 14, 1961 in her New York apartment. He then stated that Marilyn went out for entertainment afterward.

A simple fact: the people who run Marilyn Monroe's estate continually deceived the public to cover the premeditated financial exortion of Marilyn Monroe. Additionally, the story always changes; red-herrings indiscriminately thrown to the public to muddy the waters and to confuse Marilyn researchers.

If Marilyn had commited suicide after entering the Payne Whitney, then a predated will would have protected the will as it stood.

Is this just a coincidence that Marilyn was potentially incarcerated the very day her will was signed? If not, then it is damaging evidence that Dr. Marianne Kris, Aaron Frosch, and Lee Strasberg were working together to keep Marilyn off balance so they could have the will signed and immediately break her down psychologically. What better time to have her sign the will.

If Marilyn Monroe had a mental breakdown at the Payne Whitney Psychiatric Clinic thinking she would end up like her mother, she could have been compelled to commit suicide. This would have quickly ended the game. However, if Marilyn only broke down into a schizophrenic collapse, then among other legal requirements there would be the necessity of having psychological evaluation. Dr. Marianne Kris, as the "adopted" daughter of Sigmund Freud could have easily had Marilyn Monroe declared mentally incompetent for life. Marilyn would have been mentally *incompetent* to change her last will — ever.

Regardless if Marilyn will was signed on Friday January 13, 1961, Saturday January 14, 1961, or Sunday February 5, 1961, the Payne Whitney incarceration was a direct assault on Marilyn. They wanted her to commit suicide and/or go into a schizophrenia mental collapse.

On one hand it was fortunate that Joe DiMaggio intervened and Marilyn escaped the criminal ploy, however, the stakes were now critically increased — Marilyn Monroe would eventually pay with her life. Anna Freud wanted to ensure a lasting Freudian "permanent psychiatric cure," Lee Strasberg wanted his theater, and Milton Greene wanted his photographs (In fact, if Marilyn had lived, would she have challenged Milton Greene's ownership of all photographs he claims he owns today?) They would not stop until they obtained what they wanted.

Who was also Dr. Marianne Kris's patient? Jacqueline Kennedy Onassis. In the late 1960s, by "happenstance," Jacqueline "Jackie" Kennedy Onassis donated $10,000 to none other than the Anna Freud Centre, for a "permanent psychiatric cure." In a 1977 article in *The Hazelton Standard-Speaker*, it was reported that Jackie "could not shed her old memories or problems" and had to depart her office early, interrupting her workday to see Dr. Kris. Dr. Marianne Kris was culling her rich patients to fund the Anna Freud Centre!

After the Payne Whitney fiasco, Marilyn's psychological manipulation was transferred from Dr. Marianne Kris to Dr. Ralph (Romi) Greenson. What sort of relationship did Anna Freud have with Dr. Romi Greenson as described in her official biography?

"[Anna Freud] could discuss with her old friends, particularly *Marianne Kris* and Heinz Hartmann, and with her new ones, particularly *Romi Greenson*, her succession problem."[4]

Marilyn Monroe Unveiled | A Family History

Anna Freud said in correspondence that she "was placing her hopes for the future more and more on Greenson and his peers."[5]

Anna Freud had a financial need to fund her foundation after her death. She stated, "Could we not ever find in America three real millionaires who would endow the Clinic in a way which would diminish almost all of Dr. Eissler's and all of my money concerns for it, so that one could really foresee a future, at least one of ten or twenty years? Not that I wish or intend to hold out so long, but it would be so nice to know that the Clinic will."[6]

What were Anna Freud and Dr. Greenson doing to find millionaires? They were again culling their rich patients, just like Dr. Marianne Kris culled Jacqueline Kennedy Onassis. In 2007 Douglas Kirsner, PhD wrote a peer-reviewed paper titled *Do As I Say, Not As I Do: Ralph Greenson, Anna Freud, and Superrich Patients*.

Kirsner discovered, through letters between Anna Freud and Dr. Ralph (Romi) Greenson, with "full knowledge and collusion" conspired to manipulate Greenson's patients Lita Annenberg Hazen and Barbara Anderson and others for money to fund the Anna Freud Centre for "a permanent psychiatric cure."

Lita Annenberg Hazen's net worth in 1986 was $200 million.

Barbara Anderson, wife of oil executive Robert Orville Anderson, her net worth in 1982 was $500 million.

Both were Dr. Ralph Greenson's patients and both were major contributors to the Anna Freud Foundation which was searching for "a permanent psychiatric cure."

On December 11, 1972, Dr. Greenson flagrantly overstepped his position as therapist by attempting to find Hazen a companion. According to Kirsner, Dr. Greenson wrote to psychoanalyst Joseph Sandler in London. "...keep your eyes open to find a companion. It would make all our lives easier and above all, it would insure the existence of FRIP." FRIP is "Foundation for Research in Psychoanalysis."

This bears repeating — FRIP — FOUNDATION FOR RESEARCH IN PSYCHOANALYSIS. How does one obtain *A PERMANENT PSYCHIATRIC CURE?* — RESEARCH!

He then traveled, on his own accord, to New York from California to interview a possible male companion for Hazen. Dr. Greenson wrote to Anna Freud, "To me it was a chance to help Lita and help myself."

Kirsner charged, "This was beyond the call of duty for a patient — or even for a friend — would be a gross understatement, and that he communicated all this to Anna Freud also significant."

Lita Annenberg Hazen became the President of Dr. Ralph Greenson's foundation in Los Angeles. She was also funding it.

On April 28, 1979 Dr. Greenson relayed to Anna Freud about his patient Anderson, "As I told you, she is very nice woman and a very wealthy woman. I believe she will become a patron of the Anna Freud Foundation and that could be very useful."

Dr. Ralph Greenson and Dr. Marianne Kris were professionally prostituting themselves for Anna Freud and Anna Freud was clearly their *pimp*.

These letters clearly indicated that they were not only manipulating patients for money, but they were actively breaking doctor-patient confidentiality.

Anna Freud, Dr. Ralph Greenson, Dr. Marianne Kris and Dr. Margaret Hohenberg were ALL manipulating Marilyn Monroe to fund *a* "permanent psychiatric cure." Recall it was none other than Dr. Margaret Hohenberg who told Marilyn, while under duress that she wanted *a* "permanent psychiatric cure" in 1955!

By 1976 Dr. Ralph Greenson was in charge of the Anna Freud Foundation — the California Chapter, of course.

Did Dr. Ralph (Romi) Greenson begin his career culling patients for money with Marilyn Monroe? The answer is unequivocally yes! In fact, he worked with both Dr. Marianne Kris and Dr. Margaret Hohenberg. On August 1, 1962 Hohenberg submitted a bill to Marilyn three days before her death for services rendered during May, June and July of 1962 for a total of $840.00! She then submitted that bill to collect from Marilyn's Estate after Marilyn was dead!

Why was Dr. Hohenberg STILL seeing Marilyn Monroe in 1962 when Marilyn was concurrently seeing Dr. Ralph (Romi) Greenson? It does not take a rocket scientist to figure this out!

According to Kirsner, "These activities took place with Anna Freud's knowledge, approval, and collusion."

Manipulating patients for money that went well beyond the fees charged for psychological services has huge ethical and criminal implications.

Remember that Susan Strasberg witnessed and reported that her father Lee Strasberg privately took Marilyn Monroe into his living room, describing in detail what amounted to a talking therapy session. Lee Strasberg was not only practicing psychotherapy without a license, but also was clearly abusing transference dynamics with Marilyn.

Also recall, that while under duress in 1955 Lee Strasberg told Marilyn under coercive duress that he wanted a theater and that Dr. Margaret Hohenberg wanted a permanent psychiatric cure.

Marilyn was either a psychic in 1955 and could foretell the future when Lee Strasberg and Anna Freud would obtain her estate or they told her exactly what they wanted while she was under physical and mental duress in 1955! Duress that was a direct result of an illegal behavioral modification experiment conducted by them!

Kirsner emphasized about Lita Hazen, "She was tied to Greenson by transferences and he (and Anna Freud) to her through money."

Marilyn Monroe was tied to Lee Strasberg, Dr. Margaret Hohenberg, Dr. Marriane Kris, and Dr. Ralph Greenson by transferences and all of them (and Anna Freud) to Marilyn through HER money!

Follow the MONEY

It is time for Norma Jeane to come home!

On September 22, 1972, Anna Freud responded to Dr. Greenson about transference: "I was very glad too that you succeeded in making Mrs. Hazen realize that transferences are not only positive but also negative; glad for her sake, for yours and, of course, no less the Foundation. The last concern may be very mercenary of me, but after all it is for the sake of the Clinic and the work, not for myself. It is too bad that this type of work is so wholly dependent on money, and too bad that I am not a millionaire myself."

Did Anna Freud just admit to Dr. Ralph (Romi) Greenson that she would abuse transferences for the sake of the foundation? Unmistakably and emphatically — yes!

They both admitted they would abuse transferences for money!

If they were actively abusing patients for money, would Dr. Ralph Greenson murder Marilyn Monroe for money as well?

Anna Freud and Dr. Ralph Greenson have been unveiled.

The Freudians knew intimately the consequences of transference and so did Lee Strasberg who was actively working with the psychotherapist according to his own daughter Susan Strasberg. They actively used undue influence and manipulation to get what they wanted from Marilyn Monroe.

Mona Miracle, about money stated, "Marilyn sighs a mile-long sigh. 'I have no cash.' She rambles on, 'Once I gave them my AT&T stocks. Lee wanted to go to Japan.'"

The fact that Lee wanted to go to Japan was revealed in a May 8, 1959 letter to the Actors' Studio, and Marilyn offered an additional $10,000, "The full amount of these two checks, Ten Thousand ($10,000) Dollars, I wish to designate towards the trip to the Orient which Mr. Lee Strasberg is making for the benefit of the Actors' Studio."

They used coercive and illegal techniques and unethical uses of transference to continually coerce money from Marilyn Monroe.

Marilyn Monroe Unveiled | A Family History

One could surmise that as asute and professional as Lee Strasberg and the Freudians claimed to be, they could deduce that Marilyn's biographical orphan story was a fabrication as early as 1956. Yet, after seven years of "therapy" plus "talking" treatments, they failed to acknowlege anything else but the orphan story. They own it! In fact, in the documentary *The Legend of Marilyn Monroe*, we know the Bolenders would have defended Marilyn's childhood just as they did with Ezra Goodman. Yet, none of that came out. Lee Strasberg was interviewed as was Milton Greene and it was directed by John Huston. They all knew the Bolenders' story did not comform to the orphan narrative. It is clear they cherry-picked their interview with the Bolenders to defame Marilyn's grandmother Della Monroe and continued to lie to cover-up Marilyn's death. The orphan stories were their cover story to hide from the public and police their criminal ploy against Marilyn.

When Ezra Goodman did his research for the *TIME* cover story he interviewed none other than Paula Strasberg about Marilyn. They knew about Ezra Goodman's research in 1956!

If loose lips could sink ships, then Susan Strasberg, Paula Strasberg's daughter, could inadvertently help bring these ships down (The Anna Freud Centre and the The Lee Strasberg Theatre & Film Institute). Susan Strasberg (Lee Strasberg's daughter) independently verified and corroborated in her book exactly what Ezra Goodman reported concerning his research for *TIME* in 1961.

Susan reported in her own book, "[Ezra Goodman] uncovered new material on [Marilyn's] early history that showed the degree to which she had taken creative license with the facts of her upbringing. She'd borrowed some of her stories of abuse and the number of homes she'd had from a young girlfriend of hers."

Susan failed to mention her name.

Who was that young girlfriend? According to Ezra Goodman he spoke to "a blond, sad-eyed, twenty five year old movie starlet named Jody Lawrance." Jody Lawrance was none other than the stepdaughter of Grace McKee Goddard who was also Marilyn Monroe's legal guardian growing up! Her father was Ervin "Doc" Goddard. Ezra Goodman revealed, "Jody Lawrance's relationship with Monroe had been kept SECRET[i], and this was the first time she had been interviewed on the subject."

And why was it kept secret? Because it conflicted with Marilyn's fabricated orphan stories! Jody had her own foster home stories, but she was not being marketed as an orphan or as a foster child. Marilyn padded her own biographical story with some of Jody's own childhood experiences.

They were stepsisters in the Goddard family. Born October 19, 1930 as Nona Josephine Goddard she changed her name to Jody Lawrance. By 1949 she was signed for a seven year contract with Columbia Pictures and then onto Paramount Pictures and others. Some of the movies she had leading roles in: *Mask of the Avenger* starring John Derek, *Ten Tall Men* co-starring Burt Lancaster, *All Ashore* with Mickey Rooney, *The Hot Spell* with Shirley MacLaine and more.

A legal guardian to one and stepmother to the other, these two woman, both out of Grace McKee Goddard's household, became actresses and movie stars, albeit one much more famous than the other. In fact both young women ended up together in newspaper articles promoting Cinderellas at the same time! They both were actively pursuing stardom in Hollywood while a part of Grace McKee Goddard's household! The May 10, 1951 *Kingsport Times* headlined, "Film Factories Working Overtime To Turn Out Different Cinderellas."

Does that sound like Marilyn was a real abused orphan as a child or were these women crafting stories to promote themselves as Hollywood starlets?

Both Marilyn Monroe and Jody Lawrance were listed one paragraph above the other in the same article. Hollywood was indeed building Cinderellas! Grace McKee Goddard, Jody and Norma Jeane were all working the system to get into the Hollywood movie industry. And Lee Strasberg and the Freudians were mind raping Marilyn Monroe for her money using the fabricated Cinderella Story to cover up their crime!

Meanwhile, Anna Freud's official biographer Elisabeth Young-Bruehl stated, "No millionaires materialized, but, ironically enough, the clinic did get a sizable portion of the tardily settled estate of Marilyn Monroe."

---
[i] Upper case text added for emphasis.

Marilyn Monroe Unveiled | A Family History

'Film Factories Working Overtime To Turn Out Different Cinderellas'

KINGSPORT TIMES

Vol. XXXVI, No. 94   Kingsport, Tenn., Thursday, May 10, 1951   24 Pages   Five Cents

Jody Lawrence

Jody Lawrence, Hollywood's most successful "unknown" actress. She has played four starring roles, but none of the films has been released. Her studio predicts she'll hit in a hurry, though. She's a Texan, born in Fort Worth almost 20 years ago. Got her start as a swimmer in Larry Crosby's water show.

Marilyn Monroe, graduate of the school of hard knocks. Orphaned shortly after her birth in Los Angeles, she spent her youth in a number of homes and orphanages. She held a variety of jobs, from making five cents a week in an orphan home to a stock contract at a studio. Nothing much happened until John Huston cast her as the sexy moll in "Asphalt Jungle." Her blonde beauty clicked and the roles got better. Named Miss Cheesecake of 1951 by Stars and Stripes, service paper.

Grace McKee Goddard

Marilyn Monroe

Marilyn Monroe Unveiled | A Family History

"No millionaires materialized...?" Just who were Lita Annenberg Hazen and Barbara Anderson and Jacqueline Kennedy Onassis and Marilyn Monroe? Yes — Millionaires did materialize; a fact that they want to hide from the public and continue to lie to the public about their unethical funding machine!

Marilyn was indeed a millionaire when she died. Aaron Frosch, her lawyer, stated in newspapers around the country that her estate was worth upwards of a million dollars and that her assets were going to have to begin to earn an income to recover from the hit in taxes they took.

Elisabeth Young-Bruehl continued, "The actress made the bequest to her New York analyst, Marianne Kris, in a will she had made while she was with her Los Angeles analyst, Romi Greenson, who had had to live with the fact of her suicide."

Maybe Dr Ralph (Romi) Greenson had to live with the fact that he kept Marilyn addicted to barbituates and was doing everything in his power to manipulate her to keep Dr. Marianne Kris on the will for a "permanent psychiatric cure!"

Both Dr. Ralph Greenson and Dr. Margaret Hohenberg teamed up on Marilyn Monroe in the finally months right up to the day of her death. In his own words he stated, "the fact that I saw [Marilyn] professionally on 28 days from July 1 through August 4, 1962."

Sunday, July — Patient's Home
Monday, July 2 — Office
Tuesday, July 3 — Office
Wednesday, July 4 — Patient's Home
Thursday, July 5 — Office
Friday, July 8 — Patient's Home
Monday, July 9 — Office
Tuesday, July 10 — Office
Wednesday, July 11 — Office
Thursday, July 12 — Office
Friday, July 13 — Office and Patient's Home
Monday, July 16 — Office
Tuesday, July 17 — Office
Wednesday, July 18 — Office
Thursday, July 20 — Office
Monday, July 23 — Office and Patient's Home
Tuesday, July 24 — Office
Wednesday, July 25 — Office and Patient's Home
Thursday, July 26 — Office
Friday, July 27 — Office
Monday, July 30 — Office
Tuesday, July 31 — Office
Wednesday, August 1 — Office
Thursday, August 2 — Office and Patient's Home
Friday, August 3 — Office
Saturday, August 4 — Patient's Home.

Dr. Ralph (Romi) Greenson was in Marilyn's home on August 4, 1962 and August 5, 1962 and Dr. Margaret Hohenberg charged Marilyn for phone consultations in May, June, and July of 1962 right before her death!

Dr. Ralph Greenson explained, "All office visits lasted a minimum of 1 ½ hours. All visits to the home were approximately 2 hours in duration. On those days on which it was stated that the patient was seen both at the office and at her home, it means there were two separate visits on that particular day. I had arranged with Miss Monroe that her fee would be $50. per hour. However, since she

needed a great deal of extra time and since I did not want her to think I gave her extra time or made extra visits for monetary reason, I decided that I would charge her $50. for every day that I saw her professionally. The sum of $1400. therefore represents the fact that I saw her professionally on 28 days from July 1 through August 4, 1962.
    Very Truly Yours,
    Dr. Ralph Greenson"

After seven years of "therapy" and the top Freudian psychotherapists: Dr. Margaret Hohenberg, Dr. Marianne Kris, and Dr. Ralph Greenson, two of which are working directly under Anna Freud, could not even determine if Marilyn Monroe was really an orphan or not? They also could not resolve any of her so-called psychological issues. Clearly, they were not trying to help Marilyn Monroe resolve her childhood trauma. But what they were doing was helping themselves to her bank accounts! Ezra Goodman knew exactly what was going on in 1956 after only two months of research!

In 1992, Susan Strasberg, the daughter of Lee Strasberg wrote in her book *Marilyn and Me: Sisters, Rivals, Friends* about her mother Paula Strasberg. "In pursuit of the real Marilyn, Esra (Ezra Goodman) took Mother and Steffi to dinner. He plied Mom, who didn't drink, with some disgusting sweet rum drink to loosen her tongue, but to no avail. It was all much ado about nothing because *TIME* edited the piece till they had an upscale movie magazine version."[7]

Yes, *TIME* magazine edited their 1956 cover story on Marilyn Monroe and lied to the public!

She continued, "'How could he learn the truth about a girl who's such a good liar?' Mother laughed. 'If there's one truth, anyway. All those facts he collected may have less to do with the reality than her fantasies.' Mother spoke from experience. She was also a woman who more than once had molded the truth to suit her dreams."

And that is exactly what Lee Strasberg, Paula Strasberg, Arthur Miller, and Milton Greene did — they all molded the truth about Marilyn to suit their own hopes and dreams!

Elisabeth Young-Bruehl stated, "Dr. Kris was instructed to give the money to the charity of her choice, and she chose the Hampstead Clinic."[i]

Who else was Dr. Marianne Kris going to bequest the money to? As reported earlier, Dr. Marianne Kris culled her other patient Jacqueline Kennedy Onassis. Jackie gave $10,000 to none other than the Anna Freud Centre for "a permanent psychiatric cure!"

According to Elisabeth Young-Bruehl, Anna Freud wrote to Greenson, "I am terribly sorry about Marilyn Monroe. I know exactly how you feel because I had exactly the same thing happen with a patient of mine who took cyanide two days before I came back from America a few years ago. One goes over and over in one's head to find out where one could have done better and it leaves one with a terrible sense of being defeated."

Is this a conversation of plausible deniability between Anna Freud and Dr. Ralph Greeneson?

Anna Freud continued, "But, you know, I think in these cases we are really defeated by something which is stronger than we are and for which analysis, with all its powers, is too weak a weapon."

What about Anna Freud's need for money and a permanent psychiatric cure? Anna Freud and Dr. Ralph Greenson admitted that they were abusing transferences to manipulate patients to give them money. Ethical analysis is worthless and powerless and meaningless if your agenda is to manipulate and extort money from your patients no matter how important you think your cause is; it is still criminal; especially if their patient dies a highly suspicious death while under their direct care. They all had the motive to murder Marilyn!

Elisabeth Young-Bruehl wrote, "Marilyn Monroe's bequest came to the Hampstead Clinic just while the Clinic was adjusting to the tremendously influential work that Anna Freud had undertaken outside the Clinic — work in which the plight of children, like the young Marilyn Monroe, who had been bounced from one foster home to another, was central."

---

[i] The *Hampstead Clinic* is the same organization as *The Anna Freud Centre*. They changed their name after Anna Freud's death in 1982.

Marilyn Monroe Unveiled | A Family History

Remember, according to Ida Bolender and Grace McKee Goddard's official court documents, Marilyn was not "bounced from one foster home to another." Marilyn stayed with her mother Gladys and Ida Bolender, then Grace McKee became her legal guardian.

If the orphan story added to the gang's plausible deniability and if the preponderance of the evidence argues against the orphan stories, then their professional careers can no longer protect them.

On August 1, 1962, Cherie Redmond wrote what is titled an inter-office correspondence to none other than Hedda Rosten.[8]

Cherie was brought in by Milton Rudin, another one of Marilyn's lawyers, who was married to none other than Ralph (Romi) Greenson's sister. Cherie Redmond was responsible for Marilyn's appointments, mail and phone calls.

Cherie reported that she was going on vacation the next week, which was on August 6, 1962.

Recall that Marilyn Monroe died between August 4 and 5, 1962.

She also asked Hedda, to "Please let me know where you're going to be on your vacation - not that I intend calling you - but I always feel safer when I know where I can reach 'the gang'...."[9]

Cherie, using the term "gang" was referring to the herself, Hedda Rosten, and May Reis. It is an interesting term to use since we know that Milton Greene, Arthur Miller, Lee Strasberg and Norman and Hedda Rosten were the original members of the gang. Certainly, the term described how these people continued to cocoon Marilyn and how they saw themselves in relation to their employer. And again this "gang" mentality had a monetary interest tied directly to Marilyn and with none other than Hedda Rosten leading that office gang.

Who else was planning on going on vacation the week after Marilyn Monroe's death? None other than Eunice Murray, who was Marilyn's housekeeper. She was brought in directly by Ralph (Romi) Greenson. Marilyn hired her because of Greenson's recommendation.

In fact, salaries were drawn up early for eveyone's vacation the week of Marilyn's death! Another memo stated, "Since Mrs. Redmond was on vacation for this week, these salaries were drawn in advance. It is our understanding they were signed by Miss Monroe on August 3 [1962] and delivered to the payees on that date. Check number 1787 8/11 Eunice Murray - salary for w/e 8/11 [1962] 200.00."

According to the memo on August 1, 1962 by Cherie Redmond, Eunice was planning on taking a vacation to Europe on August 6, 1962.

Documenting the attempt of direct withholding of information from Marilyn, Cherie told Hedda Rosten, "I hope you didn't happen to mention anything to MM about Mrs. Murray going to Europe...Mrs. Murray told me she still had not made her reservation...it seems (to me) that her devotion to MM is so intense (that may not be the right word - but you'll know what I mean) that she wouldn't want to go away if she felt it would discommode MM."

There is no available evidence that Cherie Redmond was actively working with the gang to extort Marilyn, however, Cherie recogized that Eunice Murray was overly obsessed with Marilyn. She also captured the condescending attitude they had towards Marilyn.

Who is controlling who? Marilyn was their employer and paid their salaries and yet Cherie Redmond was suggesting to keep information away from Marilyn.

In another memo dated August 1, [1962] Cherie wrote to Helen, who was Milton Rudin's (Dr. Ralph Greenson's brother-in-law) secretary. She writes, "I certainly expect you to open an envelopes I mark 'personal' -- I just want to be sure that if you're away for a day -- for fun not because you're sick or anything -- that someone else would not open it (them ?) Because the fewer people who know about the state of MM's finances, etc., the better."

This highly suspicious and inappropriate memo demonstrates the state of Marilyn's finances were clearly being kept secret. And certainly who was the "them" Cherie Redmond was referring to?

Author Lois Banner suggested that Cherie was suspicous that Aaron Frosch or others were skimming money from Marilyn's account (which may have been true), however, she offered no evidence to back up that claim which seems as a red herring (redirecting the public away from Lee

Marilyn Monroe Unveiled | A Family History

Strasberg, Hedda Rosten, and Dr. Ralph Greenson) considering Lois Banner is affiliated with Anna Strasberg.

These memos from Cherie Redmond and Helen both demonstrated that at some level information was being kept away from Marilyn and that the state of her finances were not being addressed. All of this reeks of being highly unethical, if not intentionally criminal. But it also evidenced how these people manuvered around Marilyn.

Indeed Marilyn's finances were in complete disarray going back to 1955. There was a pattern of Marilyn being cash poor and at the mercy of others to fund her business; all of these sycophants taking money from her as it poured out of her account. If Marilyn did have a problem giving gifts and money away as is claimed, did any one of her "close" advisors resign in protest when she was living beyond her means? It is acknowledged that on June 25, 1962 Marilyn was informed by letter from Milton Rudin that her account would be overdrawn if she spent too much. But the day to day managment of her money was quite diffferent than telling her directly that she was living beyond her means and frivolously spending money.

There was a serious problem here and none of her so called advisors seriously addressed it.

Was Marilyn even informed that someone might be skimming money from her accounts?

There is no question that Hedda Rosten, May Reis, Patricia Newcomb, and Paula Strasberg all knew about Marilyn's finances, yet none of them ever demonstrated that they stopped accepting so called Marilyn's gifts or payments.

According to Lois Banner, Patricia Newcomb even wrote a letter to Marilyn telling her that she and Paula Strasberg loved her and want her to call them anytime day or night if she is feeling down.

They love someone but they kept on accepting huge gifts knowing that Marilyn has major financial problems! And further, they had discussions about keeping Marilyn's finances a SECRET! Marilyn had financial problems because they kept on extorting money from her and they did not want anyone else to know what they were doing to her!

- Paula Strasberg | $10,000 for 4 weeks of acting advising
- Paula Strasberg | $612.28 August 1, 1962
- Paula Strasberg | Check # 1791 Bel Air Sands Hotel -for Paula Strasberg bill $406.69
- Paula Strasberg| Stock bought for, November 27, 1961
- Patricia Newcomb | Mink Coat
- John Strasberg (Lee Strasberg's son) | a car
- Paula Strasberg | Mikimoto pearls (a gift Marilyn had received from Joe DiMaggio)
- The Strasberg Family | Various expensive gifts
- Ralph Greenson | Expensive household gifts and clothing. Many years later, these items were sold at auction. One item sold, a Pucci blouse, was pictured in police photos after Marilyn's body was found, and before her home was sealed. The Greenson family stole this item, while Marilyn's body was cold and later sold this stolen item.
- And much more!

Marilyn's relatives, on the other hand, did not document that they received expensive gifts, though it is known Marilyn sent clothing of her's to her sister Berniece.

On June 7, 1962 Dr. Ralph (Romi) Greenson took Marilyn to Beverly Hills, California to see Dr. Michael Gurdin, a cosmetic surgeon. She had bruises on her face. The injury was described as occuring in a late night fall that occured between two or three in the morning. There was apparent swelling and tenderness in the area of the nose. The x-ray did not show any damage to the nose at the time, however, a recent medical re-evaluation indicated that there was indeed a very small hairline fracture of Marilyn's nose.[10] Was this the first indication that Dr. Ralph Greenson had become physically abusive towards Marilyn Monroe?

On August 20, 1962, 16 days after Marilyn Monroe's death, Dr. Ralph (Romi) Greenson wrote a letter to none other than Dr. Marianne Kris. According to Donald Spoto, Greenson described August 4 (Marilyn died sometime between August 4 and August 5, 1962) as becoming an all day therapy session with Marilyn Monroe. Greenson also wrote that "I was aware that she was somewhat annoyed with me. She often became annoyed when I did not absolutely and wholeheartedly agree [with her]....She was angry with me. I told her we would talk more, that she should call me on Sunday morning..."[11]

Was Greenson's conversation with Dr. Kris another case of plausible deniability?

Dr. Ralph (Romi) Greenson admitted to Dr. Marianne Kris that on August 4, 1961 he and Marilyn Monroe had a conflict! He stated, "She was angry with me."

What was the disagreement about? Did Dr. Greenson ever tell the police that they had an argument on August 4, 1962?

With forethought, Greenson intentionally crafted a condition to plausibly avoid responsibility for what had happened. The condition? He stated, "I told her we would talk more, that she should call me on Sunday morning...."

In a statement by Theodore J. Curphey, M.D., Chief Medical Examiner-Coroner of the County of Los Angeles on August 17, 1962, he summarized a report by the Psychiatric Investigative Team which was headed by Robert Litman, M.D., Norman Farberrow, Ph.D., And Norman Tabachnick, M.D.:

> Marilyn Monroe died on the night of August 4th or the early morning of August 5, 1962. Examination by the toxicology laboratory indicates that death was due to a self-administered overdose of sedative drugs.

What was Dr. Ralph (Romi) Greenson trying to avoid the responsibility of in his letter to Dr. Marianna Kris? What had happened between August 4 and August 5, 1962 — Marilyn Monroe would die; literally hours after Dr. Ralph (Romi) Greenson admitted that he had an argument with her!

Also in the August 20, 1962 letter written by Dr. Ralph (Romi) Greenson to Dr. Marianne Kris, Greenson explicitly tells Kris, "I asked the housekeeper to stay overnight, which she did not ordinarily do on Saturday nights."[12]

Recall that Cherie Redmond stated in her memo to Hedda Rosten that Eunice was planning on taking a trip to Europe on August 6, 1962 even though she had yet to make reservations at the writing of Cherie's memo. Eunice Murray even received her paycheck in advance!

Now Dr. Greenson, who most likely knew Eunice was planning to go on vacation to Europe on Monday the sixth, essentially ordered Eunice Murray to stay overnight, which she "ordinarily" did not do on Saturday nights— the very night Marilyn Monroe died.

Does this sound like they were trying to "help" Marilyn Monroe on August 4, 1962?

Or does this sound like Dr. Ralph (Romi) Greenson set Marilyn up to die that night?

Premeditated murder!

In the most damning piece of evidence against the official story as documented by the Los Angeles Police Department, Dr. Ralph (Romi) Greenson confessed that his version of events concerning the day of Marilyn's death were incomplete (that he could not tell the entire story).

After Marilyn's death, some researchers quickly began promoting a sensational story that would act as the perfect red-herring and divert attention further away from Greenson.

The story followed that President Kennedy and some members of his family were implicated as having some level involvment in Marilyn's death.

Even Joe DiMaggio believed that the Kennedys participated in her death.

In 1964 Dr. Ralph Greenson was interviewed by William Woodfield who asked him in a telephone interview about Marilyn's last night. Greenson responded, "I can't explain myself or defend myself without revealing things that I don't want to reveal. I feel I - I can't, you know- you can't draw a line and say well I'll tell you this but I won't tell you that. It's a terrible position to be in to have to say I can't talk about it because I can't tell the whole story... Listen, you know, talk to Bobby Kennedy."[13]

In this secretly recorded statement, which is available on the internet today to Woodfield, Dr. Greenson effectively placed a incriminating wedge between himself and the official version of events the day Marilyn died.

Greenson could have told Woodfield to read the police report, Marilyn committed suicide, end of story. But instead he chose to throw a bone directly at those who supported the Kennedy theory.

Marilyn Monroe Unveiled | A Family History

It was an arrogant attempt to divert attention and scrutiny further away from his involvement.

In doing so he incriminated himself by admitting that facts were left out of the official report. He stated, "...I can't talk about it because I can't tell the whole story."

Why hasn't the Los Angeles Police Department ever made a comment on Dr. Ralph (Romi) Greenson's taped confession?

If an illegal behavioral modification technique was not working.

If the manipulation by Lee Strasberg was not working.

If Marilyn was not mentally broken in the security ward of Payne Whitney Psychiatric Clinic and did not commit suicide.

If the continued manipulation by Dr. Ralph (Romi) Greenson, Dr. Marianne Kris, and Dr. Margaret Hohenberg was not working.

Then their obsession with Marilyn Monroe moved to the next level of coersive extortion — murder.

Follow the money!

Under duress they told Marilyn what they wanted in 1955.

She wrote, "Strasberg's Dreams and Hopes for a theater fallen."

She wrote, "Hohenberg's Dreams and Hopes for a permanent psychiatric cure given up."

Marilyn Monroe was either a psychic in 1955 when she wrote those statements or she wrote down exactly what Strasberg and Hohenberg told her under psychological duress!

They would not stop until they fullfilled their dreams and hopes!

Marilyn Monroe's money and her legacy now fund The Lee Strasberg Theatre and Film Institute and The Anna Freud Centre — Foundation For Research in Psychoanalysis, or in Dr.Ralph Greenson's very own words — FRIP.

Dr. Ralph Greenson admitted that he had an argument with Marilyn the very day she died.

Dr. Ralph Greenson admitted to Dr. Marianne Kris that he had the housekeep Eunice Murray put her European vacation on hold and stay overnight with Marilyn on a night which she did not normally do. Marilyn's other staff were all already on vacation or soon would be!

Dr. Ralph Greenson admitted that details were left out of the official police report the day Marilyn died.

Dr. Ralph Greenson and Anna Freud admitted that they would abuse transferences for money and that they DID abuse transference for money!

Lee Strasberg, his daughter Susan Strasberg, and the Method actors admitted they were working directly with the Freudian psychotherapist.

Dr. Ralph (Romi) Greenson murdered Norma Jeane Mortenson (aka Marilyn Monroe) to help fund Anna Freud, Lee Strasberg, and Milton Greene!

And that certainly makes Lee Strasberg, Milton Greene, Dr. Margaret Hohenberg, Arthur Miller, Dr. Marianne Kris, and Annd Freud all co-conspirators in Marilyn Monroe's financial extortion and murder.

After Norma Jeane's death, Berniece Miracle, who was Marilyn's half-sister, and at the urging of Inez Melson, Marilyn's business manager, attempted to challenge the signing of Marilyn's will. That Lee Strasberg and Dr. Marianne Kris used undue influence against Marilyn to obtain her estate. In fact, Inez felt so strongly about it that she wrote that letter to Joe DiMaggio stating, "I know it sounds like a 'Perry Mason' television script but I am (between thee and me) very suspicious about that will..."

Their suspicions were reflected in an attempt brought to the court October 25, 1962. Arthur N. Field, a special guardian for Gladys Monroe, who was Marilyn Monroe's mother, stated that "he had been advised to file objections on the grounds that the will was prepared under the undue influence of Lee Strasberg. Miss Monroe's drama coach or Dr. Marianne Kris, her psychiatrist."

They knew in 1962 that Marilyn was unduly influenced by both Strasberg and Kris!

On December 4, 1963, in a typed memorandum, Eileen Atkinson wrote to Inez Melson that Marilyn's "will was drawn in eighteen minutes and it was just a fluke that it was done when it was." Otherwise everything was going to Arthur...no provisions for Gladys."

During the reading of the will, Berniece Miracle stated she was pressured to accept the deal.

Marilyn Monroe Unveiled | A Family History

Milton Rudin (Dr. Greenson's brother-in-law) was described by Berniece as impatient and rude. Aaron Frosch, in her view was more willing to discuss the problems of the will and that Marilyn's assets needed to produce an income before there could be payouts.

As Berniece challenged the attorney about prior wills, Frosch explained that if the current will was voided, then everthing would go to Arthur Miller, as later reported by Eileen Atkinson in her typed memorandum of December 4, 1963.

In the October 25, 1962 challenge to the will, Arthur N. Field was not presented any evidence by Berniece nor Inez Melson to support the attempt because Berniece Miracle decided to concede. She walked away not because she agreed with the state of the will, but because she did not have the resources to fight it. Berniece had no choice at the time because she was out maneuvered by Marilyn's very own lawyers, plus Arthur Miller, Lee Strasberg, and the Freudians.

What could be called the most egregious and sickingly visible case of financial extortion and murder happened to Marilyn Monroe aka Norma Jeane Mortenson right under the nose of her relatives, the public and the Los Angeles Police Department.

On August 7, less than three days after her death, it was reported that Aaron Frosch's secretary was already taking inventory of Marilyn Monroe's Manhattan apartment at 444 E. 57th Street in New York City. As Marilyn's body was cold and lifeless in the morgue, Louise White was rummaging through Marilyn's apartment counting her personal effects. She sought the items with the highest monetary value: four fur coats, seven stoles, several fur hats and articles of jewelry which were in the will and going directly to Lee Strasberg.

Now under the umbrella of Authenic Brands Group, The Anna Freud Centre, The Lee Strasberg Theatre and Film Institute, and Anna Strasberg, the third wife of Lee Strasberg, continue to all profit from Norma Jeane's estate today. Marilyn Monroe died without the right of publicity, but the hijacked estate is currently attempting to control Marilyn Monroe by manipulating trademark laws through the sale of her image, her name, and her soul. The profit is all blood money. It is all Marilyn's blood!

Detective Lester Freamon, in an episode of "The Wire" stated, "You follow drugs, you get drug addicts and drug dealers. But you start to follow the money, and you don't know where the fuck it's gonna take you."

If you follow Marilyn's money you don't get the Kennedys or the mob, you get Milton Greene, Arthur Miller, Lee Strasberg, Dr. Margaret Hohenberg, Dr. Marianne Kris, Dr. Ralph Greenson, and lastly Anna Freud.

Ezra Goodman stated in 1961 about his research for *TIME* magazine in 1956, "A good many of the people who had been involved with her... had different stories to tell. And their stories often checked out a good deal better than Monroe's."

In the following chapters it is hoped that the reader will understand that Marilyn Monroe's family story checks out better than Marilyn's orphan stories.

If Marilyn Monroe's family story does not fit the "Little Orphan Annie in Hollywood" story, then it is time for the public to stand behind MarilynMonroeFamily.com and help us take back Marilyn Monroe's history and legacy from the sycophants and suckerfish who murdered her and extorted from her estate. We are calling for the immediate cease and desist of all relations with Marilyn Monroe by The Anna Freud Centre, The Lee Strasberg Theatre and Film Institute, and Archives, LLC. We are calling for the unequivocal release of "Marilyn Monroe's estate" including all copyrights, trademarks, and all photographs taken of Marilyn by Milton Greene (while under the umbrella of Marilyn Monroe Productions), and all assets to be returned to Marilyn's rightful heirs — Berniece and Mona Miracle.

We want justice for Norma Jeane!

We also seek public acknowledgements and apologies from the Anna Freud Foundation and the Lee Strasberg Theatre and Film Institute for the unethical and criminal roles that their founders participated against Marilyn Monroe.

The evidence contained herein asserts that regardless if Marilyn wilfully, yet coersively took an overdose of barbiturates or Dr. Ralph (Romi) Greenson physically forced them down her throat, this gang actively lied, manipulated, coerced, and cocooned Marilyn Monroe to such a degree that any logically minded person could agree that Milton Greene, Arthur Miller, Lee Strasberg, Norman and Hedda Rosten, Dr. Margaret Hohenberg, Dr. Marianna Kris, Dr. Ralph Greenson, and Anna Freud set the conditions and had the motive to criminally force Marilyn Monroe into an early grave for her money and legacy. They were and are ALL co-conspirators in Marilyn Monroe's financial extortion and murder.

Norma Jeane aided the denigration of her own family history and unexpectedly entered a rabbit hole; a place where her "new" friends lived. They actively manipulated her circumstances and not only set her up for financial extortion, but also massively hoodwinked the public. Indeed, the public, by spending money on Marilyn Monroe for over 50 years, unknowingly supported and financed her murder and the co-conspirators who aided in and profited in the manipulation of Marilyn. The public should be outraged and sickened!

In a similar situation, the 1955 tragic demise of actress Sybille Schmitz, whose story was captured in the 1982 film *Veronika Voss*, the sycophants and suckerfish kept Sybille drugged while they fiscally drained her until they had no use for her, then the psychotherapist doctor mentally coerced her to overdose on drugs. They walked away from criminal prosecution just like the gang did with Norma Jeane's extortion and murder. What was the name of the psychotherapist that cocooned Veronika Voss in this 1982 film? None other than — Dr. Marianne Katz which is eerily similar to — Dr. Marianne KRIS. Coincidence? Maybe...

Nonetheless, the Anna Freud Centre, The Lee Strasberg Theatre and Film Institute, Archives LLC and descendants should not be allowed to continue to profit from the murder and financial extortion of Marilyn Monroe. And they should immediately cease and desist from their involvement with Marilyn Monroe's money and legacy. It is time for Norma Jeane to come HOME.

On September 22, 1961 Marilyn, using the alias "Mrs. Norman," sent a telegram to Joe DiMaggio stating that she loved him and that she wanted to change her will. It is suspected by many involved that Marilyn was going to remarry Joe DiMaggio at the time of her murder. Joe would place flowers on Marilyn Monroe's grave for over 20 years after her death. Did the gang? No! Not even one bloom! Plus, Joshua Greene has been known to sell items outside of the chapel during the annual memorial services for Marilyn, only steps away from her crypt.

The gang did nothing but brag that they were the recipients of Marilyn estate. In fact, Hedda Rosten had pictures of her and her smiling daughter in the newspapers as early as August 20, 1962,

The Weirton Daily Times

WEIRTON, W. VA., MONDAY, AUGUST 20, 1962

LEFT $5,000 BY MARILYN MONROE—The daughter of playwright Norman Rosten, Patricia, 16, sits with her mother, Mrs. Hedda Rosten, and the family dog at their home in Brooklyn after learning the late movie queen, Marilyn Monroe, left the family $5,000 in her will for Patricia's education.

literally days after Marilyn's death on August 5, 1962.[14] A photo statement that did nothing but crow that that they were on Marilyn's will for — Patricia's education. Why were they not in mourning? Or does a photo session in your house 15 days after after your employer (and so called "Marilyn's new friend") is dead, bragging that they were benefactors seem appropriate?

During Marilyn's funeral Lee Strasberg gave the famous eulogy where he claimed Marilyn was

Marilyn Monroe, under the alias Mrs. Norman tells Joe DiMaggio on September 22, 1961 that she wants to change her will.

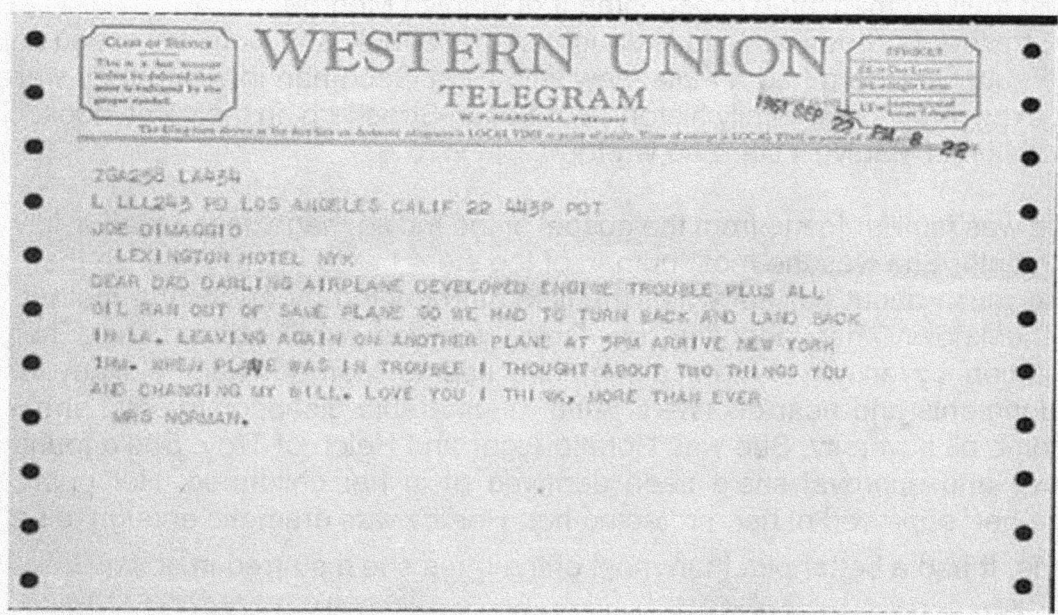

1961 SEP 22
Joe DiMaggio

Dear Dad Darling Airplane Developed Engine Trouble Plus All Oil Ran Out Of Same Plane So we Had To Turn Back And Land Back In LA. Leaving Again On Another Plane At 5pm Arrive New York 1pm. When Plane Was In Trouble I Thought About Two Things You And Changing My Will. Love You I Think, More Than Ever.

Mrs Norman.

only part of *his* family. He never acknowledged that Marilyn's sister Berniece and Grace Goddard's sister and her husband (Enid and Sam Knebelkamp) were in the audience listening to him speak the eulogy. Photos show family members were distraught that day, but Lee Strasberg and Dr. Greenson and his family members were stone faced.

That point alone should have given Lee Strasberg's motives away. The gang wanted to erase Marilyn's family and family history. Publicly they never wanted to acknowledge that Marilyn had family and admit that she was not an orphan.

Did any of them suggest to Marilyn that she should go see her sister? Or her cousins? Of course not. Doing so would have required that they admit Marilyn Monroe had family and it would have gone against their premeditated concoonment of Marilyn Monroe.

In Susan Strasberg's (Lee Strasberg's daughter) 1992 book, she both witnessed and admitted that her mother Paula Strasberg had an interview with Ezra Goodman in which they were informed that Marilyn was exaggerating her family history. Yet Susan Strasberg, in the same book, clung to the fan magazines version of Marilyn's life. She wrote:

> Her life was familiar to me from the gospel of the movie magazines I read avidly each month. She was the most human of the stars I read about because there was so much about her early life: the little girl rejected by an insane mother, father unknown; her adoption by foster families who abused her; her molestation by an older man; a meteoric rise to stardom after a litany of abandonments and near disasters. After innumerable disappointments, she'd overcome all adversity. She was Horatio Alger and Helen of Troy. She'd found the love and approval she'd been deprived of in her childhood. Her public adored her, approved of her, protected her. Her life was dramatic enough to be a movie. It had a better plot than most of the ones she'd starred in so far.[15]

The Strasberg family, the Anna Freud Centre, and Milton Greene and their descendants have made millions of dollars off of Marilyn Monroe and continue to sell the fabricated fan magazine version of Marilyn's life. They continue to reject that Marilyn Monroe had any relatives at all. They failed to acknowledge them because they knew they could cocoon Marilyn and financially extort her and then murder her. The only reason they got away with this for so long is that Marilyn's relatives who knew the most about her early years passed away before 1954. After Marilyn died in 1962, most of her cousins were so disconnected from what was really happening to her behind-the-scenes that they could do nothing after the fact. Marilyn's New York "new friends" had literally locked her down and cocooned her. Even her sister Berniece Miracle and Joe DiMaggio did not understand the extent of what was happening to Marilyn.

Marlon Brando wrote, "People don't relate to you as the person you are, but to a myth they believe you are, and the myth is always wrong. You are scorned or loved for mythic reasons...."

Help us bring Norma Jeane Back to Life.

Help us change Norma Jeane's death certificate to MURDER instead of "probable suicide."

Follow us at www.facebook.com/marilynmonroefamily and show your support.

Help us to bring Norma Jeane HOME.

Jason Edward Kennedy (Marilyn Monroe's second cousin)
and
Jennifer Jean Miller

"What you do in this life matters." Wink! Wink!

www.MarilynMonroeFamily.com

Chapter Seven Supporting Resources

[1] *My Sister Marilyn* – Berniece Baker Miracle and Mona Rae Miracle; 1994, 2003; Published by iUniverse,Inc.
[2] *MM Personal from the Private Archive of Marilyn Monroe* – Lois Banner, Page 315.
[3] *MM Personal from the Private Archive of Marilyn Monroe* – Lois Banner. Pages 314-315.
[4] *Anna Freud: A Biography* – by Elisabeth Young-Bruehl, Yale University Press, Oct 1, 2008.
[5] *Anna Freud: A Biography* – by Elisabeth Young-Bruehl, Yale University Press, Oct 1, 2008.
[6] *Anna Freud: A Biography* – by Elisabeth Young-Bruehl, Yale University Press, Oct 1, 2008.
[7] *Marilyn and Me – Sisters Rivals Friends* – by Susan Strasberg; Warner Books; 1992; Page 109-111.
[8] *MM Personal from the Private Archive of Marilyn Monroe* – Lois Banner, Page 306.
[9] *MM Personal from the Private Archive of Marilyn Monroe* – Lois Banner, Page 306.
[10] *Physician emerges as seller of Marilyn Monroe plastic surgery notes* – Reuters, Los Angeles by Eric Kelsey, Fri Oct 11, 2013, http://www.reuters.com/article/2013/10/11/entertainment-us-marilynmonroe-idUSBRE9970DE20131011#dEClUzdpYXX8ttEu.97
[11] *Marilyn Monroe: The Biography* – By Donald Spoto; Page 568.
[12] *Marilyn Monroe: The Biography* – By Donald Spoto; Page 570.
[13] *Say Goodby to the President* – Director: Christopher Olgiati, Writer: Christopher Olgiati; Voice recording of Dr. Ralph Greenson from 1964, Documentary released in 1985.
[14] The Weirton Daily Times, 20 Aug 1962, Mon, Page 3.
[15] *Marilyn and Me -- Sisters Rivals Friends* – by Susan Strasberg; Warner Books; 1992; Page 3.

Marilyn Monroe Unveiled | A Family History

CHAPTER EIGHT

You open up your local newspaper one Thursday morning as you are eating your breakfast and readying to start your day. You see her, appearing differently than the last time you met in person. The fresh-faced kid who romped on the beach or who you saw dancing through a sprinkler on a hot summer afternoons, the one who cuddled dogs and children and who played outside until evening approached.

The last time you saw her she was on her way to womanhood. Pretty, a little lipstick and mascara coated her lips and eyes, while curls were set through her usually wiry hair, of which she had a fascinator perched delicately to one side atop of it. She would soon be on the road to becoming someone's wife in a few years one imagined.

And she did become someone's bride. You had heard about their small but lovely wedding gathering. You had also learned that she was quite happy in her new marriage with a husband in the military.

Then life took a different path. A pretty blonde stares over at you from the print of your newspaper, her head resting on her shoulder. She is wearing a metallic type of bathing suit that hugs her curvaceous body, her platinum locks perfectly tumbling on to her back with a style reminiscent of Betty Grable, and she is coquettishly hiding the rest of her body from the world. That kid who you saw doing cartwheels on the beach is now modeling swimwear and is coined a "starlet" in the morning rag you are reading.

We knew she was breaking into modeling.

"Can it be? Is it?" You ask yourself.

You call your spouse into the room and ask them to confirm.

"Isn't that Norma Jeane?"

This looks just like her, but different and the caption reads "Marilyn" under her photo.

You had last heard in a letter she was modeling, yet still happy in her marriage, anticipated to live an idyllic life as a wife to a soldier. Kids were expected and the perfect suburban white picket fence life after he returned from war.

Modeling at first appeared to be a hobby.

But then you learn differently, after letters fly back and forth between relatives, when you inquire about this bathing beauty and if she is one and the same.

"Yes," you learn that is Norma Jeane. She and her husband divorced and her new name is Marilyn Monroe.

You are proud of your relative, as you watch for more news clips about her. But then you realize that fiction is soon larger than fact.

You begin reading other stories. You relative is hitting the "big time," rubbing shoulders with famous names like the Marx Brothers. You see the papers have listed her age wrong, Maybe a typo? Or was this on purpose? But they also call her a "Cinderella" and refer to her as "a ward of the state of California" until she turned 18.

"Wait," you tell yourself as a concerned look crosses your face, "that's not true."

Marilyn Monroe Unveiled | A Family History

Her star climbs as you see her listed as "cheesecake," "Miss Morale" and the "Chogie Girl" (the girl that most soldiers would like to "chogie" or climb up a hill with). She is posed more provocatively now, the front of her body visible, her curves present for the rest of the world to see, the rail-thin child you once knew, referred to now as "hour-glass figure with the sand distributed in the right places."

Wolf-whistles call out to her wherever she goes, though some have referred to her as "vulgar," something, which hurts you since you know the beauty of her heart inside. You pray her skin has toughened up and she will not be bruised by the criticism aired in some publications.

You open up the movie listing to see what is coming up for the weekend and there she is on a Tuesday, with top billing in a new picture, *Ladies of the Chorus*. You head to the darkened cinema that weekend, still in disbelief at the talent and confidence you witness dancing across the screen that once was the little girl dancing in the sprinklers on the front lawn with the other children.

Soon you begin seeing your relative's name becoming more mainstream in the papers and magazines. But you are not thrilled with what you are reading. Tabloid fodder stating that she started out as a babysitter when she was discovered, a tidbit you know is fictional.

As her star ascends you read an article that she tells a reporter that she was "orphaned shortly after her birth."

"What?" you tell yourself, your mouth dropping as you lift your coffee cup to your lips. "Who was that little girl then who jumped through the sprinkler on the lawn with her cousins?"

"Her father had been killed in an auto accident before she was born and her mother became ill and was unable to care for Marilyn," you read. "The mother is believed to have died. Marilyn spent some of her early years in an orphanage."

You think a retraction is in order because you know Gladys dropped you a line not long ago and Norma Jeane was with her. How can this be written?

But as years march on and your relative becomes a worldwide sensation, the tales become more sordid and sensationalized. Your relative is interviewed about dark tales of her family. That there was forced religion down her throat, abuse, and scullery work in orphanages like Oliver Twist, abandonment and more.

You know these stories are not true. What if you tried to reach out to her and talk to her?

Impossible. Representatives and studios are now shielding her. Messages are passed on but calls rarely returned. Your messages through switchboard operators and telegrams make it through, but her closest advisors are telling her to forget about you.

"Forget about your family, they were no good for you," the famous blonde is being brainwashed. "We are your family now, we will help you."

Opportunists close in on her like vultures to feast on her and aim for her generous heart.

Time marches on and throughout the world she is known, but hiding inside is the same young woman, Norma Jeane, while she has created an exterior character that the world knows as Marilyn Monroe. Behind the platinum hair and sequined gowns, you still see glimpses of the sweet and shy girl you once knew.

She calls one day….when the advisors are not watching. But soon, the calls cease from her again.

Then one August morning, the headlines scream she is dead. How is this possible? She was only 36, with so much life ahead of her. They say she may have committed suicide. How could the beautiful life you once knew take her life with her own hand? You know this is not true, just like the horrible tales you read about your family having been abusers and in other accounts that you did not exist.

When you try to come out and tell your side, even more than a half a century later, angry fans beat you down because the myths remain so strong.

This is what life is like to be one of the family members of one of the greatest legends to emerge from the 20th Century, Marilyn Monroe.

Many have painted Marilyn's family as "heinous," "abusive," "low class," "hillbillies," "inferior," "mental," "opportunistic" and other negative adjectives. According to her few advisors, relatives did not exist. But they sure did and they were hiding after being beaten down by those advisors who walked away with Marilyn's bank account, garnering more on Marilyn's legacy post-mortem than Marilyn did in her lifetime.

But she did have family who she loved and vice-versa. The paper trail is strong and the myths can be challenged, though some prefer to stick with the Cinderella story, because it continues to place money into their pocketbooks. They do not want the truth out there about Marilyn Monroe, because the fantasy is much more profitable.

Marilyn Monroe did have a family history and relatives that were prominent movers and shakers of society, including some who were only miles away from her but were being blocked from reaching her.

CHAPTER NINE

MANY AUTHORS HAVE taken creative liberties (which much amounts to nothing more than lies) when addressing Marilyn's ancestral line, especially when writing about Tilford Marion Hogan, her maternal great-grandfather. In return, many myths have developed about her family that they came from poor stock, were stupid and uneducated, and without ever having left a blip on the radar screen.

In Marilyn's later life when Freudian proponents began to manipulate her, using various clinical techniques and a bevy of prescription medications, they suggested they should be the replacement for her family.

When Marilyn died, the Freudians obtained 25 percent of her estate and Lee Strasberg obtained 75 percent of her estate.

"We're the only family she's ever known," were some words leaving the lips of those who were opportunists in her life: Milton Greene, Lee Strasberg and her Freudian psychotherapists including Dr. Margaret Hohenberg, Marianne Kris and Ralph Greenson.

Many iterated and reiterated how poor Marilyn never had a family experience in her life until they came along. Yet throughout her life she did with the Bolenders, Grace Goddard's family, Anne Karger and Joe DiMaggio's family just to name a few. And when Gladys was well, she experienced love and care from her mother, who struggled as a working single parent in the 1920s and 1930s. Later, she would meet her half-sister Berniece Baker Miracle, her brother-in-law Paris and niece Mona Rae, who would wrap their family love around her though they did not see one another often.

And then there was Marilyn's extended family including cousins, an uncle (who did later disappear), an aunt, great-uncles, great-aunts and so on, many in the Los Angeles area. This topic will be covered separately in a later chapter.

Many look to Marilyn's family as having been plagued with mental illness, beginning with her grandparents who both ended up dying in mental institutions, the suicide of her great-grandfather Tilford Marion Hogan, the incarceration of her mother Gladys in the mental health system and her own attachment to Freudianism. Anna Freud and her inner-circle practitioners kept her believing she was ill in order to continually extort money from her for mental health treatments, later walking away with a part of Marilyn's residual estate.

The truth of the matter is her grandfather Otis Monroe did not die from a mental illness but from paresis, which was a swelling of his brain due to neurosyphilis, a non-sexual form of syphilis that was caused from the unsanitary working conditions he experienced in Mexico. Her grandmother Della (Otis's widow) died shortly after Marilyn's first birthday from the side effects of malaria that she contracted while in Borneo, something that has been falsely reported as a mental illness.

Marilyn's great-grandfather Tilford Marion Hogan may have experienced temporary financial setbacks at age 82 and committed suicide. This too has been a source of contention for biographers, who have dwelled on the issues with Marilyn's purported genealogy of mental illness.

Marilyn Monroe Unveiled | A Family History

Tilford on the contrary was quite prosperous and socialized with the movers and shakers, unlike popular myth, which the writers will demonstrate later in this book. However, he has been written about as an uneducated and unsophisticated farm laborer. To the contrary, he had owned land, was involved in politics and community service and was constantly marketing his business, as many hardworking people do to earn a living.

In Tilford's case as it was for many during those times, the stock market crashed in October 1929, which kicked off the Great Depression, impacting all industries including income for farmers, which was Tilford's livelihood. The worst of the Depression took hold between the early winter of 1932 and before the spring of 1933. The greatest stronghold was in the cities, where "Hoovervilles" or small shantytowns that those who were homeless set up to live after losing it all, reigned.

However, life in the country where Tilford Hogan resided was not unaffected either. Though it would come after his death, the Dust Bowl circulated throughout the Midwest, impacting many farmers beginning in 1934. Overall, the climate was one of fear, as 13 million were unemployed and by 1932, 34 million families were without a full-time worker in their households. Poverty was at a height of 60 percent in the country, with two million homeless.

Farming, Tilford's industry, would naturally be impacted in the chain since in excess of five thousand banks had shut down. President Herbert Hoover's Emergency Relief and Construction Act of 1932, which was intended to offer government-secured loans to parties including farmers had not taken off in Tilford's lifetime as intended, but was incorporated into succeeding President Franklin Roosevelt's "New Deal."

If only Tilford Marion Hogan had held out hope for just a little longer, he would have experienced the upturn. But his failing health and fears about the economy captured the best of him.

Suicide was an unfortunate byproduct of the Great Depression, with an increase to 17 people per 100,000, when it had previously been 14 people. In the farming community, farmers watched other farmers have their land foreclosed on, many rallying around one another and refusing to bid on each others' farms when they went to auction, helping each other by holding on to the furniture of those evicted.

The farming community tried desperately to cling on to their own ideals, creating in Tilford's part of the country the Farmers' Holiday Association in May 1932, which endorsed a farming "holiday," where they basically were striking from sharing their produce with others to counter the foreclosures. In one instance, it turned violent, with farmers threatening to string up an Iowa judge who continued to foreclose on farms. Dairy farmers in Wisconsin were striking in February and May of 1933 before Tilford made the difficult decision to hang himself in his barn on May 27, 1933. It was much for a man who had worked hard yet experienced times of prosperity.

On March 4, 1933, the country witnessed the inauguration of Roosevelt. Many states had already experienced their own banking holidays to give their institutions time to recoup losses, as many fell apart when their monies were pulled out.

Detroit was especially hit hard and there was previously an eight day banking holiday in Michigan. Beginning on March 9, banks were closed to begin to stabilize and reopened on March 13. The stock market reopened on March 15 and saw a small gain on the New York Stock Exchange and Dow Jones Industrial Average.

By April, Americans had placed more than a billion dollars back into the banks. By June after Tilford's suicide the Federal Deposit Insurance Corporation (FDIC) was formed to protect the assets that Americans placed in banks.

Whatever happened to Tilford Marion Hogan and his fears, he experienced what the newspapers described as "worry over imaginary financial troubles, coupled with infirmatives of old age."

But Tilford Marion Hogan was not mentally ill and nor was his family as has often been erroneously reported by biographers. Nor was he uneducated or unrefined. Nor were Marilyn's other ancestors. In fact, her family line had prominence and her relatives were quite involved in the community. In the days however of the frontier, her ancestors were no different than any other people, but have been written as if they were criminal or bad.

Marilyn Monroe Unveiled | A Family History

    Her maternal great-grandfather Tilford was written as "self-educated" in a day when many were self-educated. Think of Abraham Lincoln, one of the country's most celebrated Presidents who, only earlier in the same century was a self-educated person who hailed from a Middle America farming family like Tilford Marion Hogan. Lincoln was a blend as well of bodily strength for his work in the fields, yet intellect with his love of reading and learning, much like Tilford Marion Hogan who came from the same part of the country.

    Yet why are Tilford and the rest of the family mocked and defamed by biographers, especially Lois Banner, Ted Schwarz and J. Randy Taraborrelli as exemplified below?

    Tilford was a success in business and politics. He enjoyed reading in a time when newspapers and books were a leisure activity outside of work and in a day when there was no television or YouTube. Plus it was a time when education was still limited and teachers were themselves in short supply and itinerant. Yet, the family has been portrayed as inferior people. Past writers have penned Marilyn Monroe's family in a defamatory way and the writers of this book next explore the actuality.

"We know little about Norma Jeane Mortenson's ancestors. They were poor people and their lives went unreported in the newspapers and are blurred in the memories of surviving friends. The fragments of available data compose a mosaic of misery, mental disorder, and violent death. On her mother's side, both grandparents were committed to mental institutions. An uncle killed himself. Her father died in a motorcycle accident."
– Maurice Zolotow – Marilyn Monroe – 1960

"Southwest of Los Angeles in a middle-class community of verandaed bungalows known as Hawthorne, Mrs. Grainger lived in a stucco house set among trees and shrubs. She was alone much of the time and did not make new friends easily. Except for the trips to the Angelus Temple or brief excursion to the store, she was rarely seen on the street. Although there as little socializing with the neighbors, Della was regarded with respect, perhaps because they believed she had once known wealth. But this had more to do with her manner than with reality. By 1925, she had spent twenty-one of her forty-nine years in California. Born Della Hogan, she had come from lower-middle-class stock in Missouri. The family moved to the West when she was in her teens and Della met her first husband, a man with the last name of Monroe, in the Northwest. Their marriage was terminated by divorce around the time he was committed to a state asylum. Della married again, a man only remembered as Grainger, and around 1919 they moved to Hawthorne."
– Fred Lawrence Guiles – Norma Jean: The Life of Marilyn Monroe - 1969

Marilyn Monroe Unveiled | A Family History

"If mystery surrounds Marilyn's father, the facts about her mother's side of her family are painfully well documented. Knowing what she knew of that history, Marilyn feared she was genetically prone to insanity. The fear was understandable. Her maternal great-grandfather, Tilford Hogan, hanged himself at the age of eighty-two. Suicide among the aged is not uncommon. It is certainly not necessarily a side of madness, but mental illness did run in the family. The maternal grandfather, Otis Monroe, died in an institution of general paresis, according to the death certificate. Paresis, and specifically paretic dementia, is recognized as a form of insanity provoked by syphilis in its final stage. Marilyn ran no risk of inheriting syphilis, but her maternal grandmother, Della, also died in an asylum, at age fifty-one, a year after Marilyn's birth. She had been something of a religious zealot. The cause of her death was given as heart disease, with 'manic-depressive psychosis' as a contributory factor." – Anthony Summers – Goddess The Secret Lives of Marilyn Monroe – 1985

"The responsibility of a home she could barely afford and a child she had no idea how to care for plunged Gladys into a deep depression. The news that her maternal grandfather, Tilford Hogan, had hung himself in Linn County, Missouri, confirmed her fears about the family fate. Gladys had hallucinations. Lying on the living-room sofa, kicking and screaming, she imagined that someone was coming down the staircase to murder her. One morning in January 1935, Gladys woke up in Norwalk State Hospital, where her mother had died in a straitjacket seven years previously. Doctors listed her condition as paranoid schizophrenia; Grace told Ida Bolender that a portion of Gladys's brain had collapsed. From then on, Grace never tired of repeating that she had warned Gladys against taking on too much responsibility, such as buying a house and trying to care for Norma Jeane." – Barbara Leaming – Marilyn Monroe – 1998

"Gladys's mother, Della, always caused heads to turn as she sashayed down the street. However, she was apparently as tough as she was eye-catching. Early photographs taken of Gladys's parents show a handsome, somewhat robust woman with a severe countenance – that would be Della – standing next to a gentleman who looks rather scared to death – Otis. If he ever thought he would be able to tell Della what to do, Otis soon found out it was not the case. Della was never one to acquiesce to anyone's will. Therefore, the arguments between them started on their honeymoon and never ceased. In one of the family's photographs, Otis has a deep scar on his cheek and there's no telling how he got it. However, one thing is clear: He doesn't have it in pictures taken before he married Della." – J Randy Taraborrelli – The Secret Life of Marilyn Monroe – 2009

"Shortly after the news of Jackie's death, Gladys received a phone call from a family member: Her grandfather had passed away. During the call, her cousin went on for some time about how Tilford Marion Hogan had apparently gone mad before his death. Also it wasn't a death from natural causes – he had hanged himself. Gladys believed that both her parents had gone mad, and now her grandfather too? Worse yet, she had always wondered about her own sanity. With that phone call, the question grew louder: Was she next? Gladys had tried to disregard the voices in her head for many years. But with *tragedy all around her, they became more insistent, impossible to ignore."* – J Randy Taraborrelli – The Secret Life of Marilyn Monroe – 2009

"They were an odd mix of people, Norma Jean's ancestors. They were dreamers and schemers, of course, but they were also sexual libertines and self-righteous conservatives, self-taught scholars and illiterates proud of their lack of knowledge, religious zealots and ardent nonbelievers. Several experienced ill health that affected their ability to think clearly – neurosyphilis, cardiovascular disease, multiple mini-strokes – that would lead to a misguided belief in the family that mental illness was rampant. Others were simply young moderns in rebellion against the strictures of the Victorian era, men and women who would eventually be classed as part of the Roaring Twenties. Tilford Marion Hogan was typical of Norma Jean's ancestors. He was an uneducated Missouri day laborer who supported his family with a strong back and muscular arms, working the land, taking whatever jobs he could find and using his spare time to pursue the dream of a life of scholar reflection and good works. He and his wife, Jennie Nance Hogan, could barely feed their three children, yet Tilford prided himself on inviting strangers to share a meal with them." – Ted Schwarz – Marilyn Revealed The Ambitious Life of an American Icon – 2009

"It was in October 1933 that Gladys was notified about a man who had been out of her life for many years. Tilford Hogan, her grandfather who had abandoned both her grandmother, Jennie Nance Hogan, and her mother Della May, was dead. A distant cousin had taken it upon herself to locate and notify as many of the estranged family members as possible. She found where Gladys was living approximately five months after the death." – Ted Schwarz – Marilyn Revealed The Ambitious Life of an American Icon – 2009

"Gladys soon developed schizophrenia. Her family had a history of mental instability. Both of her parents, Otis Elmer Monroe and Della Monroe Grainger, lived out their twilight years in mental institutions and her brother, Marion, had suffered from a problem best described at the time as paranoid schizophrenia. Though Gladys herself was most likely a manic-depressive, it was not uncommon during the 1930s and 1940s for those suffering from manic depression to be diagnosed as paranoid schizophrenics. Whatever the exact nature of her mother's disorder, Marilyn Monroe naturally came to possess a morbid fear of genetic insanity." – Keith Badman – Marilyn Monroe The Final Years - 2010

"On a swing through Missouri in 1898, Otis met Della Hogan. Born in 1878, she was twenty-two, still living with her mother and siblings. Her childhood had been difficult. Her father, Tilford Hogan, was an itinerant farm laborer who worked long hours for low wages, following the harvests and doing odd jobs. He married Jennie Nance, a Missouri farm girl, in 1870. Living in tenant cabins and farm shacks, they nonetheless had three children in eight years. Yet Tilford's financial woes weren't unusual in post-Reconstruction Missouri. The building of railroads as well as a dramatic population growth through immigration caused a rise in prosperity in the state – for those able to exploit it. Most Missourians remained tenant farmers or landless laborers employed part-time to harvest crops or do odd jobs. Pro-slavery and secessionist during the Civil

War, Missourians remained loyal to the South for decades. Jennie Nance, Marilyn's maternal great-grandmother, was raised in Chariton County, settled by migrants from the Upper South who owned slaves. It was called 'Little Dixie.' As Tilford's wife, Jennie often moved with him as he sought employment, often in Ozark hillbilly country, moving her children from school to school. When Marilyn played Cherie, the hillbilly singer in Bus Stop, she could draw on her family's past to create the character." – Lois Banner – Marilyn: The Passion and the Paradox – 2012

"*The circumstances surrounding that 'turbulent childhood' took shape well before June 1, 1926, the date of her birth in a charity ward at Los Angeles County General Hospital. Her mother, Gladys Pearl Monroe – she claimed to be related to James Monroe, the fifth president of the United States – came from a working-class family with a considerable history of emotional disturbance. Gladys's maternal grandfather, Tilford Marion Hogan, committed suicide in 1933, and her mother and father both spent time in mental institutions." – C. David Heymann – Joe and Marilyn: Legends in Love – 2014*

CHAPTER TEN

MANY BIOGRAPHERS HAVE described the Hogan family as unrefined, even to the point of mocking them, like Banner who eludes that Marilyn's family lived in hillbilly country.

The Hogans, however, held roles of prominence in developing the area in which they resided.

Tilford Marion Hogan was born on February 24, 1851 in Adams Illinois. Adams County is a fertile area adjacent to the Mississippi River. It was known at the time for its livestock like cattle and hogs. In terms of crops, corn, wheat and potatoes were among the bounty that grew best there.

Tilford's parents were George W. Hogan and Sarah Ann (Owen) Hogan, and he was raised among other siblings including: Mary, Newton, John, William, Amanda, Stephen and Rosa. Tilford was the first of the brood born in Illinois, the second youngest of the boys, with Rosa born in Missouri. Later in his lifetime, he would live with his elder sister, Mary Ann (Hogan) Mahurin, one of the eldest of the children born in 1844.

George W. Hogan was born in Kentucky and his mother Sarah Ann Owen in Virginia.

George Hogan was a Civil War military veteran, having served as a private in the Illinois Company I 16th Infantry Regiment, serving the Union, with that regiment considered a "twin" with the Illinois 10th regiment. He was enlisted on December 30, 1863 and served through July 28, 1865.

George's parents, Zachariah Hogan and mother Delilah (Marksbury) Hogan held an entrepreneurial spirit, having started a mercantile business in 1813, following the War of 1812. Zachariah Hogan was born in Bedford Virginia circa 1784. The possibility of Delilah's connection to Scottish Royalty is also currently being explored. He married wife Delilah August 9, 1806.[i]

The mercantile store that Zachariah and Delilah owned in Grant County Kentucky apparently thrived during the embargo of English goods, until that embargo was lifted. Then the Hogans apparently lost their business and after a go at farming, lost their farm. Delilah was the one who transferred the deed of 43 acres to a William Pierce on November 13, 1820 for $430, a generous transaction in its day.

Zachariah died in 1850. It is unclear when Delilah died. He remarried after Delilah's death to Elizabeth Doty in 1828, and she outlived him until 1886 at the age of 84.

It was Zachariah Hogan's father John and two uncles William and James, Jr. (Their father was James Hogan, Sr.) who participated in and were an instrumental part of Daniel Boone's exploration of the State of Kentucky during the years of 1775 to 1780.

James Hogan Sr. was Marilyn's fifth great-grandfather, John Hogan was Marilyn's fourth great-grandfather and William Hogan and James Hogan Jr. her fourth great-uncles.

James Hogan Sr.'s (Daughters of the American Revolution Ancestor #A056450) rank is listed as "patriotic service" on his DAR.

On April 1, 1775 Daniel Boone and Richard Henderson built a fort near the Kentucky River which was then known as Boonesborough.

James Hogan Jr. and Richard Hogan are listed as residing in or near the Fort. Bryan's Station is another settlement about 16 miles from Boonesborough. James Hogan Jr. was interestingly

---

[i] Douglas Archives- Delilah married Zachariah Hogan http://www.douglashistory.co.uk/history/articles/marksberry.htm

Marilyn Monroe Unveiled | A Family History

captured in the *Irish Pioneers in Kentucky* which documented the early dangers and clash of cultures while exploring the early North America:

"'Bryan's Station was a frontier post,' says Collins, 'and, consequently, was much harassed by the Indians and was greatly exposed to the hostility of the savages. The redmen were constantly lurking in the neighborhood, waylaying the paths, stealing horses and butchering cattle. At length it became necessary to hunt in large parties so as to be able to repel the attacks which were daily becoming more bold and frequent.' 'On May 20, 1779, two parties set out, one in command of William Bryan and the other under James Hogan. Bryan was killed, and Hogan's party, after being pursued by a band of Indians, returned to the encampment which, in the meantime, another band of redskins had attacked.' Hogan and his men soon put them to flight.'"[i]

One of John Hogan, Jr.'s other historical accomplishments was with his brother James as the two embarked on the first ferry service for the area that ferried passengers in the Kentucky River area. The trio started the service in 1785 at the mouth of Hickman's Creek, which they petitioned the Virginia General Assembly for permission to set up the service plus the rates for the ferry travel.[ii]

James Hogan, Jr. additionally served in the Revolutionary War as part the 2nd Virginia Regiment (Daughters of the American Revolution Ancestor # A056452). Though he was born in Virginia on April 22, 1752, he became a prominent Kentuckian in 1781, after receiving land grants for his service in the Revolutionary War. With the ferry service in Garrard County where he owned land (and had land in Jessamine, Laurel, Rockcastle and Scott Counties), he ferried in addition to passengers, tobacco to a warehouse he owned.

William, who was the other third of the brotherly trio that scouted with Daniel Boone and Marilyn's fourth great-uncle earned the rank of Captain (Daughters of the American Revolution Ancestor # A056467). Born in Virginia in 1750, he died in Madison Alabama in 1827. He is buried in Garrard County Kentucky. William Hogan's wife was Sarah Grant, an orphaned little girl that Daniel Boone and his wife Rebecca ending up assuming the parenting of. Sarah Grant Hogan was then, in essence, the fourth great-aunt of Marilyn Monroe by marriage. Daniel and Rebecca Boone were her stepparents.

There were other ancestors in Marilyn Monroe's family tree who held a colorful history, in spite of what has been written otherwise.

Tilford Hogan's uncle Overton Penix Hogan (born May 29, 1801) was a judge often known as O.P. Hogan. He was also a U.S. Representative candidate in 1874 for Kentucky's 6th District. He invited Grant County residents to his home in Kentucky's Grant County Anderson Grove, where they discussed the July 4th centennial celebration over a picnic. His property was under another significant property in the area known as Old Childers Farm. He also started a stagecoach line that traveled between Burlington and Covington, plus Walton and Williamstown, to connect with train lines at Walton in the late 1800s.

Returning to Tilford's generation, in the 1860 census Tilford's parents who were listed as farmers, had a personal property valued at $3,500 in Knox County Missouri's Greensburg Township. His personal estate at the time was valued at $600.

Tilford married Charlotty/Charlotte Virginia "Jennie" Nance, who was born on April 10, 1857. Her parents were Levi Nance and Sarah Caroline (Jones) Nance. She was one of nine children, with five of her siblings having passed away in early childhood.

Tilford and Jennie married and they had five children: Dora Olivia (born November 1874), Della Mae (born July 1, 1876, Marilyn's maternal grandmother), William Marion (born April 10, 1879), Myrtle Belle (born October 30, 1880) and James Berry (born August 4, 1883).

In spite of all the negativity that has been spread about Marilyn's relatives, none of these children had mental illnesses as indicated in the many biographies about Marilyn. Three of them especially (William, Myrtle and James) lived more idyllic and "normal" lives. Dora and Della the elder two siblings had more colorful existences with Dora's especially high profile.

---

[i] *Irish Pioneers in Kentucky* – by Michael I. O'Brien, Cornell University Page 33.
[ii] *Irish Pioneers in Kentucky* – by Michael I. O'Brien, Cornell University Page 17.

HOGAN FAMILY HISTORY

James Hogan Sr. | Born 1728–Died Sept 11, 1793 | Married Silence Lane

JAMES HOGAN SR. IS MARILYN MONROE'S FIFTH GREAT GRANDFATHER.

North Carolina Revolutionary War Pay Vouchers, #1226, Roll #S.115.99 | Rank Patriotic Service | Paid for Services rendered.

21 May 1761 Deed: James Hogan, wife Silanee, to John Been, all of Halifax County, for £20, 383 acres in Halifax County, on Cane Creek, adjoining Walton... /s/James Hogan, Silanne "X" Hogan. Wit: Hance HENDRICK, Wm. Cornelius, Edmund "X" Floyd. (Halifax County, VA, Deeds 3:147)

Anson County, North Carolina – Slave Holders, From Appendix VII to The History of Anson County: Based on 1790 Census of Fayette Dist.

Family Heads and Number of Slaves:

James Hogan Sr.–10 Slaves

Sons of James Hogan Sr. |

William Hogan, James Hogan Jr., and John Hogan (Marilyn Monroe's Fourth Great-Grandfather).

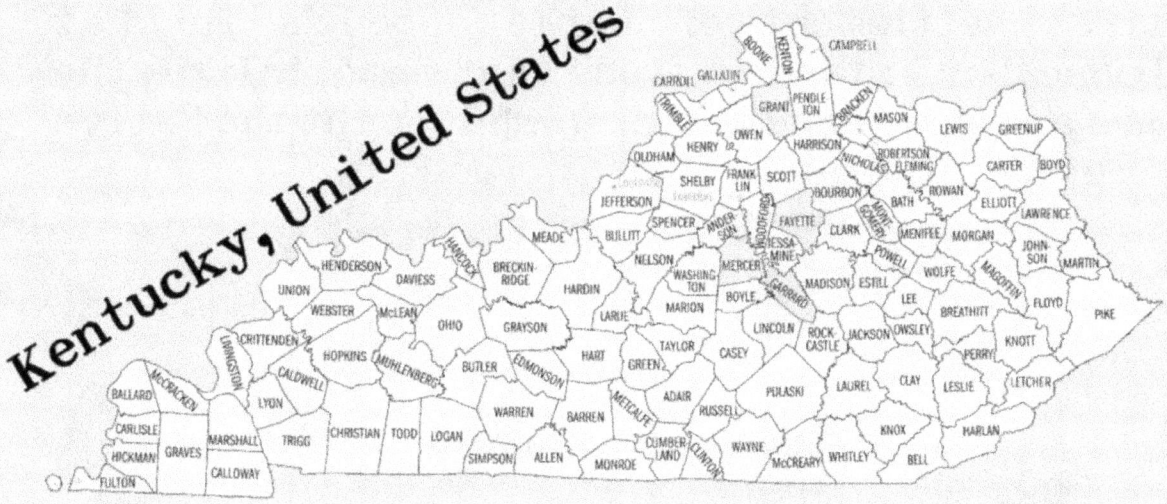

May 1995 Issue of "Kentucky Explorer" magazine:

"The Hogan brothers, William, James and John (John being Monroe's GGGG-grandfather) were members of Daniel Boone's second scouting party that came to Kentucky in 1779-1780. It was William Hogan who married Sarah Grant (the orphaned girl raised by Daniel and Rebecca Boone) afterwards settling at Bryan's Station where their first child, David was born on March 2, 1781, making him the second child born on Kentucky soil. Prior to 1779-80, other members of the HOGAN family, named Richard, Edward and Phillip joined Boone on one of his earliest explorations into the Kentucky wilderness. It was James and John Hogan, however, who began one of Kentucky's first Ferry services located at the mouth of Hickman Creek in Jessamaine County. Ferry service that was used for many years transferring pioneers back and forth across the Kentucky River."

William Hogan married Sarah Grant.

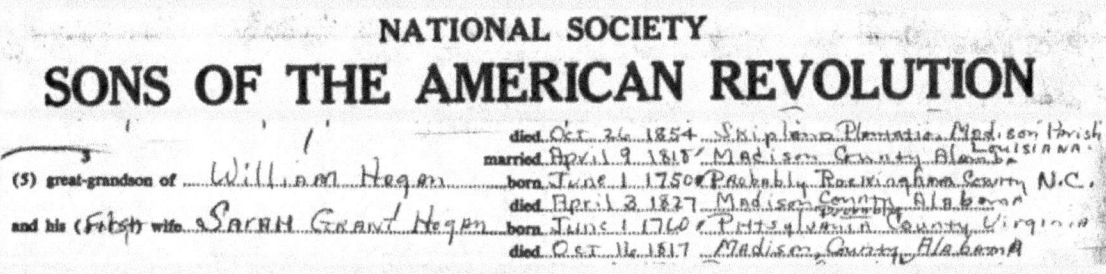

William Hogan | Militia, Fayette Co, Ky at Bryan's Station.

Rank: Captain

Located 12 miles from Richmond, Kentucky, at the first settlement of Daniel Boone's fort at Boonesboro, stands a stone that memorializes the men and women and children who fought the Native American Indians.

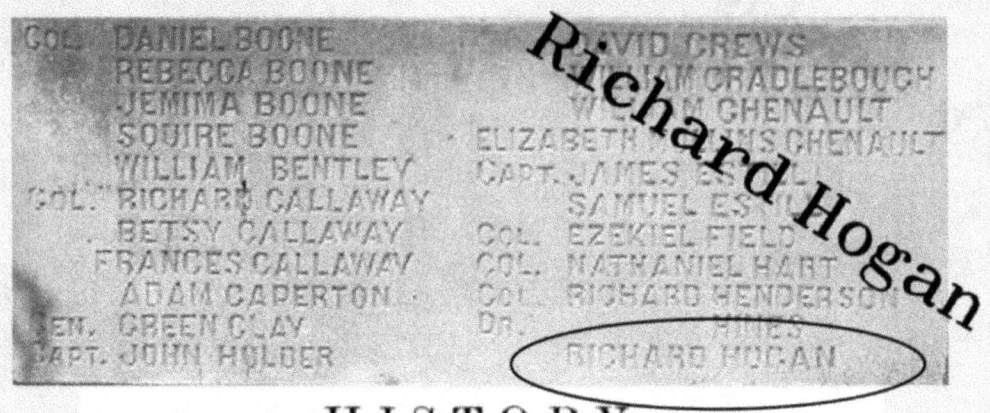

HISTORY
OF
KENTUCKY:

BY THE LATE LEWIS COLLINS,
Judge of the Mason County Court.

REVISED, ENLARGED FOUR-FOLD, AND BROUGHT DOWN TO THE YEAR 1874,
BY HIS SON,
RICHARD H. COLLINS, A.M., LL.B.

JOHN HOGAN IS MARILYN MONROE'S FOURTH GREAT GRANDFATHER.

Residents in 1777-78.—From "an account-current of provisions purchased by Joseph Lindsay, commissary, for the use of the garrison at Harrodsburg, from Dec. 16, 1777, to Oct. 16, 1778," we gather the names of part of the residents of the fort at Harrodsburg and of that neighborhood at that early day:

Elisha Bathy,	Edward Davis,	John Hogan,	Margaret Pendergrast
John Bayley,	James Davis,	Richard Hogan,	Ann Poague,
James Berry,	John Denton,	Andrew Johnston,	Robert Pruett,
Squire Boone,	William Field,	Joseph Lindsay,	Nat. Randolph,
Isaac Bowman,	David Glenn,	Richard Major,	George Ruddle,
Col. John Bowman,	John Gordon,	Robert McAfee,	John Severns,
John Brand,	John Grisim,	James McColloch,	John Shelp,
Edward Bulger,	Silas Harlan,	James McCauley,	Glenn and Stuart,
Pat. Calihan,	James Harrod,	Hugh McGary,	Abraham Taylor,
Joseph Cartwright,	John Hays,	Robert McKim,	Daniel Turner,
Ambrose Coffey,	Mary Hendrix,	William Myers,	John Williams,
William Combs,	Abram Hite,	John Montgomery,	Lot Wood,
Cornelius Coplin,	Isaac Hite,	Reuben Moscoe,	Edward Worthington.

Adventures of James Hogan Jr.

HISTORY OF KENTUCKY:

By the late LEWIS COLLINS,
Judge of the Mason County Court.

REVISED, ENLARGED FOUR-FOLD, AND BROUGHT DOWN TO THE YEAR 1874, BY HIS SON,
RICHARD H. COLLINS, A.M., LL.B.

Bryan's station, about five miles north-east of Lexington, was settled by the Bryans in 1779. In 1781, Bryan's station was much harassed by small parties of Indians. This was a frontier post, and greatly exposed to the hostilities of the savages.* It had been settled in 1779 by four brothers from North Carolina, one of whom, William, had married a sister of Colonel Daniel Boone. The Indians were constantly lurking in the neighborhood, waylaying the paths, stealing their horses, and butchering their cattle. It at length became necessary to hunt in parties of twenty or thirty men, so as to be able to meet and repel those attacks, which were every day becoming more bold and frequent.

One afternoon, about the 20th of May, William Bryan, accompanied by twenty men, left the fort on a hunting expedition down the Elkhorn creek. They moved with caution, until they had passed all the points where ambuscades had generally been formed, when, seeing no enemy, they became more bold, and determined, in order to sweep a large extent of country, to divide their company into two parties. One of them, conducted by Bryan in person, was to descend the Elkhorn on its southern bank, flanking out largely, and occupy as much ground as possible. The other, under the orders of James Hogan, a young farmer in good circumstances, was to move down in a parallel line upon the north bank. The two parties were to meet at night, and encamp together at the mouth Cane run.

Each punctually performed the first part of their plans. Hogan, however, had traveled but a few hundred yards, when he heard a loud voice behind him exclaim in very good English, "stop, boys!" Hastily looking back, they saw several Indians, on foot, pursuing them as rapidly as possible. Without halting to count numbers, the party put spurs to their horses, and dashed through the woods at full speed, the Indians keeping close behind them, and at times gaining upon them. There was a led horse in company, which had been brought with them for the purpose of packing game. This was instantly abandoned, and fell into the hands of the Indians. Several of them lost their hats in the eagerness of flight; but quickly getting into the open woods, they left their pursuers so far behind, that they had leisure to breathe and inquire of each other, whether it was worth while to kill their horses before they had ascertained the number of the enemy.

They quickly determined to cross the creek, and await the approach of the Indians. If they found them superior to their own and Bryan's party united, they would immediately return to the fort; as, by continuing their march to the mouth of Cane run, they would bring a superior enemy upon their friends, and endanger the lives of the whole party. They accordingly crossed the creek, dismounted, and awaited the approach of the enemy. By this time it had become dark. The Indians were distinctly heard approaching the creek upon the opposite side, and after a short halt, a solitary warrior descended the bank and began to wade through the stream.

Hogan waited until he had emerged from the gloom of the trees which grew upon the bank, and as soon as he had reached the middle of the stream, where the light was more distinct, he took deliberate aim and fired. A great splashing in the water was heard, but presently all became quiet. The pursuit was discontinued, and the party remounting their horses, returned home. Anxious, however, to apprize Bryan's party of their danger, they left the fort before daylight on the ensuing morning, and rode rapidly down the creek, in the direction of the mouth of Cane. When within a few hundred yards of the spot where they supposed the encampment to be, they heard the report of many guns in quick succession. Supposing that Bryan had fallen in with a herd of buffalo, they quickened their march in order to take part in the sport.

The morning was foggy, and the smoke of the guns lay so heavily upon the

"Garrard County was first settled because of its proximity to the Wilderness Road. Pioneers in the county maintained close ties with Fort Boonesborough and Logan's Station (Stanford) and had somewhat less contact with Lexington and Harrodsburg."

"Cattle, hemp, and tobacco were among the early agricultural products of the county, shipped via the Kentucky River by flatboat to downstream markets. JAMES HOGAN established a ferry in 1785 to bring Garrard County products to his warehouse across the river at the mouth of Hickman Creek in what is now Jessamine County."

James Hogan first Kentucky ferry service... With brother John Hogan.

STATUTE LAW
OF
KENTUCKY;
WITH NOTES, PRÆLECTIONS, AND OBSERVATIONS ON THE PUBLIC ACTS.

1802-1807
[585]

FERRIES.

OCTOBER, 1779, CHAP. 35, SEC. 1, CHAN. REV. PAGE 116.

An ACT for establishing several new Ferries, and for other purposes.

WHEREAS it is represented to this present general assembly, that public ferries at the places hereafter mentioned, will be of great advantage to travellers and others: *Be it therefore enacted*, that public ferries be constantly kept at the following places, and the rates for passing the same shall be as follows, that is to say: From the land of Edward West, in the county of Stafford, across the north [...] of Rappahannock

APPENDIX.

1787, CHAP. 49, SECT. 1.

An ACT for establishing several new Inspections of Tobacco, and reviving and establishing others.

SECTION 1. BE it enacted by the general assembly, That the warehouses for the reception and inspection of tobacco, shall be, and the same are hereby established on the lands of Walter Beall, on Kentucky river, near Harrod's landing, in the county of Mercer, to be called and known by the name of Harrod's landing; on the lands of James Hogan, at the mouth of Hickman's creek, on the north side of Kentucky river, in the county of Fayette, to be called and known by the name of Hogan's; on the lands of Walter Beall, at the mouth of Beech fork, on Salt river, in the county of Nelson, to be called and known by the name of Beall's; on the lands of general Charles Scott, near the mouth of Craig's creek, on Kentucky river, in the county of Fayette, to be called and known by the

Slave owners William Hogan and James Hogan with brother John Hogan.

Early KENTUCKY Tax Records

Persons Charged With the Tax	Blacks	Horses	Cattle
Hogan, Wm.	2	4	8
Hogan, John		2	7
Hogan, James (Fayette)	2	2	14

John Hogan was born 17 Feb 1756 in Pittsville, Pittsylvania Co., Va., and died 06 Aug 1798 in Garrard County, Kentucky.

Kentucky Pioneer and Court Records, Abstracts of Early Wills, Deeds, and Marriages from Court Houses and Records of Old Bibles, Churches, Grave Yards and Cemeteries.

> JOHN HOGAN, of Garrard Co., Ky.—Will Book A, page 8—Names wife, Elizabeth and children. Exec's., Jacob Black, Daniel Brown, and wife, Elizabeth. Witnesses, Nicholas Lloyd, Robert McKay, Lewis Hogan. Written Dec. 18, 1797. Probate not given.

John's son Lewis Hogan acted as a witness to his will and is listed on the 1820 United States Federal Census.

Jessamine County Kentucky River Task Force

http://www.jessamineco.com/river/guidebook5.htm

Liberty Warehouse & Richardson's Ferry

The Liberty Warehouse was located at the earlier site of John Hogan's Landing and served the tobacco farmers of the Mt. Hebron section of Garrard County.

In July of 1817 Lewis Hogan, son of John Hogan, applied to the Garrard County Court for the establishment of a tobacco warehouse on his land. The Court approved the request in October of 1817 and gave it the name, Liberty Warehouse. Located midway between the busy Hickman and Quantico warehouses, it was more local in its appeal and more limited in the area it served.

John HOGAN married Elizabeth Penax/Penix/Pinnix/Pinay/Pheonix.

Elizabeth's mother's maiden name is OVERTON. Her father was John PINNIX.

John HOGAN - Elizabeth PINAX - 12 Apr. 1781. md. by Rev. William DOUGLASS. Louisa Co., VA

Deed Book B, p. 299, Garrard Co., KY, August 29, 1801 between Zachariah Smith of the county of Mercer, State of KY on the one part and ELIZABETH, WIDOW OF JOHN HOGAN deceased; Lewis Hogan; Edmund Hogan; Elihu Hogan; *ZACHARIAH Hogan*; Elizabeth Hogan; Sarah Hogan; HEIRS OF JOHN HOGAN.

Other children of John Hogan not listed: John Hogan Jr., William Hogan.

Zachariah Hogan is named as John Hogan's son in Deed Book B, p. 299, Garrard Co., KY, August 29, 1801.

In 1755 John Pinnix, Elizabeth's father, enlisted in Capt. Samuel OVERTON's company of Rangers during the French and Indian War.

Captain Samuel Overton's Company of Rangers,

In service in 1755 to 1756

OFFICERS

Samuel Overton...............Captain

Ansolem CLARKson.........Sergeant

PRIVATES

John Penix

John PENIX, tithable in Trinity Parish, Louisa Co., VA.

Also in Trinity Parish were Zacharias COSBY and Zacharias HOGAN with John HOGAN Jr. Also GENTRY THOMASSON and James OVERTON.

Elizabeth Pinnix's father John PINNIX and her two sons Zachariah HOGAN and John HOGAN Jr attend the same Parish as James OVERTON of the Overton family in Louisa Co., VA.

13 MAR 1780 John PENIX proved in Louisa County Court by oath of William MELTON, that he had enlisted in Capt. Overton's company and had served until legally discharged and was entitled to bounty land under the Proclamation of 1763.

13 MAR 1780 John PENIX received Land Bounty Certificate No. 1189, which he later assigned to John HOGAN.

The prominent Overton family originated from William Overton of Wales who came to America and was a descendant of Maj. Gen. Robert Overton 1609 England. They were well known in Hanover Louisa Co., VA.

JEREMIAH ZACHARIAH HOGAN IS MARILYN MONROE'S THIRD GREAT-GRANDFATHER.

Zachariah Hogan's first marriage:

Zachariah Hogan married Delilah Marksberry. Delilah's father is Samuel Marksberry III.

Source Citation for Kentucky Marriages, 1802-1850
Name Delila Marksbury
Marriage Date 9 Aug 1806
Marriage Place   Garrard, Ky
Zachariah Hogan
Delila Marksbury

Grant Co. Deeds

ZACHARIAH HOGAN and Delilah his wife of Grant County to WILLIAM PIERCE**** of same, for $430, land in Grant County on the "waters of Licken" - 43 acres and 12 poles, beginning at a stone near the edge of the dry ridge road leading from Lexington to Cincinnati, to JOSHUA CHILDRES' corner, it being part of DAVID LEECH's survey of 30,000 acres. Delilah signs (X). 13 November 1820.

DELILAH HOGAN (MARKSBERRY/MARKSBURY) IS MARILYN MONROE'S THIRD GREAT GRANDMOTHER.

Kentucky Pioneer and Court Records, Abstracts of Early Wills, Deeds, and Marriages from Court Houses and Records of Old Bibles, Churches, Grave Yards and Cemeteries.

SAMUEL MARKESBERRY—Book B, page 57—Names wife, Isabella. Sons, Isaac, William, John, Samuel Marksberry. Daughters, Rachel Banks, Nancy Fugate, Jane Banks, Milly Franks, and Deliah Hogan. Exec's., Sons, John, Isaac and William Marksberry. Written Dec. 29, 1812. Probated July, 1813. Witnesses, Anna Huffman, Arthur Steen and Paisey Marksberry.

First Circuit Court held in Williamstown, Grant, Kentucky May 5, 1820.

> The first Circuit Court was held at the house of Henry Childers on the 5th day of May, 1820, Hon. John Trimble presiding. The Grand Jury of this Court were John Marksbury, foreman; Dixon Tongate, John Crook, Daniel Seward, Robert Childers, Richard Lucas, Perry Chipman, Bennett Williams, Zachariah Hogan, Lewis Gregory, John Norton, Ichabod Ashcraft, James Reed, Absalom Skirvin, John Rowland, and Thomas Thomas. This Court adjourned on the day it convened, having transacted all the business, the Grand Jury making three indictments—one against the County Court for not having the County divided into road precincts and overseers appointed.

Grand Jury of this Court | Zachariah Hogan and John Marksbury.

HISTORY OF GRANT COUNTY,

AS COMPILED BY

ROBERT H. ELLISTON,

AND READ BY HIM

ON THE FOURTH DAY OF JULY, 1876.

"A child of Mr. Samuel Marksbury…"
Samuel Marksbury III is Delilah Hogan's father.

The growth of Williamstown contains no event of special interest until the year 1856. At that time there had been erected a row of wooden buildings on either side of Main street—scarcely a brick edifice to be seen in town. A child of Mr. Samuel Marksbury was amusing himself in the basement story of his father's house, then standing where Mr Lucas has his grocery, by burning some combustible material, when the building took fire. The flames spread up and down the street, destroying every house and tenement on the west side from where P. T. Zinn's store now stands to Mill street, and on the east side from John H. Webb's store to several houses below the residence of E. H. Smith. This was the first fatal disaster to the county-seat, and thirty families were in a few minutes rendered destitute and homeless by this terrible fire-fiend. Contributions were raised for the sufferers, and the people all over the county contributed liberally. Judge O. P. Hogan made speeches in Georgetown, Frankfort and Lexington, whose people subscribed as much as seven hundred dollars to the unfortunate ones in our midst. Three thousand dollars were soon raised in their behalf, and it was not long until the clink of the hammer was heard and the mason and carpenter were busy in erecting new and better houses on the burnt ground, so that in a few years all the lots on Main street, once covered by old wooden buildings—excellent rat harbors and food for flames—were now occupied by good and substantial houses.

Judge O.P. HOGAN

Judge O.P. Hogan and Family as recorded in the 1860 Census.

Page No. 174

SCHEDULE 1.—Free Inhabitants in _____ in the County of _Grant_, State of _Kentucky_, enumerated by me, on the _22nd_ day of _August_ 1860. C.R. O'Hara Ass't Marshal

Post Office _Williamstown_

		Name	Age	Sex	Occupation	Value Real Estate	Value Personal Estate
93	1195–1197	Oristan P. Hogan	52	M		4500	3100
94		Sarah "	46	F			
95		Amanda "	17	F			
96		William "	16	M	Farming		
97		Elihu "	14	M			
98		Sarah E. "	11	F			
99		Egustus "	8	M			

Marilyn Monroe Unveiled | A Family History

Judge O.P. Hogan Sr. Slave Owner.

SCHEDULE 2.—Slave Inhabitants in _____ in the County of Grant, State of Kentucky, enumerated by me, on the 28 day of _____, 1860. N. H. Oliver, Ass't Marshal.

Page No. 1

	Names of Slave Owners	Number of Slaves	Age	Sex	Color	Fugitives from the State	Number manumitted	Deaf & dumb, blind, insane, or idiotic	No. of Slave houses		Names of Slave Owners	Number of Slaves	Age	Sex	Color	Fugitives from the State	Number manumitted	Deaf & dumb, blind, insane, or idiotic	No. of Slave houses	
1		1	25	m	B							1	7	F	B					1
2		1	20	F	B							1	7	F	m					2
3		1	17	F	B							1	3	m	B					3
4		1	15	m	B							1	2	F	B					4
5		1	12	F	B							1	10	m	m				2	5
6		1	2	F	m						Cornell N. Carter	1	44	F	B					6
7	Theodosia Lucas	1	27	F	B							1	22	m	B					7
8		1	4	F	m							1	21	m	B				1	8
9		1	13	F	m						Weeden L. Henns &	1	28	F	B					9
10		1	10	F	B						Six others	1	24	m	B					10
11		1	6	F	m							1	9	m	B					11
12		1	2	m	B							1	7	F	B				1	12
13	Overton P. Hogan	1	55	F	B						Alfred Kendall	1	50	m	B					13
14		1	35	m	B							1	40	F	B					14
15		1	30	F	B							1	30	F	B					15
16		1	25	m	B							1	25	F	B					16
17		1	20	F	m							1	23	m	B					17
18		1	22	F	B							1	22	m	B					18
19		1	17	m	B							1	22	m	B					19
20		1	14	m	B							1	14	m	B					20
21		1	14	F	B							1	15	F	B					21
22		1	12	m	B							1	14	F	B					22
23		1	11	F	B							1	13	F	B					23
24		1	10	F	m							1	11	F	B					24
25		1	8	F	m							1	10	F	B					25
26		1	6	m	B							1	8	m	B					26
27		1	5	m	m							1	4	F	B					27
28		1	4	F	B							1	3	F	B					28
29		1	3	m	B							1	2	m	B					29
30		1	2	F	B							1	2	m	B					30
31		1	1	m	B							1	1	F	B					31
32		1	2	F	B			2				1	1	F	B				1	32
33	Lewis Kendall	1	60	F	m						Esau Bryant	1	70	m	B					33
34		1	22	m	B							1	30	F	B					34
35		1	18	F	m							1	10	m	B					35
36		1	17	F	m							1	6	m	B				1	36
37		1	15	F	m							1	2	F	B					37
38		1	14	m	B						John N. Webb	1	26	F	m					38
39		1	11	m	B							1	4	F	m					39
40		1	10	F	B						Elkanah Johnson	1	8	m	m					40

No. of owners, 8
No. of houses, 11
No. of male slaves, 33
No. of female slaves, 47
Total slaves, 80

Judge O.P. Hogan Sr. is the son of Zachariah Hogan.

JUDGE OVERTON PENNIX HOGAN SR. IS MARILYN MONROE'S THIRD GREAT UNCLE.

BIOGRAPHIES OF SOME OF OUR PROMINENT CITIZENS

July 14, 1881

Overton P. Hogan the son of Zachariah and Dellah Hogan, nee Marksbury. His grandfather, James Hogan [James Hogan is O.P. Hogan's Uncle as evidenced by historical documents. John Hogan is O.P. Hogan Sr's father] served four years in the war of the Revolution, and was a native of Southern Virginia, and crossing the boundary line married a lady of North Carolina. Subsequent to this, about the close of the last century, he emigrated to, and settled near Paris, Kentucky, where he lived when the great massacre took place, but hearing in the night of the approach of the savages, he fled with his family to Boones's Fort, (now Boonesboro) where he remained some six months. The Indians in the meantime destroyed his house and personal property. On leaving the Fort he settled in Garrard County on the banks of the Kentucky River where he died. Zachariah, father of Judge Hogan, married Miss Dellah, daughter of Samuel Marksbury, an old Revolutionary soldier who emigrated to Kentucky just after the war. This branch of the family can be traced to Scotland in the person of a Miss Baxter, who was kidnapped from the Bonnie isle when but twelve years old and brought to Philadelphia Pennsylvania, Pennsylvania where she was sold into bondage until 21 years old, when she married a man named Mayfield, and emigrated to Kentucky and reached the good old age of 111 years. Zachariah was the second son in a family of five sons and two daughters, and followed farming until the war of 1812 broke out, when he and a brother engaged in mercantile pursuits in Lexington, Kentucky, and desiring to enlarge their business they established a branch store about one a a half miles north of Williamstown on the farm now owned b H. Clay White. Zachariah Hogan came with his family to take charge of this store in October 1813, it being the first one located within the present limits of Grant County. At that date this was a precinct of Pendleton County and the voting place was at the house of Old Captain William Arnold, who was a soldier of the Revolution and magistrate of the district. The mercantile venture prospered until the embargo was removed from goods, when nearly every merchant in the country failed, and among them the father of Mr. Hogan lost all he had accumulated by energy and industry. He returned to the farm, but ere long that went to satisfy the demands of creditors. But a still greater calamity befell him in 1824, when his wife died, leaving seven small children of which our subject was the oldest.

He was born May 29, 1808 in Garrard County, Kentucky. At 16 he left home to begin the struggle of life for himself, first working by the month on the farm or whatever else he could find to do at $6 per month. He worked for John Thomas, a liveryman, on the same site where his own stable now stands. He drove state for 5 years, probably during the years 1828-1833, from Cincinnati, O., to the Foot of the Ridge known as Peter Jones' Hotel, 52 miles distant, with four-horse stage. He was among the first to cross the Ohio on a small ferry boat run by a tram-wheel, impelled by four blind horses. Then Covington had but 5 houses and the principal landing was Kennedy's Ferry. The journey was made daily, carrying many passengers who were going to the north and west to locate. Mr. Hogan was a member of the Legislature in 1842 '43, and of the Senate in 1849, '50, '53 and '67. He was also County Judge and Master Commissioner one term. He claims to be the originator of the bill exempting personal property from execution. In politics Judge Hogan has always been a Democrat, and for many years was the acknowledged leader of the Democratic Party in Grant County, and chairman of the Democratic Executive Committee. After the disastrous fired in Williamstown in 1856, Judge Hogan made speeches in George, Frankfort and Lexington, and secured subscriptions amounting to $700 for the suffers. In 1836 Mr. Hogan united in marriage to Miss Sarah, daughter of Lewis Kendall, then of Harrison County, Kentucky, and after marriage kept hotel in Williamstown for several years. He has been a large farmer and has accumulated a handsome property by his industry and energy. He and his wife have been consistent and devoted member of the Christian Church since its organization in this place. He takes a great interest in Sunday Schools, and for several years past has been superintendent of the Sunday school in the above church.

Dr. Overton Pinnix Hogan Jr. is the son Judge O.P. Hogan Sr.

Dr. Overton Pinnix Hogan Jr.

BIRTH 13 MAY 1851 • Grant County, Kentucky, USA

DEATH 09 JAN 1931 • Cincinnati, Ohio

O.P. Hogan Jr. is documented in the Source Citation for U.S., School Catalogs, 1765-1935 for 1871-University of Virginia:

Hogan, Overton Phœnix, Jr.   Williamstown, Ky.,   C., MED., P. & S., AN.,   1

Physician, Farmer and Dealer in Blooded Stock

February 16, 1891

Dr. O. P. Hogan is a member of one of Grant County's oldest and most prominent families. He was born at the old Hogan homestead, north of town, now known as the Dr. Frank place, June 13th, 1851, making him forty years of age next June. Dr. Hogan is the youngest child of a family of nine children born to Overton P. Hogan and wife, Sarah kendall Hogan. Of that large family of children only three are now living, two boys and one girl, to-wit, Dr. O. P. Hogan, Ella Hogan and Mrs. G. W. Yancy of Cynthiana. O. P. Hogan Sr. was the eldest son of Zachariah Hogan.

His grandfather, James Hogan [second great uncle as denoted by historical documents], served four years in the war of Independence, and after the close of the war was one of the early pioneers of Kentucky, and had many exciting adventures with the Indians, having at one time his house burned and all his personal property destroyed. Judge Hogan was born in Garrard County in

1808 and came to Grant County when quite young. For fifty years he was one of the most progressive farmers and businessmen for the county. He was one time elected to represent the county in the State Legislature and twice elected to the State Senate from this Senatorial district. At the time of his death, October 5, 1855, he had again been elected by the Democracy of Grant to a seat in the Legislature, but death called him home before he could take his seat. Dr. O. P. Hogan spent the first sixteen years of his life on his father's farm, attending school a part of each year. In 1868-9 he attended the A. & M. College at lexington, being a classmate of Judge C. C. Cram. In 1870-1 he attended Washington and Lee University at Lexington, Virginia, at that time presided over by the venerated and world-renowned General Robt. E. Lee. While in this university he graduated in the Business Department and received a prize for the best set of books. After a two-year course in this college, he entered the medical department of the New York University from whence he graduated in March 1872. Returning to Williamstown he formed a partnership with Dr. R. H. O'Hara in the drug business, but shortly afterwards disposed of his interest in the business and engaged in various other callings until 1880, when he built his elegant home near Dry Ridge and commenced to operate the "Hogan Grove Stock Farm," dealing largely in blooded stock, especially trotting horses.

January 1st, 1874, he led to the Hymeneal altar Miss Lutie Smith, daughter of Hon. E. H. Smith and Sallie O'Hara Smith. Four children have been born to this union, three of who are now living. Mr. Hogan, in conjunction with his brother, Ella Hogan, has done a great deal to educate the people of this part of the country in merits of good blood for breeding purposes. In the last four years he has brought into this county several finely bred stallions and the improvement in the stock of horses has been very noticeable. Last spring he met with quite a calamity by the burning of his stables and eleven heads of fine horses, including Clayford and Magic Wilkes. The loss at the time was put at $12,000 to $15,000 and was about correct. Mr. Hogan was not discouraged by this great loss, but immediately wen to work and rebuilt his stables and secured other good horses. He is now building a large addition to his stables and otherwise improving his facilities for training and driving. The Hogan Grove Stock Farm has a reputation all over northern Kentucky. Mr. Hogan is the owner of 600 acres of the best land in the county and is not only a breeder of fine stock but a large general farmer. He is one of the oldest members of Centurion Lodge I.O.O.F., a consistent Democrat and good citizen, has never held office except Police Judge of Williamstown for a short time. His name has been frequently mentioned as a probable candidate for the Democratic nomination for the Legislature, and while he has not yet announced himself, it is very probable that he will be a candidate for that position.

Dr. O.P. Hogan Jr. son of Judge O.P. Hogan.

Souvenir Edition, The Williamstown Courier, Williamstown, Ky, May 30, 1901

O. P. HOGAN. Clever and sociable, with plenty of good common sense, and withal a cultured and highly educated gentleman. These qualities are rarely ever so happily blended in the same person as they are in the subject of this sketch. A graduate with the first honors of the business school, Washington and Lee University, Lexington, Va., and the Medical University of New York, a registered physician. He established the largest and best equipped breeding and sale stock farm in Northern Kentucky and operated it from 1885 to 1894. Was Judge of the Williamstown Police Court for five years and clerk and assistant to Attorneys E. H. Smith and W. N. Hogan, his brother, during this time. Represented Grant County in the General Assembly of Kentucky in 1894-95. These services seemingly developed a fondness for the law and public questions, and at the October term of the Grant Circuit Court, 1897, he was admitted to the bar, passing a most creditable examination. At that time we predicted for him a successful future, and it is being fully realized, for he has a fair share of the practice in the courts and is the attorney for several large estates, and controls and manages more property, consisting of farms and other real estate and personality than any other one person in the county, and is now regarded as one of the county's most successful lawyers and substantial business men. He is a prominent and active member of the I.O.O.F. and the Christian Church; has sometimes represented the order in the State Grand Lodge and has been Secretary or President of the Convention of Christian Churches in Grant County for the past three years. In politics he has always been a Democrat, and has rendered the party much valuable service, especially as a campaign orator. He is the youngest of nine children born to O. P. and Sarah K. Hogan (nee Kendall), and was born and reared on the farm now owned by J. B. O'Neal, in the Dry Ridge precinct. Since 1895 he has resided at the old homestead Williamstown, Ky.

THE BOURBON NEWS.

SWIFT CHAMP, - EDITOR AND OWNER

FRIDAY, APRIL 21, 1905.

O. P. Hogan, of Grant county, was unanimously nominated for State Senator from the twenty-sixth Senatorial District, composed of Bracken, Grant and Pendleton counties.

Elihu Hogan is the son of Judge O.P. Hogan Sr.

Kentucky: A History of the State, Battle, Perrin, & Kniffin, 7th ed., 1887, Grant County.

E. HOGAN, stock breeder and grain speculator, was born in Grant County, Ky., July 22, 1847. He is the sixth of a family of nine born to O. P. and Sallie (Kendall) Hogan. O. P. Hogan was born in Lancaster, Garrard Co., Ky, in 1808. He represented Grant County, Ky., in the Legislature three times, was State senator one term, and was county judge of Grant County one term. He was a large hog trader, perhaps the largest that was ever in the State of Kentucky. He died October 8, 1885, a strict member of the Christian Church for forty years. Mrs. Sallie (Kendall) Hogan was born in Harrison County, Ky., and was a daughter of Lewis and Phebe (Nelson) Kendall. E. Hogan was educated at Harrodsburg and Georgetown., Ky. He has always been a great horse man, and is one of the best judges of horses in Kentucky. He was in the livery business in Williamstown for several years and was very successful. He now has a fine farm of 410 acres between Williamstown and Dry Ridge which is called the Hogan Grove Stock Farm. He makes a specialty of raising fine horses generally. He was married, December 18, 1867, to Rose Collins, of Grant County, Ky., A daughter of James N. and Cordelia (Carslinea) Collins. Four children have blessed this union, and of these, two are living: Collins K. and Charles R. Mrs. Hogan is a strict member of the Christian Church, and her father was a thirty-second degree Mason.

Overton S. Hogan is the son of Judge O.P. Hogan Sr.

Souvenir Edition, The Williamstown Courier, Williamstown, Ky, May 30, 1901:

OVERTON S. HOGAN. The Grant County bar has always been one of the strongest in the state, and judging by the young men who have been admitted to the practice in recent years it will long retain its prestige. Overton S. Hogan is one of its youngest members, but has already demonstrated that he will be a worthy successor to the many bright lawyers who have made this bar famous in the days gone by. He comes from a long line of distinguished lawyers. His father is a lawyer of no mean ability, his grandfather, Hubbard Smith, was one of the greatest lawyers who ever practiced in a Kentucky court; his uncle, Wilbur Smith, was a great young lawyer when he died in 1885 at the age of twenty-five; his cousin, Edward O'Hara, is now a brilliant young lawyer, and his uncle, and great uncle--James O'Hara--were both great lawyers and distinguished judges. So young Hogan comes by his taste for the law quite naturally. He is a son of Dr. O. P. Hogan and Miss Lutie (Smith) Hogan, and was born in Grant County November 21st, 1847, and was raised on his father's farm at the town residence in Williamstown. He attended the common schools here, the high school, and then a two years' course at the Kentucky State College, and a two years' course at Fishburns' Military Institute in Virginia. Later he graduated in typewriting and shorthand at Nelson's Business College in Cincinnati. Coming home he entered the law office of W. W. Dickerson, and after three years' close application and hard reading was admitted to the bar some five years ago. He has been in the office of Lawyer Dickerson ever since, and has been successful in his practice. April 27, 1898, he was united in marriage to Miss Frances Halbert, a niece of Mrs. M. D. Gray. To this union one child has been born, Smith D. Hogan, born September 21st, 1900. Mr. Hogan is a Democrat in politics, a fine speaker, an active secret society worker, being a member of the local lodge Knights of Pythias. His future ought to be full of promise to him and his.

The Hogan House

Built in the mid 1800's this beautiful estate was first home to Elias Smith, a prominent attorney and his wife Sarah. Elias and his wife, gave this house to their daughter Lucy, and son-in-law Overton Hogan Jr, probably as a wedding gift in 1872. Overton Hogan Jr. was the son of Overton Hogan Sr. the owner of the first train over the southern railroad. Overton Hogan Jr., himself was an extremely successful businessman, a registered physician, lawyer and general assembly member. Overton and Lucy Hogan then passed down the house to their son Robert Dawson Hogan and his wife Josephine in 1939. While Robert Dawson was a accountant, banker and insurance agent, his wife Josephina oversaw the day to day operations of the estate then name The Broadlawn Farm. Josephine was widowed in 1987 but continued to live in the house until 1993 when she sold it to Charles and Sharon Rider. Josephina passed away only days after selling the home to Mr. and Mrs. Rider, at the age of 96. The Rider family still owns and operates The Hogan House in her honor.

Hon. O. P. Hogan, of Grant, being introduced to the Convention, made an eloquent address, which was listened to with interest and attention, and frequently and loudly applauded.

LOUISVILLE DAILY COURIER

VOLUME 31.   LOUISVILLE, KENTUCKY, FRIDAY MORNING, JULY 20, 1860.   NUMBER 17.

had room for it to-morrow or next day.

O. P. HOGAN'S SPEECH.

Mr. O. P. HOGAN, of Grant, then took the stand and spoke, as follows:

Fellow-citizens, I feel highly flattered by the call you have made upon me. It is now about ten minutes to twelve o'clock, and I reckon you are not very impatient.

I feel a little sorrowful in my heart, and why? I have got a few erring brethren who have gone astray in Kentucky, but, as I am quite forgiving to my brethren in the Democratic party as I am to my brethren in the Church, I want to take them by the hand and bring them back to the Constitution that our forefathers, eighty years ago, declared—to that Constitution which they fought a seven-year's war to maintain, against a people who were then the masters of the seas—Old England. They fought upon principles, and I stand before you to-day upon the same platform they fought for—the Constitution we live under this day, the Union and the equal rights of the States, the protection of all citizens in their lives, liberty, and property in each and all of the Territories, whether such property consist of horses, niggers, wooden nutmegs, red oak hams, fine pumpkin seed, Yankee clocks, or red flannel. [Great laughter.] When I see a Democrat in Kentucky who raises his voice against these principles, it makes the cold chills run through my heart. [Laughter and applause.] Why? I have stood thirty-two years and fought the battles of the Democratic party until my head has got a little bald, and I intend to fight them thirty-two years longer, if God spares my life. [Cheers.] I have never faltered or fallen by the roadside, and I don't intend to falter or fall until John C. Breckinridge and Joe Lane are President and Vice President of this Republic. [Great applause.]

What are we contending for? Why, fellow-citizens, I never heard of a Democratic Convention attempt to pass a resolution that did not protect all citizens in their rights in this Union, which the Constitution accorded to them, until this Convention of Douglas men in Baltimore convened. I suppose you all know the nature of the resolutions there adopted, and I will not take time to read them here. They passed a resolution that they would go to war with a whole nation to protect a foreigner, but when it was proposed to put in one to protect our own citizens it was rejected. When one of those old patriots who fought in the Revolutionary war, disfigured with the scars of British bayonets, (I believe there are a few hundred of them yet surviving), now asks to carry with him to a Territory an old and valued slave, he must be denied the privilege, if the Douglas doctrine prevails. To this result do the principles of his party inevitably tend. Are these Democratic principles?

evitably tend. Are these Democratic principles? Is there any Democrat in this Union going for Douglas? Pause, and think where you are going. Like the Prodigal Son spoken of in scripture, who left his family and spent his substance among strangers in riotous living, and who, when he reflected on his wicked course of life, he said "I will arise and return to my father's house; I will be a servant among servants." When he returned his father received him with open arms, assembled his friends, and killed the fatted calf. To the prodigal Democrats, who are rioting among strangers, we say return to your father's house, and you shall be received with rejoicings; but we will not go to you and live with you on the husks of Squatter Sovereignty. [Laughter and applause.] Come, and we will not only kill the fatted calf, but will roast Christmas bulls all over the State, and feast and grow jolly. [Renewed laughter.]

Why, fellow-citizens, I have been called a disunionist, a fire-eater, an interventionist, and all sorts of names. Mr. Douglas said, in his speech when he was serenaded on Saturday night, after they nominated him in the Baltimore Convention, that intervention was disunion. Let it be so then. I say, with respect to slavery in the Territories, "hands off, gentlemen." Let any citizen of the Union go there with whatever property he has, and enjoy it there; no power in the country is sufficient to take it from him, until the citizens of such Territory prepare a State Constitution adverse to the holding of such species of property. Let the people, under a State Government, decide whither they will have slavery or no slavery.

Mr. Douglas says Congress has no power to interfere with slavery in the Territories.— If any Douglas man will pay attention, I will prove he is an intervention man.— He says Territorial Legislatures can use unfriendly legislation to keep you out of the Territories with your negroes, and is not this intervention with a vengeance? Every single paper that pretends to give a support to Douglas, says the people of a Territory have the constitutional right to abolish slavery in the Territories. I want to know whether any man here is willing to have his slaves driven from the public domain, either by Congress or by Territorial legislation? How is it possible that any Democrat, with these plain facts staring him in the face, can go into the Squatter Sovereignty camp?

The American party of '55-6 told the Democratic party that Mr. Douglas would take them into Squatter Sovereignty, they said that whenever Mr. Douglas went there we would follow him.

We pledged the people all over the State that we never would adopt the Squatter Sovereignty, though all other Democrats in the United States became identified with the doctrine. I ask Democrats if they want us to take back all we have said, and repudiate every platform we have laid down, and adopt instead thereof the Douglas heresies?

But, fellow-citizens, there never was a word spoken by Mr. Douglas in favor of Squatterism until he got into that race with Mr. Layton. In an evil hour (at Freeport) that great statesman and talented man stepped aside. I was, before that period, like my friend Talbott. I stood up for Douglas against all others; but he stepped aside from the true principles of Democracy, and then I said "Goodbye, Mr. Douglas." [Laughter.] I told my friends, in less than ten minutes after I read Douglas' Freeport speech, he was going to give the Democratic party a great deal more trouble than Tom Benton, Sam Houston, Martin Van Buren, or all the other renegades in the country had done.

Our American friends are making a great noise about Douglas in this State; in fact, all the noise is made by them. Gentlemen, you ought to know by their movements, that they are linked with the Douglas faction to oppose Breckinridge. Whenever they find a wavering Democrat, they pat him on the back and tell him to go in for Douglas and win. My God, did you ever know a Know Nothing to tell a Democrat to vote right in your life. [Great laughter and applause.] I was in Georgetown on Monday last and heard a gentleman from Pennsylvania, but a native of Kentucky, and heard him make a speech in favor of Bell and Everett. He said it was a slander upon the Bell and Everett party to say that they went for the protection of slavery in the Territories! On the previous Monday, in my own town, a celebrated orator there took the stand for Mr. Bell, and convinced everybody there that he was for intervention in the Territories. I never heard such a jumble of contradictions in my life, as were contained in that speech. It would take a Philadelphia lawyer to understand the position of his party. In one place they are one thing, and in another place, another thing.

I stand to-day, fellow-citizens, upon the platform upon which I have always stood, and I appeal to every Democrat to rally around that platform—the platform upon which John C. Breckinridge and Joe Lane stand. I ask every speaker of all parties to point out a single sentiment contained in that platform which is not in perfect accordance with the spirit of the Constitution. The Douglas wing of the Democracy and the American party fire off their small arms against Breckinridge, but they make nothing but noise and smoke. [Applause.] They remind me of a lot of dogs [laughter] I once heard of. A friend of mine had five or six cur dogs. One night, when the light fleecy clouds were wafted by the wind across the face of the moon, partly obscuring her splendor for the moment of their passage. The dogs barked, howled, and jumped like mad at the spectacle. A neighbor inquired the cause of the singular conduct of the dogs. Their owner told him that they were barking at the moon; that the clouds obscured her brightness at the spectacle. A neighbor inquired the cause of the singular conduct of the dogs. Their owner told him that they were barking at the moon; that the clouds obscured her brightness for the moment, and the fool dogs jumped at her and howled, but she went on her course unhurt and indifferent to the attack. [Laughter.] The political curs of all kinds and colors bark, howl, and go mad, because the light clouds of faction obscure for a moment the bright light of John C. Breckinridge; but the winds blow them away, and he shines forth in all his glory, lighting up the valleys, illuminating the mountains, and spreading his genial light over the whole of his native State. [Immense cheering.] I have never before seen so much enthusiasm manifested in this State for a man as goes up wherever the name of Breckinridge is mentioned. All the boys, and girls even, lisp the name of Breckinridge; and every married Democrat in the State must vote for Breckinridge, or your wives will not let you sleep with them. [Laughter and applause.] I tell you, you might as well attempt to run the Mississippi river up to Frankfort as to prevent the people from voting for Breckinridge. [Immense applause.]

Owen, Sweet Owen, [laughter] will give about sixteen hundred majority; and if he wants any more than that, he has only to say so, and we will give him two thousand, [Cheers,] for you have only to shout "Breckinridge," and the Democrats jump out of the bushes and come up to the work. [Laughter and cheers.]

I must now close my remarks, as I wish to save myself for other occasions. It is not much use to talk to you here. I tell you, my shirt has hardly been dry since I returned from the Baltimore Convention. I am in this fight heart, soul, and hand; and if God spares my life, I intend to be in it until November. [Cheers.] I want you all to enlist in the same cause as heartily as I do, for I never before felt such interest in any cause. Like Davy Crockett, I know I am right, and therefore go ahead. [Applause.]

The members of the Convention then retired from the Hall.

AFTERNOON SESSION

The Courier-Journal.

LOUISVILLE, WEDNESDAY MORNING, MAY 3, 1893.

* * *

Mr. O. P. Hogan is a candidate for Representative from Grant county. Mr. Hogan is not a superstitious man. If he were, he would not be running for this office. His brother, W. N. Hogan, was elected to the Legislature in 1883, but died before that body convened. His father, O. P. Hogan, was elected at the August election, 1883, and died also before the meeting of that body. It is very well known that death has no terrors for an office-seeker, but Mr. Hogan is not of the kind usually included in that class. He is a doctor and a successful breeder of livestock.

* * *

Semi-Weekly Interior Journal

Stanford, Ky., November 20, 1883

W. P. WALTON — EDITOR

and the others a quarter each.

—W. N. Hogan, who was elected Representative of Grant county last August, has resigned. His health had been failing him for the past two months and has gradually grown worse, rendering him incapable of attending to any business.

LEXINGTON, KENTUCKY, SUNDAY, JUNE 14, 1908.

SENATOR HOGAN MAY RUN FOR CONGRESS

Good Chance If Convention Goes Out of Kenton or Campbell Counties.

Senator O. P. Hogan, of Grant county, remained in Lexington from the State Convention until yesterday afternoon with friends.

Senator Hogan is very enthusiastic over the result of the convention, and believes that the Democrats will carry Kentucky this year by a big majoity. He has represented his district in the Senate for the last two sessions, and there is considerable talk in the Sixth Congressional district of the possibility of his nomination for Congress by the Democrats.

The counties of Kenton and Campbell have a majority in the Congressional Convention, and if they unite on a Campbell or Kenton man they will control the situation, but there are a number of candidates in other parts of the district, and in case the convention goes outside of the two big counties Senator Hogan's friends think he has a good chance for the nomination.

A DYING LEGISLATOR.

Hon. O. P. Hogan, the Honored Representative of Grant County, at Death's Door.

[Correspondence of the Courier-Journal.]

WILLIAMSTOWN, Oct. 2.—Hon. O. P. Hogan, the honored Representative-elect to the Legislature from Grant county, is lying at death's door, his physicians having given up all hope of his recovery. Mr. Hogan is 76 years old, a fact which is against him in his struggle against disease. A strange fatality seems to hang over the family. At the August election, 1883, Judge Hogan's oldest son, W. N. Hogan, was elected to the Legislature from this county by a complimentary vote. He was a strong man physically and mentally; a lawyer with a lucrative practice; the hope and comfort of friends and family. Soon after his election his mental facilities began to fail. He forwarded his resignation to the Governor, and January 9, 1884, died by his own hand. Two years later his father was elected to the same position, and he lies now on his dying bed.

Judge Hogan has been a leading man for years. From 1845 to 1856 he served Grant county continuously in either the House or the Senate. He was also County Judge for many years. He has lived in Grant county for 60 years, and been prominently identified with its every advancement. A Democrat and a member of the Christian Church, he was true to both; a faithful, untiring friend, devoted to his family, he will be missed and mourned by a wide circle of friends and relatives.

THE COURIER-JOURNAL, LOUISVILLE, THURSDAY MORNING, JUNE 27, 1912.

THIRD ASSISTANT TO ATTORNEY GENERAL

C. S. HOGAN, OF WILLIAMSTOWN, GETS APPOINTMENT.

Frankfort, Ky., June 26.—(Special.)—O. S. Hogan, of Williamstown, has been appointed Third Assistant Attorney General by Attorney General Garnett, and has begun his duties. Mr. Hogan is a son of O. P. Hogan, who was a member of the State Senate four years ago. The place as third assistant was held by Charles Morris, of Lagrange, prior to the resignation of Judge W. R. Black, following which Mr. Morris was appointed first assistant. The place as third assistant pays $2,500 a year.

Marilyn Monroe Unveiled | A Family History

Zachariah Hogan's son was Confederate Captain Tilford Marion Hogan.

TILFORD MARION HOGAN WAS MARILYN MONROE'S THIRD GREAT UNCLE.

Hogan, Tilford
Co. H, 1 Missouri Infantry.
(Confederate.)
Captain | Captain

(CONFEDERATE)

H

Tilford Hogan,
Capt., Co. H, 1st Mos. Regt. Inf.

Appears on a
LIST
of Field Officers and Captains of the 22d Reg't. Tenn. Vols., and Officers of the 1st Reg't. Mo. Inf., Sept. 22, 1861.
List not dated.

(Confederate.)
H 1 Mo.

Tilford Hogan
Capt., Co. H, 1 Reg't Missouri Infantry.

Appears on a
Historic Roll*
of the organization named above.

Roll dated _____, 186_.

Age when enlisted 45
Nativity { State or Kingdom Missouri
          { Town or County Pemiscot
Occupation or profession Farmer
Enlisted:
When June 22, 1861.
Where Memphis Tenn
Term 1 year
Resident when enlisted:
Town or Post Office _____
County Pemiscot
Remarks: Resigned Nov. 24, 1861

*This card was made from the original record which was borrowed from Mrs. Wright L. Smith, through Capt. James W. Allen of St. Louis, Mo.—A. G. 129159½.

Book mark: _____

(653) Copyist.

135

Another son of Zachariah Hogan was George Willis Hogan.

GEORGE WILLIS HOGAN IS MARILYN MONROE'S SECOND GREAT-GRANDFATHER.

George Willis Hogan marries Sarah Ann Owen.

The U.S. and International Marriage Records, 1560-1900.

Name: Sarah Ann Owen

Gender: Female

Birth Year: 1822

Spouse Name: George Willis Hogan

Spouse Birth Place: KY

Spouse Birth Year: 1822

Marriage Year: 1843

Marriage State: KY

Number Pages: 1

Hogan, George W. & Owen, Sarah Ann – March 11, 1843.

The County Seat for Grant County Kentucky is WILLIAMSTOWN.

Documented in the Grant County Historic Marriages for GRANT COUNTY KENTUCKY:

Peter Ireland witnessed the marriage between George Willis Hogan And Sarah Ann Owen, as documented on the right. Peter Ireland married Elizabeth Hogan, as documented on the the right also. Judge Overton P. Hogan witnessed the marriage Between Elizabeth and Peter.

George, Elizabeth, and Judge Overton P. Hogan Sr. were siblings. Their father was Zachariah Hogan.

By Febuary 5th, 1825 Delilah Marksbury/Marksberry marries Johnson Simpson in Grant County, Kentucky.

After spending many years in Williamstown, Kentucky, Zachariah Hogan then moved with his second wife Elizabeth DOTY and family to Adams County Illinois. Hogan, Zachariah married Elizabeth Doty December 4, 1828.

Elizabeth's family hailed from Somerset County in New Jersey, before settling in Rowan County, North Carolina. They made their way to Grant County (formerly Pendleton), Kentucky.

Moses Doty, Elizabeth's adventurous father was the one who led the migration from New Jersey to North Carolina where he married his wife Sarah, and then headed for Illinois. However, Moses drowned in icy waters during the journey in 1811 and Sarah returned to Kentucky. She remarried Lewis Buskirk and migrated to Adams County, Illinois with Zachariah, Elizabeth and members of both the Doty and Buskirk families.

Zachariah died in 1850 and Elizabeth in 1886.

Zachariah's son from his first marriage, George Willis Hogan, eventually made his way from Kentucky to Illinois with his wife Sara Anne Owen.

Source: Adapted from Grant County News – Published in *Footsteps of the Past*, June 22, 1995.
Researched by James R. Glacking

Marilyn Monroe Unveiled | A Family History

1840 United States Federal Census for Zackariah Hogan.

-Adams County, Illinois, Quincy-

Zachariah Hogan, Marilyn Monroe's Third Great-Grandfather, purchased land in Adams County, Illinois.

CERTIFICATE No. 422

THE UNITED STATES OF AMERICA.

To all to whom these Presents shall come, Greeting:

WHEREAS Zachariah Hogan of Adams County, Illinois ha_s_ deposited in the **GENERAL LAND OFFICE** of the United States, a Certificate of the REGISTER OF THE LAND OFFICE at Quincy whereby it appears that full payment has been made by the said Zachariah Hogan according to the provisions of the Act of Congress of the 24th of April, 1820, entitled "An Act making further provision for the sale of the Public Lands," for the North East quarter of the North West quarter of Section nineteen, in Township two South, of Range seven West of the fourth Principal Meridian, in the District of lands subject to sale at Quincy, Illinois, containing fifty acres and fifty four hundredths of an acre

according to the official plat of the survey of the said Lands, returned to the General Land Office by the **SURVEYOR GENERAL**, which said tract has been purchased by the said Zachariah Hogan

NOW KNOW YE, That the United States of America, in consideration of the Premises, and in conformity with the several acts of Congress, in such case made and provided, HAVE GIVEN AND GRANTED, and by these presents DO GIVE AND GRANT, unto the said Zachariah Hogan and to his heirs, the said tract above described: **TO HAVE AND TO HOLD** the same, together with all the rights, privileges, immunities, and appurtenances of whatsoever nature, thereunto belonging, unto the said Zachariah Hogan and to his heirs and assigns forever.

In Testimony Whereof, I, Martin Van Buren PRESIDENT OF THE UNITED STATES OF AMERICA, have caused these Letters to be made PATENT, and the SEAL of the GENERAL LAND OFFICE to be hereunto affixed.

GIVEN under my hand at the CITY OF WASHINGTON, the Sixth day of August in the Year of our Lord one thousand eight hundred and thirty eight and of the **INDEPENDENCE OF THE UNITED STATES** the Sixty third

BY THE PRESIDENT: Martin Van Buren

By A. Van Buren Jr. Sec'y.

Jos. S. Wilson Acting Recorder of the General Land Office.
ad interim

1850 Federal Census for George W. Hogan and family.

George Willis Hogan followed his father Zachariah Hogan to Adams County Illinois.

[Census image: Schedule I.—Free Inhabitants in the Town of Concord in the County of Adams, State of Illinois, enumerated on the 9th day of Oct. 1850, E. H. Buckley Ass't Marshal. Entries include George W. Hogan (34), Sarah A. (32), Mary (5), John (4), William (3), Caleb (1), Edward Owen (60), Elizabeth Hogan (40), Lewis, Adaline.]

Also on the 1850 Federal Census is Edward Owen.

He is Sarah Ann Owen's father. Edward Owen's father is Zachariah Owen.

Zachariah Owen: A Patriot of the American Revolution for MARYLAND. DAR Ancestor # A085319. Service Source: BRUMBAUGH, MD RECS: COL, REV, CHURCH, VOL 2, P 255 Service Description: 1) SIGNED OATH OF ALLEGIANCE, PRINCE GEORGES CO, 1778.

ZACHARIAH OWEN

IS MARILYN MONROE'S THIRD GREAT-GRANDFATHER

Sometime after the death of George Willis Hogan's father, Zachariah Hogan, George then settled in Chariton County Missouri with his family.

The 1870 Federal Census

#	Name	Age	Sex	Race	Occupation		Value
372	Hogan, George W.	46	M	W	Farmer		300
	" Sarah A.	46	F	W	Keeping House		
	" Mary J.	26	F	W			
	" John F.	25	M	W	Farm Laborer		
	" Newton	23	M	W	" "		
	" Tilton M.	21	M	W	" "		
	" Jasper	24	M	W	" "		
	" Stephen A.	15	M	W			
	" Rosa B.	14	F	W			
	" Harriette J.	7	F	W			
	Owen, Edward	84	M	W			250
373	Magruder, Samuel	26	M	W	Wagon Maker		200
	" Amanda	19	F	W	Keeping House		
	" Laura M.	3/12	F	W			

Also on the 1880 Federal Census: Samuel Magruder married George Willis Hogan's daughter Amanda Elizabeth Hogan.

Marilyn Monroe Unveiled | A Family History

The 1880 Federal Census

George Willis Hogan and Sarah and son.

[Census excerpt — Page No. 9, Supervisor's Dist. No. 5, Enumeration Dist. No. 171. Schedule 1 — Inhabitants in Brunswick Township, in the County of Chariton, State of Missouri, enumerated by me on the 5th day of June, 1880.]

- Hogan, George W., M, 57, Farmer — Ken. Ken. Ken.
- Sarah A., F, 57, Wife, Keeping house — Vir. Md. Vir.
- Stephen W., M, 25, Son, Farm laborer — Ill. Ken. Vir.

George Willis Hogan's son Tilford Marion Hogan and family.

Also on the 1880 Federal Census for Tilford Marion Hogan is Marilyn's Great Grandmother Charlotte Virginia Jennie Nance (C.V.), Dora Hogan (Marilyn's Aunt Dora Graham), William Marion Hogan (Jason Edward Kennedy's Great-Grandfather), and Della Hogan (Marilyn Monroe's Grandmother).

[Census excerpt — Page No. 24, Supervisor's Dist. No. 4, Enumeration Dist. No. 5. Schedule 1 — Inhabitants in Flat Creek Twp, 5th District, in the County of Barry, State of Mo., enumerated by me on the 11th day of June, 1880.]

- Hogan, T. M., W, M, 29, Head, Works on farm
- C. V., W, F, 23, Wife, Keeping house
- Dora, W, F, 5, Daughter, At home
- Della, W, F, 3, Daughter, At home
- Hogan, Wm., W, M, 2, Son, At home

TILFORD MARION HOGAN
IS MARILYN MONROE'S GREAT-GRANDFATHER.

Judge O.P. Hogan Sr. is Tilford Marion Hogan's Uncle. Dr. O.P. Hogan and brothers are Tilford's first cousins. Confederate Captain Tilford Hogan is the younger Tilford's uncle.

Marilyn Monroe Unveiled | A Family History

Official Death Certificate for Tilford Marion Hogan in 1933.

Tilford's father documented as George Hogan.

Tilford's mother documented as Sarah Ann Owen.

Marilyn Monroe Unveiled | A Family History

Official Death Certificate for
Charlotte Virginia (Jennie) Nance in 1927.
Virginia used the last name of her 2nd husband SELLARS.
Virginia died in Los Angeles, California where she resided for approximately 6 years. Her father was Levy Nance And her mother was Sarah Jones.
Her daughter Dora Hogan was the informant.

George Willis Hogan's children and their spouses are all listed on this family group sheet which was documented in 1988.

TILFORD MARION HOGAN IS MARILYN MONROE'S GREAT-GRANDFATHER.

Information on this sheet obtained from

HUSBAND'S NAME: George Willis Hogan (Husband's Full Name)
- When Born: 1822-1824 Where: Ky
- Christened: Where:
- When Died: Living Chariton Co., Missouri Where:
- When Buried: Where:
- When Married: 11 March 1843 Where: Grant Co., Ky
- Other Wives (if any): None
- His Father: b. Ky — His Mother's Maiden Name: b. Ky

WIFE'S MAIDEN NAME: Sarah Ann Owen (Wife's Maiden Name)
- When Born: about 10 April 1822 Where:
- Christened: Where:
- When Died: 15 Feb. 1900 Where: Aged 77 yrs. 10 Mo. 5 days
- Where Buried: Hinckle Cem. S.E. Laclede Where: Linn Co. Missouri
- Other Husb. (if any): None
- Her Father: Edward Owen — Her Mother's Maiden Name: Rebecca White

Compiler: Mrs. Hugh Harris
Address: 4143 Vista Bonita Lane
City: Escondido **State:** Calif. **92025**
Date: 26 January 1988

Male or Female	#	CHILDREN (Arrange in order of birth)	When Born Day Month Year	Where Born Town or Place	County	State or Country	Married to	When Married Day Month Year	When Died Day Month Year	Where Buried Town or Place	County	State or Country
F	1	Mary Ann Hogan	10 Jan 1844	Louisville		Ky	Stephen Mahurin	8 Sept. 1878	28 Aug. 1930	Laclede Cem.	Linn	Mo.
M	2	John F. Hogan (Joseph?)	1845- 1846			Ky	Sarah Ann Dunkle	26 Jan. 1871	Living 1880 Chariton Co., Mo.			
M	3	William Jasper Hogan	1846- 1847			Ky	No Marriage in Chariton Co. Missouri			May have been in Tulare Co., Ca.		
M	4	Newton Hogan	3 Feb. 1850	Quincy	Adams	Ill	Eliza Josephine Switzer	31 Oct. 1873	26 Oct. 1934	Inglewood Cem.	Los Angeles	Calif.
M	5	Tilford M. Hogan	24 Feb. 1851		Adams	Ill	1. C.V. (Jennie) Nance 2. Mrs. Emma D. Wyatt	La Clede, Mo. / 17 Sept. 1928	La Clede, Linn, 29 May 1933	La Clede	Linn	Mo.
F	6	Amanda Elizabeth Hogan	12 Feb. 1854		Adams	Ill	Samuel Gowen Magruder (McGowan) (Angeline or Angies)	Chariton Co. Mo. 18 March 1869	Muskogee Okla. 3 Jan. 1929	McAlester-Pittsburg Okla.		Okla.
M	7	Stephen Arnold Douglas Hogan	34 July 1856			Ill	Anna Dunkel	Chariton Co. Mo. 5 Sept. 1910	McAlester Okla. 24 Oct. 1927	Visalia	Tulare	Calif.
F	8	Rosa Bell Hogan "Hattie"	14 Feb. 1860	Edina	Knox	Missouri	1. George P. Riddle 2. Isaac Newton Cassidy	Chariton Co. Mo. 9 Dec. 1875 / 20 July 1920 Linn Co. Mo.	Laclede, Linn, 21 Dec. 1930	Laclede Cem.	Linn	Missouri
F	9	Harriette Hogan	1 Jan. 1863		Knox		Missouri Lafayette Dunkel	Mendon-Chariton Co. Missouri 5 Jan. 1881	Randolph Co. Hunts-ville 3 Nov. 1935	Huntsville	Randolph	Missouri
	10											
	11	Amanda Elizabeth Hogan and Samuel B. Magruder are the great-grandparents										
	12	of the compilers husband.										
	13											

RECEIVED FEB - 4 1988

Charlotte (Jennie) Virginia Nance/Hogan/Sellars (far right).

Marilyn Monroe's great-grandmother.

William F. Nance (Virginia's brother) married Mary Mathey (second from left).

Captured in this Kansas City, Missouri Directory, Charlotte Virginia (Jennie) Nance and family. Virginia married Frank Sellars after Tilford Marion Hogan. Mrs. Jennie Sellars, James Sellars (Jas), Myrtle Sellars, and William Sellars.

HOYE'S 1899 DIRECTORY.

Sellars Jas. r 1634 Summit
Sellars Jennie Mrs. dressmkr 1634 Summit
Sellars Myrtle, milliner r 1634 Summit
Sellars Wm. M. lab r 1634 Summit

U.S. City Directories, 1822-1995

Marilyn Monroe Unveiled | A Family History

Ozarks ACCENT — The News-Leader
SUNDAY, JUNE 26, 1988
Weddings 3
Entertainment 6
Travel 8
F SECTION
Share an idea; call 836-1185

Looking for relatives of actress Marilyn Monroe

GENEALOGY

Genealogy queries listed below should be responded to directly to the address listed with each item. New queries which are not in response to earlier-published items should be mailed to the address at the end of each column.

RELATIVES OF THE ACTRESS MARILYN MONROE: Warder Harrison, 115 S. 4th (Utica), Jeffersonville, Ind., 47130. Anyone having information regarding the following people please write. George W. Hogan and wife Sarah Owen; Tilford Hogan and wife Emma Fisher; Dora Bruce; Pearl Sprague; Zella Dunkle; Myrtle Dowell; Avel Shively; Irene Hungate; Alfred and Earnest Fisher, all of Linn or Barry Counties, Mo.

Marilyn Monroe Unveiled | A Family History

GENEALOGY

Marilyn Monroe's Great Grandparents

Tilford Marion Hogan and Charlotte (Jennie) Virginia Nance had five children.

Dora Olivia Hogan

William Marion Hogan

Della Mae Hogan

Marilyn Monroe's Grandmother

James Berry Hogan

Myrtle Belle Hogan

Marilyn Monroe Unveiled | A Family History

ALIASES

Throughout their lives, the children of Tilford Marion Hogan and Charlotte (Jennie) Virginia Nance used aliases. Jennie also went by the name VIRGINIA SELLARS.

Dora Olivia Hogan

Dora Andros

Dora Bruce

Dora Graham

Dora Schulties

Della Mae Hogan

Della Monroe

Della Grainger

Della Graves

William Marion Hogan

William Sellars

William Nance

James Berry Hogan

James Sellars

Jimmy Hogan

Myrtle Belle Hogan

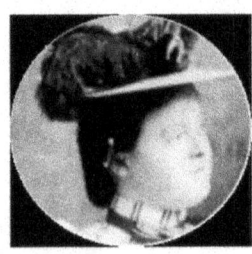

Myrtle Matheys

Myrtle Myers

Myrtle Sellars

Four of the five children born to Tilford Marion Hogan and Charlotte Virginia (Jennie) Nance were documented in a newspaper obituary for William Marion Hogan in 1947.

William M. Hogan

Brother Jimmy Hogan

Sister Mrs. Dora Graham, Portland, Ore.

Sister Mrs. Myrtle Myers, Kansas City

Missing is sister Della Mae Hogan. She passed away in 1927.

LACLEDE, MISSOURI, SEPTEMBER 28, 1928.

Tilford M. Hogan, 78, and Mrs. Emma D. Wyatt were united in marriage by Judge O. F. Libby at the home of the groom September 17. Mr. and Mrs. H. C. McCoy, neighbors, were witnesses to the ceremony.

Two of Della Monroe's (Hogan) sisters were also documented in a newspaper death notice for their father, Tilford Marion Hogan in 1933.

Two Daughters:

Mrs. Andros of California (aka Dora Olivia Hogan)

And Mrs. Myers of Kansas City (aka Mrs. Myrtle Belle Hogan)

LACLEDE, MISSOURI, FRIDAY, JUNE 9, 1933.

Card of Thanks

I wish to express my sincere appreciation and thanks to friends and neighbors for the kindness shown during the death of beloved husband. —Mrs. Emma Hogan.

LACLEDE, MISSOURI, FRIDAY, JUNE 2, 1933.

DEAD FROM HIS OWN HANDS

Despondent, and worry over imaginary financial troubles, coupled with infirmatives of old age creeping on, Tilford M. Hogan ended his life by hanging about 3 o'clock last Monday afternoon.

Returning from a business trip downtown after an hour's absence, Mrs. Hogan found her husband dead at the end of a rope hanging from the second floor joist of the barn.

Startled by the ghastly find she ran towards the house calling for help, and fell in a faint on reaching the front yard.

J. G. Clinefelter and N. B. Cross, near neighbors, hearing her cries, went to her assistance. She soon revived sufficiently to mumble, "Tilford in the barn." They rushed to the barn, and after ascertaining that Hogan was dead notified the officers and Undertaker Thorne. Mr. Thorne gave the facts to the county coroner, Dr. McLarney, of Brookfield, who instructed him to remove the body from the barn and take care of it.

On arriving here Dr. McLarney empanneled a jury composed of C. A. Felt, A. C. Windle, H. M. Standly, A. J. Caywood, W. L. Molloy and S. W. White.

After hearing the testimony of Mr. Clinefelter, Mr. Cross and Undertaker Thorne, the jury returned a verdict of suicide by hanging.

Tilford M. Hogan was born in Adams county, Illinois, February 24, 1851, and at death hi sage was 82 years, 3 months and 5 days. He had resided in this vicinity many years.

He is survived by his widow of a second marriage and two daughters, Mrs. Myers of Kansas City, who attended the funeral, and Mrs. Andros of California, by a previous marriage.

Funeral was held at the Christian church Wednesday afternoon, the services conducted by Elder C. E. Dunkleberger. Burial was in the Laclede cemetery by Director Thorne.—Laclede Blade.

Marilyn Monroe Unveiled | A Family History

MARILYN MONROE FAMILY

DORA   WILLIAM   DELLA   MYRTLE   JIMMY

   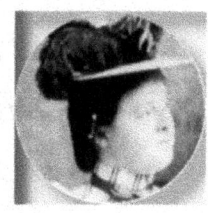 

Della Mae Hogan

Mother of Marilyn Monroe

Marilyn Monroe's Uncle
Marion Otis Monroe

Marilyn Monroe's 1st Cousin's
Elizabeth Monroe
Ida Mae Monroe
Jack Monroe

Gladys Monroe

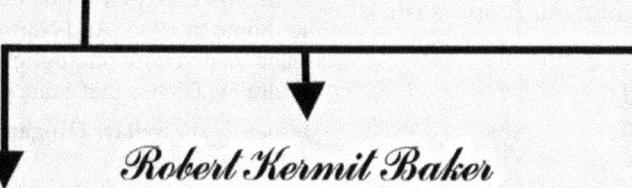

Robert Kermit Baker

Marilyn Monroe's half-sister
Berniece Miracle

Marilyn Monroe's Niece
Mona Miracle

Marilyn Monroe

Descendants are
PRIVATE.

We call her *Norma Jeane*

Marilyn Monroe Unveiled | A Family History

Los Angeles Family Network from 1926 to 1935 (Refer to pages 303-346)

A brief survey of a few quotes from various Marilyn Monroe biographies documents clear fabrication and exaggerations of Marilyn's early childhood based on new family documentation.

June 1, 1926, Norma Jeane is born.

"If it hadn't been for a crew back at Consolidated which took up a collection to foot the hospital and Doctor's bill, Gladys never would have made it."
George Carpozi| Marilyn Monroe "Her Own Story"

Della urged Gladys to consider "arrangements" to place the baby up for adoption. During the following year Gladys made little contact with the Bolenders, and rarely saw the baby."
John Gilmore| Inside Marilyn Monroe: a memoir

"Of this Gladys's own mother, Della, was similarly convinced, for as soon as she returned from her exotic South Seas adventure — when her granddaughter was a week old — she urged Gladys to place Norma Jeane in the care of a sober, devout couple named Bolender... 'I was probably a mistake,' Norma Jeane told a friend years later. 'My mother didn't want me. I probably got in her way, and I must have been a disgrace to her.'"
Donald Spoto| Marilyn Monroe The Biography

Wrong, **George Carpozi**. Gladys would have made it! Gladys's grandmother Virginia Sellars (Charlotte Virginia Nance) lived in Los Angeles for approximately 6 years prior to her passing on December 13, 1927. As documented by other evidence in this book it would have not been out of character for Virginia to take care of her granddaughter Gladys (especially during pregnancy) while her daughter Della was in Borneo visiting her husband. And she would have been present for the birth of Rebecca Esther Hogan (Baby Nance) as well on January 1,1927 at the same hospital as Norma Jeane. As noted, other close family were living near Gladys and Norma Jeane also. There was no reason for an adoption **John Gilmore**. An adoption dissolves ALL family relationships and bonds. **John Gilmore**, both Gladys and Norma Jeane were living with Ida Bolender as borders. Both the 1930 census and *TIME*'s investigative reporter Ezra Goodman verified and corroborated that fact. Ezra interviewed Ida Bolender when he researched Marilyn for the 1956 cover of *TIME* magazine. Ida Bolender stated that Gladys mostly stayed with she and Norma Jeane. Ida watched Norma Jeane while Gladys was working. *TIME* magazine rejected Ezra's Goodman's research on Marilyn and paid Ida Bolender and her husband a sum of money to extinguish any defamation claims (The fifty-year decline and fall of Hollywood-1962). **Donald Spoto**, Della came back from Borneo on September 8, 1926 and NOT a week after Norma Jeane's birth (Passport application and California Passenger and Crew Lists 1882-1959 for Della M. Grainger). Therefore your description of that period is nothing more than a fabrication. Marilyn would never have been rejected by her mother at birth when her great grandmother and other family were right there.

Myrtle Myers (Hogan): Lived in Kansas City Missouri. Myrtle filled out Virginia's Probate records when she passed away in 1927 without leaving a will. Myrtle needed special court permission to list beneficiaries. Both Gladys and Marion Monroe were documented as daughter and son of deceased daughter Della Monroe.

Norma Jeane's birth
June 1, 1926

Dora Graham (Hogan): Lived in Oregon. Dora took Gladys Monroe into her home in 1945. And Norma Jeane visited with photographer Andre De Dienes that same year.

James Berry Sellars (Hogan)-Lived in Arlington, Virginia.

Charlotte Virginia Nance (Virginia Sellars)- Grandmother of Gladys. Location: **LOS ANGELES**
   Gladys Monroe - Norma Jeane's mother. Location: **LOS ANGELES**
   William Marion Nance (Hogan) and family - Uncle of Gladys. Location: **LOS ANGELES**
   Milton and Naomi Andros and son Lee - Dora Hogan's son. 1st Cousin of Gladys. Location: **LOS ANGELES**
   Newton Hogan and family- Great Uncle of Gladys. Tilford Hogan's brother. Location: **LOS ANGELES**
   Ida Martin- Mother of Olive Brunings. Location: **LOS ANGELES**
   Olive Brunings Monroe- wife of Marion Monroe (Gladys's brother)/Children Ida Mae and Jack Monroe. Location: **LOS ANGELES**
Della Monroe - Mother of Gladys. She left for Borneo to see her husband on March 20th 1926. She returned September 8th 1926. Lived in: **LOS ANGELES**
Grace McKee Goddard - Gladys's best friend since 1921. She became Norma Jeane's legal guardian in 1935 after Gladys became ill. Location: **LOS ANGELES**

After Della died AUG 23, 1927, her mother Virginia Sellars (Nance) died DEC 13, 1927 in Los Angeles. When Gladys became ill in January 1935, Grace McKee Goddard, Gladys's best friend since 1921 was chosen as guardian of Norma Jeane, although there were still many relatives throughout the Los Angeles area who offered to take Norma Jeane under their care. Gladys and Grace continued to work together to care for Norma Jeane. The court documents prove there were only THREE people obtaining money from Gladys's estate for room and board of Norma Jeane: Grace McKee Goddard, Ida Martin, and Grace's aunt, Ana Lower. It can no longer be denied that relatives did not know and/or did not have contact with Gladys and Norma Jeane. Myrtle Myers documented Gladys and Marion on Virginia's Probate records in 1927 and Dora Hogan was listed as informant on Virginia's death certificate. In addition, Dora took physical care of Gladys in 1945. Also William Nance (aka William Marion Hogan) and spouse Clara tried to persuade Gladys to have Norma Jeane stay with them (interview with Rebecca Ester Hogan-Gladys first cousin). In reality, biographers had no knowledge of this family other than scant documentation of which they fabricated many details. Their biographical works, largely a work of fiction. Relatives such as William Marion Hogan and his spouse Clara, Myrtle Myers, and Dora Graham (Hogan) were clearly engaged with Gladys and Norma Jeane as a FAMILY.

CHAPTER ELEVEN

DORA IS THE first of Marilyn Monroe's family whose biography can disprove the myths that they were yokels and unrefined types. Marilyn's Mother, Gladys, was close to the woman she then called her Aunt Dora Graham, after Gladys was released from the mental institution in 1945. It was Dora who patiently took her niece Gladys under her wing and helped her to readjust to life outside of the hospital. Dora had a caring and intuitive spirit, after many years of evolving through the different phases of her life, after her girlhood with parents Tilford and Jennie, and her siblings in Missouri.

Dora married Louis Milton Andros on June 15, 1890 in El Paso Texas. On one of the marriage indexes he was listed as "L.M. Andras" though she was listed correctly as "Dora O. Hogan." She was 17 at the time of their marriage and he was age 28. His family, like Dora's hailed from the Midwestern part of the country, where he was born in Iowa, though he had also resided in Minnesota and later had connections to the Linn County Missouri area as his first wife did. Yet eventually, Louis Milton Andros's final resting place would be in the Hollywood Forever cemetery with his second spouse Marguerita ("Rita").

Challenging the Marilyn Monroe orphan tales is that there were relatives nearby in Los Angeles, including Milton Stores Andros, the son of Louis Milton Andros and Dora. Both father and son resided in the Los Angeles area where Marilyn grew up and passed away. Louis Milton Andros died in 1943 while Marilyn was a teenager and Milton Stores Andros, his son and Gladys's first cousin outlived Marilyn. Like Marilyn's mother Gladys he also worked in the movie industry as a set designer and plaster artist.

However, with Grace Goddard's intervention in the courts, Gladys's best friend, the tale was dreamt up that there were no relatives in the Los Angeles area. Grace took custody of Marilyn, then known as Norma Jeane, as her legal guardian. With a short stay required in Hollygrove, also known as the Los Angeles Orphans' Home, Grace assumed guardianship after Norma Jeane's stay there. However, this could have been avoided altogether if Gladys and Grace chose differently.

In fact, in the 1937 city directory for Los Angeles Milton Stores Andros and his wife Naomi were documented as residents on 1736 Hauser Boulevard, with his occupation listed as "studio worker."

The Andros family was especially prominent in the San Francisco area in the legal field. Dora would experience a very public divorce from her husband that would lead to a sensationalized kidnapping case, which is explored in a later chapter.

In the *Arizona Republic*, a newspaper for Phoenix, it is noted on June 20, 1891 that L.M. Andros headed to El Paso that previous Tuesday to "meet his better half. Mrs. Andros has been with her parents in Missouri for the past four months." L.M. Andros at that time was working as a "rear brakeman on Captain

Arizona Republican, June 20, 1891.

thing was fixed up to the satisfaction of all parties.

L. M. Andros, who does the honors of rear brakeman on Captain Mahoney's train on the Gila division, went to El Paso Tuesday to meet his better half. Mrs. Andros has been with her parents in Missouri for the past four months.

The total earnings of the Rio Grande railroad for the first week of June were

Louis Milton Andros is Dora Hogan's first husband.

The Arizona Sentinel.

"Independent in All Things."

YUMA, ARIZONA, SATURDAY, MARCH 4, 1893.

L. M. Andros, one of the trusted employes of the S. P. R. R., between Yuma and Tucson, has greatly improved in health and is now stronger than he has been for years.

Dora Olivia Hogan

Dora Olivia Hogan had four husbands.

Louis Milton Andros, Charles Bruce, Mr. Graham, and Mr. Schulties.

Louis Milton Andros — **Charles Bruce**  — **Mr. Graham**  — **Mr. Schulties**

Milton Stores Andros  — **Georgia Marie**  — **Dorothy Mary Bruce**

Gladys Monroe's 1st cousins

Tilford Bruce

14 Jul 1906 - 3 Mar 1910

Buried Laclede Cemetery;

Brookfield, Linn County, Missouri, USA

Captured in the 1900 Federal Census, Dora Hogan is listed as Daughter-in-law living in the home of Richard Stores Andros. Richard is the father of Dora's husband Louis.

90	98	Andros, Richard S.	Head	Atty at Law	
		—, Maria	Wife		
		—, Lewis M.	Son	Orchardist	
		—, Dora	D. in law		
		—, Milton L.	G.-Son	At School	
		—, Georgie M.	G.-Daughter		
		Shevelier, Delia	Servant	Servant Dom.	

State: California
County: San Bernardino
Township or other division of county: Ontario Township
Enumerated by me on the First day of June, 1900

SCHEDULE No. 1.

Richard Stores Andros's father was Frederick Andros MD who was son of the famed Reverend Thomas Andros. In 1791 Reverend Thomas Andros enlisted as a privateer and was subsequently captured and held in the Jersey prison-ship in New York. He was fortunate enough to escape and began his career in theology. His biography is located in The Ministry of Taunton: With Incidental Notices of Other Professions, Volume 2, Samuel Hopkins Emery January 1, 1853, J. P. Jewett & Company.

Massachusetts, Town and Vital Records, 1620-1988 for Frederick Andros.

```
Thomas Andros & Abigail
    Milton, Plainfield, Conn.
        16Apr1786
    Mary, same place    5Dec1787
    Abigail, Berkley   29Sep1789
    Thomas              6Mch1791
    Benedict            7Oct1792
    William            16Mch1794
    Lydia              20ct1795
    Susanna            13Jany1797
    Clarisa            25Aug1798
    Sophia Sanford Andros  23Sep1800
    Prissy Dean Andros 17Nov1802
    Frederick          14Sep1805
    Sarah              12Nov1807
    Daniel Kendrick    14Jany1811
    Leander            25Dec1814
    Richard Salter Storrs Andros
                       27Oct1817
    Milton              7Feb1823
```

Escape of Rev. Thomas Andros, from the Old Jersey Prison Ship, during the Revolutionary War. (Written recently by himself.)

Gladys Monroe's Aunt Dora Graham.

This photograph was thought to be Tilford Marion Hogan, Charlotte (Jennie) Virginia Nance, and a little Della Mae Hogan, however, it is actually

Dora Hogan son Milton Stores Andros, and Husband Louis Milton Andros. Dora is Gladys Monroe's Aunt Dora Graham and Marilyn Monroe's Great Aunt Dora.

Louis Milton Andros, Wife, Milton Andros

The original unreleased photo of Dora Hogan, son Milton Stores Andros, and Husband Louis Milton Andros. The photo was taken in Tucson Arizona.

Gladys Monroe stayed with her Aunt Dora Graham in 1945. Marilyn Monroe, who was going by Norma Jeane at that time, visited Portland Oregon while on a photography road trip with photographer Andre de Dienes.

Louis M. Andros

Mahoney's train on the Gila division." Mrs. Andros (Dora Hogan) stayed with her parents, Tilford Marion Hogan and Charlotte Virginia (Jennie) Nance.

Their son, Milton Stores Andros was born in Tucson on September 20, 1891. In what has mistakenly always been identified in biographies as a photo of Tilford and Jennie Hogan with Della is actually a photo of Dora, Louis Milton and young Milton. A copy of the actual photograph and also with the photo sleeve from a studio in Tucson, plus original notations in a scrapbook have been a longtime part of the family archives.

Only a few years later but this time in Pomona California, their daughter Georgie Marie was born on January 8, 1896. It is obvious from a later childhood photo taken in Pomona with his sister that the small child in the photo from Tucson is young Milton.

In the 1900 census, all of this new family including Louis M. (then age 37), Dora (then 25), Milton (age eight) and Georgie (age four) lived with his father Richard L. Andros and his wife Maria (ages 61 and 65 respectively). Though the Hogan family members have often been depicted as deprived, the census documents the snapshot of the life that Dora Hogan was living. Her father-in-law was an attorney and her husband was an orchardist. Delia Shevelier was also on the census after little Georgie Marie. This French woman's role was that of a "servant" to the household.

Dora and Louis Milton would duke it out in a divorce case that the papers followed diligently, which eventually would crescendo to the kidnapping case. Though Dora would remarry later, there are some indications that she and her first husband reconciled. The facts are in the form of news articles reporting the pair together in Linn County Missouri, vacationing at his family's plantation in Cuba, at their son Milton's wedding, visiting her father Tilford, and many more social notes in the papers. By 1915, however, the papers reported that the couple returned to the courtroom once again to terminate their marriage.

THE LACLEDE BLADE

Entered at the postoffice at Laclede, Mo., for transmission through the mail as second class matter.

A. J. CAYWOOD.

Friday, June 4 1915.

Louis M Andros vs Dora O Andros, divorce.

It is known based on the newspaper documentation of his kidnapping of their daughter Georgia Marie that Dora had remarried and her former husband and his attorneys attempted to smear her name in the press after the first divorce. She was then married to Scotsman Charles Bruce. They had a daughter Dorothy, born in St. Louis County on September 8, 1904 following the kidnapping.

The *Laclede Blade* reported a visit made to Tilford in Missouri after the birth of daughter Dorothy. The report from October 9, 1905 stated Dora and her husband Charles voyaged to California from Montague Michigan and on the way, stopped to see Tilford for a visit.

They had another child, a son named after her father Tilford, who was born in Montmorency County Michigan on July 14, 1906. Little Tilford sadly passed away on March 10, 1910 and is buried at Laclede Cemetery along with his grandfather, Tilford Marion Hogan, who died in 1933.

The Laclede Blade, March 12, 1910

The body of little Tilford Bruce, son of Chas. and Dora Bruce, was brought from St. Louis Tuesday and buried in Laclede cemetery. He was aged 3 years, 7 months and 19 days. The mother, who was unable to be present on account of sickness of another child at home, has the sympathy of the community in her bereavement.

LACLEDE, MISSOURI, SATURDAY, OCTOBER 20, 1906.

had not seen for thirty-five years.

Mr. and Mrs. Chas. Bruce, on their way from Montague, Mich., to California, stopped off and spent a day here the past week with Mrs. Bruce's father, T. M. Hogan, south of town.

A grading outfit of teams and wheel

The *Laclede Blade* reported on March 12, 1910, "The body of little Tilford Bruce, son of Chas and Dora Bruce, was brought from St. Louis Tuesday and buried in Laclede Cemetery. He was age 3 years, 7 months and 19 days. The mother, who was unable to be present on account of sickness of another child at home, has the sympathy of the community in her bereavement."

While some have said that Tilford Marion Hogan's children abandoned him, reality was to the contrary. The 1910 Federal Census shows that Dora Bruce actually lived with both her father and her aunt Mary A. Mahurin, Tilford's sister, in Mary's home in Jefferson Township, Linn County Missouri.

Milton Stores Andros:

Dora Graham's (Hogan) son. Gladys Monroe's first cousin. Worked as a Hollywood Plaster Artist the same time Marilyn's mother was a Hollywood Film Cutter.

Marilyn Monroe Unveiled | A Family History

The census was taken on April 21, slightly over a month after the death of little Tilford. Daughter Dorothy also lived with them at that time, while Dora was listed as "married" on the census. Charles Bruce was not with them in the household. A hired man named George Duncan additionally resided in the household, which Mary Mahurin, a widow was listed as having a fruit farm. Her brother Tilford was classified then as "single" and as a "farmer/laborer," while it was clear that George Duncan was written as "working out," likely in a position that Mary and Tilford were his employers.

Though Dora was documented as "married" on the 1910 Census, it is uncertain when she ended up back with L.M. Andros exactly. Later, she would be back with Charles Bruce in Oregon. But for now, she was referred to as part of "Mr. and Mrs L.M. Andros of St. Catherine," which was an unincorporated area in Linn County just outside of Brookfield and near Laclede. On a particular date, November 10, 1911, it was indicated that Tilford hosted a dinner at his home on Route One, with the group, including S.S. Andros and Mrs. Brooks of Hollywood the paper reported. They were all described as the "guests of Mrs. Andros' father, T.M. Hogan on Route One Wednesday."

After the kidnapping there was a divorce issue that Louis Milton claimed existed, noting that the divorce case was overturned between he and Dora, with the papers smearing her name and referring to her as a "bigamist." It is uncertain if her first divorce to Louis Milton was ever properly terminated.

Some of Dora's offspring were nearby as well during her lifetime, with Milton also in Oregon for a period when Dora resided there. Milton and his wife "Naomi E" for "Naomi Ella," lived in Bend Oregon at 644 Kansas Avenue. Milton Stores Andros did have a connection to Linn County Missouri, having married Naomi Ella Love, who was also a prominent citizen of that area. Both resided in Brookfield in Linn County Missouri on March 1, 1914, when they were married in a Methodist Ceremony by an ordained minister.

Another instance where Dora is listed as part of the Mr. and Mrs. L.M. Andros team was at the elegant wedding between Milton and Naomi. "Dorothy Andros" was also reported in the press as another guest, though her name was Dorothy Bruce. And one more guest who has been an elusive ancestor in the family's story was "Mrs. Sellars" from Kansas City, meaning Charlotte Virginia "Jennie" Nance Hogan Sellars. In other words, the mother of all the Hogan children including Marilyn's grandmother Della, and Tilford Marion Hogan's ex-wife.

Following the kidnapping, Georgie resided with her aunt Georgie Brooks (aka "Georgiana" or "Georgia") in Minnesota, her father's sister, though some thought Louis Milton would settle with his daughter in California.

Georgia lived a charmed life in spite of the kidnapping in her early days, residing with her aunt Georgia L. Brooks and her spouse, Anson S. Brooks. The 1910 Census reflected a residence in Minneapolis on 2445 Park Avenue, which was recently nominated in the city to be preserved as a local landmark and in our times is known as the "Anson Brooks Mansion," by the Department of Community Planning and Economic Development. After the family left the property in the late 1930s for Lake Minnetonka, it has been used as an educational and office facility. In its heyday, it was known as part of a prominent Minneapolis location, the "Golden Mile." The family constructed the home in 1907.

Georgie resided there with her cousin, Anson and Georgia's son Paul, who was 28 while she was 14 (Paul's brother Stanley had passed away in 1907). He was an attorney for the lumber company that his father was the owner and treasurer for. Sharing the census with the family, in addition to a boarder named Sophie Russell in 1910, were the chauffeur and three servants.

SANTA ANA DAILY REGISTER, WEDNESDAY EVENING, JULY 6, 1927

Mrs. G. E. Bruns of 1208 Spurgeon street, had as guests today for luncheon Mrs. Lee Love and Mrs. Milton Andros and her little son, all of Los Angeles. Included in the party was Mrs. Bruns' niece, Mrs. Perry Mount of Brookfield, Mo., who arrived Monday for a month's visit. Mrs. Bruns is to accompany her guests to Los Angeles to remain over the week end. Mr. Bruns will join her in that city Saturday.

* * * *

Los Angeles California, 1927, Mrs. Milton Andros (Naomi Ellen Love) and her little son at luncheon her mother Mrs. Lee Love and others.

Richard S. Andros (Milton's grandfather), Georgia Brooks, Milton S. Andros (Dora Hogan's son) and son Lee.

LACLEDE, MISSOURI, FRIDAY, JANUARY 8, 1915

A girl baby born to Mr. and Mrs. Milton S. Andros at their home just south of Brookfield on Wednesday, December 23, died the following Saturday. The remains were buried in the Laclede cemetery Sunday, December 27. Mrs Andros is a daughter of Mr. and Mrs. Lee Love and a sister of Mrs. Frank Weaver of Laclede.

Marilyn Monroe Unveiled | A Family History

Dora Hogan's son Milton Stores Andros

Married

Naomi Ella Love

in 1914.

MARRIAGE LICENSE.

STATE OF MISSOURI, COUNTY OF LINN.

THIS LICENSE authorizes any Judge of a Court of Record or Justice of the Peace, or any licensed or ordained Preacher of the Gospel, who is a Citizen of the United States, or a resident of and pastor of some church in this State to SOLEMNIZE MARRIAGE between Milton Storer Andros of Brookfield in the County of Linn and State of Mo., who is over the age of twenty one years, and Naoma Ella Love of .... in the County of Linn and State of Mo., who is over the age of eighteen years.

WITNESS, my hand as Recorder of Deeds with the Seal of Office hereto affixed at my Office in Linneus, Mo., this 27th (SEAL) day of Feb. 1914

By _____ Deputy.

W. B. M. Leyor
Recorder of Deeds.

STATE OF MISSOURI,
County of Linn } ss. THIS IS TO CERTIFY, that the undersigned an Ordained Minister did at Brookfield in said County, on the 1 day of March A. D. 1914 unite in Marriage the above named persons. And I further Certify that I am a Citizen of the United States and a resident Pastor of Methodist Church Brookfield Missouri, legally qualified under the Laws of the State of Missouri to solemnize Marriages.

Edgar P. Reed.

Filed for Record on the 24th day of March 1914

By _____ Deputy.

W B McGyor
Recorder of Deeds.

VOL. 15.

WELL KNOWN CITIZEN DEAD.

Ex-Mayor Ong Succumbed to La Grippe and Pneumonia Last Tuesday.

Ex-Mayor J. L. Ong, whose serious illness was mentioned in THE BLADE last week, passed away at the home of a relative in Rosedale, Kansas, last Tuesday morning, February 7th, at 9 o'clock. Although the end had been expected for two or three days, when the message came announcing his death, it cast a gloom over the entire city.

He left home January 23rd on a business trip and stopped in Rosedale to visit a niece and her family, where

CAPTAIN J. L. ONG.

CAPTAIN J. L. ONG.

he was taken suddenly with la grippe, which later developed into pneumonia. This, complicated with chronic heart and kidney trouble, caused his death.

The remains, accompanied by Mrs. Ong and daughter, Miss Ella, and his son-in-law, W. L. Love, and wife, of Albia, Iowa, who were with him during his last hours, arrived in Laclede Tuesday night, and were taken to the family home.

The funeral service was held at the M. E. church Thursday afternoon, conducted by Rev. Allen, assisted by the pastor, Rev. Robison. As a mark of respect to the deceased and his family, Mayor E. B. Allen issued a proclamation requesting all business houses and the public schools to close during the hour of service. The very large attendance at the funeral of sympathizing neighbors and friends attests the very high esteem in which he was held.

John Louis Ong was born at Steubensville, Ohio, July 9, 1834. In 1853 he removed with his parents to La Salle county, Illinois, where his youth and early manhood was spent.

On December 31, 1858, he was united in marriage to Miss Margaret Elizabeth Purviance, who survives him. To their union six children, one son and five daughter, were born, all now living. They are Plummer L. Ong, Sweetwater, Okla.; Mrs. Lida I. Rogers, Elgin, Oregon; Miss Ella M. Ong, Laclede; Mrs. Nellie B. Bruns, Laclede; Mrs. Edna M. Love, Albia, Iowa; and Mrs. Abbie M. Gould, Laclede.

In October, 1879, he moved with his family to Missouri, and in July, 1881, to Laclede, where he has since lived.

In 1861, he enlisted in the government service, but was rejected on account of disabilities. Later, he was appointed captain of a company of government scouts, and served with them to the end of the war. During his life he filled many places of trust and honor. He served fourteen years as mayor of Laclede. He took a pride in the discharge of his duties as chief executive of the city, and was the leading spirit in all movements for the public good. His home and social life was an ideal one. Being

LACLEDE, MISS

mill machinery for the last 24 years, he was naturally away from home a great deal of the time, but no difference how far away or how crowded with business, he always found time to write a letter home each day, and was disappointed if he didn't receive one. His wife and family and his home were always first in his mind.

He was an Odd Fellow for 47 years and was the last one of the charter members of Hiawatha lodge at Anna, Ill., at which place he held membership at the time of his death. He was also a member of the Canton at Brookfield, the funeral services being held under the auspices of that lodge, assisted by the Odd Fellows and Rebekahs of Laclede.

Capt. Ong will be missed in Laclede.

Milton Stores Andros married Naomi Love. Her Grandfather was Captain J.L. Ong who was Mayor of Laclede.

LACLEDE, MISSOURI, FRIDAY, JUNE 2, 1916

A boy baby was born to Mr. and Mrs. Milton Andros at Brookfield last Friday and has been given the name of Lee Milton. Mrs. Andros is a granddaughter of Mrs. J. L. Ong of Laclede.

LACLEDE, MISSOURI, FRIDAY, FEBRUARY 15, 1918

Mr. and Mrs. Lee Love of Brookfield spent Sunday with the latter's mother, Mrs. J. L. Ong and other relatives.

LACLEDE, MISSOURI, SATURDAY, FEBRUARY 11, 1905.

LACLEDE, MISSOURI, FRIDAY, JULY 23, 1920.

Mrs. Naomi Andros and little son of Portland, Oreg., are visiting Laclede relatives, guests at the home of her aunt, Mrs. E.E. Gould and family.

LACLEDE, MISSOURI, FRIDAY, AUGUST 19, 1921.

Birthday Dinner

Mr. and Mrs. E.E. Gould gave an elaborate dinner at their home Monday to a number of relatives in honor of the eighty-first birthday of Mrs. Gould's mother, Mrs. J. L. Ong. Those present were Mrs. G.E. Bruns, Mrs. Gussie Cribaro and daugnter, Nellie Elizabeth, of Santa Ana, Cali., Mrs. Lee Love and Mr. and Mrs. Wesley Love of Brookfield, Mr. and Mrs. Ed L. Love of Hannibal, Mr. and Mrs. Milton Andros of Brookfield, Mr. and Mrs. Ira Taylor of Sumner and Miss Ella Ong.

LACLEDE, MISSOURI, SATURDAY, NOVEMBER 11, 1905.

Louis M. Andros, formerly of Laclede, being a son of Station Agent Andros who had charge of the old B. & S.-W. business 27 years ago, is now a member of a big land syndicate at Las Ovas, Cuba. Some of Mr. Andros' advertising matter was received in Laclede this week by C. B. Welsh.

LACLEDE, MISSOURI, FRIDAY, DECEMBER 1, 1911

Mrs. Mary Mahurin and T. M. Hogan spent Monday with the latter's daughter, Mrs. L. M. Andros, and family near St. Catharine. Mr. Andros leaves this week to spend the winter looking after his tobacco plantation in Cuba.

LACLEDE, MISSOURI, FRIDAY, JANUARY 26, 1912

Mrs. L. M. Andros and son, Milton, were over from St. Catharine Monday and rented R. J. Alexander's farm northeast of town for the coming season. Mr. Andros has not yet returned from Cuba, but the family will move here in the near future.

LACLEDE, MISSOURI, FRIDAY, MAY 12, 1916

Gazette:—L. M. Andros, a prominent farmer living south of this city, returned from Hollywood, California, Wednesday, to which place he was called last November by the sickness of his mother, Mrs. R. S. S. Andros, who passed away April 8.

LACLEDE, MISSOURI, SATURDAY, APRIL 28, 1906.

The Commercial and Financial World, published at New York, contains an extensive notice of the immense business being done by the Las Ovas syndicate, Havana, Cuba; of which L. M. Andros, a former Laclede boy, is president. Mr. Andros is handling 6,000 acres of grazing, sugar cane and tobacco land in the heart of the famous Vuelta Abajo district and is an acknowledged leader in real estate matters in Cuba. Those who have once lived in Laclede are bound to succeed, no difference what part of the world they afterwards land in.

LACLEDE, MISSOURI, FRIDAY, MARCH 15, 1912

L. M. Andros returned Sunday night from spending the winter at his plantation in Cuba. Among the souvenirs Mr. Andros brought back with him was a bullet from the battleship Maine. It was found in the wreck when the battleship was raised last December. It is of steel, is badly corroded by the action of the salt water and weighs about a pound. It was intended for use in one of the rapid-fire guns.

LACLEDE, MISSOURI, FRIDAY, MAY 10, 1912

R. S. S. Andros of Havana, Cuba, is visiting his son, L. M. Andros, and family and old friends here. Mr. Andros resided in Laclede a number of years ago, but has spent several years in Cuba, where he and his son own a large plantation.

LACLEDE, MISSOURI, FRIDAY, NOVEMBER 10, 1911

Mr. and Mrs. L. M. Andros of St. Catherine and the former's mother, Mrs. S. S. Andros, and sister, Mrs. Brooks, of Hollywood, Cali., were guests of Mrs. Andros' father, T. M. Hogan, on route one Wednesday.

Uncle Anson
Aunt Georgie & Brooks

house

2535 Park Ave

Mpls, Minn

Mrs. Brooks referenced in the news clipping also resided at 2535 Park Avenue in Minneapolis. Today, that is a historic mansion in the city called the Anson Brooks Mansion. The second image is from the back of a photo in the family photo album.

The social event of the season – the wedding of Milton Stores Andros and Naomi Love. This news report shows Dora (Marilyn's great aunt) was present with her husband L.M. Andros and daughter Dorothy Bruce (mistakenly called "Andros" in the article). Also present was Mrs. Sellars, Marilyn's great-grandmother Charlotte Virginia (Jennie) Nance.

LACLEDE, MISSOURI, FRIDAY, MARCH 6, 1914

Andros-Love

Milton Andros and Miss Naomi Ella Love were married Sunday, March 1, at 2:30, at the home of the bride's parents, Mr. and Mrs Lee Love east of Brookfield, Rev. Edgar Read performing the ceremony. The bride wore a white messaline dress with jeweled net over drapery and carried white rose buds with ferns, the groom wearing the conventional black.

The bride's sister, Mrs. J. Frank Weaver, assisted by her aunt, Miss Ella Ong, served an elaborate three course luncheon. The groom's parents, Mr. and Mrs. L. M. Andros, gave a second day reception at their home two miles south of Brookfield. The young couple received a shower of lovely presents from relatives and friends consisting of linens and silverware.

Those present were Mr. and Mrs. Lee Love, Mr. and Mrs L. M. Andros, W. O. Love, Miss Dorothy Andros, and P. Kiel, all of Brookfield; and Mr. and Mrs. J. Frank Weaver, and Miss Ella Ong of Laclede; Mr. and Mrs. Ed. L. Love of Hannibal; Mrs. Sellars of Kansas City.

Mr. and Mrs. Andros are both well known in Laclede and have the best wishes of their many friends here.

1910 United States Federal Census for Dora Hogan

Mahnick Mary A	Head of	F	W	56	Wd		0	0
Hogan Tilford M	Brother	M	W	59	S			
Burke Dora	Niece of	F	W	35	M	6	2	
Dorothy	Grand Daughter	F	W	5	S			
Duncan George	Hired Man	M	W	22	S			

Georgie applied for a passport on May 3, 1920, with the purpose of traveling abroad from Seattle to Japan and China, sailing for a pleasure trip on the Katori on May 25, 1920, the duration of her trip to last six months.

In 1920, before her departure on her journey to set sail, she was also accounted for in the Park Avenue mansion, with Sophie still a boarder in the home. Her aunt and uncle were moving up in years at ages 66 and 68 respectively and her cousin Paul was no longer in the residence. However, three Scandinavian servants and a horseman also were accounted for on the census.

Georgie's uncle Anson Brooks has been described now with Minneapolis land and structure preservationists as "one of Minneapolis's most influential early residents – a commercial and civic leader of the day – and the house that he built was an elegant example of this success." His business alone the Brooks-Scanlon Lumber Company was the largest sawmill in the northwest, with sites throughout the United States and Canada, with the company remaining alive until 1994 with its last sawmill, though it merged with the Diamond International Corp in 1980.

Anson Brooks was an instrumental founding father of the city's business community and the community at large. He served on Minneapolis's Chamber of Commerce, plus was one of the parties instrumental in having the "Father of the Waters" statue imported from Italy to Minneapolis, where it is now at home in the city hall rotunda. His is one of several names at the base of the sculpture.

Their home is one of the few remaining from those opulent times, which the historians have also described as "a little piece of Venice on Park Avenue."

The home was built in a Venetian Gothic Style with intricate architecture and a magnificent front door all fashioned of stained glass. Wood accents and mahogany rounded out the lush living.

1920 United States Federal Census, Los Angeles, California, District 0163

Andros Louis M	Head	O	F		M	W	57
Rita	Wife				F	W	40
Barry Laura	Sister in Law				F	W	37
Isabelle	Niece				F	W	45
Andros Richard L.	Father				M	W	81

Eventually, Anson and Georgiana would "downsize" to another smaller residence of 12,000 square foot on Park Avenue at number 2535, which is currently the Thomson-Dougherty Funeral Home, with Paul, his spouse Hazel and their four children taking up residence in the Brooks's mansion, continuing with a legacy of deluxe living with servants, a gardener, cooks and chauffeurs. Georgie's aunt and uncle passed away in 1934 and 1937 respectively.

It was on June 9, 1920 that Georgie Marie Andros, Gladys Monroe's first cousin married William Allen Leet in Yokohama Japan in a marriage that the American Consular Service recorded. She was the fourth of his spouses and their marriage resulted in one child, Gordon Anson.

Gordon would assume the surname "Andrist," which was from Georgie's second husband, a successful businessman Victor Rudolph Andrist. Gordon would grow up to serve in World War II, the Korean War and Vietnam, serving with the U.S. Air Force.

Georgie and Victor Rudolph's daughter Cynthia was born in 1926 and by the 1930 Census, Georgie was residing in Minnesota with her two children in a home with a servant. Her daughter was

The husband of Georgia Brooks, the sister of Louis Milton Andros, Anson S. Brooks.

THE BEND BULLETIN, DAILY EDITION, BEND, OREGON, TUESDAY, AUGUST 28, 1923

Anson S. Brooks

For generations Minneapolis was the greatest single lumber producing point in the world, as well as the principal lumber market in the northwest, and among those prominently identified with that industry is Anson S. Brooks, treasurer of the Brooks-Scanlon Lumber Co. Brooks was born in Redfield, Oswego county, New York, September 6, 1852, his parents being Dr. Sheldon and Jeannette (Ranney) Brooks. In 1856 the father removed with his family to Minnesota, settling on a farm in Winona county.

In the public schools of Winona and Wabasha counties, Anson S. Brooks acquired his education and when 15 years of age took up the study of telegraphy with the old Northwestern Telegraph Company,

Treasurer of the Company

TRIPLICATE
FORM NO. 87—CONSULAR.

Enclosure with dispatch No. 775, of June 9, 1920 - Yokohama

CERTIFICATE OF MARRIAGE.

American Consular Service.
Yokohama, Japan.

Received Fee $1.00 U. S. Gold, equal to Yen 2.01. Stamp affixed to Original number of this document.

June 9, 1920.

I, H. T. Goodier, Vice Consul, of the United States of America at Yokohama, Japan, do hereby certify that, on this 9th day of June A.D. 1920, at the American Consulate General in the City of Yokohama, Japan, William Allen Let, a citizen of Nebraska, U.S.A., aged 24 years, born in Anderson, Iowa, and now residing in Yokohama, Japan, and Georgia Baird Andros, a citizen of Minnesota, U.S.A., aged 24 years, born in Ramona, California, and now temporarily residing in Yokohama, Japan, were united in marriage before me, and in my presence by written declaration, as required by Article 775 of the Civil Code of Japan, and that such marriage has been duly registered by the Mayor of the City of Yokohama Japan, and is in accordance with the laws of Japan.

IN WITNESS WHEREOF I have hereunto subscribed my name and affixed the seal of my office at Yokohama, Japan, this Ninth day of June A. D. 1920, and of the Independence of the United States the one hundred and forty fourth.

H. T. Goodier
Vice Consul of the United States of America.

Georgie Brooks (Andros) is the sister of Louis Milton Andros. Marilyn Monroe's first cousin once removed, Georgie Marie Andros lived with her father's sister, Georgie Brooks, after the kidnapping event.

MRS. ANSON BROOKS DEAD; CLUBWOMAN

Mrs. Anson S. Brooks.

CLUB, CHARITY LEADER DIES

Mrs. Anson S. Brooks, Resident 37 Years, Succumbs to Long Illness.

Mrs Anson S. Brooks of 2535 Park avenue, a resident of Minneapolis since 1897, died Monday afternoon after a prolonged illness.

Mrs. Brooks was born in Garnavillo, Iowa, the daughter of Mr. and Mrs. R. S. S. Andros, and granddaughter of Dr. Frederick Andros, the first licensed physician to practice west of the Mississippi and north of the Missouri rivers.

She married Anson S. Brooks at McGregor, Iowa and moved to Minnesota. They lived at Grand Forks, N. D. and in St. Paul for some time before moving to Minneapolis.

Mrs Brooks was a member of Sigma Alpha Iota, a national musical sorority, and of the Ladies' Thursday Musical, Friends of the Institute, Woman's club, Northwestern hospital board, Audubon society and Daughters of the American Revolution. She was interested in charity, music, art, gardening and ornithology.

Surviving Mrs. Brooks are her husband, a son, Paul Andros Brooks, and five grandchildren; a brother, Louis M. Andros of Verdego City, Calif.; a nephew, Milton Andros of Los Angeles, and a niece, Mrs. G. M. Andrist of Minneapolis. Private funeral services will be conducted at the residence at 10 a. m. Wednesday.

Tilford Hogan's granddaughter Miss Georgie Andros married William Allen Leet for a short time.

THE LINCOLN STAR—SATURDAY, DECEMBER 24, 1927.

LEET IS DIVORCED FOR FOURTH TIME

SAN FRANCISCO, Dec. 24—(AP)—William Allen Leet, member of a wealthy Omaha family, was divorced here Friday by his fourth wife, Mrs. Doris Leet, who charged cruelty, testifying they were married at Vancouver, Wash., February 19, 1924. Leet's former wives were Miss Ann Robertson of Omaha, who eloped with him in 1914; Miss Martha Byrne Ruddy of Aurora, Ill., and Miss Georgia Andros, who married him in Hong Kong in 1920 and the same year obtaining a divorce.

MARRIAGE RETURN

This return must be made to the County Auditor of the County in which the marriage took place, within five days from the date of the marriage.

1. Date of License: May
2. Full name of groom: Charles Bruce
3. Age last birthday: 47
4. Color (a): White
5. No. of groom's marriages: Second
6. Residence: Portland, Oregon
7. Birthplace (b): Glasgow, Scotland
8. Occupation: Electrician
9. Father's name: James Bruce
10. Mother's maiden name: Mary McIntire
11. Full name of bride: Dora O. Boyce
12. Maiden name if a widow: Dora O. Hogan
13. Age last birthday: 50
14. Color (a): White
15. No. of bride's marriages: Second
16. Residence: Portland, Oregon
17. Birthplace (b): Missouri
18. Occupation: Self Employed
19. Father's name: Telford M. Hogan
20. Mother's maiden name: Virginia Nance
21. Date of marriage: May 4—1925
22. Place of marriage: Vancouver, Washington — By whom married: Minister
23. Names of witnesses and their residences:
   No. 1 Adolph Trapp, Portland, Or.
   No. 2 Lizzie A. Tripp, " "

STATE OF WASHINGTON,
County of _____ ss.

I hereby certify that the above is a true return of said marriage.

Dated at _____, Wash., May 4—, 1925.

J. C. Lauthouse

NOTE—(a) State color distinctly, so race may be known as White, Black, Mulatto, Indian, Chinese, Mixed White and Indian, etc.
(b) Give State or Foreign Country, so nationality is plainly known.

CERTIFICATE OF MARRIAGE

B9432

RECEIVED JUL 5

PLACE OF MARRIAGE, County of **Clark** Town of **Vancouver**

	GROOM	BRIDE
Full Name	James Graham	Pandora O. Bruce
Residence Street and No.	S.E. 60th Ave. Portland Ore	7607 N.E. Halsey Portland Ore
Age at last Birthday	56 Years	58 Years
Color or Race	White	White
Single, Widowed or Divorced	Widowed	Divorced
Number of Marriages	Second	Third
Birthplace	Scot.	Mo.
Occupation	Machinist	Nurse
Name of Father	George Graham	Telford M. Hogan
Birthplace of Father	Scotland	Ky.
Maiden Name of Mother	Marian J. Cameron	Virginia E. Nance
Birthplace of Mother	Scotland	Virginia

Maiden Name of Bride, if She Was Previously Married: **Pandora O. Hogan**

We, the groom and bride named in this certificate, hereby certify that the information given herein is correct to the best of our knowledge and belief.

James Graham Groom   _Pandora O. Bruce_ Bride

CERTIFICATE OF PERSON PERFORMING CEREMONY

I HEREBY CERTIFY That **James Graham** and **Pandora O. Bruce** were joined in Marriage by me in accordance with the laws of the State of Washington, at **Vancouver** this **30th** day of **June** 1939

Signatures of Witnesses:
Eugene A. Hoen Res. 7607 N.E. Halsey St. No. Portland
Dorothy M. Hoen Res. 7607 N.E. Halsey No. Portland

Signature of person performing ceremony: _Paul L. Grozman_
Official Station: Minister
Residence: 1014 Franklin St

then age four, the same age as Marilyn, and her son nine-years-old. Again, in a pinch, Gladys Monroe's cousin and Dora Hogan's (Andros/Bruce/Schulties/Graham) daughter Georgie was already raising her own offspring and could have helped with Marilyn if there truly was a need.

Her next marriage again was to a prominent man, Homer Baer, with the Andrist children and his son, Homer, living with all of them under one roof, with their maid. He was the President and Owner of Security State Bank and his son a bookkeeper with the bank.

Georgie would settle in California, eventually passing away in Stanislaus in 1959.

In the 1920 census the Bruce family though appears again, this time with a residence in Multnomah County Oregon's Mount Scott. The three, meaning Charles, Dora and Dorothy, who was then 15, resided on 64 Foster Road, in a home that they owned. He was employed as an electrician at a powerhouse. Two years prior, Charles and Dora appeared in the city directory, where he was listed as an operator at PRL&P or the Portland Railway, Light and Power Company.

In the 1920 census Louis Milton Andros was living in Los Angeles California with his current wife Rita, sister-in-law Laura Barry, his niece Isabelle and his father Richard Andros.

An article from *The Bee Danville* from August 21, 1925 gives an insight into Dora's spry character, which placed her in the national spotlight, with this publication in Virginia. In Portland, escaped convicts had residents astir with fear, except for one.

"Farmers out in the brush have run like frightened rabbits, not knowing which to fear most, the escaped convicts or the pursuers, and in the midst of the tumult has bounded a red-haired woman giving the alias of Miss Billie Bruce and claiming the power to pray the murderers out of hiding. When Governor Pierce and Prison Warden Dalrymple both refused to listen to her or to promise the suspension of the death sentence for the convicts if caught, owing to her prayers, the valiant Miss Billie started out alone for the wild region known as drift wood canyon, where the desperate men are supposed to be at bay. After tramping five miles up the creek and declaring she saw the print of a prison shoe, Miss Bruce returned stating she had changed her mind about forgiving the men, as they had shot a guard through the head and she did not approve such tactics. She turned out to be Mrs. Dora Bruce, of Portland. She is interested in prison reform and humanitarian work."

It is known that her relationship eventually dissolved with Charles Bruce, because Dora was listed on family probate records in 1927 at Dora Schulties and her father's obituary in 1933 as "Mrs. Andros" and of California.

Dora's daughter Dorothy resided in Portland Oregon herself in 1937 with her husband Eugene Ibsen on 1415 NE Euclid Avenue.

That year in the same directory, Mrs. Dora Bruce was listed as an employee at Children's Home Inc., one of the non-profit groups that helped orphaned children in the area. Located at 3415 SE Powell Boulevard, this organization was one of a number that evolved into Trillium Family Services. Dora Bruce was employed as a "house mother." If Gladys had needed help with Norma Jeane, Dora would have been more than qualified. Dora was well acquainted with her great-niece Norma Jeane, who ended up visiting her aunt in 1945 with the photographer Andre de Dienes in Portland.

In 1935, Grace McKee Goddard declared to the court that her friend Gladys was deemed incompetent. There were, she declared, "no relatives entitled to the guardianship of said minor," meaning Norma Jeane (who she then called "Norma Jean Baker") aka Marilyn Monroe. Some have said that the use of the name "Norma Jean Baker," was to hide Marilyn from her biological father and relatives, but that seems unlikely.

Grace, though she was a friend, was crafty. There is no question she loved both Gladys and her daughter. She took a vested interest in Norma Jeane, with no biological children of her own. Thankfully, for Gladys while she was declared "incompetent," her friend Grace was not the type to have exploited her and handled her money accordingly, though she was an overzealous spender with the needs for Norma Jeane, buying her shoes and clothes that in some instances, would equate to about $200 for a coat in today's currency.

Many feel it was Grace's enthusiasm to groom a new and young Jean Harlow through Norma Jeane that drove her to assume the role of guardianship. She had a genuine belief in Norma Jeane and eventually became her first manager. Unlike Lee Strasberg and the Freudian doctors who would later take over the life of Marilyn Monroe and steal her legacy, Grace did no such thing and never misappropriated her funds. In fact, many will express that Marilyn may have forgotten Grace and later interviews will demonstrate that as she was recorded speaking about "this woman Grace," as if Grace was a stranger to her.

It was Grace though who was instrumental in co-signing Marilyn's first contracts for her before she was old enough to. She also helped to create the "Cinderella myth," especially honing in on the orphanage for sympathy, while Marilyn was temporarily in the Los Angeles Orphans' Home Society. As Grace assumed legal guardianship, the orphanage was part of the process required to allow that to happen.

Further details have been and are being investigated into the life of Dora. It was known by one of her nieces, Rebecca Esther Hogan (Becky Fritz), the daughter of William Marion Hogan, that she was living in Portland and married to a Scottish man. Rebecca was in Portland in 1945 for the birth of one of her children and spent time with her aunt Dora. This was at the same time that Gladys, the mother of Marilyn Monroe was also in Portland living near her Aunt Dora. Rebecca and Gladys were also first cousins.

Dora took Gladys under her wing in agreement to supervise her after her release from Agnews Hospital. It was at Berniece Miracle's urging, Norma Jeane's half-sister, and Dora requested information before she committed to helping her niece, but did so with a generous heart, helping to coordinate her release from Agnews State Hospital in the San Jose California area.

Norma Jeane aka Marilyn Monroe also visited Dora and Gladys during this period.

It was Dora who worked to supervise Gladys while she was cleaning houses. After being subjected to the techniques in the mental hospital including electroshock therapy, Gladys was initially someone battling a case of the blues when she first became ill in 1933. Now, she was a woman who advocated Christian Science to a level which was deemed fanatical and dressed in white as if she was a nurse, seeking to cure illnesses without "materia medica," as she often told her daughter Berniece, using the Latin term for prescription medications. Dora, according to Berniece and daughter Mona's memoirs, attempted to have Gladys focus on a career as a practical nurse. Eventually, Gladys left Dora's before the year was up and returned to Los Angeles, where she lived with Grace's Aunt Ana Lower and her daughter, Norma Jeane.

Dora outlived her brother William Marion, as listed in his 1947 obituary, having previously been reported as deceased in 1946. She was 72 years old at the time of her brother's death on May 5.

Dora herself now eternally rests like her famous great niece behind a slab of pink marble. The Lincoln Memorial Park in Multnomah County in Portland Oregon is her final resting place. Her marker is simply engraved "Dora O. Graham, 1875-1949." Though some believed Dora to have passed away earlier, she eerily died the day before her younger sister Myrtle on September 6, 1949 at age 75. James Graham, Dora's husband purchased the plot for her.

CHAPTER TWELVE

THOUGH NOT AS financially prosperous as her sister Dora though still well off at many times in her life, Della Mae Hogan has been the most slandered of all of the siblings of the Hogan family because of her connection to Marilyn Monroe. She was Marilyn Monroe's maternal grandmother. Many biographers describe Della in the most derogatory way, especially J. Randy Taraborrelli, who painted Della as mentally unstable, violent, tacky and promiscuous.

Taraborrelli also formed lies about the character of Della's neighbor, Ida Bolender, a gentle natured woman who was not into gossip.

However, Taraborrelli told a tall tale that Ida Bolender formed a secret alliance with another church member, Anna Raymond, who would deliver clothing her way as well as costume baubles. Apparently Raymond, a seamstress, would set aside these items for the church rummage sale. The pair conspired, according to Taraborrelli's claims, to rid of these items to the most gullible of people to buy such tackiness, with that person Della Grainger (formerly Della Hogan, then Della Monroe, who was also Della Graves in a tumultuous marriage).

Taraborrelli wrote, "Indeed, whenever Ida Bolender stood watch at her rummage-sale table, she looked forward to selling as much of her tacky merchandise as possible to one eager customer in particular – her neighbor across the street, Della Monroe."

Additionally, Taraborrelli's statement above is further inaccurate because he named her Della Monroe instead of Della Grainger which shows his lack of knowledge on the topic of Marilyn Monroe history.

Taraborrelli highlighted the snickers in his fabricated account as Della descended the steps into the church, donning fake furs and fake jewels. Allegedly, the locals in the Hawthorne California area would gossip about Della, including Bolender and considered her a drinker with a wandering eye, who was past her prime and furthermore, had suffered from postpartum depression.

Ida Bolender was also one of the most heavily misquoted members of the cast of characters in Marilyn Monroe's life. Bolender was wrongly slandered in the press as well by Marilyn herself. In the Cinderella fairy tale that Marilyn Monroe created about her earlier life as Norma Jeane, she depicted Mrs. Bolender as a heavy-handed religious woman who shoved church down the throats of the children and despised Norma Jeane. As Ezra Goodman who authored the *TIME* magazine article in 1956 noted, which *TIME* replaced with the Hollywood myth through their editorial process, the Bolenders were not the zealots that Marilyn Monroe had told him.

Nothing could have been more from the truth in fact, Ida Bolender dearly loved Norma Jeane and was hurt from these misinterpretations. Cut and paste has reigned in documentary interviews where she and husband Albert Wayne were also interviewed following Marilyn's death where their words were misconstrued and edited.

Ida Bolender was so troubled about the depiction of her family and Norma Jeane's early childhood, she penned a letter to Berniece Miracle, Della's granddaughter and Marilyn's half sister after Marilyn's death. In the letter, she explained to Berniece how she cared for Norma Jeane after Gladys brought her home from the hospital, noting the care was until 1935, which was not possible since Gladys had taken Norma Jeane to live with her in 1933.

Marilyn Monroe Unveiled | A Family History

"It has almost broken my heart to read the terrible stories that have been written about her early childhood, which I know personally they are so untrue," she wrote to Berniece.

She also enclosed a photo from the paper of a toddler Norma Jeane, enthusiastically looking ahead as she is wearing a prairie style dress and bonnet. Ida Bolender indicated that Della snapped the photo – the same Della that so many biographers have indicated was mentally incompetent.

"Your grandmother took this photo before Norma Jeane was a year old," she wrote. "She died when the baby was about 14 months old."

Della Monroe – the same woman who has been smeared with tales of near attempted murder as smothering her granddaughter with a pillow (according to Ezra Goodman, when he researched this topic the TIME cover article in 1956, he learned from psychiatrists that memories from infancy and toddlerhood are often distorted and that still holds true today). Della Monroe – the same woman who was pictured lovingly spending time with all of her grandchildren from Gladys, including young Norma Jeane, who she greatly adored.

Della was first spotted on documents on the 1880 Federal Census in Flat Creek Missouri in Barry County. Her parents were recorded as T.M. Hogan, then age 29 and the head of household and C.V. Hogan, age 23, his wife. His career was described as "works on farm" and hers as "keeping house."

The two daughters were Dora, then five-years-old and Della then age three, both described as "at home." William, abbreviated as "Wm." was listed as two-years-old and "at home" too.

Flat Creek is a township that in the 2000 census had a population of 5,642. Besides the ancestors of Marilyn Monroe having lived there, actor Don Johnson was born there, but moved away in his early childhood. It is known for its sleepy waterways where people enjoy kayaking. Farms and trees still dot the two lane local highways, which are steeped with quaintness.

The city of Branson is about an hour's ride away on MO-76 W with a range of points of interest in between in the Ozark Mountains from Mark Twain National Forest to Coney Island (a village in the area) to a range of campgrounds and resorts to the famed Table Rock Lake in Branson, an artificial body of water that offers many recreation and vacation rentals in the Ozarks.

Della has not turned up on the census for 1900 having been in Mexico at that point with husband Otis Elmer. Daughter Gladys Pearl, Marilyn's mother was born on May 27, 1902 in Porfirio Diaz Mexico. Marion Otis Elmer Monroe, Della's son was born in 1905 in Los Angeles.

At the time of Gladys's birth, the declaration noted that Otis presented his brand new baby girl to the judge in Mexico and indicated that he was a painter from the United States, age 37, and from Indianapolis Indiana, and his daughter was born at 4:30 a.m. on May 27 in Porfirio Diaz. He told the judge he was the son of Jacob and Mary Monroe, who had both passed away, and his wife Della's parents (Della was then approximately 26-years-old) were Tilford and Jennie Hogan. An interesting clue as to Della's whereabouts prior to their marriage indicated that she had previously resided in Bentonville Arkansas prior to Mexico, which was the birthplace of her youngest brother, James.

In 1910, the year following her husband's death, Della resided in Los Angeles as a homeowner who took on boarders at 1114 East 6th Street. She was listed as the head of household at only age 33 and was listed as "Della M. Monroe." Daughter "Gladys P." was listed as eight-years-old and son Marion E. was misclassified as a daughter of age five. Gladys's year of immigration, since she was of Mexican birth, was noted as 1907.

While Della has been painted by past biographers as having been a homeowner that took in boarders who were men to satisfy her personal pleasures, based on the census records, this is also an incorrect statement about the recently widowed Della. In fact, she had a family and a couple living under her roof. Samuel Evans with his wife Lois, ages 47 and 45 were among the residents, along with their daughter, May, nine-years-old. David H. Nelson and his wife Mary E. Nelson, both 28 years old, were also on her roster. Samuel Evans was a painter and decorator and his wife a music teacher who specialized in piano. The Nelsons both worked as clerks, he in telegraph and she worked in the escrow industry.

In 1912, Della married Lyle Graves, who was employed with the Pacific Electric Railway along with Otis. He was also a native of the Midwest, having resided in Wisconsin, and 29 years to Della's

35. The marriage was reportedly not a healthy one, with Graves allegedly a heavy drinker with a violent temper. Gladys later reported to daughter Berniece that he had thrown her cat against a wall.

In spite of that sad memory Gladys held onto in adulthood, she had joyful memories she shared of a stepfather not accounted for on documentation with her mother, who had a farm in Oregon. Gladys spoke of happy times in Oregon, though "Chitwood" as she called him, also drank. They lived on his family's pig farm with his parents.

In spite of the rumors that Della was never legally married to her husband Charles Grainger, the two were registered to vote in Los Angeles County in 1920, residing on 5310 Rhode Island Avenue in Hawthorne, he as an oil driller and she as a housewife. He declared himself as a member of the Republican Party and she marked "DS" or "Declined to State." She used the name "Mrs. Della M. Grainger."

[Fourteenth Census of the United States: 1920—Population record showing Grainger, Charles W. (Head), Della (Wife), Oliver A. (Son) at 1410, 74, 115.]

In the previous voter registration listed for Grainger from 1898, he was a Ventura County resident having been employed as a farmer at that time. He was also a tall person for those days, at about five feet, 10 inches in height, identified with gray eyes, brown hair and a fair complexion.

In 1917, she did attest that daughter Gladys was 18 when she married John "Jasper" Baker, who hired Della to manage the apartments for him that he owned in Venice, California, when young Gladys caught his eye. In actuality, Gladys was not even 15-years-old. Eventually, the two married, had two children and then divorced, with Jasper kidnapping the children to Kentucky. Gladys would pursue them and eventually return to Los Angeles, then start life on her own, later remarrying, then becoming pregnant with Marilyn.

Some have said that Della married Gladys off and sent son Marion away, claiming to some relatives in San Diego. Yet, no relatives have surfaced in the records from that area. In 1924, Marion ended up marrying Olive (Olyve) Brunings and by 1929 he disappeared without a trace, creating angst within the family. Olive was born in Oregon and was traced to Monterey with her mother as a little girl, where the mother Ida (Henderson) Brunings Martin was already widowed and then apparently, later remarried and divorced.

What is known is Olive and Marion were married in San Diego on September 20, 1924 by a Methodist Minister, LeRoy W. Lowell. He claimed his residence as Salinas and she San Bernardino. He was listed as a mechanic for an occupation and also attested to his age at 22, though at this point, he was barely 20 and she was 19.

Della and her husband Grainger also appeared in the early part of the year 1920 (January) in the census at 1410 Coral Court in Venice, listed as husband and wife. His son Oliver, age 21, was also residing with him, listed as an oil driller like his father. In the census, once again, they are classified husband and wife. Her name is also registered as "Della Grainger."

Some unscrupulous biographers in the past have additionally misstated that Della's husband Grainger was running away from her and that is why he took an assignment in Borneo (where Della soon followed) instead it is noted that Grainger had traveled in the past for work. He had a passport application to head to India in 1915 to drill for ore. Next was on to Burma and then travels through Hong Kong and Japan for his work as an oil driller in 1916 for an emergency passport application.

Charles W. Grainger

Charles W. Grainger was Della Hogan's third husband. She visited with him while he was on business in Borneo. The passenger list on the following page shows her return to the United States. It also shows his on June 16, 1927, about two months before Della died. While many biographers have spread the myth that Grainger abandoned Della, the passenger list with his name shows an address for Hawthorne, where she also lived.

Marilyn Monroe Unveiled | A Family History

S.S. "PRESIDENT LINCOLN"

LIST OF UNITED STATES CITIZENS (FOR THE IMMIGRATION AUTHORITIES)

Sailing from Hongkong, Aug. 15, 1926, Arriving at Port of San Francisco, Sept. 8, 1926.

Number 105   25/9/8   1926

No. on List	Family Name	Given Name	Age Yrs. Mos.	Sex	Married or Single	If native of United States insular possession or if native of United States, give date and place of birth	If naturalized, give name and location of court which issued naturalization papers, and date of papers	Address in United States
1	CONSTIEN	EDWARD THEODORE	51	M	S	Nov. 12, 1875. Ashland, Pennsylvania		Naval Dept. Washington, D.C.
2	DAWS	MATTIE D.	20	F	M	March.25th, 1906. Tennessee		2624½ E. Anaheim St. Long Beach
3	GLASS	RUTH IONE	25	F	M	MAY 7th, 1901. Utah		747 E 7st. Long Beach, Cal.
4	GLASS	LEONARD GARTH	2 6	M	S	Feb. 4th, 1924. Long Beach, Cal		747 E 7st. Long Beach, Cal.
5	MORGAN	NORMAN K.	14	M	S	June 15th, 1925. Oxnard, Cal.		7# E 7st. Long Beach, Cal.
6	GRAINGER	DELLA M.	43	F	M	July 7th 1887. Brunswick, Missouri		418 E Rhode Is. Hawthorn, Cal

S.S.

LIST OF UNITED STATES CITIZENS (FOR THE IMMIGRATION AUTHORITIES)

Sailing from COLON (Canal Zone), , 192, Arriving at Port of Los Angeles June 16th, 1927

Number 1179

No. on List	Family Name	Given Name	Age Yrs. Mos.	Sex	Married or Single	If native of United States insular possession or if native of United States, give date and place of birth	If naturalized, give name and location of court which issued naturalization papers, and date of papers	Address in United States
1	CARNAHAN	Francis M	45	M	M	Lotus (Cal.) 26/4-	458P 26135 50 2/15/26	Whittier (Cal) 448 Hevlin Ave
2	GRAINGER	CHARLES V.	45	M	M	Ventura(Cal) 25/12-82	41038 3/4/25	Hawthane(Cal) Box 277
3	GROUNT	William I.	31	M	M	Los Angeles 24/4-1896	133613 3/5/25	Long Beach(Cal) 739 S.Iris Ave
4	KUPPER	Fred	29	M	M	Look Valley (Cal) 20,5	268605 4/14/26	Orange (Cal)484 S.Shoffer Str.
5	MEYER	Carl J.	26	M	S	Edmond (Okla)1/3-901 1898	264645 7/9/26	

Marilyn Monroe Unveiled | A Family History

A consular application from 1915 notes that Grainger's first wife was deceased and he had two children including Oliver and also Elbin, who was born just after Gladys on June 7, 1902 (Oliver was born in 1899).

While some have said the husband and wife had separated, Della M. Grainger was on the "President Lincoln" roster of passengers, with her address in the United States as 418 E. Rhode Island Avenue in Hawthorne. The ship left from Hong Kong on August 15, 1926 and arrived in San Francisco on September 8, 1926.

While it is thought that Della did not see her granddaughter Norma Jeane until December of that year for the first time, she likely became a part of the child's life earlier than that. Della was reportedly instrumental in the baptism of her granddaughter, who was baptized Norma Jeane Baker on December 6, 1926 at the Hawthorne Foursquare Church, while others have said it was at Aimee Semple McPherson's Angelus Temple, with the famous evangelist performing the blessing of baby Norma Jeane herself.

While it is also often noted that Grainger and Della had called it quits before her death and he did not return from Borneo, to the contrary, he returned from the Colon Canal Zone on the S.S. M/N Fella arriving into Los Angeles on June 16, 1927, while Della died in August. His address was listed as a P.O. Box in Hawthorne, number 277, with a date on his papers of May 4, 1925, more than two years prior. In other words, Grainger was back in the area before Della's passing from malaria.

Della did spend time with Norma Jeane before she passed away and was busy fighting fevers and myocarditis, an inflammation of her heart. As she passed through delusion phases from the effects of malaria, it was mistaken as mental illness, another nail in the coffin for the family with the reputed history of emotional issues for family members.

This though was inaccurate and Gladys especially watched her mother grow sicker and sicker, as she juggled the responsibilities of work, caring for the ill Della and Norma Jeane.

On August 4, 1927, it is claimed Della experienced an emotional collapse due to the effects of malaria, on the Bolender's front porch, which prompted a call to the police. However, as noted previously in this book, Ida Bolender, when interviewed, gave no context to this event. Della was brought in to the Norwalk State Hospital, a mental institution, where she passed away on August 23 at 12:20 p.m.

Della was listed as "married" as well on her death certificate, which denoted she was a housekeeper.

One of the contributing factors was mistakenly noted as "manic depressive psychosis," another falsehood of Della's health condition, because her psychosis was caused from the malaria.

Della was buried in the same cemetery, Rose Hill in Whittier California, along with husband Otis. Records indicate that Gladys continued to make regular payments to the funeral home, White & Emerson, for her mother's eternal rest.

Charles Grainger is not documented as having remarried following Della's passing. In fact, in the 1930 Federal Census he was accounted for as a resident of Redondo Beach in California's Los Angeles County. At that time, he was still employed as an oil driller, even at age 54. He lived with other lodgers, including others who listed their employment as having been in the "oil fields" and his marital status as "widower."

CHAPTER THIRTEEN

WILLIAM MARION HOGAN was the third child in the Tilford and Jennie Hogan brood, born on April 10, 1879 and was the oldest of the two boys.

As the Hogan marriage dissolved, the three youngest children followed their mother to Kansas City after her remarriage to Frank Sellars, who was listed as "John W" on some documentation. With following their mother, that also followed with a name change to "Sellars." It is said the three were upset with their father, with the unknown if there was ever a reconciliation (though most suspect there was for William since he changed his name back to "Hogan," as well as Myrtle who attended their father's funeral).

In an 1899 directory from Kansas City Missouri, Jennie and her three children are featured. They resided then at 1634 Summit, with Jennie listed as a dressmaker, Myrtle as a "milliner" (or what is known as someone who makes or sells hats), "Jas" which is short for James and no career after his name (he was still a teen at this time) and William (with "Wm" short for William and his middle initial "M") listed as a laborer (William was 20 years old then). All the children had an "r" following their name, denoting they were each a resident of the household that Jennie headed up.

What is a fascinating point of interest as well with the Hogan family is the change of name for William, the maternal great-grandfather for Jason Edward Kennedy, one of this book's authors. While he was known as William Marion Hogan at birth, he changed his name to William Marion Sellars (his stepfather's last name) and then assumed his mother's maiden name of "Nance."

This was another complexity in connecting particular children of Tilford and Jennie's to the both of them, because of the name changes following the divorce of their parents.

However, in December 2011, a letter from the Social Security Administration connected the dots about William Marion Hogan's identity. His U.S. 8th Cavalry card listed both his alias as William M. Sellars and his legal name as William M. Hogan, and also confirmed his enlistment in the U.S. Navy.

He served honorably in both the Army and Navy, with the Navy he was on the "Lancaster," "Yankee" and the "Prairie" between 1904 and 1908. The "Lancaster" was a receiving ship in Philadelphia within Philadelphia's Navy Yard during the time of William's service.

The "Yankee" was a ship that was in the West Indies, and then headed to Newport News, before heading to Panama, as well as to League Island. In 1905, the ship headed for the Hispaniola and West Indies and returned for repairs in New York at New York's Navy Yard. Depending on William's time of service, the ship also headed to New York and was put out of commission. Its final run was with Naval Academy and militia reservists and ended up running aground in September 1908, and sinking it as it was towed through Buzzards Bay in Massachusetts.

In the 8th Cavalry, William was part of Troop A on standby in 1901 because of the uprising that they expected from Chitto Harjo, the leader of the Creek Indians, with his name literally translating to "Crazy Snake." He and his followers advocated whippings of those publicly, as well as taking off the ears of those who were for the allotment in Oklahoma. While it was expected to be a bloodbath to arrest Crazy Snake and his leaders, 96 were quietly arrested, taken into custody, tried and found guilty. After Crazy Snake claimed his group would be peaceful, that was a lie, and he continued to

Social Security application for William Marion Hogan. His father was Tilford Marion Hogan and his mother Charlotte Virginia Nance. He was Gladys Monroe's uncle and Jason Edward Kennedy's great-grandfather.

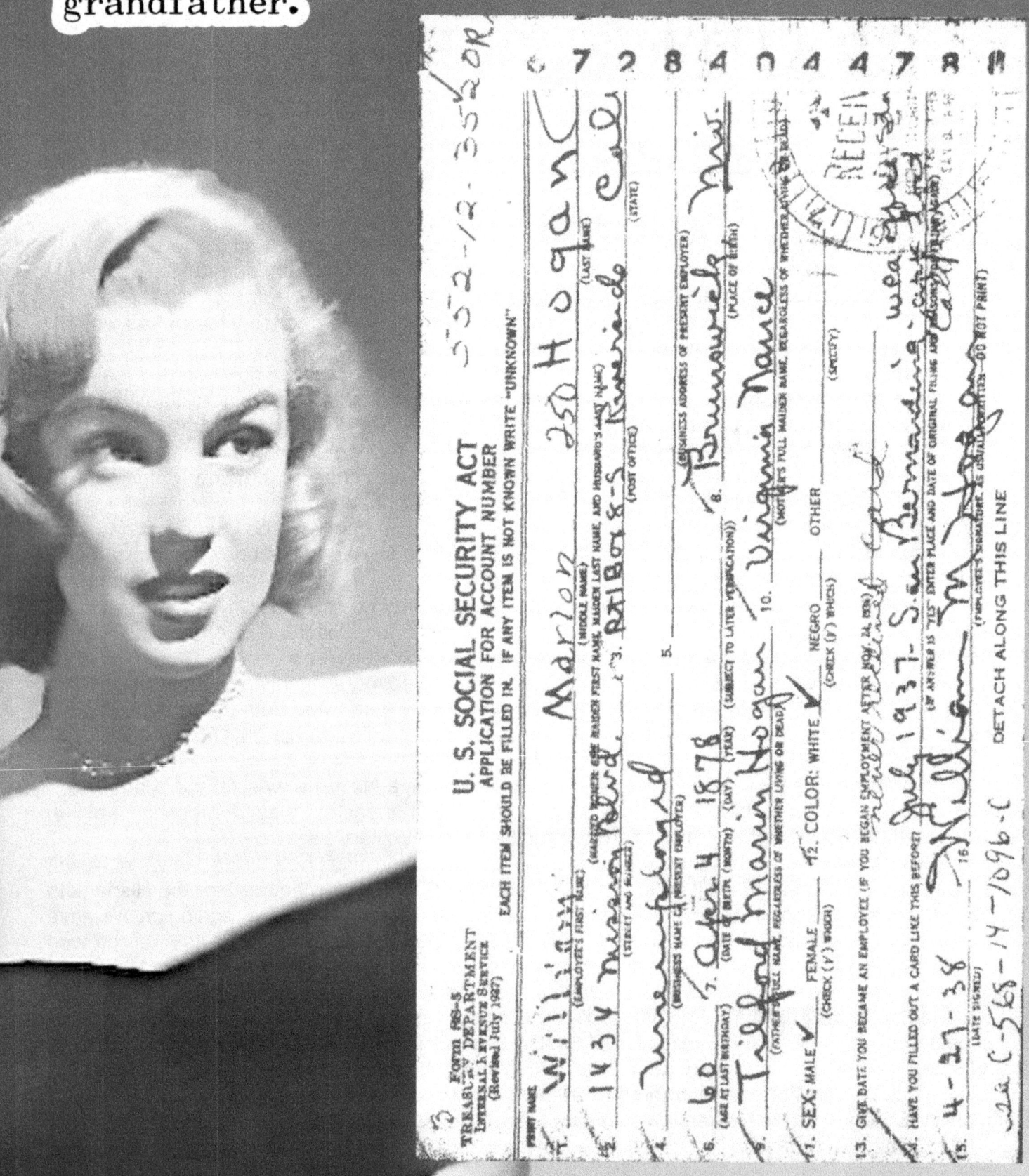

Children of William Marion Hogan

From left to right:
William Leonard Hogan,
Violet Lindsey Hogan,
Daisy Maria Hogan,
Rebecca Esther Hogan,
Robert LaVerne Hogan.
Missing from this photo is Naomi Ruth Hogan.

fight against allotment and threaten uprising. In 1902, he ended up with nine others at the Leavenworth Federal Penitentiary.

William's discharge under the name "William Sellars" was on May 6, 1902 from Fort Reno, for the reason of a disability. He left the Army as a private, and his rating was "Excellent." For Reno was located in Oklahoma in the middle of the Indian Territory and today is a preserved location. During the period when William was there, it was a location for the Cavalry and those enlisted with the Army until 1907.

While Marilyn's family has often been chastised and said they offered nothing to society, William's participation in the Navy and Cavalry reflects otherwise.

On October 16, 1912, he used the name William Marion Nance when he and Clara May Slough applied for their marriage license in Benton County Missouri (he was from Warsaw and she from Bristol). All of William Marion's children were born with the last name of "Nance" and it is said following his mother Jennie's death, the names were changed back to Hogan.

William registered for the draft in September 1918, as William Marion Nance. His occupation is listed as a farmer in Montrose Colorado. Clara was listed as "Clara May Nance."

On the 1920 Federal Census, William was listed as the head of household on a farm, owning his home and running the farm as an employer. He and his spouse, Clara, resided in Coal Creek Colorado on School House Road, with children Daisy (later known as "Marie") and Violet then ages four and two. The entire family was registered on the census as "Nance." William was then 41 and Clara, age 29.

Clara was born on April 18, 1891 in Kansas City, with her residence having shifted from Missouri to Kansas to Missouri to Texas, where Daisy Marie was born on August 17, 1915. Violet was the first child born in Colorado on January 10, 1918, with William Leonard born on June 2, 1920, the census that year preceding his birth by six months.

Son Robert followed in Colorado two years later on June 25, 1933 and then the family headed to California, where daughter Naomi Ruth was born on July 23, 1924.

Daughter Rebecca Esther was born on January 2, 1927, at the same hospital as her first cousin one time removed, Norma Jeane Mortenson aka Marilyn Monroe. Though Rebecca Esther Hogan was Gladys Monroe's first cousin, she was one year younger than Gladys's daughter and held memories of occasions spent with Norma Jeane, ice skating in the Los Angeles area at one of the public rinks and then running through the garden sprinklers to cool off together on warm summer days.

In the 1930 Federal Census, the Hogan family was six children strong, ranging in ages from three years old with Rebecca (author Jason Edward Kennedy's maternal grandmother) to age 14 with daughter Daisy. William was then 52 years old and Clara, age 38. There was even a lodger residing with them, a waitress named Bessie Davis.

The family lived a comfortable life on 37 W. Ave. 31 in Los Angeles County, with William working as carpenter. And with that comfortable life and already taking in a boarder, the family did not mind bringing others into the home. Norma Jeane was one of them they offered to help with when Gladys was busy working away as a single parent, because they were of course, nearby. William realized the strain his niece was under and offered to take his great-niece. However, Gladys declined the offer, noting that William and Clara already had many children to take care of.

The sad fact of the matter was when Gladys became ill, her friend Grace Goddard lied to the court and stated there were no other relatives nearby to take care of Norma Jeane. This was not the case at all as William was one of several.

William registered for the draft when he was living in San Bernardino on 375 Tippicanoe Street (also sometimes written as 375 ½ Tippecanoe) and registered under the name "William Marion Hogan." he was then 64 and wrote that the family did not have a telephone. The person who he documented would always have his address was the Reverend, Reverend Peterson, from the Seven Day Adventist Church in San Bernardino (the family had a strong religious conviction and the information for the funeral home for Clara Mae Slough noted that she was baptized in California in 1928). The draft registration was in 1942, five years before his passing.

TWELFTH CENSUS OF THE UNITED STATES.
SCHEDULE No. 1.—POPULATION.
MILITARY AND NAVAL POPULATION.

Name of Military or Naval Station, or Vessel: Fort Riley
State: Kansas
Country: United States

Company or Troop: A
Regiment: Eight
Arm of Service: Cavalry

81 Sellars, William M. — Private

U.S., Civil War Pension Index: General Index to Pension Files, 1861-1934

NAME OF SOLDIER: Hogan, William M. / Sellars, William M. (alias)

SERVICE: Co. 8 U.S. Cav.; U.S. Navy ("Iowa," "Yankee," "Lancaster," "Prairie")

DATE OF FILING: 1902 Oct 30
CLASS: Soldier
APPLICATION NO.: 1,292,340
CERTIFICATE NO.: 1,294,434
STATE FROM WHICH FILED: Mo.

ATTORNEY: J. H. Kennedy + Co.
REMARKS: C 2372124

MARRIAGE LICENSE.

STATE OF MISSOURI, COUNTY OF BENTON.

This License authorizes any Judge of a Court of Record or Justice of the Peace, or any licensed or ordained Preacher of the Gospel, who is a citizen of the United States, to solemnize Marriage between William Marion Hogan of Warsaw, in the County of Benton, and State of Missouri, who is over the age of twenty one years, and Clara May Slough of Warsaw, in the County of Benton, and State of Missouri, who is over the age of eighteen years.

WITNESS MY HAND, as Recorder of Deeds, with the Seal of office hereto affixed at my office in Warsaw, Mo., the 16th day of October, 1902.

Sellars, the name that I was using at the time was my step father's name; since that time I have taken my father's name Hogan.

Marilyn Monroe Unveiled | A Family History

We Remember You Sweet Carol Ann...

With Love Always and Forever...

Adopted daughter of William and Clara Hogan.

June 1, 1937 - May 17, 1940

THE BAKERSFIELD CALIFORNIAN, SATURDAY, MAY 18, 1940

BABY BURNED TO DEATH

SAN BERNARDINO, May 18. (A. P.)—An oil stove explosion which scattered flames into her crib cost the life yesterday of Carol Ann Hogan, 3.

SAN BERNARDINO DAILY SUN, THURSDAY, MAY 23, 1940

CAROL ANN HOGAN

Funeral services for Carol Ann Hogan were held at 2 p.m. yesterday from the Mark B. Shaw Memorial chapel, with the Rev. N. C. Peterson and Meller Brockett officiating. Two sacred selections, "Safe in the Arms of Jesus" and "Lead Kindly Light," were played.

Pallbearers were Esther Palhegyi, Quyla Wellage, Violet Smith, and Barbara Foster. Interment was in Montecito Memorial park.

Carol Ann was the biological daughter of William And Clara's daughter Violet Hogan. While the 1940 census listed Carol Ann as adopted, it is not known if she actually was legally adopted.

VETERANS ADMINISTRATION

WASHINGTON 25, D. C.

JUL 7 1947

Representative of the estate
of William M. Hogan (deceased)
375 Tippecanoe Avenue

San Bernardino, California

YOUR FILE REFERENCE:

IN REPLY REFER TO: 4ABA-X

XC-2 372 124
HOGAN, William M.
War with Spain

Dear Sir:

Notice of the death of William M. Hogan has been received, and it is requested that all checks issued in favor of this beneficiary subsequent to the date of death be returned to the Division of Disbursement, Treasury Department, Washington 25, D. C.

In the event such check (checks) has (have) been negotiated, refund of $ 75.00 the total amount thereof, should be made by check, draft or money order drawn to the order of the Treasurer of the United States and forwarded to Collections Division, Veterans Administration, Washington 25, D. C. for deposit to the credit of 36X0102 Army and Navy Pensions (5B).

The enclosed copy of this letter should be attached to the remittance for identification purposes.

In reply, please quote file reference given above.

Very truly yours,

L. J. Johnston

L. J. JOHNSTON,
Director,
Payees Accounts Service.

1 Enc.

FL 4-12
Mar 1946
(Replaces Form 1320)

Marilyn's great-uncle William Marion Hogan was residing in San Bernardino California at 375 Tippicanoe Street. This was his draft registration card in 1942.

Marilyn Monroe Unveiled | A Family History

TELEPHONE 9-2701

GABRIEL BROS.
4TH AND "E" STREETS • SAN BERNARDINO, CALIF.

CLARA MAE SLOUGH HOGAN

WIFE OF: WILLIAM M. HOGAN, DECEASED. 1947

BORN: KANSAS CITY, KANSAS. APRIL 18, 1891

MARRIED: BENTON COUNTY, MISSOURI. 1912.

BABTIZED: CALIF. 1928

NAMES OF CHILDREN: 6   GRAND CHILDREN: 15

MRS MARIE TRANSUE

MRS VIOLET LINDSEY

MRS NAOMI FOWLER

(MRS REBECCA FRITZ)

MR WILLIAM HOGAN

MR ROBERT HOGAN

PRIVATE

West Ave 31, Los Angeles, 1930 Census

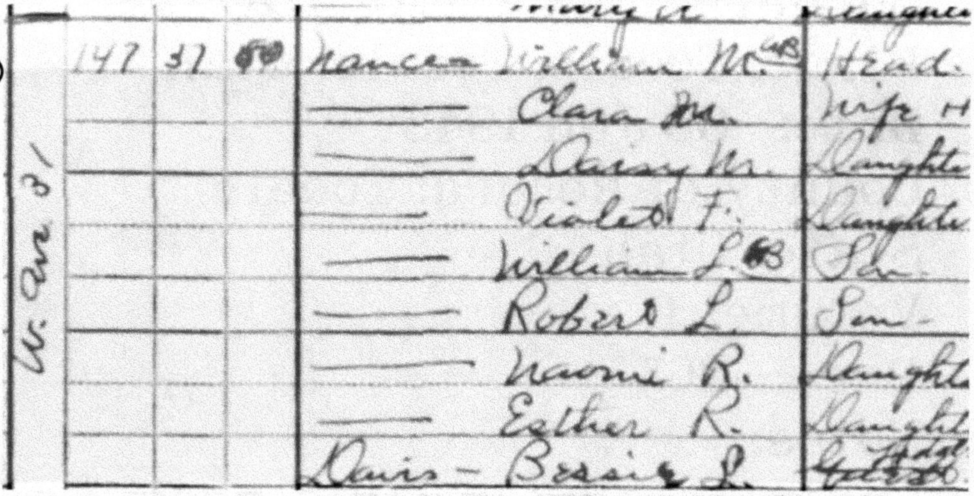

NAMES OF BROTHERS AND SISTERS:

MRS KATIE TEMPLETON

MRS BERTHA GREER: DECEASED:

MR HENRY SLOUGH

MR RITTER SLOUGH

Mr George Slough; Deceased.

Mrs. Rebecca "Becky" Esther Fritz (Hogan), noted on the previous page is Jason Edward Kennedy's grandmother. Rebecca married Richard Fritz.

Details For Marriage ID#537173
Groom Last Name: FRITZ
Groom First Name: Richard Robert (22)
Groom Residence: Buffalo, Erie, New York
Bride Last Name: HOGAN
Bride First Name: Rebecca Esther (18)
Bride Residence: San Bernardino, San Bernardino, California
Place: Tooele, Tooele, Utah
Date: 05 Jun 1945
County of Record: Tooele
State: Utah
Volume: D
Page: 263
Notes:
Certificate # 2233
THE WESTERN STATES MARRIAGE RECORD INDEX
http://abish.byui.edu/

Rebecca and Richard's daughter is Karen Mae Fritz. Karen is Jason Edward Kennedy's mother.

Marilyn Monroe Unveiled | A Family History

-Bring myself back to Life-

Through unfortunate circumstances of a divorce, Jason lost contact with his mother Karen for many years. While Jason heard rumors of his family relationship to Marilyn Monroe early in his youth, he learned his exact family connection when he was reunited with his mother and grandmother in 2011.

After rediscovering Marilyn's story in five days of research and knowing she was alienated from her family by Lee Strasberg and the Freudian therapists, Jason knew it was time for Norma Jeane to come home too. This book is the result...

One document that has been in the family archives is a letter that William wrote to the government about his military pension. He explained he was having difficulty accessing it, in spite of his years of service, injuries while serving, and age.

While he and Clara were older, they were still energetic. They obviously had the hearts to adopt children, and adopted a daughter named Carol Ann. They had offered to Gladys that they would have assisted with Norma Jeane, a gesture that she turned down while she was still working and capable to care for herself and Norma Jeane. Sadly with little Carol Ann, an accidental fire swept through the family home in 1940 and the three-year-old perished in her crib. While the 1940 census listed Carol Ann as an adopted daughter, she may have not been adopted. It is reported by family members that Carol Ann was the biological daughter of Violet Hogan. Violet was William and Clara's daughter.

William Marion Hogan died on May 4, 1947 from a "probable cerebral accident" and arteriosclerosis. He was 68 years old and was buried at the Montecito Memorial Park.

His beloved Clara Mae Slough, Marilyn Monroe's great-aunt died at age 65 and was buried alongside William following her death on June 24, 1956. The Gabriel Brothers funeral home listed her children and 15 grandchildren, with many of those grandchildren, who are the first cousins once removed of Gladys and second cousins of Marilyn Monroe, still living today.

Many of these relatives have accomplished great things, including Daisy Marie Hogan Transue, Marilyn Monroe's first cousin once removed, Gladys's first cousin, born in 1915. Daisy Marie, known as "Marie" had several poetry books published as well as having studied aeronautical engineering at the University of California.

On another interesting note one of William Hogan's children was so inspired watching Norma Jeane beginning to blossom in her modeling career, with her acting career just beginning that the daughter (who was Gladys's first cousin) named her son born on September 7, 1946 Norman Eugene, after her first cousin once removed.

William Marion Hogan and Clara May Slough were married for 35 years until his passing.

William Marion Hogan and spouse Clara Mae Slough with son William Leonard Hogan dressed in Navy Uniform.

CHAPTER FOURTEEN

A GENTLE LOOKING FACE with the profile staring off to the right, as she is seated on an elegantly detailed settee, is the first glance that many have seen of Myrtle Hogan, in a posed photograph with her elder sibling, Della.

Myrtle gazes dreamily in a pose from the photographer in a photo first publicly featured in the book, *My Sister Marilyn*, wearing a high-necked vertically striped blouse, with a tied neckline. A belt cinches her waist and her hand demurely holds a parasol handle.

On her head is a hat topped off with voluminous and curly plumes.

Perhaps the hat was her own design, as a milliner, her early career listed in the 1899 Kansas City directory. Her mother was then a dressmaker. The lovely clothes both she and sister Della wore in the photograph, which Berniece and Mona, Marilyn's half sister and niece dated around 1890, could have been their mother Virginia's creation.

It is obvious from the photo both girls are fair complected, with light brown to reddish hair that the Hogan children were noted for in their earlier years. Like her sister, Della is attired in a high-collared top and an equally chic feathered hat.

While biographers have mocked the Hogan family for their roots in the Ozarks, they were far from slouches. Evident is the photograph alone of the two sisters, when photography and photographs in a studio were luxury purchases.

Born on October 30, 1880, Myrtle and her youngest brother James, the story goes from the Sellars side, ran away together to be with their mother in Kansas City.

What is known is Myrtle married her first husband, Eugene Mathey, born in Ohio on October 16, 1872, with both of his parents from France. He was 27 when the 1900 census was taken and Myrtle was then 19. He was a coal shaft worker. Their residence was the City of Peru Illinois in the County of LaSalle.

A Baptist Clergyman married the pair in Kansas City on November 15, 1899, with Myrtle reassuming the "Hogan" name, marrying Eugene as Myrtle Hogan.

Their date of divorce is currently unknown however, Myrtle and Eugene were featured in the city directory for Peru, residing at 137 Chartres in 1905. In 1910 though, Myrtle as "Myrtle Mathey" was back in Kansas City working as a clerk for George B Peck D G Co, and residing at 1525 E 11th.

The following year though Myrtle found love again, remarrying on February 4 in front of the Justice of the Peace to Lewis A. Myers in Jackson Missouri. He was 36 and she was 30, with her husband born on February 28, 1875.

When World War I rolled along, Eugene Alfred Mathey, Myrtle's first husband, was also remarried and his wife, Florence Mathey, was listed on his registration card. He listed himself as a coal miner for Spring Valley Coal Company, residing in Spring Valley Illinois. The 1920 Census states that he and his wife, Florence, were both of French origin with their parents and they had an eight-year-old child, Viola, meaning their daughter was born around 1912. He was still working in the coal mines in those years.

Like her first husband had found with his second spouse, Myrtle also found a match who had roots in Missouri like she did, with her husband born in Moberly Missouri.

In 1920, Myrtle and her husband resided in Kansas City on 414 Lawton Place, based on the census of that year, with the 43-year-old Lewis (incorrectly spelled "Louis A" by the census taker) noting he was a detective with the city police. Then, two of his sons were living with them – a son Howard, 18, who was a mechanic in the auto industry and William, a coppersmith with the railroad, age 16. Marilyn's great-aunt Myrtle was then 38.

The two were spotted together on the 1930 Census living in Kansas City on 1125 W. 41st Street, in a home that they owned and was valued at $5,000, which would be about $71,500 in today's figures. A modest, bungalow style home built in 1924, with two bedrooms and a bathroom.

But the pair did not live alone. His grandson, William L. Myers also resided with them, a boy just shy of four-years-old. In those days, Lewis was employed as a Time Inspector and Railroad Watcher. William's son was living on West 37th Street and working on the railroad himself at age 25, while his wife Nelli, 19, was working too as a stenographer for a garment company, which explains why little William was likely living with his grandparents, so he could be looked after easily by someone who loved him. All were pictured in the photograph with Myrtle on the following page.

Nelli is also unlikely little William's biological mother, as the couple was married on August 30, 1929 when she was only 18. The 1930 Census reflects that William's mother was born in Washington, while Nellie was from Kansas.

With already taking care of a small child, if Gladys was really in a pinch, her aunt and uncle, both very reliable people with a child around the same age as Norma Jeane in their household, could have helped out.

In 1940, the trio lived only a few feet away from their previous residence, literally less than 500, and a two-minute walk on 4109 Roanoke Road. While the other house was one-story, this was a much more spacious, charmer constructed in 1890, with three levels, a cozy front porch and a more expansive backyard.

Life circumstances had treated the family kindly, as even at age 65, Lewis was again a police officer with the Kansas City Police Department. The week before the census was taken, he put in a 48-hour workweek. He also had one of the highest incomes of those who were on the census sheet, in fact the second highest on that page (the highest was $2,000 annually, while his was $1,880, which today is about $32,000).

There was a bit of a house swap in 1940 in the family with Lewis's son William now residing in their former home at 1125 West 41st Street with his wife Nellie and their son Robert, who was only two-years-old. William, like his father, was a police officer with the Kansas City Police Department and then age 35, his wife, 29. Like his father, William, who was technically Gladys's first cousin through marriage, was putting in 51 hours of work each week and taking in about $1,600 a year, or just over $27,000 for his salary.

Again, while Marilyn's family has been depicted as lowlifes, her mother's aunt Myrtle, then 59, and uncle (Marilyn's great-aunt and uncle) both lived a decent life in the thriving city of Kansas City, with he in an upstanding career as a police officer. Lewis's son was an officer as well.

Lewis worked at an elegant location, the Ambassador Hotel in Kansas City, a column laden building with plush amenities today as it was in those days.

The hotel was near demolition condition until recently at 1111 Grand Boulevard, though it still had its stately signs from the old days, the $8 million renovations drew it back into its elegance. With the upgrades, some of the building's glamour from its construction in 1906 like the old fireplace from the ballroom, some of the original molding and some of the stairwells, were preserved with upgrades. The original stately columns in the front have blended in with modernity, with the authentic beauty of the building retained with the new. With many of the floors one could imagine how Lewis kept a watch over the halls of the stunning apartment hotel.

Lewis's life though was a different one and that was due to his occupation at the hotel, which was not a traditional one like a bellhop or manager, but his role was as a house detective. As a retiree, he was in a different level of his career, with such a fine establishment trusting his expertise so greatly that he was employed at one of the finest Kansas City hotels in the role of plainclothes sleuth to watch over the safety of guests and investigate any odd happenings. In those days, it was common for upscale hotels to hire their own internal investigative staff.

Marilyn Monroe Unveiled | A Family History
Myrtle Hogan – Gladys Monroe's Aunt and Marilyn's Great Aunt.

Myrtle Hogan and Della Mae Hogan

Myrtle's husband Lou was a Kansas City Police Officer & House Detective

William Myers, their son (step-son to Myrtle), was a Kansas City Police Ballistics Expert

In 1940 Myrtle's husband Lewis Myers was a Kansas City Policeman.

In 1955 Myrtle Hogan's stepson William Myers was a Ballistic Technician for the Kansas City Police Department.

THE KANSAS CITY TIMES, SATURDAY, JANUARY 22, 1955.

TELLS OF FATAL SHOT

WYANDOTTE JURY HEARS A BALLISTICS EXPERT.

Sergt. William J. Myers Says a Revolver Found Near Tanner Bryant Fired Bullet Which Killed Man.

A revolver found within a few feet of Tanner Bryant, former Kansas City patrolman, after he had been wounded by Kansas City, Kansas, police, fired a bullet found under the body of Dan Matthews, a ballistics expert testified yesterday.

Matthews was slain the night of November 10, 1953, near his liquor store at 400 Minnesota avenue, Kansas City, Kansas. Bryant, 61, of 3509 Smart avenue, is on trial before a jury in Judge Willard M. Benton's division of the Wyandotte County District court on a charge of murder in connection with his death.

Sergt. William J. Myers, ballistic technician of the Kansas City police department, testified the bullet turned over to him as being found under Matthews's body was fired from the revolver which police said was found near Bryant. He was shot in the right shoulder by police in an alley south of Minnesota avenue and west of Fifth street.

Other witnesses yesterday afternoon included Patrolman Robert Brazelton, Detective Gaylord Brown and Charles S. Matthews, father of the slain man.

Elmer C. Jackson, jr., special prosecutor, and Donald E. Martin, county prosecutor, said they would complete presentation of the state's case Monday morning, when the trial will be resumed.

Harry H. Hayward and Buford E. Braly, attorneys for Bryant, then will outline their defense to the jury. The attorneys said it will be a self-defense plea.

Marilyn Monroe Unveiled | A Family History

THE KANSAS CITY TIMES, SATURDAY, NOVEMBER 26, 1960.

TWO SOUGHT IN KILLING

Police Widen Search in Trying to Capture Men Who Are Said to Have Been With LeRoy Lee Larson When He Slew Officer.

Larson said, "I got excited and scared and pulled the gun out of my waist band—it was under my coat. I reached under there and pulled the trigger. I didn't know I hit him. He ran away."

Larson said he then got out of the car and ran to the Downey home and hid in the garage.

Kansas City, Kansas, police said the pistol used by Larson was pawned July 5 for $6. Through a sporting goods shop in Kansas City, Kansas, it was sold November 23 to a man who gave his name as John Carlyle. Larson told police he paid $25 for it.

William J. Myers, police ballistics expert, said the weapon found on Larson is a Czechoslovakian 7.65 millimeter automatic. That size weapon is equivalent to the .32-caliber pistols of this country.

Myers said that tests prove that the cartridge casings found at the scene of the shooting definitely were fired from Larson's automatic.

Sadly, this is the location where Myrtle's husband passed away from a "coronary occlusion," best known as a heart attack. According to his death certificate, he succumbed to the heart attack within 15 minutes, though he had about a two-year battle with arteriolosclerosis, or a hardening of the arteries. That was complicated as well with diabetes that he also apparently suffered with for over 18 months.

Lewis Arnotte Myers passed away on February 17, 1951 in Kansas City Missouri only ten days shy of his 76th birthday. The informant was William J. Myers, his son. Lewis was listed as a widower, born in Moberly Missouri and having been married to Mrs. Myrtle Myers.

"Services Today at Kansas City for Lewis A. Myers, 75," noting a service for Lewis was held on February 19, the Monday following his sudden death. This notice was published in the *Moberly Monitor-Index* because of his former presence there.

He was lauded in a blurb with many other prominent citizens, a spread that carried from the first page of *The Kansas City Times's* New Year's Day Edition on January 1, 1952, that stretched throughout the paper. "Many Able Hands Go," the headline wept, "City's Loss Through Death in 1951 Is Great."

"Lewis Arnotte Myers, 75, one of the better known city detectives," was what the praises about him gushed.

Myrtle predeceased her husband by a couple of years, passing away on September 7, 1949. She was not ill for long, having been ill from July 22 of that year until she succumbed to her illness at Kansas City General Hospital No. 1. An autopsy was performed and the coroner discovered "carcinoma of the rectum with metastases," in other words, rectal cancer that had metastasized. Curiously, her great-niece Marilyn Monroe would be diagnosed with ulcerative colitis in the late 1950s, which could be a potential health tie between the Hogan women.

Her simple headstone simply features her name "Myrtle Belle Myers" etched into it, with an emblem in the middle, that of the Order of the Eastern Star, a sect of the Freemasons, an organization for both men and women that famous Missourian Laura Ingalls Wilder, who outlived Myrtle by about a decade, was also a member.

Her death certificate noted "James Hogan" as her father and her mother unknown, though it is known that Myrtle showed to Tilford's funeral in 1933 as a "Mrs. Myers of Kansas City" is listed as one of the children who attended, along with his daughter Dora, then known as "Mrs. Andros," residing in California. It is uncertain why Myrtle's mother's name is listed as "unknown," because at one point the city directory showed Jennie lived with daughter Myrtle and Lewis Myers.

The symbol on Lewis's grave was also a Masonic emblem, with the scimitar, crescent and star, belonging to the Shriners, another arm of Freemasonry. He was, according to one of his obituaries, "the oldest member of the Milton Masonic lodge and recently received his 50-year-pin from that lodge."

For Myrtle, being a member of the Order of the Eastern Star was so significant that at her funeral they held a special Eastern Star service for her the Saturday after her death on September 10 (she died on a Wednesday). The Westport Chapter No. 345 was the group that celebrated her life with the special service at the Newcomer's Chapel.

Myrtle outlived most of her siblings, but brother James Berry, outlived all of them and passed away at age 99 on March 23, 1980.

However, it seemed as if the Myers legacy lived on for some time in Kansas City. William J. Myers who was the informant on the death certificate for Lewis Arnotte Myers, resided at 1125 West 41st Street, which was the first residence that the family lived in during the 1930 Census. This was also home address for Lewis, who probably moved back in with his son following Myrtle's passing (which his home then with Myrtl was listed as 4109 Roanoke Road on her death certificate).

The newspapers from that period offer insight into a man who was about 20 years older than Norma Jeane Mortenson, aka Marilyn Monroe. Like his famous relative by marriage Marilyn Monroe, William J. Myers earned his own headlines, including "Sergt. William J. Myers," when he was interviewed as a Kansas City Police Department ballistics expert cited in *The Kansas City Times* simultaneously as Marilyn was making the paper herself as a supernova movie star in the 1950s.

tember 10, 6:30 p. m. Third degree. Visitors welcome; refreshments. Joseph F. Janes, W. M.; Leonard T. Gillham, Sec'y.

GATE City Lodge 522, 903 Harrison — Special communication Saturday, September 10, 5:30 o'clock. Third degree. Brethren welcome. Fred C. Wade, W. M.; Fred H. Knight, Sec'y.

WESTPORT Chapter 345—Members attend funeral services for Myrtle Myers, 2 o'clock Saturday, Newcomer's Chapel. Eastern Star services. Dollie Smith, W. M.; Ann Clarke, Sec'y.

HARMONY Chapter 162, Eastern Star. Members attend Star services for Sister Ray Vanice, Freeman's, 12 o'clock noon Saturday. Roberta Gordon, WM.; Constance Miller, Sec'y.

KANSAS CITY Lodge No. 1, Knights of Pythias, 3301 Woodland. Regular meeting this Saturday evening, 8 o'clock. Pythians invited. Donald L. Rockey, C. C.; William T. Wood, sec'y.

JACKSON COUNTY Odd Fellows Assoc., I. O. O. F., meets Sat., Temple, 13th and Troost. Business session 4 o'clock. Delegates please be present. Basket dinner 6 o'clock. Evening program and dance. Vivian Hopper, Sec'y.

JACKSON COUNTY Odd Fellows Assoc., I. O. O. F., will sponsor a dance tonight, Temple, 13th and Troost. Victory Tones orchestra. Everyone welcome. Vivian Hopper, Sec'y.

NOTICE.
Lafayette Lodge of Perfection of the Valley of Kansas City, Kansas, will be host to all Master Masons, including their members in the Grand Lodge District 4 and 76 and other Districts of Kansas, who care to come, at a reception and program of entertainment, this Saturday evening at 7:30 o'clock.

Marilyn Monroe Unveiled | A Family History

THE DIVISION OF HEALTH OF MISSOURI
STANDARD CERTIFICATE OF DEATH

FILED SEP 23 1949
State File No. 30475
Reg. Dist. No. 149
Primary Reg. Dist. No. 1002
Registrar's No. 3903

1. PLACE OF DEATH
a. County: Jackson
b. City or Town: Kansas City
c. Length of Stay in this place: 1 mo 3 years
d. Full Name of Hospital or Institution: K.C. General Hospital No. 1

2. USUAL RESIDENCE
a. State: Missouri b. County: Jackson
c. City or Town: Kansas City
d. Street Address: 4109 Roanoke Road

3. NAME OF DECEASED
a. (First) Myrtle b. (Middle) Belle c. (Last) Myers

4. DATE OF DEATH: Sept. 7th 1949

5. SEX: Female
6. COLOR OR RACE: White
7. MARRIED, NEVER MARRIED, WIDOWED, DIVORCED: Married
8. DATE OF BIRTH: Oct-30-1880
9. AGE: 68 years

10a. USUAL OCCUPATION: Housewife
10b. KIND OF BUSINESS OR INDUSTRY: ----
11. BIRTHPLACE: Brunswick, Missouri
12. CITIZEN OF WHAT COUNTRY? U.S.A.

13a. FATHER'S NAME: James Hogan
13b. MOTHER'S MAIDEN NAME: Unknown
14. NAME OF HUSBAND OR WIFE: Lewis A. Myers

15. WAS DECEASED EVER IN U.S. ARMED FORCES? No
16. SOCIAL SECURITY NO.: None
17. INFORMANT'S SIGNATURE OR NAME: Lewis A. Myers
ADDRESS: 4109 Roanoke Road, Kansas City, Mo

18. CAUSE OF DEATH
I. Disease or Condition Directly Leading to Death (a): Carcinoma of rectum with metastases

22. I hereby certify that I attended the deceased from 7-22 1949, to 9-7- 1949, that I last saw the deceased alive on 9-7- 1949, and that death occurred at 3:16 P.m., from the causes and on the date stated above.

23a. SIGNATURE: Wm. W. Hart M.D.
23b. ADDRESS: Med. Dir. K.C. Gen. Hospital
23c. DATE SIGNED: 9-8-49

24a. BURIAL, CREMATION, REMOVAL: Burial
24b. DATE: Sept. 10, 1949
24c. NAME OF CEMETERY: Mt. Moriah Cemetery
24d. LOCATION: Kansas City, Missouri

DATE REC'D BY LOCAL REG.: 9-10-49
REGISTRAR'S SIGNATURE: Geraldine Holmes
25. FUNERAL DIRECTOR'S SIGNATURE: D.W. Newcomer Sons
ADDRESS: 1331 Brush Creek Blvd, Kansas City, Mo.

Marilyn Monroe Unveiled | A Family History

THE DIVISION OF HEALTH OF MISSOURI
STANDARD CERTIFICATE OF DEATH

No. 30D 10.48 — FILED MAR 17 1951 — State File No. 8698
BIRTH NO. ___ REG. DIST. NO. 149 PRIMARY REG. DIST. NO. 1002 Registrar's No. 769

1. PLACE OF DEATH
a. COUNTY: Jackson
b. CITY OR TOWN: Kansas City
c. LENGTH OF STAY (in this place): 45 Years
d. FULL NAME OF HOSPITAL OR INSTITUTION: Ambassador Hotel

2. USUAL RESIDENCE
a. STATE: Missouri b. COUNTY: Jackson
c. CITY OR TOWN: Kansas City 2048
d. STREET ADDRESS: 1125 West 41st Street

3. NAME OF DECEASED
a. (First): Lewis b. (Middle): Arnotte c. (Last): Myers

4. DATE OF DEATH: February 17, 1951

5. SEX: Male
6. COLOR OR RACE: White
7. MARRIED, NEVER MARRIED, WIDOWED, DIVORCED: Widowed
8. DATE OF BIRTH: Feb-28-1875
9. AGE: 75

10a. USUAL OCCUPATION: House Detective
10b. KIND OF BUSINESS OR INDUSTRY: Ambassador Hotel
11. BIRTHPLACE: Moberly, Missouri
12. CITIZEN OF WHAT COUNTRY: U.S.A.

13a. FATHER'S NAME: Porter D. Myers
13b. MOTHER'S MAIDEN NAME: Unknown
14. NAME OF HUSBAND OR WIFE: Mrs. Myrtle Myers

15. WAS DECEASED EVER IN U.S. ARMED FORCES? No
16. SOCIAL SECURITY NO.: 488-32-9998
17. INFORMANT'S SIGNATURE OR NAME: William J. Myers
ADDRESS: 1125 West 41st St., Kansas City, Mo.

18. CAUSE OF DEATH
I. DISEASE OR CONDITION DIRECTLY LEADING TO DEATH (a): Coronary Occlusion — 15 minutes
ANTECEDENT CAUSES DUE TO (b): Arteriosclerotic heart disease — 2 Years +
DUE TO (c):
II. OTHER SIGNIFICANT CONDITIONS: Diabetes Mellitus — 18 months +

20. AUTOPSY? No

22. I hereby certify that I attended the deceased from 4/22, 1949, to 2/15, 1951, that I last saw the deceased alive on 2/15, 1951, and that death occurred at 11:40 A.m., from the causes and on the date stated above.

23a. SIGNATURE: R.R. Becker, M.D.
23b. ADDRESS: 4000 Baltimore, Kansas City, Mo.
23c. DATE SIGNED: 2/17/51

24a. BURIAL, CREMATION, REMOVAL: Burial
24b. DATE: Feb. 19, 1951
24c. NAME OF CEMETERY OR CREMATORY: Mt. Moriah Cemetery
24d. LOCATION: Kansas City, Missouri

DATE REC'D BY LOCAL REG.: 2-19-51
REGISTRAR'S SIGNATURE: Geraldine Holmes
25. FUNERAL DIRECTOR'S SIGNATURE: D.W. Newcomer's Sons
ADDRESS: 1331 Brush Creek, Kansas City, Mo.

CHAPTER FIFTEEN

THERE IS CONFLICTING information about Tilford's and Jennie's marriage date as well as the location. Though the first four children have been attributed to the Tilford and Jennie relationship, there has been some disputes over the parentage of James Berry, who some have attributed to the relationship between Jennie and her second husband, Frank Sellars (documented on the Kansas City City Directory as "John W.").

The stories vary as to the reasons of the dissolution of marriage between Tilford and Jennie Hogan. What is known is that the younger children William, Myrtle and James aka Jimmy took on the Sellars last name on the advent of their mother's second marriage.

One of the challenges and "blanks" from this period as well is the 1890 Federal Census as having been incomplete, due to a fire in 1921 at the Commerce Department in Washington, DC.

With those records missing, many remain unaccounted for, to the tune of 6,000 of more than 62 million people.

Members of the Sellars family have always stated that James was a Hogan and Tilford his father, based on family knowledge passed through the family history. James was a common name in the Hogan family, as it was during the time period overall, with Tilford's uncle, second great-grandfather and second great-uncle (the one who scouted with Daniel Boone, started one of the first ferry services in Kentucky, prominent land owner and served honorably in the Revolutionary War) all named James.

Other evidence is that the Hogan family, including two elder children, were born in Arkansas. It was also after his birth that newspapers reported his sister Dora, visited Tilford and Jennie, which meant they were still a couple.

James's birth date is confirmed as noted on August 4, 1883 from paperwork where he documented his own birth date. He listed his birth in Bentonville Arkansas and employer as Bureau of Entomology and Plant Quarantine in Washington, DC as an auditor.

Relatives within the Nance family line believe that James was not Tilford's son, while many things point that he was. Those of the Sellars line always said that Jimmy was the spitting image of Tilford and many have also said bore a striking "full brother" type of resemblance to his brother, William.

Jennie Sellars was listed once again in the Kansas City Directory from 1901 under the designation of "widow" with only

James (Jimmy) and brother William Marion Hogan.

Sellars relatives stated that Jimmy Hogan was the spitting image of Tilford Marion Hogan (Marilyn's great-grandfather).

Gladys Monroe's Uncle James Hogan took the last name of his stepfather: SELLARS.

On the left, Alton Wise, Margaret Sellars Wise, their son Bobby Wise, Mabel Sellars, Ruth Adele Sellars, Virginia Sellars, James Sellars (James Hogan), and Dorothy Sellars.

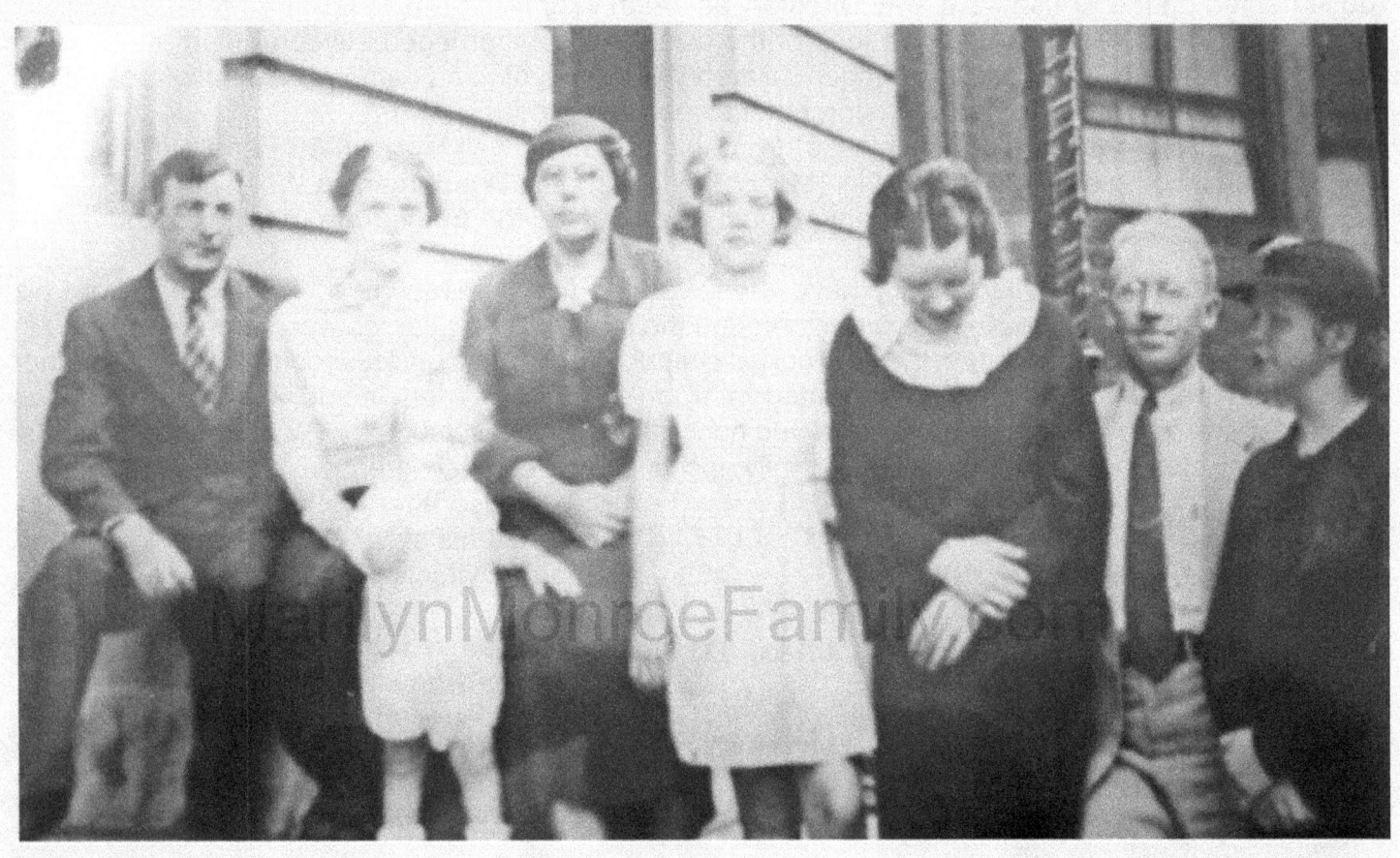

Marilyn Monroe Unveiled | A Family History

James Berry Sellars aka "Jimmy Hogan." His mother is documented as Virginia Nance. He is Gladys Monroe's Uncle.

COMMONWEALTH OF VIRGINIA—CERTIFICATE OF DEATH
DEPARTMENT OF HEALTH—BUREAU OF VITAL RECORDS AND HEALTH STATISTICS—RICHMOND

State File Number: 80-010603
Registration Area Number: 136
Certificate Number: 38

DECEDENT
1. Full Name of Deceased: James Berry Sellars
2. Sex: Male
3. Race: White
4. Date of Death: March 23, 1980
5. Age: 96 years
6. Date of Birth: Aug. 4, 1883
7. Was decedent ever in U.S. Armed Forces?: No

PLACE OF DEATH
8. Name of Hospital or Institution of Death: Walter Reed Memorial Hospital (Inpatient)
9. County of Death: Gloucester
10. City or Town of Death: Gloucester (inside city or town limits: no)

USUAL RESIDENCE OF DECEDENT
12. State: Virginia
13. County: Middlesex
14. City or Town of Residence: Deltaville (inside city or town limits: no)
15. Street Address: Box 266
Zip Code: 23043

PERSONAL DATA OF DECEDENT
16. Name of Father of Deceased: Unobtainable
17. Maiden Name of Mother of Deceased: Virginia Nance
18. Citizen of What Country: U.S.A.
19. Birthplace: Arkansas
20. Married
21. Name of Spouse: Mabel L. Sellars
23. Usual or Last Occupation: Auditor
24. Kind of Business or Industry: U.S. State Dept.
25. Informant: Mrs. Mabel L. Sellars

MEDICAL CERTIFICATION
26. Cause of Death:
Immediate Cause (A): Cardiorespiratory failure
Due to (B): Aspiration
Due to (C): CVA

26i. To the best of my knowledge, death occurred at 9:50 p.m. on the date and place and from the cause(s) stated.
Actual Signature: Thomas H. Young
Date Signed: 3-31-80
Name of Attending Physician: Thomas H. Young
Address: P.O. Box 1160 Gloucester, VA

FUNERAL DIRECTOR
27. Burial
28. Place of Burial: Philippi Memorial Gardens, Deltaville, Va.
Name of Funeral Home: Bristow-Faulkner Fun. Home, Saluda, Va. 23149
Signature: Robert H. Faulkner

REGISTRAR
Signature: Sue B. Keefer, Deputy
Date Record Filed: 4/2/80

her son "Jas B" with her, the two living at 400 Landis Court, with James as a resident under her roof.

In the 1900 census, both Jennie and Jimmy were listed under the Sellars name in Kansas City Missouri, with his birth date as 1884 and age 15, with her marital status shown as "widowed" with "John W." named as her husband. They both have an "r" after their names.

Jennie Sellars was also in the city directory for 1902 in the business section under "tailors." Her residence was her business address at 604 W 14th. And there was a second entry for her in the residential section as the widow of John W, with her son "Jas B" now as a printer.

James married Mabel Lois Fox in Jackson County Missouri on May 31, 1911, where again he was calling himself James Sellars.

In the 1920 census James was accounted for as residing in Fairfax Virginia and married. His father's and mother's birthplaces were documented as Missouri (Tilford was born in Illinois though Frank Sellars was reportedly born in Missouri), with their three daughters Margaret, Virginia and Dorothy all on the census. It was then he was working as a clerk for the U.S. Department of Agriculture, with his birth estimated at about age 36. Ten years later, the paper trail reflects he was as an auditor in Arlington Virginia, claiming the same with both parents reportedly born in Missouri and his age then approximately 46.

He died on March 23, 1980 at Walter Reed Memorial Hospital of Cardiorespiratory Failure where he is named on the document as James Sellars, with Virginia Nance as his mother and the name of his father "unobtainable."

However, on another document, the obituary for his brother William on May 5, 1947, who changed his name to Nance and then changed his name back to Hogan following the passing of his mother, his surviving siblings are Myrtle Myers, Dora Graham (always written up previously as "deceased" in 1946) and brother "Jimmy Hogan."

An obituary is an intimate document with information supplied by family members who hold first hand knowledge about their own families. That knowledge would include the information about Dora as still living and Jimmy's actual name.

Update 6/3/2017: James Berry Sellars is confirmed through DNA testing of his descendants to be the son of Tilford Marion Hogan.

CHAPTER SIXTEEN

THE MONROE SIDE of the family has been more elusive than the Hogan side and with good reason. Though the Hogan side has been wrongly fingered for abusing their relative Marilyn Monroe, the Monroe side of the family has received a greater backlash because of a biographer's misinterpretation, which has led to greater speculation of one Monroe relative in particular.

However, what the authors of this book have discovered is that the Monroe side of the family, much like the Hogans, were upstanding individuals very involved with their communities, plus with each other. Additionally, members of the Monroe and Hogan families intermingled, beyond just Otis Elmer Monroe and his wife Della, Marilyn Monroe's maternal grandparents. Something that will also come as shocking to those who have especially followed the life of Marilyn Monroe in its longtime regurgitated form is that the Monroes, like the Hogan relatives, were deeply rooted in the State of California, even during Marilyn's lifetime.

Discovering Marilyn's family roots has been a labor of love for all of her family lines as with most genealogical research, it can turn into a treasure hunt, especially when details have not been correctly documented. However, in genealogy, uncovering one lead can turn into a positive domino effect and uncover a wealth of information about family members.

But, one misconception about Marilyn's family roots on the Monroe side must be cleared up and that is the tale that she was related to fifth President James Monroe. Marilyn is not directly related to James Monroe. Accordingly, in biographies this fallacy has been regurgitated over and over, plus has been spewed out of the mouths of fans as fact. This was tabloid fodder to make Marilyn's life appear more interesting to her fans, plus was an invention that hailed from Milton Greene in his book, *My Story*, which he claimed when it was released in 1974 to have been the very words of Marilyn Monroe. The authors also unravel this work of fiction in a later chapter of this book, but in one section of *My Story*, "Marilyn" claimed that Grace Goddard told her that she was holding onto family documentation for Gladys about the direct relation to President Monroe. This fabricated detail about Marilyn's genealogy exists in the most current edition of *My Story*, and has been regurgitated over the years, to perpetuate the fraud.

While Marilyn's relatives on the Monroe side, like the Hogans, were mainly from the Midwest and then some of them migrated west to California, the fifth President of the United States was born in Virginia, and naturally as a President of the United States, his ancestry has been well tracked. Yet, prior to coming to the central part of the United States, Marilyn's ancestors did arrive on the East Coast.

James Monroe was born on April 28, 1758 in Westmoreland County, Virginia on his family's estate property. His parents, Spence Monroe and Elizabeth (Jones) Monroe were lifetime residents of the state. They had four other children.

President Monroe's grandfather and great-grandfather were also from the Westmoreland Virginia area, but his second great-grandfather Andrew Monroe, may have emigrated from Scotland to Virginia.

One of the founding fathers of the United States and a Revolutionary War veteran, James Monroe met Elizabeth Kortright (sometimes spelled "Cortright") and the two married on February 1786.

Marilyn Monroe Unveiled | A Family History

Elizabeth, who was born in 1786 and they had three children. Elizabeth was born in 1768 in New York (the city where she and James also married) was the daughter of Captain Lawrence Kortright and Hannah (Aspinwall) Kortright. At this stage, he was a part of Virginia's legislature and New York City was then the capital. In marrying Elizabeth, he resigned from his seat and returned to Virginia.

The Monroes first child was a daughter, Eliza Kortright, born on July 27, 1787 in Virginia.

Their second child was a son named James Spence, also known as "J.S." who was born in 1799 and died at 16 months old from whooping cough. This child would have been the only Monroe namesake to have carried on the legacy and to have been the direct connection to President Monroe, enabling Marilyn's family to have inherited their name from this family tree.

The next child born was Maria Hester. She was born in 1804 while the Monroes were in Paris and was about 18 years younger than her sister.

Eliza married attorney George Hay in 1808, who was the prosecutor in the Aaron Burr trial. Their daughter Hortensia Eugenia Monroe was born circa 1809.

President Monroe began his term in the White House in 1817, and served through 1825. During his time there, daughter Maria made history as the first child in the White House to be married there in March 1820. She married her first cousin, Samuel Gouverneur.

Hortensia was the only child of Eliza and George. She was married in 1829 at her grandparents' estate Oak Hill, to Lloyd N. Rogers, an attorney from Maryland.

Elizabeth, President Monroe's spouse died in 1830 at the family estate. Daughter Maria took care of her father at her home in New York, where he died on Independence Day 1831.

Eliza, who reportedly shunned tradition and the genteel dispositions of her mother and sister, departed the United States and moved to Paris, where she had been schooled during her childhood and felt most comfortable. Her husband George passed away in 1830, and she died in Paris a decade later.

Maria, the third child of President Monroe had three children, two sons and one daughter. Their three children were: Samuel Lawrence Gouverneur, Jr. (born 1820), then James Monroe Gouverneur (born 1824), and Elizabeth Kortright Heiskell (born 1826). Samuel, Jr. died in Washington, DC in 1880. James Monroe Gouverneur died in 1858, unmarried and reportedly in an institution in Maryland, housed there because he was unable to speak and hear. Elizabeth, one of President Monroe's two granddaughters was born in New York and died in Washington, DC in 1868. Their mother died in 1850 and their father in 1867.

The analysis of President Monroe's genealogy demonstrates clearly how far removed his family line was from Marilyn Monroe's. Currently, no evidence exists shows she is related to him. Nonetheless, Marilyn's genealogy on the Monroe side is still impressive and fascinating.

Marilyn's direct line begins with her grandfather, Otis Elmer Monroe, with the lineage tracing from Indiana, and Otis reportedly born in Indianapolis on May 14, 1866. His father (Marilyn's great-grandfather) was Jacob Monroe, born circa 1831 in Indiana and who died in approximately 1872. His mother was Mary E. Appleton (Marilyn's great-grandmother) born in 1841, also in Indiana.

Jacob's parents (Marilyn's second great-grandparents) were named William and Mary. He was born in Indiana as well his wife, both circa the late 1700s.

William Monroe's father was reportedly Sergeant Alexander Monroe, born in Fauquier Virginia in March 1756. He married Elizabeth Chenowith and in addition to William, there were sons Alexander and George and daughter Elizabeth. When William's father Alexander died on November 20, 1842, it took nearly a century later, according to the War Department records, that a stone was placed on his grave in Southport Indiana. The application showed he served in the Revolutionary War, having been in the 2nd Virginia Regiment (marked as the "2 Va Brigade"). An exciting piece to Marilyn's family history on the Monroe side, to have a third great-grandfather who served honorably as a Revolutionary War Sergeant. By the time he was counted in the 1840 Census in Perry, within Marion County Indiana at age 85, he was noted as a "Veteran."

In 1820, Alexander was deposed under oath for his military pension for the Revolutionary War service, at age 62, because he was requiring assistance. He told the courts that at the time, he and wife Elizabeth, then age 56, were beginning to deteriorate in health, and his profession was then as

Application for Headstone

WAR DEPARTMENT — O.Q.M.G. Form No. 623
Approved Aug. 12, 1913
Revised July 15, 1929

Rev War ORIGINAL

40069
(A12)

(PLEASE MAKE OUT AND RETURN IN DUPLICATE)

Name	Rank	Company	U.S. Regiment, State Organization	Date of Death
Monroe, Alexander	Sgt.	John Steed's	2 Va Brigade — Enlisted from Virginia	Nov. 20, 1842

Name of Cemetery	Located in or near — City	State	If World War Veteran — Division	State	Emblem
Southport, Indiana.	Southport	Indiana			Christian / Hebrew / None

TO BE SHIPPED TO Luther Wallace (Name of consignee) at Southport, Marion Co., Ind. (Give town, county, and State)

POST OFFICE ADDRESS OF CONSIGNEE R.R. 1 Box 387, Indianapolis, Ind.

DO NOT WRITE HERE
Verified _____
Ordered LEE, MASS. SEP 20 1930
Shipped 10/1/30

I hereby agree to accept the headstone at above destination, freight prepaid, and properly place same at decedent's grave.

This application is for the UNMARKED* grave of Monroe Alexander. It is understood the stone will be furnished and delivered at the railroad station or steamboat landing above indicated, at Government expense, freight prepaid, and agreed it will be promptly removed and set up at private expense.

200364 Leona Wallace Schilling, Applicant
Address 322 Grant St, Sidney, Ohio   Date June 23, 1930

*Stones must not be requested for any grave at which a private stone, monument, or other permanent marker is already erected or is to be erected.
†State whether soldier, sailor, marine, Army nurse, etc.

Statement, &c. of Marion county, Indiana.

NAMES.	Rank	Annual allowance	Sums received.	Description of service	When placed on the roll.	Commencement of pension.	Ages.	Laws under which they were formerly inscribed on the pension roll; and remarks.
John Hume	do	24 66	73 98	N. Jersey St. troops	Ap'l 14, 1834	do	76	
Alexander Monroe	Sergeant	96 00	171 12	Virginia militia	Jan. 6, 1819	do	-	March 18, 1818. Dropped under act May 1, 1820.
Do	do	120 00	260 00				70	

a farmer. His daughter then resided with them, along with a grandson and granddaughter. The next year, he deeded 50 acres to son, George Monroe, in Pendleton County, Kentucky, where the family had also resided prior to Indiana. Previously, that was where he received his pension, before moving to Indiana, and was receiving $8 monthly. He explained during the Revolution, he entered in the 16th Virginia Regiment in 1777 as a private. He was promoted in 1778 to Sergeant. He served in the Battle of Brandywine, plus German Town, Monmouth and Stony Point. He required the assistance of John Lawless, who served with him, to back his testimony, since his records of service, he believed were burned in Richmond Virginia following his discharge. By 1831, the court records show that he received $120 yearly pension, and was a Baptist Minister. His spouse Elizabeth, Marilyn's third great-grandmother, predeceased him.

It was Marilyn's fourth great-grandfather who was potentially from Scotland, though by some accounts Alexander Monroe, Sr. was only in Scotland for a trip, but it was also where he picked up his bride, Margaret Lang, Marilyn Monroe's fourth great-grandmother. If Alexander was born in Scotland circa 1705, it was likely in Inverness-shire in the Highlands, though he is currently believed to have been born in Virginia. Margaret was born in Edinburgh circa 1715. He died in Carters Run Valley, Faquier Viriginia in 1786. His wife Margaret died in Fauquier County's Town of Warrenton.

The Last Will and Testament of William Monroe, Marilyn's second great-grandfather, executed in Marion County, Indiana on September 12, 1831, gives some insight into their lives. He asked that his wife Mary retain all of his personal property after debts were paid, unless she was to remarry, in which case then she would keep one-third would remain with Mary and the remainder would be equally divided between children Sarah, Marguerite, George, Louisa, Orilla and Jacob. At her discretion, he suggested that Mary could sell his wagon and oxen.

It was obvious that William owned a considerable plot of land, mentioning in his will that Mary should keep his 80 acres of land, as long as she remained a widow, and it could be sold to support she and the children. If Mary remarried, then she could only keep one-third of the land, and then partition the other two-thirds to be sold when the youngest child, assumedly Jacob, "comes of age," with the proceeds equally divided among all the children.

In the 1850 census, Mary Monroe was then enumerated, her birth then calculated at 1794, since she was listed there at 56 years old. She was living with her daughter Orilla Hollingsworth, then 21, and her son-in-law Joseph Hollingsworth, age 22. The couple was married in Marion County on August 12, 1849.

Joseph and Orilla were tracked on the 1860 census, this time without their mother-in-law. There would be three other children, nine-year-old Jacob, seven-year-old Olive, and three-year-old Martha (Martha J (Hollingsworth) Avery was born on February 19, 1857 and who died on March 8, 1931, also in Indianapolis).

Orilla died on September 20, 1862 and where she lies in eternal rest, her place is marked with an ornate headstone. Her husband would live until February 3, 1914, even outlasting his second wife Nancy (born February 2, 1834, and passing away on April 24, 1906). He and Nancy would minimally have three daughters together as well.

Mary Monroe's/Jacob's mother's whereabouts are currently uncertain after the 1850 census.

Mary E. Appleton (Marilyn Monroe's great-grandmother and Jacob's wife) was on the census in 1850, with her mother, Elizabeth Jane Appleton (Marilyn Monroe's second great-grandmother) and the Smith family (Elizabeth's parents/Marilyn's third great-grandparents) in 1850. Hugh P and Polly Smith were their names, then ages 62 and 65. Nancy Ann Smith, age 10, also lived in the household. Of the Appleton children, Mary was then the oldest. There was also eight-year-old Nancy Ann Appleton, six-year-old Lucinda Appleton, four-year-old Eliza Jane Appleton and John W. Appleton, who was less than a year old. The family was located then in Hendricks County, Indiana.

Elizabeth and James Appleton (Marilyn's second great-grandfather) married in Hendricks on June 16, 1839. James, a blacksmith who had been born in Kentucky in 1818, died the same year that their baby John was born, 1850. The cause of death was listed as "bilious fever," which meant that it was a high fever, often accompanied by diarrhea, vomiting or nausea.

Mary and Jacob were married in Boone County Indiana on December 30, 1858.

William Monroes Last Will and Testament.

17th September 1831

In the name of God, Amen:— I William Monroe of the County of Marion and State of Indiana, being at this time weak in body, but of sound mind and Memory do make this my last Will and Testament.

First— it is my desire that all my personal property shall belong to my wife Mary, while she remains my Widow, after all my just debts are paid, and if she should marry then she is to have one third of my personal property and the remainder of my personal property to be equally divided among my six children, namely, Sarah, Harriett, George, Louisa, Orrilla and ___. It is my desire that there should be a Vendue made and that my Waggon and Oxen should be sold & any other property that my Wife should think proper to sell.

2nd It is my desire that my real Estate to wit the West half S.W. 2— Sec 1. T.16. N.R. 2. East containing 80 acres, shall belong to my Wife while she remains my Widow, for the support of herself and the children, and in case she should Marry, then she is to have the third of said land, and the remaining two thirds to be sold when the oldest child comes of age, and the money when collected to be equally divided among the six children, named above.— 3rd It is my desire that my wife and Adam Wright shall be my Executors to settle my Estate.

Signed in the presence of

Louis Mitchell
George L. Hollingsworth

William Monroe [Seal]

Indiana to Wit
Marion County. Before me James M.

The Last Will and Testament for William Monroe, Marilyn's second great-grandfather.

Marilyn Monroe Unveiled | A Family History

The first time Jacob and Mary (Appleton) Monroe's family appeared on the census together was in Hendricks County in 1860, with Jacob a 29-year-old farmer living with his wife, Mary, and son Thomas Allen, then seven months old. Thomas, who was born on October 14, 1859, simply went by the name "Allen," a name used even later on a census and his death certificate.

The entire family unit made the census together in Indianapolis in 1870, before Jacob's death. Jacob was then 39 and Mary, 29. Another two children were on this census, Otis, then five, and John A, age two. John was born July 28, 1868 in Indiana like his brothers.

All three boys were listed "at home," with Jacob a laborer and Mary recorded as "keeping house."

Jacob's death date is not currently known, though it is estimated at 1872, however it is known that Mary remarried on June 22, 1873 in Hamilton County, Indiana. Her second husband was James H. Stewart. Mary was not his first bride, with his first marriage also in Hamilton County to Susan H. Wageman.

On the 1880 census, which was taken in Chetopa Kansas's Neosho County that June, J.H. Stewart, then 50, a farmer, was living with his wife, Mary, a "house keeper." There were three sons in the house, two listed as James's stepsons. One of them was Otis Monroe (Marilyn's grandfather), then age 16, with his occupation classified as "work on farm." The other Monroe child was then age 11, and recorded "at home." That child was enumerated simply as "Monroe, A," who was age 11. This was John Monroe, who like his brother had a middle name beginning with an "A," Alva. The third child was James's son, Eddie, who was then age eight. Eddie is believed to be the child between James and first wife, Susan.

James Stewart died in Neosho County, Kansas in 1884.

In 1885, Otis was recorded as a painter "O.E. Monroe" and age 21, for the Kansas Census of March 1, 1885. He was living in Cherryvale, Montgomery County. However, a widow, age 45, was recorded on the line above his, named "M.E. Stewart," his mother Mary.

At the current time, this is the last time that Mary has definitively appeared on documents with her whereabouts. Yet in those days, proper recording of life and death was still occasionally scant.

But Marilyn's ancestors on the Monroe side were not mysterious with their whereabouts, as readers will learn later in this chapter.

Della's husband, Otis Elmer Monroe is listed in the Kansas City directory as well in 1888 and 1889, under the name "Otis E. Monroe" and "bds" meaning he was a boarder at the residence 1234 Walnut in 1888. His employer was "K.C.C. Ry." likely meaning the Kansas City, Clinton and Springfield Railway (K.C.C. & S), which was a line that ran from the Kansas City area and eventually met with the Frisco line. If it is the same line, it was known as the "Leaky Roof Railway" because of the clay tiles that were implemented in the cars that did not handle the rain well.

The next year, Otis was still working for the same company but had moved as a boarder to 539 Locust.

In 1891, Otis E. Monroe is a name that showed up in the San Antonio City Directory as a "coach painter." This documentation would make sense that this is Marilyn's grandfather since he painted railcars for a living. "G.H. & S.A." after his name is short for the Galveston, Harrisburg & San Antonio Railway.

Otis's following stop in a city directory was in 1897 in Houston. This time, he is a painter for the Houston and Texas Central Railway ("H. & T.C.") and again a boarder with the "bds" abbreviation. His residence was 605 Silver, likely today's 605 Silver Street, near Downtown Houston.

His next appearance in a city directory made available to the public is in the Los Angeles Directory for 1904 at 1308 E 17th Street, where his occupation is chronicled as a painter for the Pacific Electric Railway Company. He has the abbreviation "h" after his name as the owner of the home. At this stage, he and Della had already been married several years, Gladys was about two-years-old and son Marion was about to make his debut into the world.

In addition to Tilford Marion Hogan (Otis's father-in-law) being constantly and wrongly defamed in the family lines, Otis Elmer Monroe's memory is also constantly under attack.

Marilyn Monroe Unveiled | A Family History

Otis Monroe, Marilyn's grandfather was eulogized in this article in 1909.

LOS ANGELES HERALD: SUNDAY MORNING, JULY 25, 1909.

Officials Who Are Alert in Their Efforts to Promote the Modern Woodmen of America

ONE of the busiest Woodmen in Los Angeles is J. I. Taylor, clerk of Golden State camp, No. 7110, M. W. A. He is found in his office at 431 South Hill street, room 112, from 9 o'clock in the morning until 6 in the evening, and often until late hours at night. It is largely through the cooperative work of Neighbor Taylor and Deputy Herbelin that Golden State camp has made the splendid record of growth it has in the last year or more.

Neighbor Taylor became affiliated with the order in 1900 by joining camp No. 9446 at Coalinga as a charter member. He was made the first consul of that camp and has been active in the work of the order since. He joined Golden State camp in 1902, transferring his membership from Coalinga to this camp. He soon became active in the affairs of the camp, serving on important committees, was a member of the board of managers one year, and is serving his camp now the third consecutive year as clerk. During the two and a half years he has been clerk he has had the pleasure of seeing the membership of his camp increase from 1050 to more than 1800. He realizes keenly the responsibility of handling the accounts of a membership of over 1800 members, but enjoys the work and never tires when doing work for the upbuilding of the camp or the accommodation of a Neighbor.

Taylor is chairman.

By the death of Neighbor O. E. Monroe, who died Thursday at Patton, the camp lost a loyal member and a good Neighbor. His body was buried yesterday at Rosedale cemetery, from the undertaking parlors of Neighbor W. H. Sutch. The ritualistic service of the Modern Woodmen of America was used at the burial in the beautiful spot where the beloved Neighbor now sleeps. He leaves a widow and two children to mourn his loss; but he was thoughtful enough while in good health to provide for them in the event of his death, means by which they will be able to provide for themselves, by taking out a policy in the M. W. A. Neighbor Monroe leaves a host of friends who mourn with the members of his family over his early taking away. But the widow and family will know what it is to have the protection of the Modern Woodmen of America.

Marilyn Monroe Unveiled | A Family History

Otis has often erroneously been accused of having a mental disorder, and is part of the concocted drama that Marilyn's relatives were no good and emotionally unstable. This is untrue and all part of the narrative used to create her Cinderella story, a legend that has endured through time. This fable has permeated between all of Marilyn's family lines, as well as those intermingling with them. For example, her grandmother Della was also incorrectly painted as mentally rocky.

What is known about Otis is at the end of his life is he suffered greatly from general paresis (muscular weakness and nerve damage) due to the non-sexual syphilis he contracted while working in Mexico. "Exhaustion" was a contributory factor in his death. The medical affliction impacted his brain and he ended up in Patton Hospital, a psychiatric hospital in San Bernardino County. However, there is no notation that Otis died of psychosis as many biographers have alluded to.

In fact, there was even an obituary published for Otis in the *Los Angeles Times* on July 25, 1909, days after his passing on July 22, when he passed away at 43. It was the day of his funeral, at W.H. Sutch Funeral Chapel on 842 South Figueroa Street, an elegant building with stately columns in the front. A *Los Angeles Herald* newspaper article from 1903 described the chapel within the funeral home as "very handsome, with rich furnishings and pleasing and harmonious fittings." As Marilyn's family has often wrongly been described as deprived and unrefined, the venue where Otis's funeral was held does not fit that mold.

Another clue of Otis's importance in the community is a small writeup in the *Los Angeles Herald* that gives a nod to the legacy he left behind. The obituary in the *Los Angeles Times* referenced a group known as the "The Golden State Camp of the M.W. of A" which planned to oversee the services for Otis at Rosedale Cemetery, his final resting place.

In the *Herald* July 25 edition, a column by the Modern Woodmen of America eulogized Otis. The group is still in existence today and was founded as a membership only fraternal financial organization that originally only offered a place to those wishing to join if they lived in Midwestern states, including Otis's home state of Indiana. The group specialized as well in paying life insurance to its members, and helping them with hospitalization, specifically tuberculosis, when they were ill. Members of the group, specifically those in the "Golden State Camp" who wrote this column, referred to Otis (Marilyn's grandfather) and all others honored in the article as "Neighbor."

They wrote:

> By the death of Neighbor O.E. Monroe, who died Thursday at Patton, the camp lost a loyal member and a good Neighbor. His body was buried yesterday at Rosedale cemetery, from the undertaking parlors of Neighbor W.H. Sutch. The ritualistic service of the Modern Woodmen of America was used at the burial in the beautiful spot where the beloved Neighbor now sleeps. He leaves a widow and two children to mourn his loss: but he was thoughtful enough while in good health to provide for them in the event of his death, means by which they will be able to provide for themselves, by taking out a policy in the M.W.A. Neighbor Monroe leaves a host of friends who mourn with the members of his family over his early taking away. But the widow and family will know what it is to have the protection of Modern Woodmen of America.

What this article about Otis proves is the opposite of what nearly all biographers have penned about Marilyn's family for years. Otis Monroe was not an irresponsible husband or father, in fact, this longtime membership signified that he instead cared about the future for Della, his daughter Gladys and son Marion, and providing for them financially. This sendoff into eternity also meant that he was cherished in the community at large and by fellow "Neighbors." At this stage, he was also surrounded with family in Los Angeles, including Della's uncle Newton Hogan, who was a mover and shaker in Los Angeles.

Marilyn Monroe Unveiled | A Family History

Photos also show Gladys and mother Della sophisticatedly attired, with photos by harbor locations and in sunny yards, snuggling with the family babies before Marilyn was born. Della's passport photo as "Della Grainger" shows a bespectacled lady with a strand of pearls around her neck and a fur coat draped over her shoulders. Later pictures of Della showed her in a chair lovingly holding granddaughter Norma Jeane, who delicately held her grandmother's hand with her tiny fingers. Norma Jeane appeared to wear a christening gown, and this photo may have been taken on this very occasion.

Later, biographers, especially Donald Spoto, slandered son Marion for his disappearance. And then Spoto wrongly attacked Jack, who was still living at the time that Spoto's book was published. Marilyn's family instead was beaten down in print, subjected to years of undeserved defamation.

After they had long been married, Marion and wife Olive were listed in the Santa Monica California City Directory for 1928, with Marion having been employed as a lifeguard.

"Mrs. Olyve Monroe" was listed as a registered Republican and housewife as a voter on 660 West Jefferson Street in 1928.

They had three children, John Otis Elmer "Jack" born April 29, 1925, Ida Mae born March 21, 1927 and Olive Elizabeth "Betty" born February 11, 1929. The family dynamics were shattered only a few months after young Olive's birth when Marion disappeared without a trace.

The branch of the Monroe family, including Gladys and brother Marion, had enjoyed times of togetherness. Photos show Gladys toddlers Norma Jeane and cousin Ida Mae, Marion and Olive romping on Santa Monica Beach with each other in bathing suits. Also in the beach photos, Gladys, Olive and the girls wore dresses and Marion was attired in a dress shirt and trousers. Gladys especially appeared radiant, as if her health woes were also far away from striking her.

No one to this day knows why Marion disappeared and to where. But he has been unfairly painted as a deadbeat who did not care for his family. Yet, he had a job, and according to paperwork, there were no marital problems and he was anticipated to return home and never did. Photos also show a man who enjoyed time with his wife and children, making his disappearance even more mystifying. Photos that had also been in Marilyn's own photo collection, show her mother in Hawthorne during the 1920s with her cousin, aunt and uncle Marion. On another day, Monroe sister-in-laws (Olive and Gladys) and daughters Ida Mae and Norma Jeane pose for a photo in pretty dresses once again. Rather than suggesting that Marion left on his own accord, perhaps past biographers should have taken a different stance and assumed that he may have instead disappeared due to circumstances beyond his reach, such as a murder, rather than a voluntarily missing person. Yet, biographers and fans alike have accepted the narrative and allowed Marion Monroe to be continually defamed over decades, and defamed him too when no one knows what really happened to him.

After his disappearance, Olive petitioned the court in 1935, noting that on November 20, 1929, Marion left home at 2 p.m. and told Olive he would return around 5:30 p.m., but was never heard from again. He was employed at that point with the Union Storage and Transfer Company with Joe Zerboni. The next day, she reportedly was in touch with the Bureau of Missing Persons. Olive petitioned not just Zerboni but Gladys (although at this point she was hospitalized and her address was named on Olive's court document as 549 E. Rhode Island in Hawthorne), the California Motor Vehicle Department in Sacramento and the United States Social Security Department.

Olive's mother Ida Martin enlisted the assistance of Westwood California's Shayer Detective Service, but the agency came up with no leads about Marion Otis Monroe.

Olive asked the court to declare Marion deceased because she had difficulty supporting the children, and was receiving some minor aid from the County Welfare Department. Declaring him dead would have helped her in receiving additional benefits.

On the 1930 Census, the Monroe children were residing with their grandmother, Ida Martin. Ida's son John also lived with them. Her mother Olive Henderson (also divorced) who was then 72 lived with the family too. Her industry was as a Christian Science Practitioner, the same as Ana Lower, who was Grace Goddard's aunt who took Marilyn and Gladys both under her wing.

Olive and Marion's children were all on the 1930 Census at ages five, three and one year and one month for Jack, Ida Mae and Olive. However, mother of the three children Olive was not listed on the census as a resident. Some have said she was a worker picking fruit at the time to earn an income.

Marilyn Monroe Unveiled | A Family History

On the 1940 Census Olive was the head of household at number 3265 Greenfield Avenue and as "WD" or "widowed" as her status. Her mother Ida Martin resided with her, as did son Jack and daughters Ida Mae and Olive, then ages 15, 13, and 11.

Both Olive and her mother would be documented at that address in 1940 as registered voters, both as Republicans, with Ida's employment as a housewife and Olive (then as "Olyve" as well as a "Mrs." with the full name of "Olyve L. Monroe") disclosed her occupation as a dressmaker. Additionally residing with them was "John E. Martin," Ida's son, who lived with Ida, her mother and the three children. John was also a registered Republican and his occupation a "salesman."

Interestingly enough, Marilyn told sister Berniece after they met in person for the first time that Olive had made "two white batiste blouses with handiwork" for her, though she claimed not to have been close to her cousins, who she referred to as Betty, Ida Mae and John, but pointed out how he was referred to as "Jack." Of course though, Marilyn had lived with her cousins, Aunt Olive and Ida Martin for a stint. Records show that Gladys's friend Grace Goddard paid monies to Ida Martin on Gladys's behalf when she was hospitalized, for room and board for Norma Jeane, known later to the world as Marilyn. Ida Martin was paid for nine months, from December 1937 through August 1938. Grace also reimbursed Ida for expenses in 1938 on February 14, April 30 and July 14. These monies eventually came from Gladys's savings from monies from her house and car sale, as well as other funds she held prior to her hospitalization.

Both mother Olive and daughters Ida and Olive, but not John, were shown again in the same neighborhood and residence as registered voters and occupations in 1942, 1944 and 1946.

In 1948, she was listed as "Mrs. Olyve L. Monroe" at 3654 Ocean View Avenue and a Republican, but her mother was no longer at the same residence or page (Ida Martin died in 1952). "Mrs. Olyve L. Monroe" registered to vote in 1950 and lived on 819 S. Irolo Street. And "Miss Olyve L. Monroe" was living in 1952 at 9430 Washington Boulevard in Los Angeles County.

On December 7, 1963, Olive remarried in Nevada to Ivan K. Saltzman, more than thirty years following Marion's disappearance. From then on, she took her second husband's last name, "Saltzman." Ivan and Olyve were tracked as residents of Oxnard California on 5540 West 5th Street in 1977 and 1980.

One of the difficulties that the Monroe family has especially endured have been the rumors that commenced in some books about a rape, namely in the Donald Spoto book.

According to Roy Turner, who had traced some of Marilyn's genealogy and interviewed Ida Mae himself, Spoto had misinterpreted his notes to the dismay of Ida Mae.

Though Spoto claimed that Marilyn was sexually assaulted, taking the accounts from Norman Rosten and Eleanor "Bebe" Goddard, while Marilyn's first husband Jim Dougherty claimed she was a virgin when they married, Spoto fingered Jack Monroe as the perpetrator in an accusatory and derogatory way. This was while Jack Monroe was still alive when the book was published in 1993.

First, there were claims that Doc Goddard, Grace Goddard's husband had sexually abused Marilyn. However when Marilyn was married to Jim Dougherty, letters between Grace Goddard and Marilyn (then Norma Jeane) were gushing and loving, with Marilyn asking Grace to send love to "Daddy," meaning Doc Goddard.

"I shall be so happy to see you again dear and to see Daddy and Bebe, because I love you all so much," Norma Jeane wrote to Grace in 1945.

This was the man that Spoto claimed so violently assaulted her without acknowledging the adoring correspondence from Marilyn herself to Grace and Doc.

Of Jack he introduced, "The second episode involved a violation that was even more traumatic than Doc Goddard's crude and abusive advance."

Spoto elaborated that before Marilyn's twelfth birthday in 1938 "a cousin forced her into some kind of violent sexual contact."

"The importunate cousin," he penned, "was thirteen-year-old Jack, of whose later life nothing is known; by his twenties he seems to have imitated his father's disappearing act. The incident reinforced her sense that she was desired as an object, but she was left feeling abused; she was after all only eleven years old."

Marilyn Monroe Unveiled | A Family History

Jack Monroe is Marilyn Monroe's first cousin.

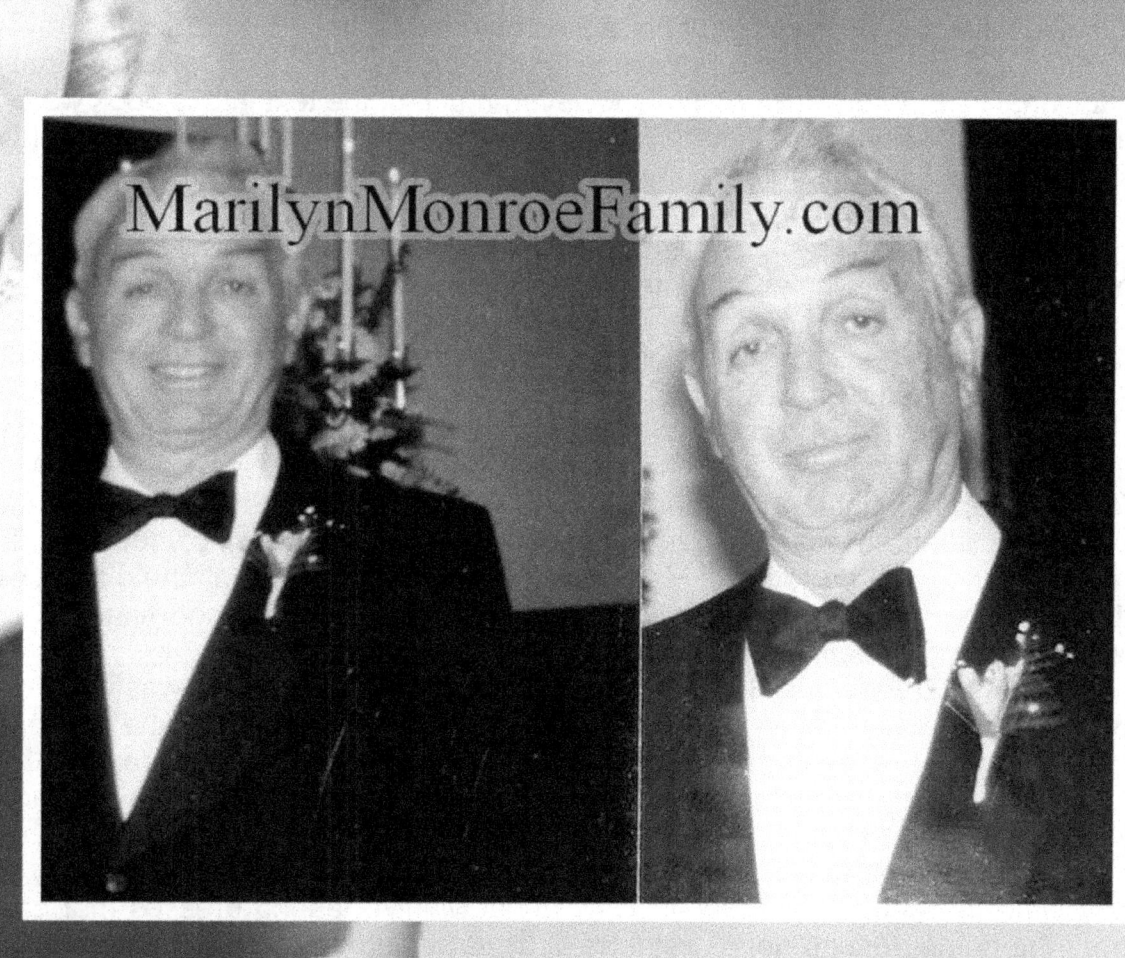

Marilyn Monroe Unveiled | A Family History

Part of the problem that Roy Turner told one of the authors of this book was that in his interview with Ida Mae, notes that he furnished to Donald Spoto for his book, Ida Mae referenced how Marilyn told her of a sexual assault she endured and how she "bathed obsessively for days after that."

Ida Mae never referenced her brother in any way as the assailant who harmed Norma Jeane. She was apparently furious to learn that she was misquoted.

Author Michelle Morgan also covered the topic in her 2007 book noting "the raft of stories and rumors have hurt the family to such a degree that Jack Monroe refuses all requests for interviews."

In her updated versions, Morgan removed all references to the rape topic, but addressed the Monroe family as having upset Norma Jeane with accusations of tearing a dress and making her bathe last in filthy water.

What is known and is something that one of the authors of this book, Jennifer Jean Miller, previously noted about the topic in her book on Marilyn is that in Marilyn's 1962 address book, Jack Monroe was the only cousin who was listed in the book itself, with this book now in the hands of memorabilia collector Ted Stampfer.

A typed message to "Mrs. DeMaggio" from November 8, 1954, also in Stampfer's collection, reads: "Her cousin Jack Monroe called from Jacksonville, Florida. Please call at VE 8-7202."

Apparently, the two cousins had contact with one another that continued into adulthood. Why would Marilyn remain in contact with cousin Jack if he had assaulted her? That makes little sense. She could have erased him from her life, but she chose not to, and he remained the only cousin in her address book.

For the record, in spite of what Spoto wrote about Jack disappearing, he in fact did not. Records show he was married in Duval County Florida in 1952 where Jacksonville is the county seat. Children were born in this family line and grandchildren later emerged. Jack honorably served in the military as well, though Spoto never bothered to check into his whereabouts and continued to defame him.

Other sordid and untrue tales have emerged from Marilyn's childhood, some from the Hollywood machine and others potentially uttered from her lips, about the Monroe family abusing her. Marilyn did also cover up the truth about her ancestry and relatives. But the actual provenance of *My Story* is so muddied, as the authors will describe later in this book it is hard to believe that these were Marilyn's additional true words. It is doubtful, however, much of the text in this book were Marilyn's own words because the manuscript generated from her conversations with writer Ben Hecht was never supposed to be released in book form. His widow also countered "the finished product" did not resemble her husband's own manuscript.

Many of Marilyn's childhood "memories" were also implanted and reinforced by the Freudians and Lee Strasberg, who also mentally controlled her while she was alive and hijacked her legacy after her death. Strasberg purposely misinterpreted Marilyn's will, claiming he exerted her right of publicity (which a judge told Strasberg's heir, his third wife Anna Strasberg, that the right died with Marilyn in 1962 and she had no access to it). Lee Strasberg was also behind the publication of *My Story*. Milton Greene was the one who claimed it was the manuscript and Marilyn had given it to him to "do the right thing" during her partnership with him, though they were not partners when Marilyn and Ben Hecht forged an agreement together and Marilyn and Milton Greene's partnership ended badly many years before her death. It was important then, and remains important now for the heirs of these grifters to retain the incorrect narrative of Marilyn's life. That narrative is that she did not have a family and that they became her surrogate family. This is how they have retained financial control over Marilyn's legacy since her death.

In the Greene and Strasberg book, "Marilyn" claims that she was in one household where she was forced to bathe last in putrid water. The book also alleges that she was berated for flushing the toilet at night because of the expense. Additionally that an old great-grandmother over 100 years old (Olive Henderson taking the fall) sent Marilyn back to the orphanage "in disgrace" for tearing a dress. This is assumed to be the Monroe household, and is a runaway tale that has remained.

The Monroe family has continued to absorb the heat from these tales, having been the ones that were erroneously accused of lying about Marilyn tearing dresses that earned her banishment from the home, forcing her to bathe in dirty water and of course, the rape. Both the Monroe family

Marilyn Monroe Unveiled | A Family History

(including Ida Martin and her mother) and Ida Bolender's family had been wrongly written about as abusive.

In discussing Monroe relatives further in this chapter, readers will learn that these ancestors, like the Hogans were wrongly smeared, and were upstanding people in society.

Returning to the immediate childhood family of Otis Monroe (Marilyn's maternal grandfather), he had two siblings, Thomas Allen, often known as "Allen" and John Alva. Both of these gentlemen, who were Marilyn's great uncles had their own lives as productive members of society, as well as their own families.

Jacob's and Mary's first child was Thomas Allen Monroe. Thomas was born on October 14, 1859 in Marion County Indiana and like his brother Otis, he had his own connections to the State of California in his later years. He was the first of the Monroe brood who was on the census with the family in 1860 when they lived in Hendricks County Indiana's Brown Township. In June 1860, Thomas was only seven months old and father Jacob worked as a farmer.

According to the book *History of Hendricks County Indiana* published in 1885, Jacob Monroe was one of the volunteers from Indiana who mustered on July 29, 1862 as a Private in Company K, as part of the 70th Indiana Infantry Regiment during the Civil War. He was discharged at the end of the war on June 8, 1865. This fact about Jacob is also referenced in the book The Seventieth Indiana, from 1900. He served while wife Mary was home with Thomas, and less than a year after the war ended, son Otis would be born. Jacob was involved with the regiment nearly the entire time it was active (it became active a week prior to his mustering), and left Indiana on August 13, 1862, under Colonel Benjamin Harrison, and then Lieutenant Colonel Samuel Merrill. Benjamin Harrison would later become the President of the United States in 1889. There were skirmishes throughout Kentucky and Tennessee that the regiment participated in, continuing through the Carolinas, and some active engagements including the Siege of Atlanta, Sherman's March to the Sea and the Carolinas Campaign. Jacob's service concluded exactly with the most of the group when his term expired on June 8. Prior to that, he was able to join his regiment and company for the Grand Review of the Armies in Washington, DC in May 1865, to celebrate the Union victory, before Jacob headed home to Mary and Thomas.

Who would have ever known that one of Marilyn Monroe's great-grandfathers served honorably in the Civil War, having a chance to celebrate victory?

In 1870, Jacob, Mary and the boys were now living in Indianapolis. Thomas was 11, Otis was five, and the toddler of the household, John was then two.

During the 1880 Federal Census, Thomas would have been about 21 years old, but at the current time has not been located.

In 1885, he married Mary Louisa Rooke, a woman from England, who was born in 1865.

The special Kansas census from 1895 showed that Thomas now had a family, and lived with them in Emporia, which was in Lyon County, Kansas. He was then 35, and Mary was 30. He was identified as "T.A. Monroe" and she as "M.L. Monroe." By then, their two daughters were born, Otis's nieces, Nellie, then age eight, and Lottie, then age six. Nellie was erroneously identified on the 1895 census as "M. Monroe," and Lottie correctly as "L. Monroe."

The census in 1900 showed that at that point, the couple had been married for 15 years.

On the 1900 Census, they were counted in within Doyle Township in Marion County, Kansas. He was written as "T.A." Monroe and Mary as "M.L." His occupation was that of a railroad conductor. His death certificate reflected that he conducted for the Santa Fe Railroad.

The census also showed two daughters who were students. Both of the daughters were born in Kansas, with Nellie, then age 13 and Lottie, 11.

The paper trail takes the family from Kansas, to Kansas City in 1904, where they lived on 1716 Broadway, with Thomas A. Monroe as a conductor. In 1908, he was still working as a conductor and living with the family at 3231 E 6th Street. In 1909 through the 1913 city directories, the family home was still at this location. At the time of Thomas's death in 1942, he resided at 5436 Virginia Avenue, though he was at the Clark Convalescent Home on 2843 Troost Avenue for his final four years.

Nellie Monroe, Marilyn Monroe's first cousin once removed was one of the editors of her 1906 high school yearbook. She was a lifetime Los Angeles resident after growing up in the Midwest.

BOARD OF EDITORS

Carl Dixon, Irene Shepard, Edgar Farney, Nellie Monroe, Harold McKibben
Frank Wilkinson, Edwin Patterson, Chas. Byers, Hugh Pinkerton, Roy Dietrich
Harold Richards, Marion Fox, Homer Berger, Katherine King, John McCoy

Nellie and Lottie Monroe were sisters and both involved as officers of the Central Choral Club in their high school.

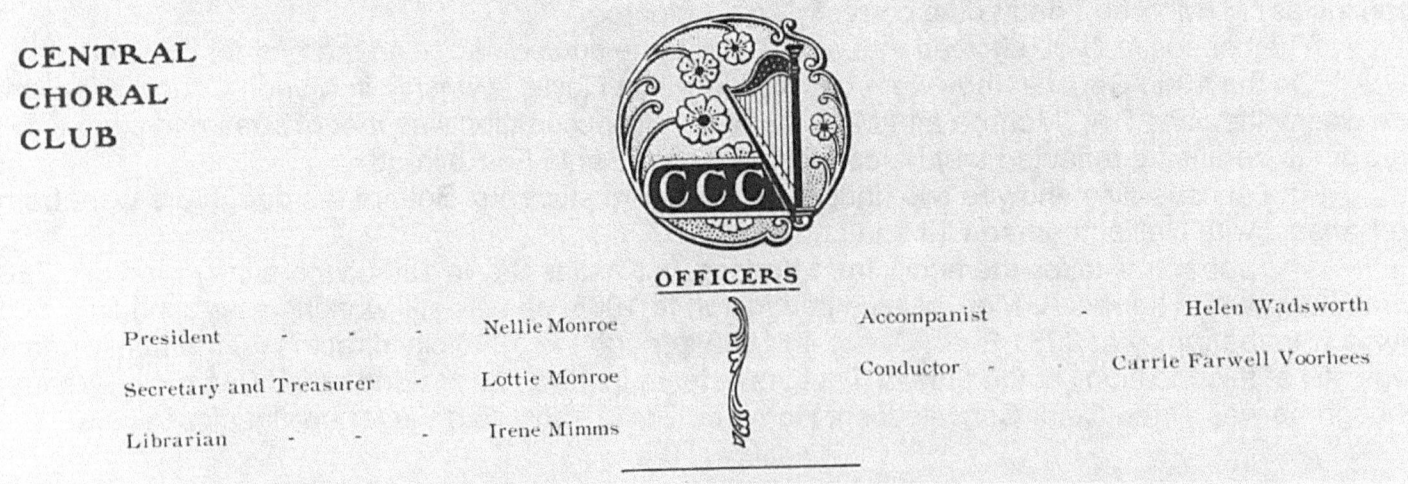

CENTRAL CHORAL CLUB

OFFICERS

President - Nellie Monroe
Secretary and Treasurer - Lottie Monroe
Librarian - Irene Mimms
Accompanist - Helen Wadsworth
Conductor - Carrie Farwell Voorhees

SOCIETY OF LITERATURE AND HISTORY

CENTRAL CHORAL CLUB
MEMBERS

Ambie McMican   Edith Wedge   Genevieve Roff   Katherine Siersdorfer   Esther Hughes   Jessie Briggs   Grace Dahn   Nellie Monroe
Edith Foster   Freda Dietrich   Ethel Kagy   Irene Mimms   Myrtle Molli   Estelle Rubin   Edith Barker   Ethel Darst   Carolyn Lewis
Grace Suiter   Hazel Brawner   Lela Lancaster   Lottie Monroe   Nellie Caleb   Hazell Chandler   Lou Bell Wherritt   Helen Wadsworth

MEMBERS.

First Sopranos: Gladys Greever, Zola Sweet, Lotta Dahn, Nellie Monroe, Pauline Post.

Second Sopranos: Irene Cozad, Mabel Bradbury, Edith Foster, Laura Campbell, Sadie Lowe, Irene Mimms, Ethel Darst, Isabel Barton.

First Altos: Mayme Roberts, Bertha Smith, Mary Noble, Bun Humphrey, Ora Davis, Helen Wadsworth.

Second Altos: Lottie Monroe, Elenore Canny, Anna Burris, Julia Wischropp, Edna Clark.

MUSIC

TO charm many with the grandeur or the sweet sympathy of a beautiful voice is the hard-earned reward of few aspirants for musical excellence. The years of study, although filled with the rich pleasure attendant upon conscientious labor, more often than not, culminate in disappointment and apparent failure. It is necessary that the person who enters upon the study of music should hold in mind certain vital principles. If he honestly lives up to these principles, then that study, while it may never accord fame, will, beyond a doubt, assure success—the success that is worth while, whose most essential attribute is satisfaction, untinged by disappointment or regret.

First of all, for the study of music, there must be a receptive mind, one that, though it does not, at first, appreciate Wagner or his "Parsifal," still is not unwilling to recognize the possibilities which are now beyond him and to follow even afar off an enthusiastic leader until those possibilities are within his grasp. The candidate for success, therefore, must cultivate a keen enjoyment of the best of music; he must determine that he will be satisfied with nothing but the best as he shall receive it from the testimony of cultured instructors. With this thought inspiring his efforts, he will ever persevere, earnestly applying his energies to grasping and assimilating the most beautiful and sublime in music, without despising, meanwhile, the labor necessary for perfect attainment.

But what is the most beautiful and sublime in music? Is it an educated understanding of harmony and thorough bass? Is it the power to execute, with the utmost precision,

This is a piece written by Nellie Monroe in 1906 about music.

the world's exquisite masterpieces? Is it the ability to sing a melody so that it shall satisfy all the requirements for accurate rendition? No. It should be a comfort, and it truly is, to the sincere lover of music to know that, even though he lacks the power of adequate expression of his emotions, there is, from the very fact of his love, a glorious prospect that he may yet achieve the highest in music. To perform the mental and physical gymnastics of music is, indeed, a rare accomplishment. Infinitely better, however, is that noble ability to attain and apply the vitalizing *spirit* of music, the spirit which cheers and comforts and sympathizes, which is able to discern the ever-present, though often undiscovered melodies of the universe—in the heart of a flower, in the busy market place, in the bosom of a friend. "Heart melodies are sweet, but those unheard are sweeter."

The privilege of becoming masters of these masterful soul melodies is the common heritage of all mankind. Attainment and use in the every-day life, of this atmosphere (the truly important phase in music study) becomes, then, alike the aim and the reward of every conscientious musician.

In truth, the study of music is an essential factor in the development of character, not so much in music that enriches the powers of the occasional genius, as the accompanying spirit of music that generates within the hearts of all, a keener love of the good and beautiful in life. Then, if at last, no world-wide tribute rewards the struggle in pursuit of the former, the contented joy which proclaims the accomplishment of the latter is sufficient recompense for all the labor spent.

NELLIE MONROE, '06.

"THO'TS FOR A YOUNG GIRL,

S VARIED and more compensating vocations come into prominence with developments in the scientific and in the business world, music as a genteel means of livlihood is gradually falling into disuse. For financially, mediocre music does not pay as well as in former years.

As requirements for distinction are becoming more and more strenuous, the profession is being relieved of the incapable who follow it for the money alone.

This elimination is being carried on further within the very field of music itself. Physical conditions limit, to a great extent, the number of the musically excellent. Vocal study, it is true, is often recommended for people who have lung trouble, but, generally, the attendant strain on the nervous system is such as is compatible only with a strong, sound physique. Too, unfavorable home environments, the financial question, or even limitations in a good voice (in the vocalist), or a combination of these difficulties, cause many to drop out of the race for musical distinction.

After taking an honest survey of the external conditions, the girl looking on music as a vocation would do well to examine herself to see if she fulfils the two internal requirements, absolutely necessary for success: namely, the intellectual, and the artistic.

On the intellectual element of musical study, the young girl cannot place too high an estimate. She cannot learn too early that there is

LOOKING ON MUSIC AS A VOCATION"

no stability in mere talent or a good ear for music. Intelligent perseverance and honest work are important in the development of a successful musician; and on them is dependence chiefly to be placed. Intimate acquaintance with the works of the masters of music is an aid the girl with a keen appreciation of the value of intellect in music will not neglect. She will read of their lives, their purposes, their philosophies; she will hear good artists perform, even at personal sacrifice, because she realizes the spur such things are, both to the ambition and to the intellect.

The other requisite which the aspiring young girl must comply with, and that, innately, is artistic temperment. As voice without intellect is insufficient, so intellect without temperment is dead. Artistic susceptibility is indispensable to success. The songs that are loved most are the ones that some singer has brought into living reality by the power of a mighty and sympathetic soul. So lives that beautiful aria from St. Paul, "The Lord is Mindful of His Own," through Mme. Schumann-Heink's soulful interpretation of it.

Then, if to all these essential attributes, both within and without herself, the girl will add sincerity, sincerity in her allegience not to the public but to music, ever, bright things are in store for her, from the view-point of the world probably;—from her own view-point surely, in the conscious joy of being a laborer in a beautiful and elevating work.

N. M.

Nellie Monroe, Gladys Monroe's first cousin and Marilyn Monroe's first cousin once removed, wrote this piece about music as a career in 1906.

Marilyn Monroe Unveiled | A Family History

Other relatives on Marilyn's family tree were, coincidentally living in Kansas City as well during this time, from the Hogan family. Technically, these two family lines were related by marriage, because of the union between Otis Monroe and Della Hogan. Virginia Sellars (Otis Monroe's mother-in-law) and her children were in the 1899 Directory on 1634 Summit. In 1901, the directory showed that Virginia and son James lived at 400 Landis Court. Two years later, she and James were at 604 W 14th Street. Myrtle Hogan, Virginia's and Tilford's daughter (Otis's sister-in-law), later known as Myrtle Mathey, then Myrtle Myers, was also a longtime Kansas City resident, making a reappearance in city directories around 1910, at 1525 E. 11th. Virginia, aka Jennie was also located in city directories in the early 1920s, only five years before her death in 1927. In 1921, she was at 414 Lawton Place, which was Myrtle's home address with second husband Lewis. In 1922, she resided at 4236 Wyoming. Myrtle later lived on 1125 W. 41st Street and then later on 4109 Roanoke Road.

Thomas and Mary Monroe's house in the 1940s at 5436 Indiana Avenue and Myrtle (Otis's sister-in-law) and Lewis Myers's house in 4109 Roanoke Road, were only less than five miles apart.

Virginia, daughter Myrtle and son-in-law Lewis are all interred in Kansas City's Mount Moriah Cemetery.

Nellie and Gladys were the first cousins of Gladys and Marion Monroe, as well as the first cousin once removed of the children in Marilyn's generation.

Nellie M. Monroe was born on December 13, 1886. Her younger sister Lottie was born in 1888. The two girls were very involved during their school days in music. The sisters were featured in the Kansas City Central High School Yearbook in 1905.

The sisters were in the yearbook together as part of the Society of Literature and History.

Like their first cousin once removed Marilyn Monroe, both Nellie and Lottie had affinities for literature, music and writing. In 1905, Lottie was noted in the yearbook as a member of the Second Alto section, while older sister Nellie was a First Soprano. Nellie, a member of the class of 1906 at her high school, wrote a piece for the yearbook about the study of music, which offers a reader insight into the love of the arts that the Monroe family appreciated.

"The privilege of becoming masters of these masterful soul melodies is the common heritage of all mankind," she wrote. "In truth, the study of music is an essential factor in the development of character, not so much in music that enriches the powers of the occasional genius, as the accompanying spirit of music that generates within the heart of all, a keener love of the good and beautiful in life."

In 1906, Nellie was the editor of the Art section of her yearbook, *The Centralian*. Ironically that year, Nellie wrote the piece in the Art section on music as a vocation for young women, a thoughtful writing about how a young girl knows she is suited to follow the career path in music. One must wonder if Marilyn ever had an opportunity to read her cousin's insightful thoughts on the topic, which are in the photo in this book, and identified with the writer's initial's "N.M." That same year, Nellie was the President of the Central Choral Club and her sister Lottie, following in her elder sister's footsteps as the Secretary and Treasurer. Nellie's 1906 senior portrait in the editor section radiates sophistication and a gentle beauty that weaves its way through the women in both the Hogan and Monroe sides of Marilyn's genealogy.

Nellie married two years following high school to Dr. William Day Moore in Kansas City on September 16, 1908. William, a Topeka resident was seven years her senior at the time of the marriage, born on March 14, 1880 in Kansas. By the 1920 Census, Nellie and William relocated to the Los Angeles area and lived in the San Pedro District of Los Angeles City on 565 W. 40th Street, a modest residence near San Pedro's coast. He was a physician in his own practice. By then, they had two sons, both born in California. Their elder son was William D., Jr., then close to three years old, and Byron A., just under one year old. William was born on February 13, 1917. His brother Byron was born on January 18, 1919.

The directory for the California Board of Medical Examiners of 1919 has Dr. William Day Moore's office located at 329 8th Street in San Pedro. He earned his degree from Washington University in St. Louis in 1908. He was also the M.D. Health Officer for San Pedro, but the California State Journal of Medicine noted in 1922, he "resigned in order to give his entire time to his private practice."

Otis Monroe's niece Lottie married a banking executive named Percival Adam. He received an employment promotion in 1921.

P. A. ADAM RESIGNS; TO RETURN TO K. C.

RESIGNATION AS A VICE PRESIDENT OF CONQUEROR TRUST IS EFFECTIVE.

P. A. Adam, a vice president of the Conqueror Trust Company, resigned yesterday to accept a position with the Fidelity National Bank and Trust Company of Kansas City. He will leave Joplin at 11 o'clock this morning for central Kansas in connection with his new position.

Although Adam's resignation was effective immediately, he had made known his intention to officials sometime previously and it came as no surprise to them.

Returns to Former Position.

In becoming connected with the Kansas City institution, Adam resumes a connection broken four and a half years ago when he became identified with the Conqueror Trust Company. He was with the Kansas City bank twelve years.

William Houk, president of the Conqueror Trust Company, said last night that Adam's position probably would not be filled before the first of the year when the board of directors meets.

Adam will make the trip to central Kansas in his motor car.

Mrs. Adam will leave this morning for California, accompanying her mother, Mrs. Allen Monroe, who is going to that state for her health. Mrs. Adam will be in California two months, after which she will join her husband in Kansas City.

Mr. Adam was prominent in church affairs here. He is a member of the Presbyterian church and president of the board of trustees of that congregation.

He is treasurer of the Loyal Order of Moose lodge and a director and treasurer of the Missouri Storage Battery Works.

Marilyn Monroe Unveiled | A Family History

Dr. Moore dedicated his lifetime to medicine, with even his tombstone referring to him as "Wm Day Moore, MD."

The location on the 1920 census where the Monroe/Moore clan resided was approximately a 20-mile distance from the Hawthorne neighborhood where Norma Jeane would spend her earliest years with the Bolenders and her mother, Gladys.

In 1930, the family was living at 402 Meyler Street, less than three miles from the other home in San Pedro. This was actually slightly closer to where Marilyn and Gladys, Nellie Moore's first cousins, were living. This home was on a more expansive lot in Central San Pedro. The family was recorded in this home, one that they owned, in the 1940 census. William was now 60 and still employed as a physician, now noted for the Board of Education. Nellie was 53. Son William, 23, was living with his parents, while younger son Byron had already moved out.

William's work with the Los Angeles City Schools as a physician was confirmed in 1942, when he registered for the draft in April 1942. He was then 62, and the residence with Nellie was the same as 1940. His work address was the Los Angeles Chamber of Commerce Building, located between First and Second Streets, on Broadway. By chance, this building was located in Los Angeles on the same street as the Copp Building, another Broadway building that was owned by other members of Marilyn's family through marriage on the Hogan side, the Copp family (Ethel Hogan's spouse was Joseph Copp).

In the meanwhile, Nellie's younger sister Lottie had moved on in her life, and married too. On October 14, 1914, she married Percival A. Adam, 28, while she was 25.

While residing in the Kansas City area near her parents, Lottie and her father Thomas "Allen" Monroe (Otis's brother) and mother Mary, still had a connection to California, because of Nellie. In 1921, Percival made headlines in the *Joplin Globe*, the paper for Joplin, Missouri, indicating that he was departing from his job at the Conqueror Trust Company, where he was Vice President, to return to a job he had held with the Fidelity National Bank and Trust Company in Kansas City. He had worked with Conqueror for four and a half years, while prior to that, he had been with Fidelity National Bank for 12.

The article also indicated that Percival was a member of the Presbyterian Church in Joplin, as well as on the board of trustees for the church. He was also the treasurer for the local Loyal Order of the Moose, and director and treasurer for the Missouri Storage Battery Works.

The news report also provides information about Lottie's activities and reads:

> Mrs. Adam will leave this morning for California, accompanying her mother, Mrs. Allen Monroe, who is going to that state for her health. Mrs. Adam will be in California two months, after which she will join her husband in Kansas City.

It is evident that both of these women were devoted daughters. Lottie lived with her parents, according to the 1910 census, when they resided at 3233 E. 6th St. The 1920 census, reflects that she and Percival were residing at 95 Inger Place in Joplin, Missouri, and confirmed he was the bank's vice-president. Lottie's occupation was that of a homemaker, since the census indicated she was not employed outside of the home. He was 33 and she was 31.

A special census taken in 1925 shows the couple was residing in Kansas in Holton, with his career in banking and hers as a housewife. He was 38 and she 36. She was documented by the name "Charlotte M. Adam."

Lottie and Percival did not have any children, according to the paper trail.

The 1930 census places them back in Kansas City, at 5035 Troost Avenue, with his employment as an accountant for a storage company. Current real estate records describe the residence as part of a "three-story, symmetrical three-bay domestic building built in the period 1910-1919." It is a stone and brick building, with the original windows still retained, and described as a "colonnaded apartment" style of architecture, which is classified as historic architecture.

Marilyn Monroe Unveiled | A Family History

In 1940, their residence was 5436 Virginia Avenue, another colonnade brick building. Percival was 53 and Lottie 51, and he was still working in the role of accountant in the "household storage" industry. However, there was an interesting exception noted in that Thomas, then 80 and Mary, 75, were living with them. The census noted in 1935 that Thomas and Mary's residence then had been in San Pedro, the city where daughter Nellie lived.

Lottie and Percival's 1930 residence at Troost Avenue was approximately a three-mile distance from another Kansas City resident and relative by marriage, Myrtle Myers. Myrtle was Otis's sister-in-law and Lottie his niece. In 1940, while Thomas "Allen" and Mary were living with Lottie and Percival Myrtle was situated about four miles away at 4109 Roanoke Road. Coincidentally, Myrtle had another relative by marriage named Nelli, a daughter-in-law who lived with her stepson William, also in Kansas City in the same neighborhood.

Sadly, on December 7, 1942, Thomas Allen passed away at the Clark Convalescent Home at 2843 Troost Avenue in Kansas City. He was buried in the Maplewood Memorial Lawn Cemetery in Emporia Kansas. On his death certificate, as well as on his headstone, he was referred to as "Allen," and was nearly two months passed the age of 83. The informant at the time of his death was Mary, residing at 5436 Virginia Avenue, evidently where Lottie and Percival still resided. His cause of death was "acute dilation of heart," as well as "old age" and "general arteriosclerosis."

The next to pass away was the first of Lottie's and Nellie's generation, and that was Lottie's husband Percival. He died in Kansas City's St. Joseph Hospital on September 10, 1949. He was 62-years-old and passed from a cerebral hemorrhage, as well as "arterial hypertension." He had been employed at A.B.C. Fireproof Warehouse, which his occupation was then listed as "secretary." He and Lottie, who was the informant at his death, lived at 300 West Armour Boulevard, a stately brick apartment building.

An eerie coincidence is that just three days earlier, Myrtle Myers had also passed away at Kansas City General Hospital, on September 7, 1949, from rectal cancer.

Myrtle Myers was laid to rest at Mount Moriah Cemetery on the day of Percival's death, and Percival, the same cemetery as Thomas in Emporia. As both of these deaths were reported, Marilyn Monroe's star was just beginning to rise. Myrtle was Marilyn's great-aunt and Percival, her first cousin once removed by marriage.

The Kansas City Times reported the news on June 22, 1954 that "Mrs. Allen Monroe Dies." The paper shared the information on a Tuesday, and Mary died the previous Friday was June 18. Mary was then 90, and considered a former Kansas City resident. Based on the news article, Mary was then residing in San Pedro, where she died at Nellie's home. She had lived in Kansas City for 38-years before moving to San Pedro. She had a brother, George, who was living in Rhode Island, and then Lottie, at 424 West 35th Street. Lottie was then 66, and her sister, 68. Mother Mary was also buried in the Maplewood Memorial Lawn Cemetery. The family's request at the time of Mary's passing was that no flowers be sent.

Both of the sisters, Marilyn Monroe's first cousins once removed, would coincidentally pass away in 1971, only a month apart from each other. Though the papers reported that Nellie was still living at the time of Lottie's death on Friday, June 11, 1971, the California Death Index shows that Nellie M. Moore, born December 13, 1886 in Kansas, died on May 19 of that year in Los Angeles. Lottie, like her father, mother and husband, was laid to rest on Tuesday, June 15 during a graveside service at the Maplewood Memorial Lawn Cemetery. She had been residing at a nursing home in Olathe, Kansas, though her address was still at 424 West 35th Street in Kansas City. She was described as a member of the Second Presbyterian Church, and a Red Cross volunteer. Lottie died at age 82. Nellie, who was six months shy of turning 85, was buried at the Green Hills Memorial Park, Rancho Palos Verdes, in California. Her epitaph is simply marked "Mother." Husband William Day Moore, MD, outlived Nellie by almost three years, passing away on April 15, 1974. He is buried at the same cemetery.

While there was yet another Monroe generation living in California at the same time as Marilyn, and the authors will delve into them later in the chapter, Thomas Allen and Otis had one remaining sibling, who also made his way to California, after residing in Iowa for most of his adult life. He was brother John Alva Monroe, born in Indiana on July 28, 1868. John was also Gladys's uncle and Marilyn's great uncle. When he made his way to California, he ended up in Long Beach, residing at one point at 3446 Cerritos Avenue with wife, Florence in the early 1950s, then 3539 Olive Avenue at his death in 1959, less than 20 miles from where his niece, Nellie, had lived in San Pedro in the 1940s.

As readers will learn overall, Marilyn was surrounded with relatives throughout the country, as well as in the Los Angeles area, though she was advised by the Hollywood and New York elite to disregard her family. Later, it was her "friends" in New York who hijacked the role of family, from Marilyn's blood relatives.

As the third child of Jacob Monroe and Mary Appleton (Marilyn's great-grandparents) and born on July 28 1868 in Indiana, he squeaked onto the census in 1870 with his parents and brothers in Indianapolis. John was only two years of age at that time. With his mother's remarriage following his father's death, he moved along with she and her brother into his stepfather's home, like Otis, since he appeared with them there on the 1880 census from Chetopa, Kansas, when he was 11. However, he was only identified by the name, "A. Monroe."

In 1894, he married Florence Thomas, born in 1876, and by 1900, they were located on the census in city of West Point, in Lee County, Iowa. By this stage, they had one child, Ervin Monroe, then five years old. At this time, he was employed as a farmer. The following year, his son, Lloyd Monroe was born.

In 1910, they were living in Grant Township, in Buena Vista County, Iowa and were working in the farming industry. Grant Township clocked in on the census in 2000 with 297 residents. Son Ervin, Marilyn Monroe's first cousin once removed (he was her mother Gladys's first cousin), then 15, was counted in on the census as employed in the farming industry, as a home farmer. Thomas was classified in working as a "general farmer." Lloyd and Florence were also counted in on the census but without occupations (Lloyd was then nine years old).

The unique point about this census is there was a "hired man," then 18, by the name of Milton Andros on there. Milton Andros was accounted for twice in that census, once where he lived and once

Cordelia Monroe, the spouse of Marilyn's first cousin once removed Ervin Monroe, worked at this department store.

where he worked. He worked with John's family, but he was also related by marriage on the Hogan

128	21	Monroe, John	Head	M	W	49
		— Florence	wife	F	W	33
		— Ervin	son	M	M	15
		— Lloyd	son	M	M	8
		Andrus, Milton	Hired man	M	W	18

side, since he was now Otis and Della Monroe's nephew (the child of Della's sister, Dora).

In 1920, John had switched industries and like his brothers, now was part of the railroad laborer, at age 51. By this stage, they resided in Winthrop Minnesota, within Sibley County, and owned their own home, which they were mortgaging. Today, even this city enumerated at 1,399 residents on the 2010 census. Florence, 42, was on the census, and son Lloyd, 19, then employed as a mechanic.

In 1940, John and Florence returned on the census, located now in Estherville, in Emmet County, Iowa, a residence where they had reportedly been residing in as well during 1935. John was 71, and Florence, 60. They had two residents with them, who were in a few places too on this census, son Lloyd, 40, and grandson William, 15. Lloyd had divorced his first wife, and remarried around the time of the census. Grandson William was their son Lloyd's child.

At least by the early 1950s, John, like his brothers Thomas and Otis, had made his way to California. John and his wife Florence, showed up on the Long Beach City Directories in 1951 and 1953, while only slightly geographically north, John's great-niece, Marilyn Monroe, was catapulting into fame.

Within a month of Marilyn making headlines with her marriage to Joe DiMaggio on January 14, 1954, her great-aunt Florence Monroe passed away in Long Beach on February 9, 1954, and was buried on February 12.

Those who opened up their newspapers in the Long Beach area on Christmas Day, 1959, learned from the *Independent* that John Monroe, Marilyn Monroe's great uncle, of 3538 Olive Avenue had passed away two days prior on December 23. Though others outlived him, those listed in his obituary included his son Ervin, his grandson John E. Monroe, and his niece, Stella Lady. Stella was Florence's niece, also living in Long Beach, who had settled there as a longtime resident with a family of her own. Stella's mother who was Florence's sister, also lived in Long Beach on Olive Avenue. John's funeral took place the following day and he was laid to rest in the same cemetery as his spouse and many of the other Monroe relatives, Green Hills Memorial Park in Rancho Palos Verdes. Stella, an extended member of the Monroe clan through marriage, would also start her eternal rest there in 1986.

There were yet other generations of Monroes who belonged to Gladys's and Marilyn's eras.

Thomas and Florence had two sons, with the first, Ervin Wesley, born April 17, 1895. Ervin was Gladys's first cousin, and Marilyn's first cousin, once removed. By 1920, Ervin had settled in Minnesota, in Sibley County's Winthrop, with his first wife, Cordelia Olivia Anderson, a Minnesota native with Swedish ancestry. They were married on May 24, 1916. His draft registration for World War I in 1917 showed that they were then married, and she was fully dependent on Ervin for support, with his work as a repairman in the Winthrop Canning Company. His draft also gives details about his physical appearance, which indicated a medium build, light brown hair and gray eyes.

Sadly for Ervin, his wife Cordelia was ill, and passed away from cancer on October 24, 1932. A news report described the church as "crowded with friends and neighbors who had known and highly respected this lady." At the time of her death, they were residing in Little Sand Lake, and previously had been in Park Rapids. She worked in the ladies' clothing department at the Glantz Brothers Department Store in Park Rapids, Minnesota.

Marilyn Monroe Unveiled | A Family History

The Park Rapids Enterprise further described Cordelia, Marilyn's first cousin once removed by marriage, as follows in the October 27, 1932 obituary:

> Mrs. Monroe, having a most pleasant personality, made friends with all with whom she came in contact and their home at the lake was the scene of many happy gatherings among the young folks.

It was in August 1931, the paper said, that after surgery there were hopes she would recover from her illness, but later that month, "her condition was found to be so serious that no hopes were given as to her recovery. She was most patient and uncomplaining during her last illness, being resigned to her fate."

Ervin did not face this tragedy alone, and the obituary noted that in addition to her family, John and Florence, then still living in Estherville, Iowa and Elvin's brother Lloyd Monroe, of Spencer, Iowa, were in attendance at Cordelia's service.

About two years after Cordelia's death, Ervin picked up the pieces and married for a second time to Agnes L. Berlin, on February 8, 1934, back in his hometown of Estherville, Iowa, where Agnes resided. It was a second marriage for her too. The papers reported that the couple married at the Methodist parsonage, enjoying the wedding and then a dinner reception with guests. There was also a wedding shower for Agnes.

Currently, the information available for Ervin shows that he and Agnes moved to Park Rapids in 1934, and then was found in the city directory for Davenport, Iowa, as a machinist in 1944, living on 637 Kirkwood Boulevard. His last known residence was at the time of his death in 1987, Olney Springs, Colorado.

Ervin also had a younger brother named Lloyd, Otis's nephew, Gladys's first cousin, and Marilyn Monroe's first cousin once removed. Lloyd was born in Iowa on August 5, 1899, coincidentally the same day 63 years later that the world would learn about Marilyn's untimely death.

Lloyd was only nine-years-old when he was living on his family's farm in Iowa, and recorded on the census with Milton Andros, the relative by marriage from the Hogan side who worked for his family.

In 1920, Lloyd still lived with his parents, and was 19, and working as a mechanic.

By 1921, he was married to Henriette Lydia Timmerman, a woman from Minnesota. That year on March 24, he was recorded as crossing into Canada, with plans to farm in Humboldt, Saskatechewan, where his mother-in-law resided. A few months later on June 18, their son John Everett was born in Humboldt. Five years later, son William Lloyd was born on February 9, 1925.

The 1930 census in Clay County's Spencer Iowa showed that Lloyd also served in World War I. He served between 1918 and 1919. In 1930, he was working in the telegraph industry as a telegrapher. Lloyd was then 30, Henriette 29, John age eight, and William, age five.

By 1940, the family had relocated back to Estherville, Iowa, at least partially. Henriette, 40 and Lloyd were divorced, and she stayed behind in Spencer, living with her sister Virginia, and working as an office assistant in a doctor's office. Both John, 18 and William, 15 were counted on the census as occasional residents in their mother's household. In October of that year, Henriette applied for a marriage license with a man named Claude B. Robison 48, from Sioux Falls, South Dakota.

Lloyd, on the other hand, was like son William, counted on the census in two locations. First was with his parents, John and Florence Monroe in Estherville on 1701 Central Avenue, where he was noted as "divorced." However, there was a second location, where he was documented as a resident and William's third, on the same street but house number 432. He had remarried to a woman named Hilma. The two were both 39, and Hilma had a daughter named Lois, who was 16. Previously, Hilma had been married to a man by the name of Ralph Anderson, living in Gibbon, in Sibley County, Minnesota, the same location where Lloyd's brother Elvin had resided. In fact, Ralph was the younger brother of Cordelia, Elvin's first wife. In essence, Cordelia was Lois Anderson's aunt and she was Lloyd's stepdaughter. This was one of the many connections within the Monroe Family Tree.

Marilyn Monroe Unveiled | A Family History

In 1955, while Lloyd's first cousin once removed, Marilyn Monroe was a main headliner in every paper worldwide, in spite of popular misstatements from many biographers that her family never made the papers, Lloyd was given his own headline. On November 23, 1955 the *Estherville Daily News* in Estherville Iowa reported that Lloyd E. Monroe had passed away.

Lloyd had been an impatient at age 55 at the Veterans Hospital at Ft. Snelling in St. Paul Minnesota. He died the prior day from "a heart ailment and complications." His obituary sung of his accomplishments, including his work as a telegrapher for the Rock Island Railroad, with the railroad a career for many Monroe relatives. He had also been a station agent. Plus, even more interestingly, both Lloyd and Hilma operated the Monroe Cabins in Estherville, which were rental homes. However, in his final year of life, they were residing in Walker, Minnesota.

Lloyd's obituary showed that his father, John, Otis's brother, had outlived his son and was residing in Los Angeles, plus, he was the grandfather of two. His son John Everett Monroe, referred to as "Jack," was also stated as living in Los Angeles. A daughter was also listed, who was his stepdaughter Lois, identified as "Mrs. Kennedy" of Walker Minnesota.

The only one sadly missing was son William, aka "Billy," with whom the paper identified as "killed in World War II and was returned to Los Angeles for burial."

Lloyd Monroe was given a hero's sendoff to eternity in the Fort Snelling Memorial Cemetery, located at Fort Snelling in Minnesota. The Report of Interment indicated that he left the military with the rank of private, after having enlisted on February 28, 1918, and was discharged on April 11, 1919. He was laid to rest in grave number 824, and grave number 825 was reserved for later use for his widow, Hilma M. Monroe. Eventually, she was buried there on February 23, 1987, after having passed away on February 18 of that year, and was identified as "Wife of Monroe, Lloyd E."

There was yet another generation that could be considered Marilyn's contemporaries, as they were born within the Monroe family lines within ten years of Marilyn.

First were the children of Nellie (Monroe) Moore. Nellie resided near Marilyn with her husband Dr. William Day Moore throughout Marilyn's entire time on earth, having relocated to San Pedro as early as 1920. They had two sons, William Day Moore, Jr., born on February 13, 1917, and Byron A. Moore, born March 18, 1919. Nellie was Otis's niece, Gladys's first cousin and Marilyn's first cousin once removed. Her sons were Marilyn's second cousins.

William and Byron were both with their parents on the 1920 census, with William only two years old, and Byron less than one-year-old. *The San Jose State College* yearbook shows a handsome young graduate named William Moore, among education graduates in 1937. His specialty was "General Junior High." Later, William Day Moore married Wilma Beth McKinney on July 14, 1942 in Long Beach by a Unitarian Minister a month after Marilyn married her first husband Jim Dougherty, also in Los Angeles on June 19, 1942. He was then residing with his parents at 402 South Meyler Street in San Pedro, with his occupation listed as "U.S. Navy," with his wife Wilma Beth also a resident. Brother Byron was living in San Francisco at the time and signed the certificate as a witness.

William's brother Byron was born January 18, 1919. He and his brother were both living at home with their parents in 1930 at the Meyler Street home in San Pedro. At that time, William was 13 and Byron, 11. In 1937, the University of California at Berkeley's Omega Chapter of Phi Sigma Kappa showed a handsome young freshman among its membership named Byron A. Moore. Two years later, the same good-looking young man was featured among the sophomores of the same fraternity.

According to the 1940 census, Byron Moore was living up in San Rafael near San Francisco on the San Quentin State Prison Reservation, where his father-in-law, Ralph New was a police captain at the prison. Byron was 21, and his spouse Helen the same age.

His life path did show some travel between San Francisco and Hawaii in 1940, with some travel on April 17, 1940 between the two locations on the ship "Matsonia."

By 1946, Byron was divorced Helen and residing back with his parents in San Pedro. He applied for and was accepted for a certificate of staff registry as a Junior Assistant Purser with the Merchant Marine. His application reflected employment at Federated Metals in San Francisco as an accountant from March of 1940 to December of 1942, before he relocated to the same company in Los Angeles from January of 1943 through September of the same year. His job history showed work at Shell

An article about the return of soldiers who died abroad, including Marilyn's second cousin Sgt. William L. Monroe. His father Lloyd Monroe is also documented in the article.

Dec. 28, 1948 — Mason City Globe-Gazette, Mason City, Ia.

War II Dead Due to Arrive

North Iowans Among Bodies on Way Home

Washington—Among the bodies of 4,384 World war II dead due to arrive from Europe aboard the U. S. army transport Barney Kirschbaum are 76 Iowans, according to announcement by the department of the army.

Armed forces dead originally interred in temporary military cemeteries in France, Belgium, Holland and Luxembourg are among those being brought back to this country.

North Iowans in the list include the following, together with the next of kin:

Pvt. Orval R. Alden; Milton L. Alden, Thornton.

Pvt. Wayne W. Dale, Mrs. Nettie D. Felkey, Armstrong.

Pfc. Neil L. Gilbertson; Jane Gilbertson, Burr Oak.

Pfc. Royal A. Jacobs; Hezzie R. Jacobs, Rudd.

1st Lt. Alan R. Jacobson; Chris Jacobson, Britt.

Sgt. William L. Monroe; Lloyd E. Monroe, Estherville.

1st Lt. Robert L. Sill; Nina S. Christopher, Eagle Grove.

S/Sgt. Edwin E. Sowles; Mrs. Mary F. Sowles, Mason City.

2nd Lt. Robert L. Van Horn; Carl C. Van Horn, Hampton.

1st Lt. Jens T. Weiby, Jr.; Jens T. Weiby, Sr., Armstrong.

Chemical in Torrance California from October of 1943 to the time of his application in 1945, in the role of an expeditor, or the person who handled the shipping logistics. He received letters of recommendation for the post, including with a fellow employee of his from Shell Chemical Company.

On November 21, 1948, as Marilyn was making strides in her career slightly north of San Pedro, Byron was married in Long Beach for the second time to Sydell A. (Mador) Garrison. He was working as a salesman of concrete blocks and she, a bookkeeper in an appliance business. It was also her second marriage.

In 1951, the *Compton City Directory* unveiled that Byron and Sydell were living at 534 West Almond Street, only about 15 miles north of his parents. His cousin Marilyn's star was beginning to rise around this time, as she lived on 8573 Holloway Drive that year in West Hollywood with Shelley Winters, about an hour north of Compton, plus 611 North Crescent Drive with acting coach Natasha Lytess, in Beverly Hills.

Before his death on March 13, 1959, Byron would father at least one child. He lays in eternal rest with other Monroe relatives at the Green Hills Memorial Park in Rancho Palos Verdes, California, with "In Loving Memory" as his epitaph. Eventually, his father's sister, his mother and his father would also take their final rest near him.

John Alva Monroe, Otis's youngest brother, would eventually settle in the Long Beach area himself, and have two sons. John was Marilyn's great uncle, and his sons her first cousins once removed. His son Lloyd would have two boys too, who would be Marilyn's second cousins.

William Lloyd Monroe was the first of these boys, born in Sibley, Minnesota on February 9, 1925, slightly over a year prior to his famous cousin. William was Lloyd's child enumerated on the census in three places in 1940; with his mother,

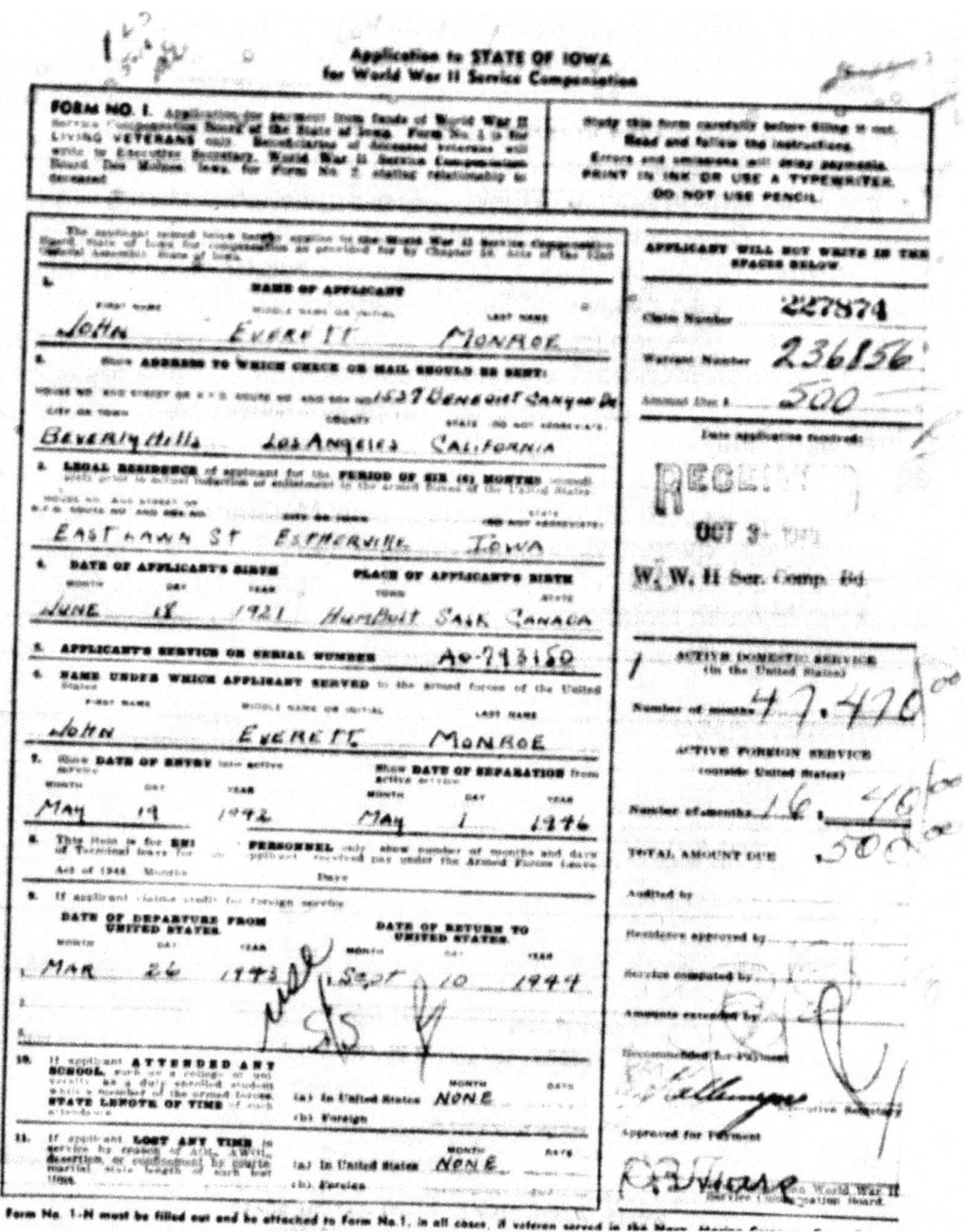

John Everett Monroe, Marilyn's second cousin, had his checks/mail send to 1527 Benedict Canyon, Beverly Hills, Los Angeles, California on September 28, 1949.

with his grandparents, and then with his father and Lloyd's second wife.

The Estherville Daily News in Estherville, Iowa reported on March 11, 1943 the names of the 18-year-olds who registered for the draft. William Lloyd Monroe registered in February of that year, his birthday month. He was killed in action during World War II on January 20, 1945.

The Department of Veterans Affairs remembers him as Sgt. William L. Monroe of the United States Army. *The Estherville Daily News* remembered him on May 26, 1947 as one of the young brave men from his area "who gave their lives in the service of their country in World War II."

The *Mason City Globe Gazette* reported on December 29, 1948 that Sgt. William L. Monroe, the son of Lloyd E. Monroe, was among North Iowans whose bodies were being returned to Washington, DC among 4,384 of the dead from Europe. Many of the deceased soldiers were buried temporarily in cemeteries in Europe during the war, in France, Holland, Belgium and Luxembourg. His body was among 76 from Iowa on the U.S. Army Transport, Barney Kirschbaum.

William L. Monroe was buried with honors in the Golden Gate National Cemetery near San Francisco, his white grave marker reading that he died with the 452 AAF Bomb Group in World War II.

William's younger brother John Everett Monroe was born on June 18, 1921 in Canada, nearly five years prior to his second cousin Marilyn Monroe.

Like his brother, he also honorably served in the military, enlisting on May 19, 1942, while his cousin Marilyn in Los Angeles was nearing the age of 16 and her first marriage to James Dougherty. He was a member of the Air Corps and ranked a Corporal, with one year of college under his belt. Records show after his enlistment a departure from the United States on March 26, 1943, with a return on September 10, 1944. His date of separation from the war was May 1, 1945. His final installment with the military was in Hammer Field in Fresno, with his address in Los Angeles as 1527 Benedict Canyon Drive in Beverly Hills in 1949 at the time of his paperwork. His cousin Marilyn was only about four miles away in 1949, living for a stint at the Beverly Carlton Hotel at 9400 West Olympic Boulevard. The distance between the two cousins became closer that year, while Marilyn lived at the home of Johnny Hyde, at 718 North Palm Drive, only about three miles from Marilyn's location.

John Everett Monroe, then known as "Jack," may have resided with a spouse named Violet, up in Monterey in 1947 and 1951. His employment also shows him potentially having worked in Monterey and Gilroy areas (Gilroy in 1968) in the meat industry. If he was married to Violet, the couple divorced by 1970.

What is known is that John married Gladys M. Grant on October 4, 1973 in Carson City, Nevada.

John "Jack" Everett Monroe died on February 8, 1988, more than two decades after his cousin Marilyn, in Rancho Mirage, Riverside County California. His wife, Gladys M. Monroe died on April 18, 2003. They are resting together in the same crypt at Green Hills Memorial Park, with the other Monroe relatives, including his mother Henriette Monroe, who also died in Riverside County in February 19, 1987.

CHAPTER SEVENTEEN

While Gladys Pearl Monroe, Marilyn Monroe's mother, was still a twinkle in her mother's eye, her aunt Dora (maiden Hogan) Andros was fighting a battle of her own.

Dora married into the powerful Louis Milton Andros family, a prominent San Francisco family, which reigned with doctors, lawyers and politicians. Their family was far-reaching with their power and Dora, who held the feisty Hogan fervor, was not taking the abuse she was doled out lying down.

Dora Olivia Hogan was born to Tilford Hogan and Jennie Nance in November 1874 in Chariton, Missouri. At 16, she married Lewis Milton Andros, 12 years her senior. In 1891, their son, Milton Stores Andros was born on September 20 in Tuscon, Arizona.

The couple commemorated their growing family with a portrait in a Tuscon photography studio, which, the sepia toned photo has been lost in time and misidentified for years as Tilford Hogan, Jennie Nance and one of their children. However, a descendant of Dora Hogan's has retained the family albums and has the original sleeve that the picture was placed in from the studio and then was retained with the family archives.

Daughter Georgia "Georgie" Marie was born in Pomona, California about five years later.

A "Court Brevity" from *The San Bernardino California Sun* from April 6, 1902, still almost two months away from the birth of Dora Andros' niece Gladys Pearl in Mexico, shows that she had filed for divorce from husband L.M. (often known as "Milton") Andros.

Later newspaper accounts would not print the sordid details about the dissolution of their marriage but it was later revealed it was due to Milton Andros' infidelity to Dora. He had made some money as an orchardist in California and then opened a saloon in the downtown Los Angeles Skid Row area, which brought about temptations for the husband and a rift in their marriage.

With the children now ages 9 and 6, it was too much to bear.

The reporters described the court event on June 17, only days after Dora's niece Gladys was born to her sister Della and brother-in-law Otis is Porfirio Diaz, Mexico, as "the star attraction of the usually quiet calendar."

In Andros vs. Andros Dora sought alimony and the enterprising reporter stated, "All had not been peaceful in the

---

The San Bernardino Daily Sun.

FRIDAY, JULY 18, 1902.

GRANTED A DIVORCE

ANDROS VS. ANDROS ENDED

Case Was One in Which the Evidence Was Heard Behind Closed Doors.

The Wife Gets the Children.

The notorious divorce case of Andros against Andros, which has dragged its slimy course through the Courts for the past two days, has at last been concluded and the plaintiff, Dora Andros, granted a separation from her husband and given the custody of the two minor children.

The case has been decidedly sensational at times, but the evidence was mostly of such a nature as to render it unprintable and every Court official in Judge Oster's department was glad when the last argument had been concluded and the decision rendered.

The parties are residents of Ontario, but the husband is at present a saloon keeper in the tenderloin district of Los Angeles, and it is because of the associations which he has formed in his new vocation that all the trouble in the Andros household arose.

THE CHICAGO DAILY TRIBUNE: THURSDAY, DECEMBER 10, 1903.

WILD CHASE AFTER CHILD

FATHER KIDNAPS LITTLE GIRL FROM SCHOOL YARD.

Playmates, Principal, Police, Carriage, and Automobile Join in Pursuit of Georgiana Andros, but Her Captors Elude All—Later Attorney Explains to Police That Case Is One of Disputed Control During Divorce Litigation.

While playing in front of the Goethe school, North Rockwell street and Fullerton avenue, before the morning session of school yesterday, Georgiana Andros, 8 years old, was kidnaped by two strangers who drove up to the school in a closed carriage.

One of the men rushed into the group of children, seized the child, and placed his hand over her mouth to stifle her cries. The other remained near the carriage, and when the child was safely inside ordered the driver to whip up his horses. As the carriage was driven away Prof. Charles S. Bartholf, principal of the school, was attracted by the screams of the other children and hurried to the street. With the school children following at his heels he started in pursuit of the carriage.

Many Vehicles Join in Chase.

The police of the Atrill street station, a block away, were notified, and a patrol wagon filled with policemen was sent in pursuit of the carriage. A policeman in a borrowed buggy, the driver of a milk wagon, and a physician in an automobile joined in the chase. After driving for several blocks along Fullerton avenue the driver of the carriage turned down a side street and eluded his pursuers.

The kidnaped child is the daughter of Mrs. Charles Bruce, 1749 Milwaukee avenue. Mrs. Bruce was formerly Mrs. Andros, and when she called at the police station a few minutes after the kidnaping she told the police that her former husband had recently arrived in Chicago from Los Angeles and that she believed he had taken the child. All the police of the city were notified to arrest Andros, and detectives were sent to the railway stations to frustrate any attempts to take the child out of the city.

In the afternoon Attorney Charles H. Hamill held a conference with Lieut. Rohan of the detective bureau and as a result the police dropped the case. Attorney Hamill, who represents Andros, the father, told Lieut. Rohan that the father had taken the child and that attempts to find him would be useless. "He is already out of the state on his way back to California," the attorney said.

Father's Lawyer Explains Case.

The story told by Attorney Hamill, and later verified by Mrs. Bruce, was to the effect that a divorce suit is still pending in one of the higher courts in San Francisco. Andros and his wife, who recently married Charles Bruce, lived for a number of years in Minneapolis, but afterward moved to San Francisco. There their domestic troubles ended in Mrs. Andros' application for a divorce. The decree was granted in the lower court and Mrs. Andros was awarded the custody of the child. Meanwhile the husband took an appeal, and the case has not yet been decided. Attorney Hamill told Lieut. Rohan that until the higher court has passed on the case the father has as much right to the possession of the child as the mother.

San Bernardino Daily Sun.

SAN BERNARDINO, CALIFORNIA, WEDNESDAY MORNING, FEBRUARY 25, 1903.

NOT SATISFIED WITH DECREE

L. M. Andros Wants Divorce Case Opened Whereby His Wife Was Given Freedom From His "Protecting" Arm.

Not satisfied with the decree of the court which severed the matrimonial bonds existing between L. M. Andros and his wife, Dora Andros, Henry W. Nisbet and F. B. Daley, attorneys for the husband, yesterday made a motion before Judge Oster for a new trial. The motion was opposed by C. L. Allison and R. E. Bledsoe, attorneys for the wife. After hearing the arguments Judge Oster took the case under advisement.

The decree of divorce was granted to Mrs. Andros. She charged her husband with extreme cruelty and the evidence introduced at the trial proved the allegation to the satisfaction of the court. The cruelty was said to be of a most aggravated character. Mrs. Andros resides at Chino.

Tourist—No trouble here to get

PECULIAR TANGLE IN ANDROS DIVORE SUIT

The Court of Appeals will have to pass upon a queer situation today at Los Angeles, when the divorce suit of Dora Andros against L. M. Andros will be heard. For nearly two years ago, in the Superior Court of this county, Mrs. Andros was granted a divorce, and six months later went to Chicago and remarried. The husband appealed, and if the Appellate court should reverse the lower tribunal, the position of Mrs. Andros, that was, will become somewhat perilous.

The case caused considerable of a sensation when it was tried, two years since, the Andros family being a rather prominent one about Ontario, they having lived between Ontario and Pomona, on the western extreme of the county. By the decree, Mrs. Andros was given custody of the two minor children, and she took them with her to Chicago, although there is some question as to her right to have taken them out of the State. But be that as it may, Andros went quietly to Chicago, watched at the school where his little girl was attending, and seizing her, was driven to a railroad station and escaped with her, bringing the daughter back in triumph to California.

He had already appealed from the judgment of the Superior Court, and now his appeal comes up in Los Angeles today. In the meantime, the whereabouts of Mrs. Andros, under her new name, have been lost, at least to Andros and his attorney, H. W. Nisbet. Perhaps her attorneys have later information. In the Superior Court she was represented by R. E. Bledsoe and C. L. Allison.

In that trial Andros was not asking for divorce himself, but he opposed her being granted one, on the charges she made against him.

THE INTER OCEAN, FRIDAY MORNING, DECEMBER 11, 1903.

The market is also being loaded with ground pine, mistletoe, magnolia leaves, and needle pines, all of which find ready buyers.

DETERMINED TO GET KIDNAPER.

Stepfather of Abducted Child Says He Will Use Violence.

"If the Chicago police persist in refusing to aid us in the search for Georgia, we shall have to resort to violence, though I dislike to do it."

This was the assertion made by Charles Bruce, stepfather of little Georgia Andros, who was kidnaped from the doors of the Goethe school Wednesday by her father. Attorneys in Los Angeles, Cal., and in Minneapolis, Minn., have been advised to be on the lookout for Andros and the little girl. If caught Andros will be arrested and the child returned to her mother in Chicago. Attorney Hamill's talk of Andros' going to California is discredited by Bruce, who calls it a bluff and believes that Andros has gone to Minneapolis.

DONATES FORTUNE TO SCHOOL.

Aged Lady Presents $10,000 to Drake

THE INTER OCEAN, THURSDAY MORNING, DECEMBER 10, 1903.

LAWYER AND POLICE AID IN KIDNAPING

Charles H. Hamill Assists Lewis Andros in Stealing and Spiriting Away Little Daughter.

MOTHER'S APPEAL FOR HELP VAIN

Woman Had Been Divorced from Husband in California and Given Custody of Children—Andros Steals Girl on Way to School.

Distracted with grief and with eyes red from futile tears, Mrs. Dora Bruce implored the Chicago police to search for and attempt to arrest a former husband who had stolen their little flaxen-haired daughter yesterday morning. Police captains shrugged their shoulders and remained passive, for they had received orders from Lieutenant Andy Rohan to take no action.

The semi-chief of the detective bureau in turn had received his orders from the divorced husband's attorney, Charles H. Hamill, law partner of State's Attorney Deneen, that this kidnaping of a 7-year-old child on the streets of Chicago was not an outrage in which the police should take an interest.

Lieutenant Andy Rohan sat in his front office and "did nothing." He also sent one of his "do nothing" messages to those police officials who, not approving of child steal-

THE EVENING TRANSCRIPT. MONDAY, JUNE 16, 1902.

OVER

The Tea Cups is Where Andros and His Wife Quarrelled.

Application For Matrimony Was Denied—Departed With the Children.

"Should the defendant in a divorce suit pay alimony?"

That was the question which furnished a whole lot of material for argument in the suit of Dora Andros against L. M. Andros. R. E. Bledsoe and Charles L. Allison argued for the plaintiff and H. W. Nisbet presented the argument for the defendant. From the scant bits of evidence introduced it is learned that the defendant is a rancher of fair circumstances who resides at Ontario. He has been married for two years and got along well with his wife until last spring. One evening at supper the quarrel took place when Mrs. Andros asked her husband why Mr. Madison had to stay at their house. The words that followed ended in the departure of Mrs. Andros and her children to the home of a neighbor where they have since resided. The case will come to trial in two weeks and Judge Oster denied the application for alimony.

The date for the trial of the divorce suit of Johnson vs. Johnson was vacated and reset for Saturday, June 28, department one.

The date for the trial of Manvel vs. Adams, set for June 19, has been vacated.

The San Bernardino Daily Sun.

TUESDAY, JUNE 17, 1902.

SHE WANTED SOME OF HUBBY'S MONEY.

Judges Oster and Bledsoe Hold Court in Banc and Dispose of Several Cases.—Only One of Interest.

The calendar was called in Department One of the Superior Court yesterday morning with Judges Oster and Bledsoe sitting in banc.

The first matter to occupy the attention of the Court was the case of Manuel vs. Adams, in which an order had been previously made setting the case for trial on June 19th. This order was vacated and the case restored to the trial calendar.

Next in order was the matter of Ward vs. Ward, which was passed.

The case of Johnson vs. Johnson was set for trial on Saturday, June 28, in Department One.

The star attraction of the usually quiet calendar was the case of Dora Andros vs. L. M. Andros. This was an action in which the plaintiff claimed that she was entitled to alimony. From all the evidence introduced in the hearing of the motion, it was evident that all had not been peaceful in the Andros household for some little time past. Mrs. Andros, by her attorneys, Charles L. Allison and R. E. Bledsoe, asked a balm for her wounded feelings in the form of good and lawful coin of the realm to be paid by her much disturbed "hubby," but after some argument attorney Henry W. Nesbit, who appeared for the husband, succeeded in convincing the court that the fair lady's demand was rather unreasonable and her attorney's motion was accordingly denied.

SHUDDERS AT HIS PAST.

Georgie Marie with her aunt Georgie Brooks at their home in Minneapolis.

The Brooks' Mansion in a family album. Georgie Marie Andros lived here with her aunt and uncle Georgie and Anson Brooks, throughout her childhood.

2445 Park Ave. Minneapolis, Minn.

Milton Stores Andros and Georgie Marie Andros. Children of Dora Hogan and Lewis Milton Andros.

Andros household for some little time past. Mrs. Andros by her attorneys Charles L. Allison and R.E. Bledsoe asked for a balm for her wounded feelings in the form of good and lawful coin of the realm to be paid by her much disturbed hubby." However, the court did not rule in her favor, listening to Mr. Andros' attorney Henry W. Nesbit, and in Victorian fashion the reporter noted, "the fair lady's demand was rather unreasonable and her attorney's motion was accordingly denied."

In the following day's report in *The San Bernardino County Sun*, the paper headline screamed to weekend readers that Friday morning looking for local gossip, "Granted A Divorce," on June 18, 1902, in the case Andros vs. Andros.

"The notorious divorce case of Andros against Andros, which has dragged its slimy course through the courts for the past two days, has at last been concluded and the plaintiff, Dora Andros, granted a separation from her husband and given the custody of her two minor children."

The paper described the case as "sensational at times" with the nature "as to render it unprintable."

However, this case was not put to rest as it was too much for the controlling Louis Milton Andros to bear that his wife was as the headline noted on Feb. 25, 1903 "given freedom from his 'protecting' arm."

Seven months later, Louis Milton Andros decided to upset the apple cart and have the divorce case reopened again, seeking a new trial. The judge decided to take it under consideration, though Dora Andros' attorneys contested the idea, because the initial case proved he had acted towards her with "extreme cruelty."

After her divorce, Dora took the children towards the middle section of the country, where she married Charles Bruce, a man who took both young Milton and Georgia under his wing.

This action alone infuriated Louis Milton Andros, with Charles Bruce with a fiery Scottish personality that matched the spark of wife Dora's.

It was in December of 1903, when Dora's niece Gladys was only about a year and a half old and newly relocated to Los Angeles and her nephew Marion was still about a year from being born in Los Angeles, that her own daughter would disappear from under her nose at the hand of ex-husband and his thugs. Later, Dora would sympathize with her own niece when Gladys' children Berniece and Jackie were snatched from under her nose and whisked away from Los Angeles to Kentucky by their father.

It was an early December morning in 1903 when a flaxen-haired Georgia ("Georgie") Marie was heading to the Goethe School in Chicago with her friend, Charley Monk. The little girl held a familial resemblance in photos to a little girl who would be pictured in studio portraits years later, also flaxen haired, named Norma Jeane Mortenson, her first cousin once removed (in other words her first cousin Gladys' child, Norma Jeane).

After Louis Milton Andros was humiliated in his divorce case and his sour grapes prompted him to attempt to overturn the case, he sought revenge on Dora, who was now happily remarried in a life away from the sordid saloon keeping life that Andros had subjected Dora and the children to.

Little did she realize though that she was to be out-lawyered, humiliated in the press and have her daughter snatched out from under her in a case that was highly reported on in the Chicago area.

The powerful Louis Milton Andros and his lawyer, Charles Hamill, helped him to reclaim Georgia and rush her back to California. Hamill had connection to the California State Attorney Deneen and when Dora later pleaded with Chicago Police to retrieve her child and press charges, they shrugged her off.

Basically, Hamill of Deneen & Hamill called the Chicago Police and told them it was a "family affair." Police asked how they could trust Hamill and the slimy attorney told them because "I'm a pretty reliable person."

He told police it was not really a kidnapping but had been planned and Louis Milton Andros had been in Chicago for several days, even purchasing clothing and toys for Georgia before rushing off with her by train back to California.

Allegedly, Hamill had spoken with young Milton Andros, then 13, asking if he would like to live with his father. Young Milton told them "no" and Hamill told police "so we did not attempt to take him."

Georgie Marie Andros is Gladys Monroe's first cousin.

Marilyn Monroe Unveiled | A Family History

The press reported that Dora Andros received her divorce and custody two years ago and because the case was overturned and appealed, she should not have left the state to marry Charles Bruce, an employee of the Union Traction Company.

Hamill also inferred he had somehow heard the children were not well cared for, blaming Dora's mother Jennie, another excuse to kidnap Georgie and that there were plans to take young Milton from the home.

"Yes, there may be two sides to the story," Hamill told the press, "I never heard the woman's side of the story until today," he reported on December 10, 1903.

That side?

Georgia Andros was walking to school and a carriage was waiting in front of the Goethe School, only less than a half a block from her home. Georgia, who was known as the "prettiest girl in the class" was about to the school when a carriage adjacent to it held lurking figures, Louis Milton Andros, Charles Hamill and a driver. Andros stepped out and Charley Monk screamed out about the kidnapping, attempting to make a valiant rescue of his young friend.

"Get out of this!" Adults screamed at Charley as Andros lifted his daughter into the carriage, while the brave young boy held tightly to Georgia.

If it is any indication of the character of Louis Milton Andros to knock anyone out of his way, he struck young Charley Monk in the face and knocked him to the sidewalk, with the child still yelling, "Kidnapper!"

School administration jumped into action after Charley Monk dusted himself off, with police officers pursuing the buggy, but losing father and daughter when they headed into the Chicago law offices of Deneen & Hamill.

Dora Bruce had been following her daughter to school that day, fearing a potential kidnapping, but the papers reported, "was far too behind to rescue her," as a "frail woman in delicate health."

She was hysterical as she told her tale, but the cruel Hamill noted that if the upper court decided to reverse the divorce, Dora Bruce "will be a bigamist."

Hamill's attitude?

"A father has as much right to a child as a mother has. I told him that he has a right to get his child in any manner he wished."

Charles Bruce, little Georgia's stepfather did not agree as reported the following day in *The Inter Ocean*.

"If the Chicago police persist in refusing to aid us in search for Georgia, we shall have to resort to violence, though I dislike to do it," Bruce told the press in a blurb that landed several pages back one Friday.

The publication did note that if Louis Milton Andros was caught, he would be arrested in Chicago and Georgia would have been returned to Dora. The Bruces' felt that attorney Hamill was bluffing and that Louis Milton Andros had only gone to Minneapolis and not California, but wanted to make the search trail for Georgia a cold one.

But Georgie did end up in California, as was told in the previous chapter and later in Minneapolis with her aunt Georgiana Brooks, one of the city's most prominent families. She grew up surrounded with maids, gardeners and chauffeurs.

Georgie married several times, traveling to Japan for her first marriage. She had three children over the duration of those marriages, living plush lives with her children that continued to be laden with maids and other household helpers living with them. One of her husbands Homer Baer was a bank president. She was shown married to him during the 1940 census as well as a 1942 city directory for Bemidji Minnesota.

When she died in 1959, she took the name of her second husband, being recorded as Georgie Marie Andrist.

Later in life, Dora was linked back to Andros, the papers reporting that Dora was at events with him and that Tilford Hogan entertained them both in his home, along with other relatives of his.

Later on, she was recorded as having been in Portland Oregon, living with Charles Bruce.

CHAPTER EIGHTEEN

MARILYN MONROE'S MOTHER Gladys could likely hold the title of the most misunderstood mother of the 20th and 21st Centuries.

Fables and sordid tales have prevailed in the myth of Gladys because of many stories told during Marilyn Monroe's lifetime that have proliferated about her whole family.

Most recently, J. Randy Taraborrelli's biography *The Secret Life of Marilyn Monroe* sparked a *Lifetime* biopic, starring Susan Sarandon as Gladys. Even in an interview, Sarandon said that she "felt sorry" for Marilyn after taking on her role as Gladys.

However the incidents in the biopic were not accurately portrayed (for example Marilyn having a discussion with Gladys about *The Seven Year Itch* and seeking advice about her marriage to Joe, both untrue scenarios) and most of this film was dramatized to sell, as is the Taraborrelli book itself, with many parts of it fictionally sensationalized.

Again, as in much of the life of Marilyn Monroe, when she has been portrayed as "interesting" with juicy and sordid details in her life, especially trauma in her childhood, it sold her and continues to sell her. This was something started in Marilyn's lifetime, which has continued with those who hijacked her estate and have made more off of Marilyn's legacy than she did in her whole lifetime.

The authors of this book are not stating that Marilyn's childhood and life were easy. And they do not discount that there were some issues existing with Gladys. Everyone has "stuff." However, many things were blown out of proportion and even invented to create a greater Cinderella story, to sell magazines and to invent the Cinderella image. Marilyn herself actively participated in exaggerating her childhood (with her mother's best friend Grace Goddard bragging to Marilyn's half sister about how she and Marilyn ameliorated the fable about the orphanage in order to craft a biographical story and gain public sympathy. Marilyn's stint in the orphanage was mandated by the court for a brief while in order for Grace to become her legal guardian after Gladys was hospitalized).

Yes, Gladys was inpatient at several hospitals during her lifetime after an emotional collapse. However, some of the strongest people are the ones that end up the most fragile after they finally break.

What many have ignored nearly 90 years later is that Gladys worked incredibly hard. She was responsible though she has been painted as a woman who abandoned her daughter. She held down a job, she purchased a home, she owned a vehicle, she did things with and for her daughter, and she tried with her previous two children who were ripped from her arms by their own father.

Gladys was literally battling a case of the blues when she was first hospitalized. She worked in the dark recesses of the film industry as a negative cutter, around chemicals and with little light.

Some have stated that Gladys was even dealing with an undiagnosed Seasonal Affective Disorder because as she worked, she was unable to get out as often and absorb her regular dose of sunshine and Vitamin D. Today, we know that could have a great impact on one's moods.

She ran her own household, having purchased a home on 6812 Arbol Drive in 1933. The brilliant arrangement Gladys made was to lease out most of her three-bedroom home to the Atkinson family who lived with she and daughter Norma Jeane (with whom she supervised and paid totally for Norma Jeane's stay at the Bolender household in Hawthorne, while she worked full-time those first seven years of Norma Jeane's life).

```
"   Gladys clk Henry's Cafe
"   Gladys film ctr RKO Studios r Hawthorne
"   Gladys sten r3628 W 58th pl
"   Gladys M Mrs br mgr Style Fame Dress Shop
      r5315 9th av
"   Gladys S Mrs sten Sou Cal Lndy Owners Assn
      r No Hollywood
"   Glenn clk r214 W 50th
"   Glenna C smstrs r2628 W Av 31
```

Several who were close to Norma Jeane during her childhood including Bebe Goddard, the stepdaughter of Gladys' best friend Grace, said that part of Gladys's collapse was a result of strikes in the film industry, which impacted Gladys's employment. Gladys was said to have received medication to help with her temporary case of depression, and instead it had an adverse effect on her.

Back in that day, mental health treatments and the mental health system were greatly flawed. Even today, some things are far from perfect but back then, being in the mental health system was a bit of a death sentence. Most patients were not treated with dignity and experimentations with a "poke and hope" kind of approach were more common.

Think Rosemary Kennedy who only a few short years following Gladys's incarceration in the mental health system was unsuccessfully lobotomized. Her father, Joseph Kennedy, did not alert Rosemary's own mother, Rose, when he took her for the procedure in 1941 as a way to "calm" the girl's moods. The pioneer surgery, doctors told him, would help to mellow their daughter. He took her to a psychiatric hospital, where one of the doctors later described that Rosemary was administered the procedure with only a mild sedative and a cut in her head. They asked Rosemary to sing "God Bless America," and decided how much to cut into her brain tissue based on her response and after she lost coherence, they stopped. Following her lobotomy, Rosemary's mental capacity, which had been previously bright, became that of a two-year-old and she was deemed incompetent, spending the remainder of her life in institutions.

Gladys's first hospital stay was only seven years prior in barbaric times like this. She was often medicated and was said to have even received electroshock treatments, as she was misdiagnosed with schizophrenia, a myth that has continued about both Gladys and Marilyn. These tales persist in the Taraborrelli book and in the many written words about Marilyn Monroe's life that have been regurgitated by a steady stream of authors and reporters, and of course even filmmakers, but never explored carefully by most. Electroshock therapies can leave a person incapacitated from the effects and honestly, with issues and difficulties.

It has become all about selling films and copy at the expense of Marilyn Monroe, her mother and the rest of her family. To paint her family as crazy has been more interesting than the truth, while the fact was that there was some misfortune that had come their way.

After her collapse, in spite of the tales that she was taken out of the home in a violent way in January 1934 to the most serious hospital facility, Gladys was first taken to the Cedar Lodge Convalescent Hospital and then the Santa Monica Rest Home for Ladies to recuperate. Her condition, however, did not improve but worsened. It was said before she was even hospitalized that she suffered a reaction to the medication she was taking for depression and it made her symptoms worse. In "the system" she was subjected to more medication and her mental state declined.

Norma Jeane reportedly visited her mother with Grace Goddard, with visits even from her daughter and best friend not lifting her spirits. She was transferred to the Los Angeles General Hospital and later to the state hospital in Norwalk.

One of her other visitors was a man in love with Gladys who is discussed later in this chapter.

In those days the hospital, now known as Metropolitan State Hospital, was located on a farm property that supplied food for the patients. To give an insight into the possibilities of what Gladys and also Della may have previously experienced there, in 1975 and later 1976 (the 1976 coverage from Walter Cronkite), the hospital was the subject of two television exposes about the drugging of the patients there. *Hurry Tomorrow* covered the medicating of the patients, in some cases where they were tied down and forced drugs in what the filmmakers described as "psychiatric rape."

Some of the patients endured lobomoties and electroshock. One of the medical technicians when the film crew shadowed staff there told the filmmakers as they dragged a patient to a medication room after he refused to take his dose that "I don't mind losing my job but if you film what goes on inside here I might lose my license to practice."

In the valiant attempt to film, the filmmakers tried to capture the scene through a mirror through the cracked door, but were unable to. When psych-tech students defended the patient's rights to the technicians, one of them stated, "I used to be like you when I started, but you'll learn."

Eventually, the students became as unethical as the technicians in their treatment of patients after they softened to the ways of the "system" and would be the ones forcing medications, including the antipsychotic Prolixin, which would force a patient into zombie-like lethargy.

The filmmakers also witnessed violence against an older patient who only fell on the ground and technicians roughed him up. They had alleged he had smashed windows just prior, an action which the filmmakers did not witness.

In Gladys's day, some of the medical treatments for schizophrenia, of which they diagnosed she was suffering with, was to medicate those with that diagnosis with insulin in higher doses, which would make the recipient comatose.

While Gladys may have not entered the hospital as a schizophrenic, she worsened under "medical" care and the treatments she received altered her brain.

Eventually it is said that her former husband Martin Edward Mortensen aka "Eddie" sought her out in the hospital, though he had been wrongly reported to her as deceased in a motorcycle accident in 1929 following their divorce. Gladys was allegedly so hysterical at the thought of being rescued she plotted an escape, as many in Norwalk did at that time, and according to the filmmakers almost 40 years later, patients still felt compelled to break out.

However, Gladys was viewed even deeper in schizophrenia since "Eddie" was believed deceased, so they thought Gladys was the one experiencing hallucinations. She was transferred to a higher security facility in the San Jose area to Agnews State Hospital. She would be there until her eventual release when her aunt Dora Hogan (Andros/Bruce/Schulties/Graham) rescued her.

Gladys was legally declared insane on January 15, 1935, when Grace Goddard (then Grace McKee) assumed legal guardianship and then sought guardianship over Norma Jeane.

Gladys endured many difficulties and was looked to as someone beloved before she was hospitalized. And following a long stint in the hospital, she was out of the system for some time, holding down a job and living under her Aunt Dora's supervision in Oregon. She even lived with Norma Jeane/Marilyn for a period in Los Angeles as Marilyn was kicking off her career. She was not an invalid the entire time as has been painted.

One person who truly loved Gladys came to the surface following Marilyn's death and was looking to reconnect with her. Harry Wilson wrote to Gladys's eldest daughter and Marilyn's half-sister, Berniece in 1962. Wilson had received Berniece's address years' prior from Grace Goddard as he sought out Gladys, and had been friends with both Grace and Gladys.

"She [Gladys] was the nicest girl I have ever known," he wrote. "I knew her a long time ago and had hoped we would get married."

Wilson poured out in his letter how he enjoyed Christmas 1935 (likely Christmas 1933 since Gladys was first hospitalized in 1934) with both Gladys and Norma Jeane. His letter is accurate and believable because it aligns with Gladys's journey and talks about time periods in her life. He did visit her in the hospital in the San Jose area and also had written to Berniece per Gladys's request. He acknowledged receiving a letter from Gladys in 1945 from Oregon after she was released from the hospital and living with her Aunt Dora, but had issues strike him and lost many of his letters. He traveled to Oregon in search of Gladys but was unable to find her.

"I have prayed for her many times and cried myself to sleep in lonesomeness for her," he wrote.

He told of a cherished memory of times spent with a young Norma Jeane and Gladys, but feared writing because he was concerned when Marilyn became famous he might be looked on as an opportunist and misunderstood. So instead, he sadly kept quiet until after Marilyn's death.

Wilson shared a fond memory about the Christmas parade on Hollywood Boulevard with Gladys and Norma Jeane, holding Norma Jeane high on his shoulders so she could see it. He went to Gladys' home and Norma Jeane sang for him by the Christmas tree at Gladys's insistence. He said the whole experience enchanted him. When little Norma Jeane went to bed, he talked to Gladys about marriage.

"I told her I was very much in love with her and her little girl," he wrote.

He fondly recalled times spent around the area with Gladys and Norma Jeane, including trips to restaurants.

"In the old days when the three of us went places together I felt like they were my little family, especially when we went into restaurants together," he wrote. "I hoped then that people watching us would think they both belong to me and they were mine."

He described how tragedy struck right after Christmas of 1933 when Gladys experienced her first hospitalization and "I almost lost my mind over it."

Another person who spoke only with fondness about Gladys was a former co-worker of Gladys's who was interviewed by biographer Maurice Zolotow, Leila Fields, who was employed as a negative cutter. While Zolotow interviewed Fields, she pointed out the small room in RKO where Gladys used to sit. Norma Jeane, she said, also often watched the women work.

"She [Gladys] was a beautiful woman, one of the most beautiful women in was ever my privilege to know. She had a good heart and was a good friend and was always happy until she got this sickness," Fields told Zolotow. "Before that, she was lively and always had a joke to make you laugh. Marilyn is the pitting image of her mother, except the hair and eyes. Her mother's eyes were green. You don't see eyes like hers often. Marilyn's are more blue."

Right before Gladys was hospitalized for the first time, both her son and grandfather Tilford Marion Hogan, died. A few years prior, she watched her mother Della succumb to the effects of malaria, though Della's death has often been painted as from mental illness. Della's brain was impacted from malaria, yet she was not mentally ill. And Gladys covered the cost of her mother's funeral, making payments to the funeral home herself until everything was paid off.

Yet, Marilyn's family, right up to her mother and then later Marilyn herself, has been painted as "cursed" and "mentally ill" in the entire line, when they have endured instead, a number of illnesses disguising as severe mental illness.

Gladys had survived a mix of ups and downs in her younger years, including the death of her father who died of a syphilis infection from the conditions he was subjected to during work in Mexico, which was later coined as insanity because of its attack on his brain.

Otis and Della had lived in Mexico, where he painted railway cars and also supervised work crews. Gladys was born there in 1902. Otis also enjoyed painting for pleasure, with a landscape scene that he created and Gladys had hanging on the wall at Ana Lower's.

The family moved to Los Angeles to a one-room bungalow 1903 and Marion was born in 1905.

In 1904, the Los Angeles City Directory placed the family in a home with the address of 1308 E 17th Street, with Otis listed as a painter for the Pacific Electric Railway Company.

Apparently, Otis built a home for the family completely by hand near Folsom and Soto Streets, which he constructed from the ground up by each piece. The Los Angeles City Directory from 1906 confirms this and that the residence was on 2511 Folsom Street. The residence maps out today between N. Mott and N. Fickett Streets. Current day records place the home constructed in 1905 and currently at 2,339 square feet, which has been subdivided into a multiple family house. Today, the home has six bedrooms and four baths.

At this stage, Otis was not only a painter for the Pacific Electric Railway, but had been promoted to an assistant foreman, according to this listing.

The family was listed again in the Los Angeles City Directory for 1909, with Otis listed as a "painter" and the family residing at 2440 Boulder Street.

Gladys attended school in Los Angeles, though she recalled spending most of her first grade year in Missouri, where she visited Tilford. This may have coincided with a short time during her father's illness or after his death.

Though some have wrongly accused Della of abandoning Otis in Patton State Hospital as he was dying in 1909 from his paresis and even having been abusive to him throughout their marriage, Gladys said of her mother that she "loved him [Otis] until he died. He was good."

Sadly, the 1909 city directory no longer reflects the address as listed to Otis, but to "Mrs. Della M." with the residence at 2440 Boulder Street. One can imagine the heartache the family must have experienced without Otis.

In 1904 Tilford Marion Hogan, Marilyn's great-grandfather lived with Otis Monroe in Los Angeles, California.

LOS ANGELES CITY DIRECT 1904

Hogan Tilford M, carp, bds 1308 E 17th.

Monroe Otis E. painter Pac Elec Ry Co, h 1308 E 17th.

COMMERCIAL NATIONAL BANK
CAPITAL AND SURPLUS 25,000.00 — 423 SOUTH SPRING STREET

1194   LOS ANGELES CITY DIRECTORY

BRENT'S THE GIANT STORE — Not In the TRUST PRICES

J. U. TABOR & CO.
TELS 127   COR. 7th AND LOS ANGELES STS.
MANUFACTURERS OF
AUTOMOBILE TOPS
OUR REPAIRING, PAINTING, WOODWORK AND TRIMMING IS STRICTLY UP-TO-DATE   See Page 2

MONROE
" Mattie (wid James), res 431 N Beaudry av.
" Otis E, asst foreman P E Ry, h 2511 Folsom.
" Susan (wid Andrew P), h 1511 W 28th.

MONTCRIEF
Montcrief Wm, emp Levy's Cafe, res 348 E 4th.
Monte Jesse P, mach P E Ry, h 1010 N St Louis.
" Mina S, nurse, res 1622 S Hill.
" Rudolph C, packer Western Whol Drug Co, res 1213d W 7th.
Montebello Land and Water Co, Frederick H Howard pres, Morris Klein sec, 415 N Main.
Montee Francis A, h 2323 E 4th.
" Henry W, printer Common Sense Pub Co, res 4500 Pasadena av.
Monteith Geo E, h 1414 W 23d.
" Mrs Lida, fur rms 207 N B'way.
Monteleone Antonio, driver Ludwig & Matthews, h 936 Rirch.

" Oscar L, clk Henry J Pauly Co r 2009 New Jersey
" Otis E painter h rear 2440 Boulder
" Thos F slsmn Mullen & Bluett Clo

MONROE see also Munro
" Agnes M lndrss r 282 Av 25
" Bertha F steno Santa Fe r 1118b E 27th
" Birdie M asst F C Shurtleff r 319 W 8th
" Briggs h 754 E Vernon av
" Carl R porter r 621 S Hope
MONROE CHARLES, judge Superior Court Dept 6, h 729 W 28th
" Clark B optician r 754 E Vernon av
" Mrs Cornelia fur rms 643½ N Main
" Mrs Della M h 2440 Boulder
" Earl F firemn r 1310½ S Los Angeles

W. W. MONTAGUE & CO. Tels Main 508 Home Ex. 508
IRON PIPE
Plumbing Goods and Iron Pipe. 122-124 N. Los Angeles St.

1032 LOS ANGELES (1910) CITY DIRECTORY

R. C. Hamlin, Agt. Phones: Main 404; F 1735

IVERS & POND / PEASE PIANOS
HOLMES MUSIC CO.
422 S. BROADWAY

Monge Benson stripper h 612 E 21
Mongerson John carp r 1115 Maple av
Mongoni Louis pdlr h 709 Castelar
Mongoslo Giovanni clk Fazzi & Co r rear 618 Macy
Monical Mrs Mary C dept mgr Lane's r 712 California
Monje Josephine phone opr r 123 S Bunker Hill av
Monjoy Mrs Annie h 1529 E 12th
Monk Anna (wid Fredk) h 942 W 36th pl
" Arthur cementwkr r 942 W 36th pl
" Chas art repr 826 S Grand av
" Clara A dressmkr r 942 W 36th pl
" Edwd B clk First National Bank r 1611 S Flower
" Edwd R atty 355 S Main rm 203 r 1613 S Flower
" Geo B real est 508 S Spring rm 908 r 427 S Olive
MONK HENRY M, mgr John J Newbegin subscription books 207 S Hill
" Jane E h 1345 W 37th pl
" Lillian (wid E H) h 1611 S Flower
Monkhouse Fred J A car inspr h 1534 Henry
" Fredk E r 1534 Henry
Monkman Geo R meatmkt 2523 Pasa-

Monona The fur rms 105½ N Los Angeles
Monreal Albt car repr r 1711 Brooklyn av
" Albt lab r 1431 Pennsylvania av
" Augustine saloon h 1243 E 9th
" Donila A (wid Teodoro) h 1431 Pennsylvania av
" Eleuterio A clk Columbia Phonograph Co r 813 McGarry
" Frank lab h 813 McGarry
" Lola clk Jacoby Bros r 746 S Central av
" Manuel lndymn r 1243 E 9th
" Petro butcher r 1431 Pennsylvania
MONROE see also Munro
" Adaline bkpr E J Elson Co r 135 N Olive
" Allene supervisor girls work Playgrounds Dept r 1546 St John
" Alvin eng r 1618 Avalon
" Bertha F steno Santa Fe r 1165 E 34th
" Carl R painter r 621 S Hope
MONROE CHARLES, judge Superior Court Dept 6 h 729 W 28th
" Chas D h 157 Parkside av
" Chas J jr brklyr r 730 Ceres av
" Clark B optician Fred Detmers r 321 W Pico
" Danl A brakemn r 200 Sotello
" Mrs Della M apts 1114 E 10th
" Earl r 1021 Wall
" Edwd clk h 138 N Ditman
" Mrs Ella h 1720 S Hobart blvd
" Fannie (wid C J) r 730 Ceres av
" Forrest r 301 S Boyle av
" Frank C v-pres Wm R Staats Co r Pasadena
" Geo r 738 Merchant
" Geo carp h 826 Francisco

Marilyn Monroe Unveiled | A Family History

Della and her two children buried her husband and their father up at the Angelus Rosedale Cemetery.

In 1910, Della was listed at 1114 E 10th Street in the Los Angeles City Directory under "apts," when she and the children lived with boarders in their home, a way she helped to make ends meet.

The year 1911 places the family back at the 2440 Boulder Street location with it noted they were living in the rear section of the home.

The 1912 directory when Gladys had attained her first decade of life lists her mother Della as a Widow for "O.E." with their home still at 2440 Boulder Street.

Then Gladys endured the remarriage of her mother to one man in particular who she told daughter Berniece was abusive, Lyle Graves, a man who reportedly threw one of Gladys's kittens against a wall. Though Della is no longer in the city directory alone in 1913, Lyle Arthur Graves (listed under "Graves Lyle, A") is listed in the city directory in 1913 at 1832 Pasadena Avenue. When they married, however, at 1324 ½ So Hill Street. In 1913, this was when she apparently left him, after the marriage became too painful due to his drinking.

She told Berniece though that Della eventually married a man in Oregon named "Chitwood" who Gladys liked and there is an entry in the Multnomah Oregon marriage records of a "Monroe, Della M.," marrying on July 26, 1916. So far, the Oregon records do not turn up a man with the same date as the Della M. Monroe listed, but turn up the following men that may have been potential spouses: Ernest Sherley Brown, Clay C. Davis, Gifford Nils, Willie D. Peasley, S. Neilson, Charles Julian Williams and Charles E Young.

If there was a marriage for Della in Oregon, it was short-lived because she ended up later marrying Charles Grainger.

For Gladys, there was the return to California with her mother and brother to Venice, where she was married off early to a man named Jasper Baker before her fifteenth birthday.

It would have been scandalous for a young girl, barely fifteen, to be married to a man over ten years her senior. But Gladys was a beautifully captivating brunette who John "Jasper" Newton Baker took notice of.

On May 17, 1917, ten days shy of her fifteenth birthday, she married Jasper Baker. Her mother, Della, attested that Gladys was already eighteen.

While conflicting dates exist for the birth of her first child Robert Jasper Kermit Baker, also known as "Jackie," the half-brother of Marilyn Monroe, his death date was known as August 16, 1933, in which his death certificate attested to his age at 15. The young boy died of tuberculosis of the bone, which impacted his kidneys. He had difficulty with his gait after a fall as a youngster. Not to mention he was missing his right eye after a firecracker accident (which sister Berniece ran for cover from) when the firework blew up in a Coke bottle. Jasper insisted on caring for the child at home, even performing unsuccessful urinary catheterizations on his own son, rather than returning him to the hospital.

Perhaps Jackie's birth was hidden because Gladys was so young at the time of his birth, which could have resulted in her husband being found on charges of statutory rape had the child's birth been reported properly.

However, the child's existence is duly noted on the 1920 Venice California Census, showing he was born around 1918, though other sources place his birth the same year as his parents' wedding. His birth dates also conflict, with some sources listing him as born on November 10, 1917 and his death certificate listing his birth date as January 16, though the year is not given it would deduct at 1918. The other discrepancy is his mother is not listed as "Gladys" but "Bernice Monroe" on the death certificate.

On the other hand, when Gladys' second child Berniece Inez Gladys Baker was born on July 30, 1919, she was listed as the only living child and the only child born to Gladys, while Jackie was accounted for on the census. Even Gladys' age was altered on Berniece's birth certificate, with Gladys actually just over seventeen years old at the time of Berniece's birth, when she was listed as nineteen years old.

G. W. WEIK   **J. A. SCHWARZ**

ARTELS, WEIK & SCHWARZ
SUCCESSORS TO G. W. WEIK CO.

EXCHANGES, LOANS, INSURANCE
404-405 Douglas Building
Telephones   Home F 4468   Main 1709

1006   LOS ANGELES (1911) CITY DIRECTORY

California Wall Paper Co.
G. J. VIEIRA, President
816 S. BROADWAY

MONETA—Continued
" Sweet Shop (Misses A L and L L Hoskinson C P Bergstrom) 4428 Moneta av
" Theatre J J Tully prop Moneta av ne cor 45th
Monette Julia B tchr r 817 W 23d
" P r 918 W 1st
Money Harry N lab r 1016 E 7th
Mong Edgar W driller r 320 E Emilita av
" Harry plumber r 244 E 5th
" Ray R driller r 320 E Emilita av
" Wm E driller h 320 E Emilita av
Monge Benj stripper r 363 Aliso
" Benson cigar mfr 363 Aliso
Mongie Frank cook 732 E Hollywood blvd
Mongosio Giovanni clk R Fazzi & Co r rear 618 Macy
Monheim Robt meatctr r 502½ N Alameda
Monia U S h 146 S Alameda
Monical Mrs Mae slswmn Wetherby-Kayser Shoe Co h 712 California
" Mrs Mary C h 322 W 51st
Monich Nicholas lab r 126 N Rio
MONICO See Mounicou
Moninger John A (Hollywood Pharmacy) r 132 N Whitley
Monino Bogio lab r 2226 E 8th
Monir E r 1000 Wilde
Monje Josephine phone opr r 529 California
" Raymond fdymn r 1217½ N Main
Monjos Louie h 628 Mateo
Monjoy Anna wid Jerry h 1529 E 12th
" Robt waiter r 1529 E 12th
Monk Anna wid Fredk h 942 W 36th pl
" Arthur cementwkr r 942 W 36th pl
" Cattle Co F R Monk mgr 201 Grant

MONNETTE MERVIN J, broker and banker, 1019 Wright & Callender Bldg and v-pres Citizens Nat Bank tel Home 14391, h 911 S Western av
MONNETTE ORRA E, attorney-at-law, 1017-1018 Wright & Callender Bldg 405 S Hill, h 3101 Wilshire blvd
Monnier Lys lab r 149 Rose
Monnin Geo D gardener h 1819 W 25th
Monning John C slsmn Geo J Birkel Co h 1206 W 51st
Monnschreck Otto baker r 502½ N Alameda
Mono Mining & Milling Co F E Woodley sec 356 S Spring rm 531
Monohan Thos hlpr r 1739 E 37th
Monona The fur rms 105½ N Los Angeles
Monreal Alberto car bldr r 1711 Brooklyn av
" Donila A wid Teodoro h 1711 Brooklyn av
" Lola seam Jacoby Bros r 743 E 9th
" Manuel lndymn r 1243 E 9th
" Mary student r 1239 S Vermont av
" Nellie h 1243 E 9th
" Peter lab Cudahy Pkg Co
" Rosa G lndrss r 759 Wall
MONROE See also Munro
" Adaline bkpr Elson Ptg Co r Glendale
" Addison D carp r 449 Mt Washington dr
" Belle r 5311 S Figueroa
" Bertha F steno Santa Fe r 1165 E 34th
" Birdie M steno C C Browning r Monrovia
" Carl mach r 621 S Hope
MONROE CHARLES, judge Dept 6 Superior Court h 729 W 28th
" Chas eng r 769 Ceres av
" Chas distributer r 347 S Los Angeles
" Chas D h 159 Parkside av
" Clara B clk Paris Cloak S & M Hse r 1400 W 7th
" Clark B optician Detmers Optical Co r 735 Francisco
" Mrs Cornelia fur rms 643½ N Main
" Mrs Della h rear 2440 Boulder
" Mrs Dexter h 920 W 55th

Marilyn Monroe Unveiled | A Family History

The only place where her age was accurate anywhere was the 1920 census where she was listed as having been a native Spanish speaker, having been naturalized from Mexico and she was eighteen years old.

Things were tumultuous in the Baker household, with Jasper reportedly abusive to Gladys. Jasper accused Gladys of having an interest in his brother, Ardry, who was two months older than Gladys and actually lived with them in Venice. Allegedly, when there was a visit in Kentucky before the divorce, Gladys and Ardry went hiking in Flat Lick, Kentucky, which struck a jealousy chord in Jasper over his younger sibling, who was said to be very handsome. Jasper reportedly beat Gladys on the back with a bridle, causing her to bleed and leaving Gladys emotionally scarred. A widow named Maggie Mills, who eventually married Jasper and was 13 years older witnessed this event from a grocery store that she owned. According to memoirs from daughter Berniece, Maggie excused the beating because Jasper said that Gladys "wouldn't cook and wouldn't clean house."

It was also on this trip that young Jackie reportedly fell from the vehicle onto a roadway and injured his leg, resulting in his permanent limp.

The divorce papers, filed after the trip to Kentucky, are also a proof of Jackie's existence. Filed on June 14, 1921, it notes that the marriage produced "Jackie Monroe Baker" then age three (which might place his birth at 1918) and "Bernice Gladys Baker" listed at about two years.

Gladys confessed to her daughter Berniece when the two spent time together in Los Angeles during the fall of 1946 that her first husband, Berniece's father, was "a ladies' man" and although he beat on Gladys following his concerns about the hike with Ardry, Gladys told her daughter that she witnessed her husband walking down the street one day with another woman while she was with Berniece and her older brother Jackie.

Gladys also told her daughter that Jasper had a drinking issue, something Berniece was already well aware of in her adulthood.

The marriage at that point had exceeded more than five years and in the time, Gladys accused him of mental cruelty, physical cruelty, the use of vile names, hitting her in the face, and kicking her in the body. Her lawyer asserted she was a "good and loyal wife" to Jasper. Jasper was ordered to pay Gladys $150 monthly in child support plus reimburse her attorney fees of $250. At the time, he was not permitted to sell their game business on the Pickering Pleasure Pier in Santa Monica, until a further court action took place on June 20, in which he could defend himself as to why he did not have to pay child support, or offer proof why he needed to sell his business. The divorce was granted on March 8, 1922.

With Gladys granted physical custody of the children, on one day when Jasper had visitation for the weekend he took them from Gladys and headed for Flat Lick, never turning back. Gladys headed after in pursuit, while Jasper had already settled with the children at his mother's home. However with Jackie's limp, Jasper delivered him to a Louisville hospital, where his leg was placed in a cast, and he remained a patient for a lengthy term.

Gladys showed up at Jasper's sister's house, reportedly pleading for help to have the children again and the sister Myrtle alerted her brother of Gladys's arrival. Berniece was kept sequestered and when Gladys learned that Jackie was hospitalized, she stayed near him in Louisville to visit him daily.

In the meantime, Jasper and his new spouse Maggie played parental alienation games between Berniece and Gladys, following their move to Harlan, Kentucky. After Gladys felt she could no longer sustain herself, she returned to Los Angeles, but before she did, she attempted to see Berniece. She ascertained her daughter was being cared for. It was allegedly in 1923 when Gladys said "goodbye" on a Kentucky bridge, something that Maggie emphasized throughout Berniece's childhood was Gladys's grievous error.

Gladys felt bullied and outnumbered, while Maggie frequently told Berniece over the years, "I just don't see how a mother could turn her back and walk away from two children like that."

Jasper's explanation to Berniece was that her mother was "beautiful" but "too young," and without knowledge to care for children. Jasper explained that was why he brought the children to their grandmother and married Maggie, who was much older. From there, despite Berniece's questions, he would drop the subject, and all Berniece had was Gladys' photograph and questions left unanswered.

Gravers Alida student r 1320 E 15th
GRAVES, see also Greaves
" Addie E wid Howard nurse r 4478 W Rosehill dr
" Adeline wid J C h 219 W 47th
" Alla wid D M h 251 S Bunker Hill
" Anna M Mrs wid Myron h 6433 Santa Monica blvd
" Anthony F contr h 2219 7th av
" Arthur H teller All Night & Day Bank r Long Beach
" Asa B pdlr h 425 N Breed
" Avard R cond h 144 E 53d
" A F mill hd r 951 E Vernon av
" Benj F barber 317 S Hill h 212 S Flower
" Bert C (Cunningham & Graves)
" Byron L mgr Ford Motor Co h 3928 Normandie av
" Carrie Mrs lndrss r 1331 Wall
" Catherine Mrs steno Los Angeles Map & Address Co r 1018 S Hill
" Chas lab L W Blinn Lbr Co
" Chas A colln clk L A Gas & Elec Corp h 3933 Dalton av
" Chas C chief clk to supt W F & Co Exp r 2156 W 31st
" Chas C motrmn **h 128 N Av 59**
" Chas D baker h 873 N Figueroa
" Chas N slsmn r 544 Gladys av
" Chas R trav pass agt S P L A & S L R R r Huntington Park
" Chas S h 470 E 41st
" Chesley R real est 610 S Bway rm 627 r 251 S Bunker Hill av
" Clarence photo Express r 1502 W 47th
" C D clk Santa Fe r 7614 Whittsett av
" C H slsmn Claude Mathewson r 255 S Bunker Hill av
" Della M Mrs gro 1832 Pasadena av
" Earl h 212 S Bunker Hill av
" Earl A clk Percival Apts r 470 E 41st
" Edith M Mrs public steno and notary 542 Douglas Bldg 257 S Spring h 523 W 41st
" Effie steno W N McKee r Pasadena
" Jos K packer Cooper, Coate & Casey r Pasadena
" J A clk Barker Bros r 832 W 54th
" J Monroe motrmn h 1029 E 45th
" Laura A wid G W r 928 S Hope
" Lemuel F mgr E Graves h 126½ S Fremont av
" Lida J wid C M real est 5601 S Central av h 1054 E 56th
" Letitia M wid C M h 1445 W 25th
" Louis S insp City Elec h 1742 Morton av
" Louise Mrs dressmkr h 1324 Bond
" Louise M Mrs relish mfr 947 S Normandie av
" Lyle A r 1832 Pasadena av
" Lyman S mech r 931 S Hill
" McKenzie N h 4211 Morgan av
" Marcus M switchmn h 923 W 50th
" Madge J clk Hamburgers r 752 S Main
" Mary A wid Franklin r 960 E 20th
" Mary A phone opr R A Rowan & Co r Sawtelle
" Mary F wid H E h 2047 S Harvard blvd
" Mary R wid F W r 1345 W 38th
" Minnie V steno r 1543 W 8th
" Mose W saddle mkr r 538 S Flower
" M Mrs h 453 S Hope
" M O atty 205 S Bway rm 703 r Whittier
" Nellie A Mrs r 5742 Carlton Way
" Nellie N phone opr Bullock's r 219 W 47th
" Orlo B tinner h 2815 Michigan av
" Ray B druggist B & B Drug Co h 809½ W 12th
" Ray T elev opr r 470 E 41st
" Richd W elec r 3418 4th av
" Robt r 322 E 4th
" Robt G pressmn r 726 W 23d
" Rosebelle H wid John demonstrator r 601 Edgeware rd
" Sarah E wid C M h 2025b E 2d
" Stephen D pres Sun Land Co h 542½ Gladys av

Marilyn Monroe Unveiled | A Family History

When Berniece finally met her mother, she learned of Gladys's perspective and defeat. Gladys admitted that she felt obliged to leave her children there, but eventually envisioned returning without anyone's knowledge, to keep watch from a distance. This tore at Berniece's heart.

"Mamita's been through so much," she told Grace Goddard, using the pet name that she and her daughter Mona Rae had adopted for Gladys. "Just having your children stolen would be enough to drive any woman crazy!"

Grace sided with Berniece's sentiments and then offered words of praise about her friend, through teary eyes noting, "And yet Gladys held up through the loss of her children. And many other things. There's a lot in her to admire. She's stronger than we realize."

Gladys returned to Los Angeles and began working at CFI (Consolidated Film Industries) as a negative cutter. It was there she met friend Grace McKee, who would later become Grace Goddard.

It was in 1924 that she somehow Gladys connected with Southern California Gas Company meter man Martin Edward Mortensen. He was a stable man who was apparently very fond of Gladys.

Mortensen and Gladys Pearl Baker were married on October 11, 1924 in a Presbyterian ceremony. He was listed as a meter man and she a negative cutter, he then living on West Santa Barbara Avenue, likely today's Martin Luther King Boulevard, while Gladys lived on Hyperion Avenue. If the house was what it is today, where Gladys lived was a cute bungalow that now has an orange tree in the front and had a Tudor style to it. This is a place where Gladys' friend Grace Goddard also resided.

Mortensen's residence is also confirmed in the Los Angeles City Directory for 1925 on 721 ½ West Santa Barbara Avenue, listing him as a meterman for the L A Gas & Elec Corp. And the year of Marilyn's birth, he is listed as "Martin R" on 4937 1st Street.

It was Mortensen who gave up and filed for divorce, noting "desertion" as the reason. In his complaint, Mortensen stated on May 26, 1925 that Gladys deserted the marriage "willfully and without cause," through his attorney, denoting that as the date of separation. The document also claims that "no children have resulted from said marriage" and "there is no community property."

However, while they were technically still married, as the paperwork was filed and granted on August 15, 1928, Norma Jeane Mortenson was born, slightly over a year following the separation date Mortensen claimed.

Some biographers have written that Martin Edward Mortensen perished in a motorcycle crash in the late 1920s, which was also untrue. He was also reputed born in Norway, though that is not fact. Martin Edward Mortensen was born in fact in California where he lived out his life until his death in 1981. Among his belongings were news clippings and papers, including Norma Jeane's birth certificate and divorce papers with Gladys Pearl Baker, who identified herself on the birth certificate of daughter Marilyn Monroe as "Gladys Monroe," her maiden name. While Gladys was married to "Eddie" and he was said to be enamored with her, the feelings were not reciprocated. The couple was allegedly separated when Norma Jeane was born though he was listed on the birth certificate and did attempt to make contact with the child during her lifetime, advances Marilyn reportedly rejected.

There was speculation on the other hand that Mortensen was not the father of Marilyn Monroe at all, but Charles Stanley Gifford was. Marilyn often told stories of seeing a photograph in her mother's room of a man resembling Clark Gable. She had an affinity for the actor, who was her co-star in the last final film that they both completed, *The Misfits*. And while some have vouched that Gifford was Marilyn's father, he, unlike Mortensen, reportedly rejected her advances to contact him. He apparently became a dairy farmer in Hemet, California, where Marilyn has also been rumored several times to have tracked him down.

Charles Stanley Gifford was born in Rhode Island and was married in 1919, where he had listed on his marriage certificate to Lillian M. Priester that he was a "Laboratory Worker, Motion Pictures," when the two were married on July 26 of that year.

Some have reported that Gifford had an affair with Gladys and they lived in the same building after Priester left him in October of 1923. The pair worked together at Consolidated Film Industries. He was a philanderer by nature, unlike Mortensen who was said to have been loyal to a fault. Priester filed on the grounds of "extreme cruelty," according to divorce documents from May of 1925. Two children were a result of the Gifford and Priester union, so if he was the biological parent of Marilyn Monroe, she had two half siblings, Doris Gifford, born 1920 and Stanley Gifford, born 1922.

The divorce decree and testimony from Lillian Priester filed on her behalf from attorney Andrew J. Copp depicts a man who treated his wife with extreme cruelty as Jasper Baker did with Gladys during their marriage. Priester, who filed under the name of Lillian Gifford, described that he used "vile and approbrious (sic) epithets, profanity, disgusting and vulgar names and references" towards his spouse.

Priester also claimed that he has "been guilty of habitual intemperance to such an extent that the same reasonably inflicted a course of great mental anguish upon the plaintiff, and has boasted of his conquests of other women, shamelessly boasting of his power to be intimate with other women."

And there was more. There were claims he exhibited to Priester "marks on his body and declaring that same were caused by a hypodermic injection of narcotic drugs, and boasted that he was addicted to the use thereof, and wrongfully and untruthfully charging plaintiff with being the cause of the defendant having been addicted to the use thereof."

The divorce decree shows Gifford was abusive in language, calling his wife a "little whore" in front of their daughter and threatening to hit her in the jaw and with a gun. Additionally, during the birth of their son, he dropped her off to the hospital but did not stay for the baby's birth. In 1923, he did in fact hit Priester in the face for which she required medical attention.

The divorce documentation points in the direction of potential affairs with his co-workers, one of them Gladys, because of Gifford's disappearances. "Plaintiff has been informed and believes that during such absences defendant was carousing with persons who were employed with him in the laboratory and others, both male and female, drinking intoxicating liquors, dancing and otherwise indulging in recreation apart from the plaintiff."

Gifford has been seen in photos enjoying alcoholic drinks and in a fancy suit with other men beside him.

Gladys did not publicly divulge that Gifford fathered Norma Jeane, nor did she ask for support and Gifford reportedly broke off his affiliation with her when he learned she was pregnant.

Later photos show a man who was more casually dressed and who was outfitted in the Red Rock Dairy uniform, where he started over and lived with his wife and children from his third marriage.

Gifford's son Charles Stanley Gifford Jr. claimed to a biographer that the stories of Gifford having fathered Marilyn Monroe were untrue. He said reporters harassed he and his family, including his stepmother Mary when they owned the dairy, because of these tales. Some have reported that Marilyn herself visited the dairy and received a business card from Gifford's lawyer, which the son also denied his father would have ever done. Another action was a claim that Gifford tried to contact Marilyn on his deathbed and she told the representative who reportedly reached her that they would need to contact her lawyer. Gifford's son denied this to be true as well, but also, knowing Marilyn's kind heart, this would not have been something she would have done and would have consented speaking to someone who was ill if she was able. That being said, Marilyn would have had a representative deal with a representative of her's, not her directly.

Whether or not Gifford was the father of Marilyn Monroe, those who are his descendants wear this potential as a badge of honor and also connect Gifford to her on genealogy forums. Additionally, they will note his Mayflower connection and attach Marilyn to it, based simply on the speculation. Upon removal of his name from genealogical attachments to Marilyn Monroe since he is only a potential father and not confirmed, while Mortensen had legitimately been married to Gladys and was the legal father on the birth certificate, Gifford relatives often take offense and have sent inflammatory emails to those who correct them on genealogy forums, including one of the book's authors, who manages both Marilyn's and Gladys's profile on one forum. In some cases, representatives of the genealogy software company have blocked these parties from adding their relative on as Marilyn's parent or Gladys's husband (which he definitely was not). On these forums, they still attempt to connect Gifford even as an "ex-partner" though his relationship with Gladys may have been little more than one of his flings.

Regardless of his connection, Gifford died in 1965.

Marilyn Monroe Unveiled | A Family History

However, when Gladys learned of her pregnancy with daughter Norma Jeane, she was said to have approached Charles Stanley Gifford, who denied the baby she was carrying was his and disappeared from Gladys's life. Gladys' mother Della also ended up out of the picture temporarily, though she had been present for Gladys when Jackie and Berniece were small. Della, who listed herself a "housewife," applied for a passport under the name Della M. Grainger to visit Borneo on what was said a travel trip to "Join husband" (though some have contested the couple was unmarried she attested it happened on November 25, 1920), signing her name on the dotted line in flowery penmanship as "Della M. Grainger," of which she planned to leave for her trip on March 20, 1926.

Grainger was traveling for work with Shell Oil in Borneo. While some have said he was "running away" from Della, he joined her on the return trip home in December of that year. She passed away in August 1927 from a series of respiratory infections and a heart issue triggered from malaria.

However, while Della was still well she was photographed enjoying her visits in Asia and even sent a postcard on May 27, only days away from the birth of her third grandchild, to her first two grandkids, Jackie and Berniece. The card had a large snake on the front and she wrote to the children, "This is the kind of big snakes they have here. They are big enough they could swallow you & Jackie and so could the alligators."

But Gladys was not totally alone at the birth of her daughter, Norma Jeane. And though she had been written as a "single mother," she was not technically divorced, but unaccompanied by any man at that time. Grace McKee was her best friend, a friendship that would last until Grace's passing in 1953. Plus, friends at Consolidated reportedly gathered up money for Gladys prior to her maternity leave to help her.

It was on Saturday, June 1, 1926 at 9:30 a.m. that Norma Jeane Mortenson entered the world at Los Angeles General Hospital, with Dr. Herman Beerman performing the honors of bringing one of the world's most famous movie stars into existence.

Baby Norma Jeane Mortenson was born to her mother, Gladys Monroe, who told those who registered the child's birth certificate that her daughter was the only surviving child of her three live births. Plus, Norma Jeane's last name is misspelled with a "son" instead of a "sen" as should have been documented. Throughout biographies recorded during Marilyn's lifetime, those were other myths as Marilyn herself did not recognize these siblings and there were conflicting tales of their existence in biographies where she was directly interviewed.

The certificate noted that Gladys Monroe resided at 5454 W. Boulevard (many say 5454 Wilshire though the "W." is often written up as an abbreviation for "West" and could also mean "West Boulevard"). If it was West Boulevard it was a quaint Los Angeles neighborhood that is still in existence today with sleepy bungalows from that time. If 5454 Wilshire Boulevard, as some attributed her address to, that is part of the area's business district now.

Her birth certificate also offers information about the man who was legally her father, Edward Mortensen (his name was spelled incorrectly on the birth certificate too, as "Mortenson"), whose name was actually Martin Edward Mortensen. Though Gladys referred to herself as "Monroe" during the time of her daughter's birth, she was actually Gladys Mortensen at the time. Additionally, there is a nod to her first ex-husband in there, with Mortensen's occupation noted as "Baker."

Some have said that the stigma attached to single parenthood back in that day was the reason that Gladys included Mortensen on the birth certificate and the possibility that Gifford could have been Marilyn's father. Interestingly enough, nearly 20 years after her death, *The New York Times* published an *Associated Press* article discrediting Marilyn's birth as "illegitimate," as many had been led to believe. There were copies of her birth certificate found in Martin Edward Mortensen's apartment in Riverside County, California, along with his divorce papers with Gladys. How Martin Edward Mortensen acquired a copy of Marilyn's birth certificate is another mystery. Did he request it? Or did Gladys deliver a copy to him? Norma Jeane was supposedly named after a little girl that Gladys was a nanny for when she lived for the stint in Louisville while tending to Jackie, with her name spelled exactly that way.

At times, Norma Jeane was known as "Norma Jeane Baker" for cohesion and again, so it was not pointed out that she came from another relationship, though her only relation to the Baker line

BAKER GIRARD F, Attorney-at-Law, 925 L A Stock Exchange Bldg 639 S Spring, Phone Met 4707 h9029 Vista Grande, Phone Oxford 6898
" Gladys clk r1451½ E 51st
" Gladys film wkr r237 Bimini pl
" Gladys typist r116 W 48th
" Gladys typist r1727 S Vermont av

were her two half-siblings and nothing else. At some point, Gladys had hope that she could bring her other two children back to live with her, which was another reason for using "Baker" as an alias for Norma Jeane.

Norma Jeane was reportedly baptized under that name as well. Some have said that Grace insisted on her being registered under the name "Baker" with the fears that Mortensen was allegedly seeking claim to the child while Gladys was hospitalized. However, later legal documents like her marriage certificates would show her under the name "Mortenson." In the 1942 Chieftain yearbook, Marilyn was listed as "Baker, Norma," and was already a standout in front of the camera lens with a mass of curls cascading from her head and a sweet smile.

After Norma Jeane's birth, Gladys delivered her to Ida and Albert Wayne Bolender, neighbors of her mother, Della. In spite of popular belief though, Gladys never abandoned her youngest child. In fact, Gladys spent the first two months following Norma Jeane's birth on her maternity leave and stayed with the Bolenders herself.

Once Gladys returned to work, she made regular payments for Norma Jeane's care to the Bolenders of $25 monthly, which totals to about $340 by today's standards.

While the stories of abuse and neglect persist, they are untrue. Marilyn and the Hollywood machine perpetrated these longstanding rumors.

If we consider it by today's standards, Gladys was a working single mother who, in her case, dropped her child off to a daycare situation, where she was in loving care. Many parents today do that and do not face a backlash as Gladys has for nearly a century. She checked in regularly as she could have while working. In 1927, she was around even more as her mother Della grew ill with malaria and she took the time to care for her ill mother.

Gladys's funds helped to pay for material to make clothing for Norma Jeane (Ida sewed the clothes on her Singer machine and Gladys provided the funding for the fabric). Norma Jeane was also pictured in a swimsuit on the beach with her mother and family, a swimsuit that Gladys herself purchased for her daughter.

Norma Jeane attended Sunday School and later school, with her "brother" Lester, a boy that the Bolenders eventually adopted. Lester and Norma Jeane were called "the twins," because of their blonde hair and pale complexion. The two were inseparable.

Norma Jeane also had a puppy named Tippy, a dog that followed Albert Wayne home from work one day as a postman. The dog took a liking to Norma Jeane and she was photographed with him. One evening, Tippy ran off and was shot by the neighbor who was upset with his barking in the night streets. Albert Wayne found the dog in the morning. However, what is often not told was that Gladys comforted Norma Jeane following Tippy's death and helped her to bury her beloved pet. Gladys had initially told Norma Jeane she was purchasing a home that she could reside in with her daughter and Tippy could come too.

There were weekend trips to the beach together, as well as time spent at movie theaters with Grace and Gladys, who were obsessed with the movie stars of their day. They often took little Norma Jeane on excursions to Grauman's Chinese Theater, where they would all attempt to fit their hands and feet in the prints of their favorite stars.

In the 1927 Los Angeles City Directory a Gladys Baker, a "film worker" is listed as a resident on 237 Bimini Place, with Grace McKee Goddard also residing with her at the same address in 1928.

In 1927, Grace lived at 1350 Wilshire Boulevard and was listed as a "film inspector," moving in with Gladys the following year.

Gladys was said to have excelled at her job, including having helped her crew at Consolidated Film Industries to safety when there was a major fire at the facility that entirely destroyed the lab. On October 24, 1929, an explosion rocked the laboratory, the independent company used to process many of the studio films. Though some film was saved, others were feared destroyed then, including *Hell's Angels* and *The Taming of the Shrew*. The estimated damages to the building were $400,000 and to the films lost approximately $1 million.

McKEE FRANK Dist Mgr California Development Assn Suite 100 W M Garland Bldg, 117 W 9th, Phone Trinity 3236 r239½ S Berendo
" Frank slsmn h353 S Fremont av
" Frank M r317 E 6th
" Frank S home bldr h1909 W 82d
" Frank S printer h1542 W 65th pl
" Frank W h623 W 5th
" Frank W phys h1101 Gramercy dr
" Frank W slsmn h875 El Paso dr
" Geo T drftsmn Dept Pub Serv h127 Muriel av Brentwood Hts
" Geo W h1129 Mignonette
" Geo W (Wallace McKee) h5765 Aldama
" Gerhard C firemn L A F D r368¾ S Burlington av
" Gladys clk Sec Tr & Sav Bk r1007 W 36th
" Gordon J clk h1135 W 50th
" Grace h237 Bimini pl
" H Stewart jr r434 S Rimpau blvd
" Harry L h1227 N New Hampshire av
" Harvey R firemn h920 Sheffield av

One man was killed during the fire, and the *Santa Cruz Evening News* reported, "Explosion and fire which wrecked the laboratory of the Consolidated Film Industries, Inc., today passed miraculously by fifty men and women workers in the building, with a toll of only one death."

Though film cutters were unnamed, *The Lincoln Star* stated, "Two women workers, who ran as the first flash of flame spread through the building said they saw the first explosion occur in a pile of chemicals near one of the polishing machines in an assembly room."

The person who died, Albert Lund, was near that machine.

"C.M. Lockwood, a film company executive, working in a projection room, said 35 women and fifteen men were in the structure when the first explosion occurred and that he had accounted for them all except Lund."

Another interesting note and one wonders if any of the film cutters quoted could have been Gladys, read, "Film cutters told of many feet of film lying loose on the floors of cutting rooms, which they had not time to gather up."

The 1930 Census is another piece of physical proof that there was never an abandonment issue on Gladys's part. In fact, both Gladys and Norma Jeane were listed as "boarders" in the Bolender home. The census is a treasure that reflects Albert Bolender's role as Head of Household on 459 Rhode Island Avenue. It is often listed though as 459 East Rhode Island Street and then 215 East Rhode Island Street.

On the census, Gladys was referred to as "Gladys Baker" and her daughter "Norma Jean Baker."

What is strange about this census is while Gladys is of her age at 27 and showing divorced, as well as having she and her parents both born in England, "Norma Jean" was recorded as a 63-year-old widow. However, it was definitely them because Albert is listed as a "Letter Carrier," and Gladys a "Developer" in "Motion Pictures."

Gladys's residency there is backed up in the 1930 Los Angeles City Directory that shows she is a "cutter" with RKO Studios, living in Hawthorne.

Lester is also on the census as a child of just under four years of age, and Ida is listed as "Edna E."

The street was renamed East 134th Street as the family resided at 459 East 134th Street in the 1940 Census, with Ida listed correctly and Albert Wayne as a postmaster. Lester was then 12-years-old and their adopted daughter, age eight. There were supplemental questions about Nancy and the birthplace of her parents, which were Ohio and New York.

When Marilyn died, Ida penned a letter to Berniece, from the address 455 E. 134th Street, which showed another renumbering of the streets.

While Gladys and Norma Jeane were with the Bolenders, they were not alone and without their families. In fact, her great uncle William Marion Hogan was then residing nearby in Los Angeles with his family and wife Clara. And Gladys's cousin Milton Andros was additionally on Hauser Place and working in the motion picture industry himself as a plaster artist. It was then a downright untruth after Gladys was "adjudged insane" and Grace sought guardianship over Norma Jeane in 1935 (which the application stated "Norma Jean Baker" also known as "Norma J. Mortenson") that there were no relatives who could have helped out with Norma during Gladys's illness.

Gladys's first cousin Milton S. Andros was a resident of Los Angeles and most specifically at his address on 1736 Hauser Boulevard in 1930, with later listings in 1936 and 1937 in city directories, long after Norma Jeane spent time in the orphanage. His son was additionally living with them and listed as a member of the Navy in 1936. It was only 10 miles from where Gladys resided with the Bolenders.

"That your petitioner is advised and believes and therefore alleges that there are no relatives entitled to the guardianship of said minor residing in the state of California except the mother of the said minor; that the address of the father of said minor is unknown," was written. Though they made it sound as if Gladys picked up and walked Norma Jeane out from the Bolender residence one day, she was still a resident of Hawthorne in 1932 and holding down a job as a film cutter for RKO. Gladys is often portrayed as unavailable to her daughter, unstable and unable to hold down work, which are all incorrect.

Gladys took Norma Jeane to live with her 6012 Afton Place, a home that was demolished in the 1960s. Gladys then acquired her home at 6812 Arbol Drive in Hollywood, renting a portion of it to the Atkinson family.

All was well and she was settling in to life with Norma Jeane and the Atkinsons. There was even a piano in the home that Gladys had purchased for Norma Jeane. Eventually, as Grace assumed guardianship, she handled the sale of the items including the property at 6812 Arbol Drive, a 1933 Plymouth Sedan, a small radio and a Franklin Baby Grand Piano. There were gifts from friends, insurance checks and a small amount of money in the bank to help, totaling over $5,000.

Grace dispersed the monies to care for Norma Jeane and for Gladys.

Grace's Aunt Ana actually purchased the piano and kept it in storage to set aside for Norma Jeane. However, *My Story* erroneously accounts that Marilyn tracked down the piano in an auction room and reacquired it.

What is known is that the pressure became too much for Gladys. As it was for the rest of the country, she was dealing with financial woes. Some have said that Gladys buckled from a job loss and was attempting to hold herself together. Over the previous summer, there was a major strike in the film industry reported nationwide that on July 24, 1933 all union employees were ordered to strike. Some have said that Gladys refused to strike and even climbed the fence to go to work.

One newspaper the *Mount Carmel Item* reported that it was sound engineers striking that day.

"Because sound technicians were indispensible to taking pictures, no cameras were grinding in the 14 major studios," it was written. "In an admitted possibility that any attempt upon the part of the producers to use non-union men in this highly organized craft would result in a wholesale walkout of cameramen, projectionists, script-girls, make-up and wardrobe men, carpenters, electricians, film cutters and property men, all of whom are organized and affiliated with the American Federation of Labor."

Two days later, the papers reported that workers were still striking, though some of the activities at slightly picked up at the studio.

By early September, 1935, Grace reported to the court that the items of Gladys's had been sold and she was able to be reimbursed by the court for payments she made on Gladys's behalf to "preserve the estate." Car payments, payments for the radio, payment of the piano, car insurance, care of Gladys and care of Norma Jeane were among the expenses.

While Norma Jeane has often been portrayed by many as neglected the record showed she was not. There were checks written for clothing and Christmas gifts. She enjoyed items like scrapbooks and also photo sessions. Grace bought her a bathing suit and cap. There was even a breakdown for medical bills for care of Norma Jeane's injured foot.

In 1936, she made a payment to a lawyer regarding guardianship for Norma Jeane. Then there were payments to the Los Angeles Orphans' Home in 1936. Grace visited her regularly and was consistently in touch with the supervisors of the home regarding her care, unlike the accounts that Marilyn was basically locked away with the key thrown out.

The Atkinsons and Grace cared for Norma Jeane for some time before she was required to enter the orphanage for the period of beginning September 1935. She remained in the orphanage, unlike many accounts, for nine months until full guardianship was established. Following, Norma Jeane stayed with family members of Grace's, with Grace herself and with Ida Martin, which the accounting shows payments to all of the women at various times from 1936 to 1940 for Norma Jeane's care.

While Gladys was hospitalized, Norma Jeane did visit with her mother, as there was a trip accounted for to San Francisco in June 1939.

Of course, with those years locked away there were various events that Gladys missed. Her daughter Berniece had grown up, married and had a daughter, with Gladys soon reconnecting with her via a letter from Agnews. Then Norma Jeane married in 1942, shortly after she turned 16. It was Ana Lower who gave away the bride, with most of the wedding guests present at the event Jim Dougherty's relatives.

Marilyn Monroe Unveiled | A Family History

When Gladys returned to Los Angeles she had the opportunity to live a life with her daughter Norma Jeane and her other daughter, Berniece, who visited for several months.

She was frustrated and angry at times after her release from the hospital, some say because of the impact of the treatments she endured. Sometimes Marilyn admitted to her sister Berniece, it was hard to reach her emotionally.

Gladys grew easily frustrated and was often calmed by Ana Lower, with whom both Marilyn and Gladys resided. She held down a job placing tags on clothes after her return to Los Angeles, which according to daughter Berniece, she was let go from her job soon following.

There are other pictures from that time too of a woman with a genuine smile posing for photos between her daughters, her arms proudly around each of their waists and vice versa. Another photo shows a mother and both of her daughters attired in bikinis and sitting in the sand together, all elegantly enjoying a day at the beach.

Another photo shows a woman appearing younger than her years although she was a grandmother, enjoying dinner with her daughters, granddaughter and good friends.

Following Berniece's departure from Los Angeles, Gladys also left, reportedly to head back towards Oregon. But she returned to live again with Ana and refocused on cleaning houses, a vocation that she called "practical nursing." Marilyn was living in her own apartment then.

In March 1948, as Marilyn was beginning to spread her wings in her film career, Ana Lower passed away.

On May 30, 1948, Gladys mailed a letter to Grace. Though Gladys may not have been herself, the letter, mailed from the Dalt Hotel in San Francisco reflected a jovial spirit, still reflecting a quick wit.

"Dear Grace and all," she wrote, "Get ready for a surprise as I guess you are surprised to hear from me. For goodness sake Grace dear why didn't you let me know of Aunt Ana's passing away? Didn't you have my address or what?"

Gladys had apparently been writing Grace and asked her to handle her belongings. She also thanked her for "all your goodness to me."

In the letter, she asked after Norma Jeane and apologized for not staying in touch. She asked to pass on her love to everyone.

It was after Ana's passing that Marilyn landed her first starring role in the *Ladies of the Chorus*. Though Gladys told her daughter Berniece that she was upset with the movie industry and Marilyn's choice of a career, author John Gilmore interviewed Marilyn's co-star Rand Brooks from *Ladies of the Chorus*. He told Gilmore he "met this frail lady named Mrs. Baker who hardly spoke but her eyes got big…She was nervous to be on a set, watching her daughter work in the movie. Marilyn was so proud of herself and eager for her mother to see how she had become a success. Mrs. Baker didn't say very much. She was polite but withdrawn, like in awe over the whole experience."

Gladys ended up marrying again in 1949 to a man named John Stewart Eley, who passed away on April 23, 1952. She moved back in with Grace. At this stage, Gladys immersed herself deeper in Christian Science.

Grace kept careful notes about things Gladys did after she began living with her, because she knew that her personality had changed. Gladys had become averse to Catholics. She told Grace no one should listen to the radio broadcasters because everyone is drunk. She told Grace that her emotional state had deteriorated because of union organizations. She no longer was eating meat or fish and was often eating spaghetti, bread, potatoes or salad only. She accused people of stealing her items when they were actually lost.

"[She] sleeps with her head at the foot of bed so as not to look at Marilyn's pictures, they disturb her," Grace documented.

Gladys showed up in Florida to visit Berniece following the death of her husband and spent seven weeks with her. It was a challenging situation, though Marilyn had suggested Gladys take an apartment in Florida, where Berniece was now living. It did not work and Gladys took a train back to Grace in Los Angeles.

However, on her return, Gladys was angry with Grace for sending her a ticket for the train rather than a plane and screamed relentlessly outside of her home. Grace and her husband Doc called for an ambulance and Gladys was taken to the hospital.

Grace mailed a letter to Berniece in July 1953 that Marilyn and Doc worked through a pile of fan mail that had been sitting for a year.

On September 28, 1953, Grace Goddard passed away. She had been struggling with cancer and her final cause of death was barbiturate poisoning, with an ingestion of phenobarbital. The other condition her autopsy uncovered was "fatty metamorphosis of liver," a byproduct of alcohol abuse. However, while Marilyn never knew her exact cause of death, Berniece was shocked to learn what the real cause was many years later.

By this time, Grace and Marilyn were hardly in touch as Marilyn climbed the ladder of success and she was whisked away by the Hollywood machine, one that Grace also helped to create as one of the crafters of Marilyn's Cinderella story.

It was Grace who also helped to architect the story about Gladys, with some saying it was a way to protect her best friend's privacy. The movie magazines truly portrayed Marilyn as an orphan, even noting that Gladys had died when she was a child.

However, the same year that news broke that Marilyn had posed nude for a calendar, which simultaneously leaked around the same time that she began dating the man who would become her second husband, Joe DiMaggio, an enterprising reporter had found out that Gladys was living.

Marilyn explained in a 1952 *Screenland* article that the studios told her to "forget the past, everybody thinks you're an orphan, so let it stay that way. It's good copy."

Marilyn told a white lie to the press about her relationship with her mother, though she had lived with Gladys on and off for several years after her release from the hospital in 1945.

"My close friends know that my mother is alive," she said. "Unbeknown to me as a child, my mother spent many years as an invalid in a state hospital. I haven't known my mother intimately, but since I have become grown and able to help her, I have contacted her. I am helping her and will continue to help her when she needs me."

Marilyn asked Inez Melson, her business manager to handle guardianship and she visited Gladys frequently on her behalf at Rockhaven Sanitarium in Glendale, which is now a site slated for historic preservation in the city.

Gladys regularly sent letters and cards from Rockhaven to her family members, including Marilyn over the years.

Though it has been said that Joe DiMaggio never spoke unkindly of Gladys, on the other hand, it is known that third husband Arthur Miller despised her and wrote poorly of her in his book, *Timebends*.

"Her past would not leave her even for this private affirmation of her value, and that past was murderous. Something like guilt seemed to suppress her voice. It was not merely her mother's malign influence – the woman had always been paranoid, an institutionalized schizophrenic who tried to smother her in her crib as an infant; it was also the condemnation of religion that she had to defend herself against. And the stain kept reappearing like a curse."

These were the tales that the likes of people like Arthur Miller, Lee Strasberg and others who controlled Marilyn's life would tell of her later. Perpetuating the myth that Gladys was detrimental to Marilyn and alternating the story that either Gladys or Della had tried to smother her with a pillow, this is what has created the damaging tales about Marilyn's family. In a 1956 *TIME* article about Marilyn the purported pillow attacker was described as a deranged neighbor, who later evolved in stories as Della and then with Arthur's account, to Gladys.

In 1957, Inez provided Marilyn with a progress report on Gladys that she kept in her files. Inez expressed how Marilyn had become like a "daughter image" to her and in return "it gives me a warm feeling to be able to do little things for your mother."

It was Inez who would challenge Marilyn's will because she believed there was undue influence that Lee Strasberg and her doctors placed on her to sign it (and afterward Marilyn herself was wrongly incarcerated in a mental hospital), and Inez attempted to protect Gladys's interests.

Marilyn Monroe Unveiled | A Family History

At Rockhaven, Gladys was occupied with activities, including fashioning tablemats from a loom, which Inez reported that Gladys's were the loveliest on display at the Rockhaven Craft Bazaar. Inez purchased four that Gladys made and told Marilyn she would send them, suggesting Marilyn use them on her table for informal dinners with Arthur and his children.

Inez told Marilyn that Gladys also copied a candy wreath that she had given to Gladys for Christmas the year prior, fashioning her own similar one with peppermint candies. Gladys followed the candy's pattern so that there was a design on her wreath from them.

At the craft event, Gladys helped to oversee the coffee urn at the refreshment table, as well as arrange the cookies and sandwiches. Inez told Marilyn that this was an enjoyable activity for Gladys as she spent time in the facility's garden for the afternoon. Plus, she reported, a black cat at the facility "Bobby" seemed to take a liking to Gladys, with Gladys responding positively to him.

Inez would shop for Gladys too on Marilyn's behalf, even purchasing boots and a raincoat for her since she enjoyed walks in the facility's garden. It was a better arrangement than the state run facilities and patients were treated with respect and dignity. Gladys enjoyed car rides with one of the employees and walks around the garden.

After Marilyn's death in 1962, Berniece suggested to Inez that she take Gladys to live with her in Florida. Inez countered that it was not advisable because Gladys was comfortable there, even when Berniece suggested that outside of her husband and daughter that Gladys was her last immediate family link.

Berniece visited Gladys while she was in Los Angeles for Marilyn's funeral and they spent time together, with Gladys wearing all white, an outfit she wore often to assimilate into her role of nurse. Gladys seemed unaffected that her daughter was dead.

Rare film footage of Gladys exists walking around the grounds of Rockhaven with Inez Melson holding her arm. Gladys is elegantly attired, her hair pulled back into a chignon, her arm linked with Inez as the two women casually walk and talk. She carries a purse, something she had also requested years ago as a purchase from Grace when she was hospitalized in her early years.

While Marilyn had provided for Gladys's care when she became wealthy and set up a trust fund for her mother, none of the payments could be made to Rockhaven for her care since Marilyn's estate was still in turmoil until nearly 20 years after her death.

Rockhaven preservationists have told the story of Gladys's stay there, which was at no cost until 1967 when Berniece assumed responsibility for Gladys's care.

As a small wisp of a woman with the same sense of adventure that she had in her younger years to hit the road, Gladys, now 63, finagled her way through an 18-inch window in her closet. She navigated over a fence with her knotted nurses' dresses and walked about 15 miles to a church, where she slept behind a hot water heater.

Until Berniece could assume guardianship, she had Gladys transferred to Camarillo State Hospital. When Gladys attempted suicide, Berniece assumed custody of her mother.

Gladys lived with Berniece for some years, though it was difficult and there were mishaps, like the iron left burning while Gladys was absorbed reading her Christian Science books.

Berniece arranged for Gladys to live in a senior citizens' complex, which she was consistently leaving. At some point, Gladys vanished altogether and later reappeared in the Florida town, Gainesville where they resided, with someone who knew Berniece spotting Gladys and informing her.

In those final years, Gladys would still be properly attired, wearing a jacket, carrying a purse and a hat on her head, even as she sat in a wheelchair.

She died on March 11, 1984, with the Florida Death Index noting her name as "Gladys P. Eley." Her burial location has never been specified.

"Even when she was bedridden in the nursing home to the end of her days," her daughter Berniece and granddaughter Mona Rae wrote, "she would jump the bedrails and make her way to the hall."

Some of their final words about Gladys summed up her life and spirit, though the ravages of the mental health system quashed her in some ways, "Her drive for independence never faltered."

CHAPTER NINETEEN

BIOGRAPHER DONALD SPOTO wrote about Tilford Marion Hogan (Marilyn Monroe's great-grandfather), "He was a generous man who shared spontaneously from his own meager supplies of food and fuel. His empathetic nature was perhaps all the more remarkable since his entire adult life was blighted by severe rheumatoid arthritis and chronic respiratory infections, conditions exacerbated by hard labor, poor diet and a ceaseless rhythm of poverty."

The man you are going to meet in this chapter was certainly a generous man, however, Donald Spoto took serious creative liberty (as did every so called biographer for the last 55 years) characterizing someone he knew very little about and creatively making that person "fit" Marilyn Monroe's orphan stories. This same sort of pattern of concocting fabricated biographical narratives has continued to promote and perpetuate the deception and myth surrounding Marilyn and all of her relatives. Tilford Marion Hogan was not the man Donald Spoto described in his biography of Marilyn Monroe.

Tilford Marion Hogan came from an upper class prominent family. His grandfather Zachariah Hogan was a business man who was involved with his community and politics. Some of his uncles such as Dr. O.P. Hogan Jr. and other cousins were very well educated and involved in law and politics. His family line was instrumental in the settling of early America and they were participants in the Revolutionary War and Civil War; in short, they were active American patriots.

With Tilford's hard work in the farming industry, Tilford Marion Hogan was wrongly portrayed as someone with an itinerant nature and unable to make money no matter how hard he tried.

He has also been painted as someone who did little else with his life; that he was uncultured and died a frustrated old pauper who hung himself in the end.

Those falsehoods are far from the truth based directly on Tilford's activities reported in the newspaper *The Laclede Blade*.

Tilford was also portrayed as someone without his family in his life. While his children lived out of the area and perhaps that was difficult, nonetheless it is documented that he was actively engaging with relatives. His daughter Dora Hogan and grandson Milton Stores Andros was living in Laclede for some time. He was also visited by his niece Miss Alice Hogan from California. Rather than being alone, Tilford Marion Hogan can be characterized as being sociable and was actively engaged with his family and community.

Many unethical biographers had Tilford never leaving the Ozarks, or the borders of Missouri for that matter and bounced from shanty town to shanty town. On the contrary, Tilford did his share of traveling and even moved out of the

> LACLEDE, MISSOURI, SATURDAY, FEBRUARY 7, 1903.
>
> At the same time and place of the above sale the following property of T. M. Hogan will be offered for sale on same terms: One black stallion, 5 years old; saddle horse, 4 years old; single buggy and harness, saddle and bridle, sleigh.
>
> T. M. Hogan will leave about the 16th of this month for California where he expects to locate.

area to California in 1903. In fact, he advertised in the paper that he was ready to sell all of his property and move to California.

On one such occasion on February 7, 1903, Tilford was planning on leaving for California on February 16 and he returned on May 9.

Prior to his first trip, Tilford advertised in the *Laclede Blade*, his black stallion, saddle horses, a buggy, a harness and a saddle for sale.

In 1907, the paper noted on January 5 that Tilford was heading for a "land hunt" in Indian Territory.

He and his sister also traveled together, according to the paper, to Muskogee Oklahoma on October 9, 1909.

> **LACLEDE, MISSOURI, SATURDAY, JULY 30. 1904.**
>
> **Notice.**
>
> Notice is hereby given that all persons indebted to me for berries or on any other account, are forbidden to pay my husband, C. M. Williams.
>
> MARY ANN WILLIAMS.

He also had visitors in the early part of 1910, in addition to entertaining daughter Dora, her family (including son Milton, daughter Dorothy, and even Louis Milton Andros and his side), his niece Alice reportedly visited, as well as visiting her Aunt Mary Ann Williams from August 1904 through February 1905. Mary Mahurin married C.M. Williams on June 19, 1903 though later that year on behalf of the fruit farm, she told the public that anyone indebted to her directly for blackberries was not to pay her husband and signed it "Mary Ann Williams."

Later that year the paper reported on August 16 of that same year, Tilford was "expected to locate" to Visalia California. This was an area with a rich agricultural history including livestock, grapes, citrus and olives. The papers indicated he did and then returned.

In January 1910, there was even word that he had purchased property in Cottonwood Kansas and was planning on relocating that spring.

One of the fascinating points of the old newspapers was how they chronicled someone's life, similarly to how people of today may use social media. The papers might have reported if a person was traveling in or out of town, if they planned to leave the area, who they dined with, who they celebrated with, their tragedies and much more. Many of these tidbits provide an interesting insight into an ancestor's life.

Tilford was one of these people who, contrary to popular reporting from the biographers who did not explore his background, was very busy and his activities recorded often in the newspapers.

Part of Missouri's heritage that Tilford helped to forge was the "U-Pick" farms. Today throughout the state farmers invite the public to their farms for a fee as Tilford advertised himself to pick a range of berries and apples.

> **LACLEDE, MISSOURI, SATURDAY, JUNE 3. 1905.**
>
> THE BLADE received a box of fine cherries yesterday from Mrs. M. A. Mahurin. T. M. Hogan, who brought them in informs us that prospects are good for a fine raspberry crop and that the blackberry bushes also promise a big yield.

"The *BLADE* family have had several batches of strawberry shortcake this last week and made from the best berries ever," the paper reported. "On Monday, T.M. Hogan brought in a quart from Mrs. Williams's fruit farm."

The paper also crowed on June 3, 1905, "The *BLADE* received fine cherries from Mrs. Mary Mahurin. T.M. Hogan who brought them informs us that prospects are good for a fine raspberry crop and that blackberry bushes also promise a big yield."

During the first two decades of the century, Tilford's crops were regularly bragged about in the paper.

Surprisingly in the winter months of 1906, Tilford advertised raspberry plants on February 17 and March 6, in limited supply. He even provided a phone line "Locust Line Mahurin," and the address Route 1 Box 24. As Tilford's business grew and he was advertising, his ads noted that they had a telephone. Phones were becoming more commonplace in the U.S. though many still did not have them among the 85 million inhabitants in the country (there were about three million phones).

In September 1906, Tilford advertised apples for sale. On July 7, 1906 "reasonable blackberries."

In Tilford's own words in an advertisement on July 17, 1907, reflected a man with a purpose, a vision and confidence: "If you want blackberries come at once and get the best they are now ripe. Pickers wanted."

On June 4, 1908 the farm was open too "for those who wish to pick blackberries."

In April of 1910, he advertised Timothy Hay, which today is the type sold for small animals. Beginning in the early 1700s, this type of hay was recommended for cattle.

In August 1910, Tilford advertised corn for sale and a telephone number "505 Laclede."

Hogs were another specialty of Tilford's, especially in 1911 that Duroc Jersey Gilts and Boars, a reddish colored hog, were for sale. The paper also noted that year that Tilford butchered three of them, ranging between 281 to 307 pounds, which he supposedly fattened up within seven and a half months.

In 1912, Tilford advertised that he would be leaving the farming industry and would sell everything and later in the month of September, advertised that a large auction sale would take place at the Mahurin Fruit Farm with an auctioneer and lunch provided from the ladies of the nearby Christian Church.

Tilford's work in farming did not stop though. In 1921, he was back on the radar advertising everbearing strawberry plants and in September of that year, earned second place in a contest for his tomatoes.

In 1914, he also listed his stalls for rent to students who needed to ride to the Laclede schools.

While Tilford was actively engaged in his farming business, both independently and with his sister Mary, he was also actively investing in real estate properties.

Biographers have always depicted Tilford as subservient to others, on the contrary Tilford owned his own farm. It was in 1907, there was the purchase made for nine acres of land in Brookfield to create a small fruit farm. In September of 1913, he was noted as purchasing the Van Valkenberg property for $1,500. In 1919, Tilford purchased another two residential properties. One other investment Tilford made was in 1921 with the Eliza Wait residence for $950. That same year, Tilford and his sister bought Laclede Mayor Plowman's property for $1,200, another specified as an investment.

The church was something that Tilford was also involved with. A minister of the Christian Church named J.A.W. Brown purchased one of Tilford's properties as well for $1,600 for his home and headquarters. Tilford was a church leader himself having been elected a church elder on January 27, 1911.

Marilyn Monroe Unveiled | A Family History

Democratic Convention: Tilford Marion Hogan, Marilyn Monroe's Great Grandfather, was elected as a man delegate to the county convention.

Laclede Blade 1920

Democratic Convention

At the democratic township primary held at the opera house Saturday afternoon, Harry Landree, George Calhoun, G. O. Plowman, and T. M. Hogan were elected the men delegates to the county convention held at Linneus Monday, and the women elected Mrs. W. R. Barton, Mrs. H. D. Hall and Mrs. J. E. Welsh. 'Squire J. T. Cushing attended the county convention as alternate for Hogan and H. C. McCoy went in place of Landree.

At the county convention held at Linneus Monday Senator Fields was chairman and C. A. Johnson, secretary.

The resolutions were short, just enough to show, as one delegate expressed it, that the convention was "agin" Senator Reed, although he was not mentioned.

The men delagates to the state convention are Walter Brownlee, T. P. Burns, Brookfield; J. I. Harman, Browning; G. L. Joyce, Bucklin; H. C. Taggert and L. F. Kelly, Linneus; T. M. Ludden, Marceline.

The women delegates are Mrs. T. P. Burns and Mrs. Robert Haley, Bookfield; Mrs. E. B. Fields, Browning; Mrs. G. L. Joyce, Bucklin; Mrs. Lillie Hall, Laclede; Mrs. Ruth Hayes, Linneus; Mrs. D. J. Buckley, St.

Not only was Tilford a farmer, he was a leader in the community in both the church and politics. At the county's Democratic convention, Tilford became one of its delegates on April 2, 1920. He also attended local political meetings, having attempted to spearhead a petition against an ordinance the town was attempting to pass in Laclede to oil the roads and on May 27, 1921, the 70-year-old Tilford complained to Laclede officials about it at the meeting and helped with the petition, which, unfortunately for Tilford and the citizens against the measure, failed.

It was not all business and community service for Tilford though. In 1909, he was one of many citizens listed as enjoying the Locust Creek District Thanksgiving Oyster Supper. Fresh oysters were part of the thanksgiving stuffing in those days as part of a rich meal that all in the Locust Creek District enjoyed on their holiday. Today, the Locust Creek's heritage is honored through the Locust Creek Covered Bridge State Historic Site and Park in Laclede itself. This covered bridge constructed in 1868 is one that all of these residents used in one of the first transcontinental roadways then known as Route 8. This truss bridge is only one of four left in Missouri.

One of the last myths to put to bed about Tilford, Marilyn Monroe's great-grandfather, was that he never met his granddaughter, Gladys, Marilyn's mother. Many biographers have incorrectly noted this.

The paper however reported otherwise, noting twice in 1913 that Della and the children visited Tilford. On June 27, 1913, Della and her children Gladys and Marion were recorded as having visited Tilford and other relatives. Another woman traveled with them named Virginia Nelson, also from Los Angeles. The paper recorded their return to California on August 15.

In 1928, Tilford, who had been divorced for most of his remaining years stood before the Justice of the Peace in Linn County with Emma D. Wyett of Brookfield. The two lived with his sister in 1930, Mary, who was then 86. Tilford and Emma were 79 and 67 years respectfully. At that time the 1930 Census recorded none of them had occupations listed at their home, where Tilford was the head of household.

The census that year was taken on April 17 and sadly, Tilford's sister died at home on August 28. Tilford was the informant, a melancholy task to have to take with the sister that he spent many years working, traveling and socializing with. Her cause of death was "Paralysis Agitans," what we know today as Parkinson's Disease.

And then three years later, the inevitable happened. The paper reported that Emma headed out to town for a business trip and then returned at 3 p.m. on May 29, 1933. She called for Tilford and he did not respond. She headed for the barn and found him hanging with a rope around his neck that was attached to one of the joists on the second floor.

Already battling heart troubles, Emma and Tilford's neighbors J.G. Clinefelter and N.B. Cross heard her cries and found Emma had fainted on the ground. After they revived her she uttered, "Tilford in the barn."

The neighbors rushed to the barn and contacted local police and the town's undertaker, Mr. Thorne. County Coroner of Brookfield Dr. McLarney instructed the undertaker to remove Tilford's body from the hanging position.

An investigation ensued between a jury of locals, who spoke to the gentlemen neighbors who came to Emma's aid. The jury with C.A. Felt, A.C. Windle, H.M. Standly, A.J. Caywood, W.L. Molloy and S.W. White concurred Tilford's death was a self-inflicted passing by hanging. Both Dora and Myrtle attended their father's funeral, which a fellow elder from the Christian Church, C.E. Dunkleberger, conducted. Neither of his sons were listed on the obituary, and nor was his deceased daughter, Della, Marilyn's grandmother. Plus, he had grandchildren like Gladys, and great-granddaughter Norma Jeane, who was then a few days shy of her seventh birthday. His tragic death, which also occurred only two days after granddaughter Gladys's 31st birthday, was said to have upset her greatly, with memories of time spent with Tilford.

In Laclede Cemetery, a pillar monument marks in capital letters "BROTHER TILFORD M. HOGAN 1851-1933."

Even in death he and his sister were inseparable, since the headstone lists his sister Mary

Marilyn Monroe Unveiled | A Family History

The Laclede Blade, November 27, 1909.

Tilford Marion Hogan and sister Mary Mahurin attended the Thanksgiving Oyster Supper.

LACLEDE, MISSOURI, FRIDAY, DECEMBER 2, 1910

The annual Thanksgiving oyster supper of the Locust Creek neighborhood was held Thursday evening of last week at the home of Mr. and Mrs. L. E. Eichman south of Laclede. Those who have attended these events in the past know how pleasant they are and this one was perhaps even more enjoyable than usual. Those present were: Mr. and Mrs. W. S. Mahurin, Mr. and Mrs. W. O. Anderson, Mr. and Mrs. J. M. McDonnell, Mr. Andros and family, Mrs. Mary Mahurin, T. M. Hogan, Misses Louise Brenner, Betty Anderson, Rose Lloyd, Leota and Leo Foster, Maude, Edith and Effie Mahurin, Mae Curtis, Orliva Anderson, Bertha and Nellie Harris, Margaret Daniels, Emma, Bessie and Ada Perry, O. Y. Watson, Rufus and A. C. Lloyd, Harry Perry, Clyde Balcom, Carlos Anderson, San McDonnell, Carl Harris, Orville Mahurin, George Dunkle, George, Henry and Charley Brenner, Ralph and Elmer Kling, Roy Howard, Landa Lloyd and Roy Transburg.

THE LACLEDE BLADE.

T.M. HOGAN

Marilyn Monroe's great-grandfather

Tilford Marion Hogan the Farmer.

LACLEDE, MISSOURI, SATURDAY, MAY 27. 1905.

The BLADE family have had several extra batches of strawberry shortcake the past week and made from the best berries that ever grew. On Monday T. M. Hogan brought in a quart from Mrs. Williams' fruit farm southwest of town, and on Thursday H. B. VanValkenburg brought in a box rounded up with berries as large as hen eggs, and the same day Mansur Benson placed on our desk a quart fresh from the family patch that couldn't be beat in any market. When we get a chance at a quarter-section of short-cake made from such luscious berries as these were, our only regret is that we haven't the capacity for storing it away that our friend Northcott of the Sumner Star has.

LACLEDE, MISSOURI, FRIDAY, APRIL 15. 1921.

Everbearing strawberry plants that bear, for sale by T. M. Hogan, Laclede.

LACLEDE, MISSOURI, SATURDAY, FEBRUARY 17. 1906.

Those wanting raspberry plants should send in their orders at once as our supply is limited. Call Mahurin 'phone, Locust line, or address T. M. Hogan, Route 1, Box 24, Laclede.

LACLEDE, MISSOURI, SATURDAY, APRIL 16. 1910.

Some good timothy hay for sale by T. M. Hogan.

THE LACLEDE BLADE

Entered at the postoffice at Laclede, Mo., for transmission through the mail as second class matter.

J. B. JONES, Editor and Publisher.

FRIDAY, JANUARY 13, 1911

Last week T. M. Hogan of route one butchered three hogs 7½ months old, which weighed from 281 to 307 pounds each. They were of Duroc-Jersey breed and those who have claimed that hogs of that breed could not be fattened under a year were evidently mistaken.

LACLEDE, MISSOURI, FRIDAY, SEPTEMBER 1. 1911

Duroc-Jersey gilts and one Duroc-Jersey boar for sale by T. M. Hogan.

LACLEDE, MISSOURI, SATURDAY, JULY 7. 1906.

Blackberries are now ready for picking at the Mahurin fruit farm. Those wishing to pick and get berries should apply at once to T. M. Hogan. The crop is good and price for berries reasonable.

Tilford Marion Hogan the Farmer continued...

LACLEDE, MISSOURI, SATURDAY, JULY 4, 1908.

Notice to Berry Pickers

My blackberries will begin ripening next week. The usual opportunity is given to those wanting berries to come and pick them.

T. M. HOGAN.

LACLEDE, MISSOURI, SATURDAY, SEPTEMBER 29, 1906.

second.

CLASS G.

Best fall apples, J. W. Wallace: winter apples, T. M. Hogan; plums, Florence Moss; peaches, A. L. Loomis; pears, Miss A. E. Ransom; display of apples, not less than six varieties, T. M. Hogan; cider vinegar, Mrs. L. T. Rowland; sorghum, W. N. Harter.

LACLEDE, MISSOURI, FRIDAY, DECEMBER 12, 1919.

Manager Patterson took one car of hogs and one car of hogs and sheep to the St. Joseph market Saturday night for the following members of the association: Elmer Kling, Geo. McGhee, A. H. Farrar, L. T. Ringland, Orvil Mahurin, Dave E. Stark, Robinson Bros., Mrs. Mary Baskin, Landa Lloyd, Mrs. E. J. Morris, Ross Glenn, E. B. Gudgell, Arthur Swank, E. F. Brenner, F. G. Adams, W. H. Glover. One mixed car was sent out Monday night in charge of Earnest Adams for the following members: Mrs. E. B. Skulley, T. M. Hogan, Ervin Griffin, J. W. Moberly, L. T. Ringland, E. B. Gudgell, Carl Wilson, F. G. Adams, J. M. McDonnell, Byron Lamme, Karl Jones, Geo. L. Farrar, Ralph Neal, W. H. Robbins, W. O. Anderson, A. H. Farrar, J. Ed. Downey.

Tilford Marion Hogan traveling...

THE LACLEDE BLADE.

A. J. CAYWOOD, Editor and Publisher.

Entered at the Laclede postoffice for transmission through the mails as second class matter.

SATURDAY, JAN. 5, 1907.

T. M. Hogan has gone on a land hunt to Indian Territory.

LACLEDE, MISSOURI, SATURDAY, AUGUST 15, 1903.

T. M. Hogan left Wednesday night for Vasalia, Cali., where he expects to locate.

LACLEDE, MISSOURI, SATURDAY, OCTOBER 9, 1909.

T. M. Hogan and his sister, Mrs. Mary Mahurin, left Tuesday for a visit at Muskogee, Okla.

THE LACLEDE BLADE

Entered at the postoffice at Laclede, Mo. for transmission through the mail as second class matter.

J. B. JONES, Editor and Publisher.

Friday, September 20, 1912

Public Sale

T. M. Hogan has decided to quit farming and will sell his live stock, including horses, cattle and pure-bred Duroc-Jersey hogs, farming implements, etc., at public auction at the Mahurin Fruit farm two miles south and one mile west of Laclede, on Tuesday, Oct. 1. Sale begins at 10 a. m., and lunch will be served by the ladies of the Christian church. Nine months credit will be given on sums over $10 on approved note; 4 per cent discount for cash. Col. D. G. Shiflett is the auctioneer.

LACLEDE, MISSOURI, OCTOBER 10, 1930.

Mr. and Mrs. T. M. Hogan, with the latter's grandson, Ola Sprague and wife, of Brookfield, motored to Glasgow last Sunday and spent the day with relatives.

Station Agent Moore spent Saturday and Sunday in St. Louis and witnessed two of the world series baseball games and no doubt did his share of rooting for the Cardinals.

LACLEDE, MISSOURI, SATURDAY, MAY 9, 1903.

T. M. Hogan has returned from California after an absence of two months. He expects to locate here.

LACLEDE, MISSOURI, FRIDAY, JANUARY 27, 1933.

Mrs. T. M. Hogan was at Linneus Monday on business at the court house.

Marilyn Monroe Unveiled | A Family History

Tilford Marion Hogan as Real Estate Investor.

Title: U.S., Indexed County Land Ownership Maps, 1860-1918

Owner's Name: T M Hogan
State: Illinois
County: Adams
Town: Concord
Year: 1901

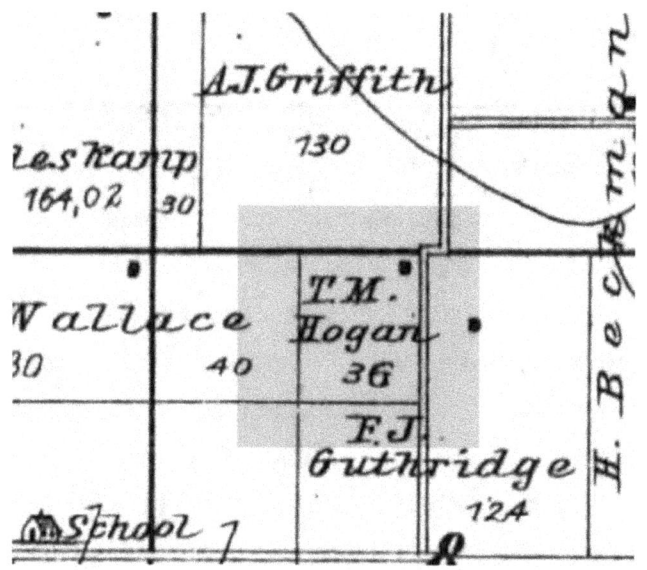

LACLEDE, MISSOURI, SATURDAY, FEBRUARY 23, 1907.

T. M. Hogan and Mrs. Mary Mahurin have bought the W. B. McGregor place of nine acres in Rose Hill, Brookfield, and expect to convert it into a small fruit farm. They have rented the place for the present year to Silas Mahurin.

LACLEDE, MISSOURI, FRIDAY, SEPTEMBER 13, 1912

T. M. Hogan has rented out his farm for the coming season and will hold a public sale of his stock and implements about the first of next month. Watch for announcement of date later.

LACLEDE, MISSOURI, FRIDAY, SEPTEMBER 13, 1912

T. H. Dunkle and family, who have been living on T. M. Hogan's farm southwest of town, have moved to the Polson residence on North State street.

Thomas Henry Dunkle Sr. was Tilford Hogan's nephew.

LACLEDE, MISSOURI, SATURDAY, JANUARY 15, 1910.

W. P. Bottiger, who recently sold his property here in town to T. M. Hogan, has bought a sixty acre farm near Cottonwood Falls, Kansas, and will move to that place the coming spring.

L. B. Allen, who recently sold

Tilford Marion Hogan as Real Estate Investor continued....

LACLEDE, MISSOURI, FRIDAY, SEPTEMBER 5, 1913

T. M. Hogan has bought the VanValkenburg place of three acres in the northwest part of town for $1500. He will set it to raspberries and other small fruit.

LACLEDE, MISSOURI, FRIDAY, NOVEMBER 1, 1918.

J. Q. Aber has sold his residence property to T. M. Hogan who bought it as an investment.

The Laclede Blade, October 03, 1919.

Tilford M. Hogan invested in two pieces of residence property this week, buying the Robert Wilson place in the southwest part of town and the cement block house in the north part of town of J. E. Kent.

The Laclede Blade, January 28, 1921.

Mayor Plowman has sold his residence in the southwest part of town, now occupied by J. B. Chapman and family, to Mary Mahurin and T. M. Hogan for $1,200. They bought it as an investment.

The fourth and last number of the season's lyceum course will

LACLEDE, MISSOURI, FRIDAY, FEBRUARY 15, 1918

Rev. J. A. W. Brown, evangelist for the Christian church, is a newcomer to Laclede, having bought the Van property of T. M. Hogan at $1660.00. Evangelist Brown's work is in Minnesota, Missouri and Kansas and this will be his home and headquarters. He has no family but the property will be occupied by his sister, Mrs. A. H. Cooper and family who now live on H. M. Standly's farm southwest of town. Rev. Mr. Brown is a pleasant and courteous gentleman, is a strong preacher and will no doubt be a great help to the local Christian church.

The Laclede Blade, September 09, 1921.

Mrs. Eliza Wait has bought the residence in the southwest part of town occupied by Ward Stutsman and family of T. M. Hogan for $950. Possession to be given next month.

Tilford Marion Hogan giving to charity.

LACLEDE, MISSOURI, FRIDAY, NOVEMBER 30, 1917

Y. M. C. A. WAR FUND

$681.50 Subscribed at Last Sunday Night's Meeting

FIVE DOLLARS

W. L. Sensintaffer, Mrs. J. H. Brown, Mrs. R. Estes, G. W. Estes, Wm. Lomax, Allie Harter, L. E. Eichman, Mrs. A. J. Caywood, Emma Gould, Cornelia Welsh, Geo. Plowman, M. E. Sunday school class 11, G. A. R. Post, F. F. Welsh Sunday school class, Mrs. Idah Moore, T. M. Hogan, J. Q. Aber, M. E. Sunday school class 17 Carl Wilson, Helen McKee, Mrs. E. B. Skulley, Geo. Kranz.

RED CROSS ACTIVITY

New Members and Donations For The Past Week

President Allen is still active looking after the financial part of the work and his appeals are meeting with a liberal response.

In addition to the $375.00 reported last week the following have since been secured:

Ten dollar subscriptions:
 Cyprus Lodge A. F. & A. M.
 Shelby Cross

Five dollar contributions:
 Cecil Welsh
 T. M. Hogan
 Chas. Cotter
 W. S. Cotter
 Max Jones
 J. L. Ritchey
 L. B. Jones
 C. F. Sayles
 E. Thurman
 C. E. Tracy
 A. J. Harter
 J. Boesiger
 W. O. Anderson
 H. L. Crooksbank
 C. B. Welsh
 Laura Lloyd
 J. G. Clinefelter
 J. E. West
 O. A. Potter
 W. S. Maburin
 David Perry
 L. E. Libby
 J. A. Henry
 J. Hetrick
 F. G. Adams.

Marilyn Monroe Unveiled | A Family History

Laclede Blade, May 05, 1921

Tilford Marion Hogan

Marilyn Monroe's Great Grandfather.

Street Oiling to Proceed

"When the council met last Monday night to hear complaints a remonstrance to the oiling in district two was presented by T.M. Hogan."

LACLEDE, MISSOURI, FRIDAY, MAY 20, 1921.

Street Oiling to Proceed

Laclede streets are to be oiled according to the ordinance published in The Blade the past two weeks. When the council met last Monday night to hear complaints a remonstrance to the oiling in district two was presented by T. M. Hogan. As it carried the signatures of only fourteen of the 33 property owners in the district it did not constitute a legal barrier and the work will proceed. There was no objection from district one. At this meeting J. T. Cushing presented a petition signed by five of the seven property owners effected asking that the oiling be extended two blocks farther north on State street. An ordinance providing for this extension to be known as district three was prepared and is published in The Blade today.

Visitors to see Tilford Marion Hogan captured in the Laclede Blade: Miss Alice Hogan his niece, Mrs. L. Dunkle (his sister) and family, Mrs L.M. Andros (Dora Hogan his daughter and family, Della Monroe (his daughter) with her two children Gladys Monroe and Marion Monroe, and of course his sister Mary Mahurin.

LACLEDE, MISSOURI, FRIDAY, JUNE 27, 1913

Mrs. Della Monroe and children and Mrs. Virginia Nelson of Los Angeles, Cali., are visiting Mrs. Monroe's father, T. M. Hogan, and other relatives.

LACLEDE, MISSOURI, FRIDAY, AUGUST 15, 1913

Mrs. Della Monroe and two children, who were visiting her father, T. M. Hogan, and other relatives, left Tuesday for their home at Los Angeles, Cali.

LACLEDE, MISSOURI, FRIDAY, AUGUST 28, 1914

Mrs. Monroe and two children who have been visiting her father, T. M. Hogan and other relatives, left Thursday for Portland, Ore.

Visitors continued...

THE LACLEDE BLADE.

A. J. CAYWOOD, Editor and Publisher.
A. J. BAUM Local Editor.

Entered at the Laclede postoffice for transmission through the mails as second class matter.

SATURDAY, AUGUST 27, 1904.

Miss Alice Hogan arrived Thursday to visit her uncle, T. M. Hogan, and her aunt, Mrs. Mary Williams.

LACLEDE, MISSOURI, FRIDAY, MARCH 1, 1912

L. Dunkle and family have moved to Mrs. Mary Mahurin's farm on route one,

Tilford's daughter
Myrtle Myers and family
visited.

LACLEDE, MISSOURI, FRIDAY, JULY 18, 1924.

Mr. and Mrs. L. A. Myer of Kansas City made a short visit here Monday with T. M. Hogan and Mrs. Mary Mahurin, Mrs. Myer being Mr. Hogan's youngest daughter. Mr. Myer is a member of the Kansas City police force and is on a vacation recuperating from a revolver wound in his arm received last March in a gun battle with a negro buglar.

LACLEDE, MISSOURI, SATURDAY, OCTOBER 20, 1906.

Mr. and Mrs. Chas. Bruce, on their way from Montague, Mich., to California, stopped off and spent a day here the past week with Mrs. Bruce's father, T. M. Hogan, south of town.

LACLEDE, MISSOURI, FRIDAY, SEPTEMBER 24, 1920.

Mrs. L. Dunkle of Brookfield spent Sunday here with her sister, Mrs. Mary Mahurin.

S. A. Hogan
(aka Steve A. D. Hogan)
Is
Tilford Marion Hogan's brother.

LACLEDE, MISSOURI, FRIDAY, SEPTEMBER 16, 1927.

S. A. Hogan is here from California visiting his brother, T. M. Hogan and sisters, Mrs. Mary Mahurin and Mrs. I. N. Cassity of Laclede, and Mrs. Thos. Dunkle of Brookfield. The five of them spent Sunday at the Cassity home, the first time they had all been together in 47 years. Mr. Hogan has been in the fruit growing business in California for many years.

Visitors continued...

Tilford Hogan's grand-daughter Georgie Marie, and great-grandchildren Cynthia and Gordon.

Georgie Marie, Louis M. Andros, Cynthia, Georgie Brooks, Gordon.

LACLEDE, MISSOURI, FRIDAY, NOVEMBER 10, 1911

Mr. and Mrs. L. M. Andros of St. Catherine and the former's mother, Mrs. S. S. Andros, and sister, Mrs. Brooks, of Hollywood, Cali., were guests of Mrs. Andros' father, T. M. Hogan, on route one Wednesday.

Louis Milton Andros and his sister Georgie Brooks.

Mrs. Andros is Dora Hogan.

LACLEDE, MISSOURI, FRIDAY, DECEMBER 1, 1911

Mrs. Mary Mahurin and T. M. Hogan spent Monday with the latter's daughter, Mrs. L. M. Andros, and family near St. Catharine. Mr. Andros leaves this week to spend the winter looking after his tobacco plantation in Cuba.

LACLEDE, MISSOURI, FRIDAY, JANUARY 2, 1925.

Local and Personal News

Mrs. Dora Bruce of Portland, Oregon, is here visting her father, T. M. Hogan and other relatives.

LACLEDE, MISSOURI, APRIL 11, 1930.

Mrs. Myrtle Meyers and small son Billy of Kansas City spent Tuesday here with her father, T. M. Hogan and his sister, Mrs. Mary Mahurir.

Tilford Marion Hogan took on the responsibilities of a municipal Judge for the city of Laclede.

THE LACLEDE BLADE

Entered at the postoffice at Laclede, Mo., or transmission through the mail as second class matter.

A. J. CAYWOOD.

FRIDAY, MARCH 18, 1921.

City Council Meeting

At the March meeting of the city council an election was ordered held in each ward of the city on Tuesday, April 5. One alderman is to be elected in the west ward to succeed Joe Albin and one in the east ward to succeed F. W. Groes. The judges appointed for the west ward are L. M. Wilson, J. R. Hawes and A. D. Jacobs, and in the east ward John Nelson, T. H. Barbee and T. M. Hogan.

At this meeting the following ordinance was passed and the marshal instructed to enforce it:

Be it ordained by the board of aldermen of the City of Laclede, as follows:

Sec. 1. It shall be unlawful for any person to allow his or her cattle, hogs, horses, mules, sheep, goats or other domestic animals; also geese, ducks, chickens, turkeys and all other domestic fowls to run at large within the corporate limits of the City of Laclede, and any person who allows his or her domestic animals or fowls to be at large contrary to the terms of this ordinance shall on conviction be fined not less than one nor more than twenty dollars for each offense.

Adopt and approved this 7th day of March, 1921.

G. O. Plowman, Mayor.
Attest: M. P. Benson, Clerk.

Tilford Marion Hogan elected Deacon for Christian Church.
Laclede, Missouri in 1911.

LACLEDE, MISSOURI, FRIDAY, JANUARY 27, 1911

Christian Church Notes

Church officers were elected Jan. 22, as follows: Elders: D. B. McKisson, J. B. Patrick, L. M. Wilson and D. E. Polly. Deacons: H. Eccles, B. F. Thompson, L. W. Libby, G. F. Lewallen, John Murphy and T. M. Hogan. Trustees: L. W. Libby, B. F. Thompson and J. N. Wilson. Miss Bertha Libby, organist; Mrs. Rebecca Libby, treasurer; Mrs. J. R. Renoe, clerk; J. R. Hawes, janitor.

We cordially invite all those who are not attending services at other churches to meet with us.

Sunday school 10 a. m.

Endeavor meeting 6:30 p. m.

Preaching services second Lord's day of each month.

Prayer meeting Wednesday evening at 7 p. m.

Willing Workers meeting every Thursday.

Tilford Marion Hogan's grandson Milton Stores Andros married Miss Naomi Ella Love in Laclede.

Dora Hogan and her daughter Dorothy Bruce attended the wedding as Mr. and Mrs. L.M. Andros and Miss Dorothy Andros. Also in attendance was Mrs. Sellars of Kansas City. Mrs Sellars is Marilyn Monroe's great-grandmother - Charlotte Virginia Nance.

LACLEDE, MISSOURI, FRIDAY, MARCH 6, 1914

Andros-Love

Milton Andros and Miss Naomi Ella Love were married Sunday, March 1, at 2:30, at the home of the bride's parents, Mr. and Mrs Lee Love east of Brookfield, Rev. Edgar Read performing the ceremony. The bride wore a white messaline dress with jeweled net over drapery and carried white rose buds with ferns, the groom wearing the conventional black.

The bride's sister, Mrs. J. Frank Weaver, assisted by her aunt, Miss Ella Ong, served an elaborate three course luncheon. The groom's parents, Mr. and Mrs. L. M. Andros, gave a second day reception at their home two miles south of Brookfield. The young couple received a shower of lovely presents from relatives and friends consisting of linens and silverware.

Those present were Mr. and Mrs. Lee Love, Mr. and Mrs. L. M. Andros, W. O. Love, Miss Dorothy Andros, and P. Kiel, all of Brookfield; and Mr. and Mrs. J. Frank Weaver, and Miss Ella Ong of Laclede; Mr. and Mrs. Ed. L. Love of Hannibal; Mrs. Sellars of Kansas City.

Mr. and Mrs. Andros are both well known in Laclede and have the best wishes of their many friends here.

Marilyn Monroe Unveiled | A Family History

Documented evidence for the middle name of Tilford Hogan's father: George WILLIS Hogan.

BROOKFIELD, MISSOURI, FRIDAY, JUNE 1, 1934

THE FUNERAL TOMORROW.

For Mrs. Emma Hogan, Esteemed Laclede Woman.

Mrs. Emma D. Hogan passed away Thursday morning, May 31, after a brief illness, at her home in Laclede, where she had lived for the past six years.

Funeral services will be held at the Park Baptist church, Saturday afternoon, at 2:30 o'clock, conducted by Rev. C. O. Hardgrove. Interment will be made at Rose Hill cemetery.

Emma D. Hogan was born in Howard County, near Fayette, Missouri, December 3, 1861, the daughter of George and Sarah Levell, who came in the pioneer days from Kentucky to Missouri, to make their home. When 18 years of age she was united in marriage with Augustus Fisher, also of Howard County, who preceded her in death in 1915. To this union seven children were born. The living children are: Mrs. Ben Sprague, of this city; Mrs. Ella Duncie, Triplett; Mrs. Jacob Shively, of Glasgow; Mrs. L. O. Dowell, of Laclede, and Charles Fisher, of St. Joseph.

Six years ago Mrs. Fisher was united in marriage with T. M. Hogan, of Laclede. Mrs. Hogan was an estimable woman, a devoted Christian mother and will be missed by those who knew her.

LACLEDE, MISSOURI, SEPTEMBER 5, 1930.

Death of Mrs. Stephen Mahurin

Mrs. Mary Ann Mahurin, widow of the late Stephen Mahurin, passed away at her home in Laclede on Thursday, August 28, at the age of 86 years, 7 months and 18 days, after a long illness.

Mary Ann Hogan was born near Louisville, Ky., and moved with her parents to Knox county, Missouri, when she was about ten years old. She was united in marriage to Stephen Mahurin, September 9, 1878. Her husband preceded her in death in 1897. She leaves to mourn her going two brothers, Newton Hogan of Los Angeles, Calif., and T. M. Hogan of Laclede, and two sisters, Mrs. Rosa Cassity of Laclede and Mrs. Hattie Dunkle of Cairo, Mo., besides other relatives and friends.

Funeral was held at the Baptist church, the services being conducted by the pastor, Rer. J. W. Trower, and burial was in Laclede cemetery by Director Thorne.

LACLEDE, MISSOURI, OCTOBER 30, 1931.

Notice of Final Settlement

Notice is hereby given to all creditors, and others interested in the estate of Mary A. Mahurin, Deceased, that I, Tilford M. Hogan, Executor, of said estate, intend to make Final Settlement thereof at the next term of the Probate Court of Linn County, State of Missouri, to be held at Linneus, on the 9th day of November, 1931.

TILFORD M. HOGAN, Executor.

LACLEDE, MISSOURI, DECEMBER 26, 1930.

Passing of Mrs. Cassity

Mrs. Rose Bell Cassity, widow of the late I. N. Cassity, passed away at her home here last Sunday evening, after a brief illness.

She was born near Edina, in Knox county, Missouri, February 14, 1860. Was the daughter of Willis and Sarah Hogan. She spent her early life in the county of her birth after which the family moved to Chariton county, near Brunswick, where she was married to Geo. P. Riddle of Marceline, Illinois. Four children were born to this union, two preceding her in death. She leaves to mourn her death one son, B. F. Riddle of St. Joseph, and one daughter, Mrs. Peter Thompson of the home, and fifteen grand children; one sister, Mrs. Hattie Dunkle of Moberly, and two brothers, Newton Hogan of Los Angeles, Calif., and T. M. Hogan of Laclede, besides a host of friends in Linn and Chariton counties.

She was converted and united with the Baptist church at an early age and never faltered from that faith to the end.

Funeral services were held at the Baptist church Tuesday afternoon, conducted by the pastor, Rev. J. W. Trower, after which the remains were laid to rest in the Laclede cemetery.

LACLEDE, MISSOURI, FRIDAY, JUNE 9, 1933.

Card of Thanks

I wish to express my sincere appreciation and thanks to friends and neighbors for the kindness shown during the death of beloved husband.

—Mrs. Emma Hogan.

LACLEDE, MISSOURI, FRIDAY, AUGUST 18, 1933.

Rooms, Barn and Garage For Rent

Two front rooms partly furnished; two stalls in good barn and garage for rent. Have chest of carpenter tools and some farm tools for sale. Mrs. T. M. Hogan, Laclede.

LACLEDE, MISSOURI, FRIDAY, DECEMBER 25, 1942.

REVIEW OF THE PAST IN LACLEDE

From Blade Files of 1897—1907—1917

Forty-Five Years Ago This Week—1897

Mrs. M. J. Mouser entertained a number of friends at a birtday dinner at her home southwest of town. Those present were Mrs. E. J. Watson, Mrs. Jas. Skulley, Mrs. Anna Nelson, Mrs. James Quillen, Mrs. Wm. Mahurin, Grandma Hogan, Mrs. Steve Mahurin, Misses Ellen and Zella Watson, Laura and Kate Skulley, Chas. Berry and wife, W. O. Anderson and wife, Pink Mahurin, Misses Kate and Barbara Sasell, Tilford M. Hogan, Mrs. Rachel Huddleston, Hulda Inman, Mrs. Geo. Anderson, Mrs. C. O. Warner, Miss Addie Warner, W. N. Harter and wife, Mrs. Mary Tharp, Master Orbid Burnett, Mrs. A. J. Caywood and little daughter, Vivia; Miss Effice Mahurin, Silas Sharp and family, Miles Weston and wife, Miss Lillie Weston, Mrs. J. R. Wells and daughter, Miss Bessie; Mrs. C. C. Bigger, Ortha Nelson and C. M. Burnett.

The rephublican vote in Linn county at the presdential election in 1896 [...] 120; Jack[...] 328; Locust [...] 285; Parson Creek, 80; North Salem, 166; Benton, 173; Clay, 129. Only the men voted at that time.

Eighteen local young people appeared in curious, brilliant, unique, rich, gay costumes under tinted calcium lights in a Burmese wedding at the Methodist church.

Thirty-Five Years Ago This Week—1907

1897 is the earliest documented date for Tilford Marion Hogan in The Laclede Blade newspaper. "Grandma Hogan" is believed to be Tilford's mother Sara Ann Owen.

Marilyn Monroe Unveiled | A Family History

Marilyn Monroe's California Relatives

From Norma Jeane's birth and throughout her movie career... and while telling the public orphan stories, HOGAN and MONROE relatives were living literally steps away from her in Los Angeles, California and surrounding cities. Norma Jeane would have <u>never</u> been adopted as a child. An adoption would have severed all of these family relationships.

-I've Been Living a Lie-

Marilyn Monroe Unveiled | A Family History

RELATIVES IN CALIFORNIA – 1920's THROUGH 1950's.

Note: Relatives were present in Los Angeles previous to 1920 and most died in Los Angeles during the 1950's, 1970's or later. Many descendants are still living around the country. This list does **not** reflect all relatives or addresses.

Name	Relation	Year	Address	Source
Gladys Monroe, Jasper Baker, children Berniece and Jasper	Marilyn's mother and daughter of Della Hogan	1920	342 Fifth Ave, Venice, CA	1920 United States Federal Census
Milton Stores Andros	Son of Dora Hogan	1924	1416 Cloverdale Ave, Los Angeles, CA	U.S. City Directories, 1822-1995
Chester Hogan	Son of Newton Hogan	1924	610 Camden Dr. Beverly Hill, CA	California, Voter Registrations, 1900-1968
Norma Jeane Mortenson	NORMA JEANE	1926	1100 Mission Rd, Los Angeles, CA	Birth Certificate
Marion Monroe	Son of Della Hogan	1927	Hawthorne, CA	Probate Estate Document for Virginia Sellars
Gladys Baker (Monroe)	Marilyn's mother and daughter of Della Hogan	1927	Hawthorne, CA	Probate Estate Document for Virginia Sellars (Nance)
William Nance (Hogan)	Son of Tilford Marion Hogan	1927	Hawthorne, CA	Probate Estate Document for Virginia Sellars (Nance)
Milton Stores Andros	Son of Dora Hogan	1928	625 Buckthorne St., Los Angeles, CA	California, Voter Registrations, 1900-1968
Milton Stores Andros	Son of Dora Hogan	1930	1736 Hauser Blvd, Los Angeles, CA	1930 United States Federal Census
Newton Hogan	Brother of Tilford Marion Hogan	1930	W 35th St, Los Angeles, CA	1930 United States Federal Census
Olive Monroe	Wife of Marion Monroe	1930	2013 Selby Ave, Los Angeles, CA	1930 United States Federal Census
Ethel Copp (Hogan)	Daughter of Newton Hogan	1930	352 Van Ness Ave, Los Angeles, CA.	1930 United States Federal Census
William Nance (Hogan) and Family	Son of Tilford Marion Hogan	1930	W. Ave 31, Los Angeles, CA	1930 United States Federal Census
Ida Bolender and Gladys Monroe with Norma Jeane.	NORMA JEANE	1930	4201 West 134th St, Hawthorne, CA	1930 United States Federal Census
Ervin "Doc" Goddard and Grace McKee	NORMA JEANE	1936	3107 Barbara CT, Los Angeles, CA.	California, Voter Registrations, 1900-1968
Alice Hogan	Daughter of Newton Hogan	1937	348 N Van Ness Ave, Los Angeles CA	U.S. City Directories, 1822-1995
Milton Stores Andros	Son of Dora Hogan	1937	1736 Hauser Blvd, Los Angeles, CA	U.S. City Directories, 1822-1995
Chester Hogan	Son of Newton Hogan	1937	2621 Rutherford Dr., Los Angeles CA	U.S. City Directories, 1822-1995
Olive Monroe	Wife of Marion Monroe	1940	3265 Greenfield Ave, Los Angeles CA	1940 United States Federal Census
Chester Hogan Jr.	Son of Chester Hogan	1940	7859 Hillside Ave., Los Angeles, CA	U.S. City Directories, 1822-1995
Joseph Copp, Jr.	Son of Ethel Hogan	1940	5054 Sunset Blvd, Los Angeles, CA	1940 United States Federal Census
Ethel Copp (Hogan)	Daughter of Newton Hogan	1940	352 Van Ness Ave, Los Angeles, CA	1940 United States Federal Census
Milton Stores Andros	Son of Dora Hogan	1942	1760 El Cerrito Pl, Los Angeles, CA	U.S. City Directories, 1822-1995
Chester Hogan	Son of Newton Hogan	1942	6342 Mulholland Dr. Los Angeles, CA	U.S. City Directories, 1822-1995
Ethel Copp (Hogan) and family	Daughter of Newton Hogan	1946	424 Muirfield Rd, Los Angeles, CA	California, Voter Registrations, 1900-1968
Dr. Newton Hogan Copp	Son of Ethel Hogan	1955	1819 Coldwater Canyon Dr Beverly Hills, CA 90210	U.S. City Directories, 1822-1995
Ethel Copp (Hogan)	Daughter of Newton Hogan	1956	223 Bentley Circle, Los Angeles, CA 90049	U.S. City Directories, 1822-1995
Joseph Copp Jr.	Son of Ethel Hogan	1956	11950 San Vicente Blvd, Los Angeles, CA	Westwood City Directory

Marilyn Monroe Unveiled | A Family History

RELATIVES IN LOS ANGELES CALIFORNIA and surrounding cities – 1920's THROUGH 1950's. (CONTINUED)

Norma Jeane Mortenson	NORMA JEANE	1926	1100 Mission Rd, Los Angeles, CA	Birth Certificate
Nellie Monroe Moore and Dr. William Day Moore Sr.	First Cousin Once Removed and Spouse	1930	402 Meyler Street, San Pedro, Los Angeles County	1930 United States Federal Census
George W Dunkle	First Cousin Twice Removed	1930	228 E Wilshire Avenue, Fullerton (Anaheim, Orange County)	Anaheim, California, City Directory, 1930
Thomas Allen Monroe and Mary Monroe	Great Uncle and Aunt	1935	402 Meyler Street, San Pedro, Los Angeles County	1940 United States Federal Census
Nellie Monroe Moore and Dr. William Day Moore Sr.	First Cousin Once Removed and Spouse	1940	402 Meyler Street, San Pedro, Los Angeles County	1940 United States Federal Census
William Day Moore, Sr.	Spouse of First Cousin Once Removed (Nellie Monroe)	1942	Los Angeles Chamber of Commerce Building, 1151 S Broadway, Los Angeles (Office)	Draft Application
William Nance (Hogan)	Son of Tilford Marion Hogan	1940	375 1/2 Tippecanoe Avenue, San Bernardino	1940 United States Federal Census
William Day Moore, Jr.	Second Cousin	1940	402 Meyler Street, San Pedro, Los Angeles County	Marriage Application
Byron A. Moore	Second Cousin	1942	402 Meyler Street, San Pedro, Los Angeles County	Merchant Marine Application
Byron A. Moore	Second Cousin	1948	402 Meyler Street, San Pedro, Los Angeles County	Marriage Application
John Everett Monroe	Second Cousin	1949	1527 Benedict Canyon Drive, Beverly Hills	Application to State of Iowa for World War II Service Compensation
John Alva Monroe and Florence Monroe	Great Uncle and Aunt	1951	3446 Cerritos Avenue, Long Beach – Long Beach	California, City Directory 1951
Byron and Sydell Moore	Second Cousin and spouse	1951	534 W. Almond Avenue – Compton California	City Directory, 1951
John Alva Monroe and Florence Monroe	Great Uncle and Aunt	1953	3446 Cerritos Avenue, Long Beach – Long Beach, California	City Directory 1953
Mary (Rooke) Monroe	Great Aunt (Wife of Thomas Allen Monroe)	1954	402 Meyler Street, San Pedro, Los Angeles County	The Kansas City Times, June 22, 1954
Naomi R Fowler (Hogan)	First Cousin Once Removed	1955	5383 Kent Ave, Riverside, CA	Riverside, California, City Directory, 1955
John Alva Monroe	Great Uncle	1959	3528 Olive Avenue, Long Beach	Independent (Long Beach California), December 25 and 26, 1959

LOS ANGELES RELATIVES MAPPED
1920'S - 1950'S

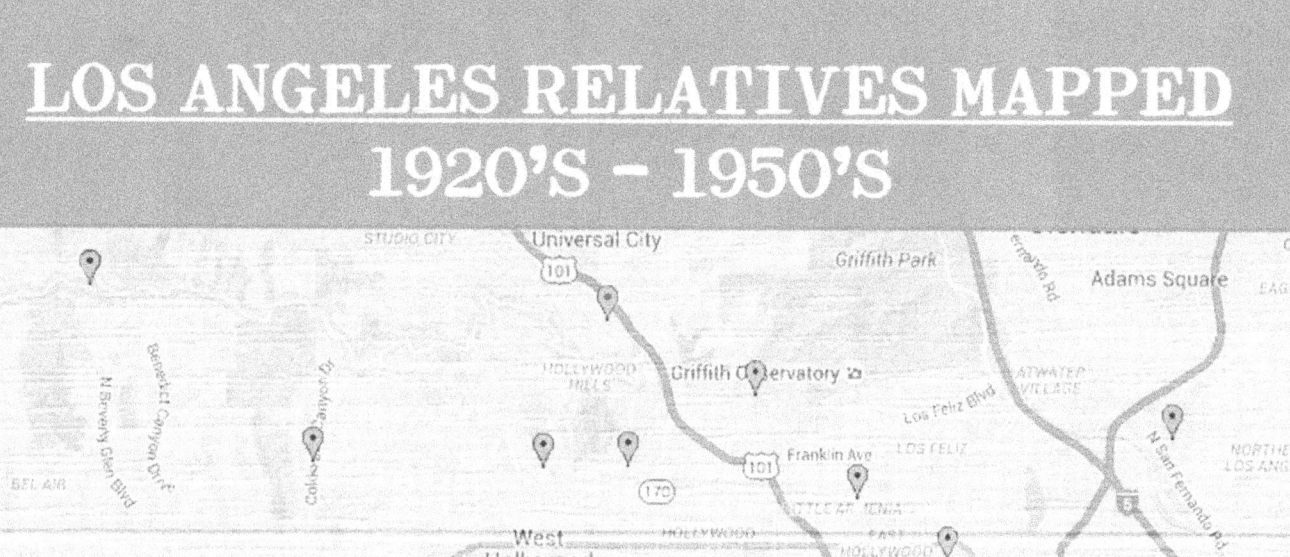

DECEMBER 13, 1927 CHARLOTTE VIRGINIA (JENNIE) NANCE DIED IN LOS ANGELES.

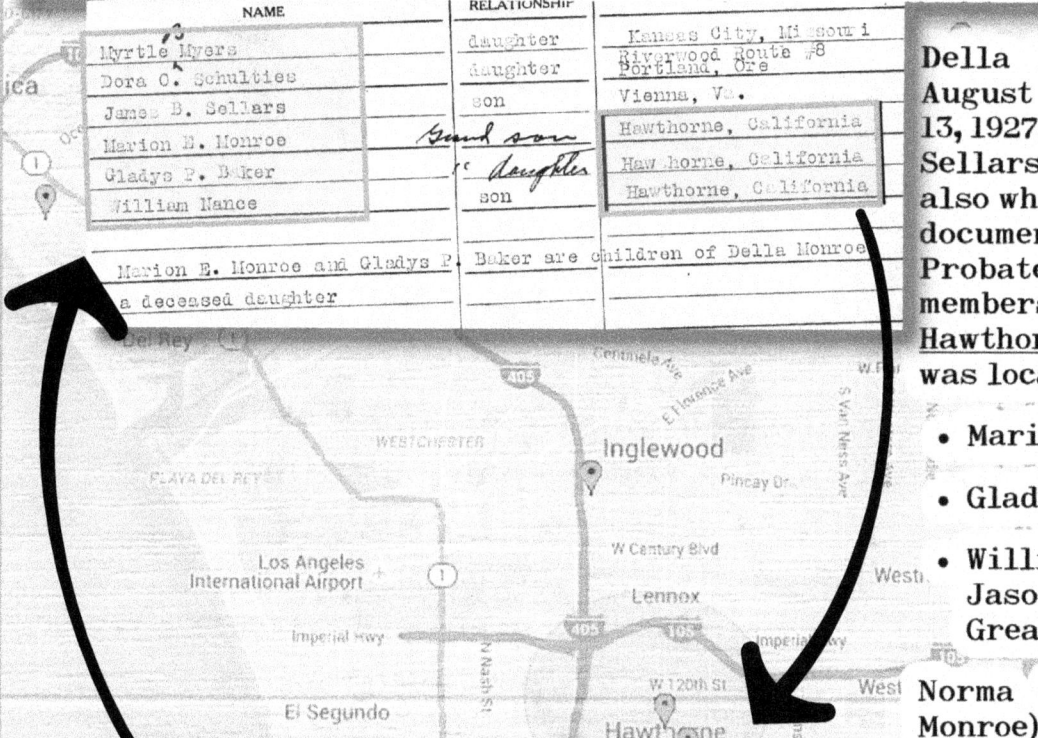

Della Mae Hogan died in August 23, 1927. By December 13, 1927, her mother, Virginia Sellars (Nance) passed away also while in Los Angeles. As documented by Virginia's Probate Records, family members were present in <u>Hawthorne</u> where Della's home was located:

- Marion Monroe
- Gladys Baker
- William Nance (Hogan)- Jason Edward Kennedy's Great-Grandfather.

Norma Jeane (aka Marilyn Monroe) was one year and six months old.

MARILYN MONROE'S FAMILY

Application for Letters Testamentary or of Administration

In the Probate Court of Jackson County, Missouri, at Kansas City.

In the matter of the Estate of Virginia Sellars .... Deceased

Now comes Myrtle B/Myers and states that deceased died on the 13th day of December, 1927, intestate and was at that time a resident of Kansas City, Jackson County, Missouri

That the probable value of her estate is: Personal, $ 3850.00 ; Real, $ 500.00

That the names and residence of the widow, heirs, or legatees and devisees of deceased are respectively as follows:

NAME	RELATIONSHIP	RESIDENCE
Myrtle B Myers	daughter	Kansas City, Missouri
Dora O. Schulties	daughter	Riverwood Route #8 Portland, Ore
James B. Sellars	son	Vienna, Va.
Marion E. Monroe	Grand son	Hawthorne, California
Gladys P. Baker	" daughter	Hawthorne, California
William Nance	son	Hawthorne, California

Marion E. Monroe and Gladys P. Baker are children of Della Monroe, a deceased daughter

DEBT OR CLAIM OF	NATURE OF CLAIM	AMOUNT
O. V. Mast	Undertaker	150.00
W. M. Strother, Los Angeles	"	517.48

For complete Probate records for Virginia Nance, see companion guide.

That affiant will make a perfect inventory of and faithfully administer all of the estate of deceased and pay the debts as far as the assets will extend and the law direct, and account for and pay all assets which shall come to his possession or knowledge.

Subscribed and sworn to before me, this 19th day of December, 1927.

Myrtle B. Myers
Residence 1125 West 41st, Kansas

Durward P. Strother, Notary Public

Chester Campbell, Atty. for Estate

My Commission Expires April 27, 1929

The building at lower left was W.M. Strother Inc., the funeral home where Jennie's body was prepared. Dora accompanied her body back to Kansas City and Myrtle reimbursed her the travel expenses. This was known as the funeral home to the stars, and the Pantages Theatre is across the street. Copyright unknown, Los Angeles Public Library WPA Collection.

Charlotte Virginia (Jennie) Nance- Marilyn Monroe's great-grandmother. She was also known as Virginia Nance, Virginia Sellars, Virginia Hogan, or sometimes just called Jennie...

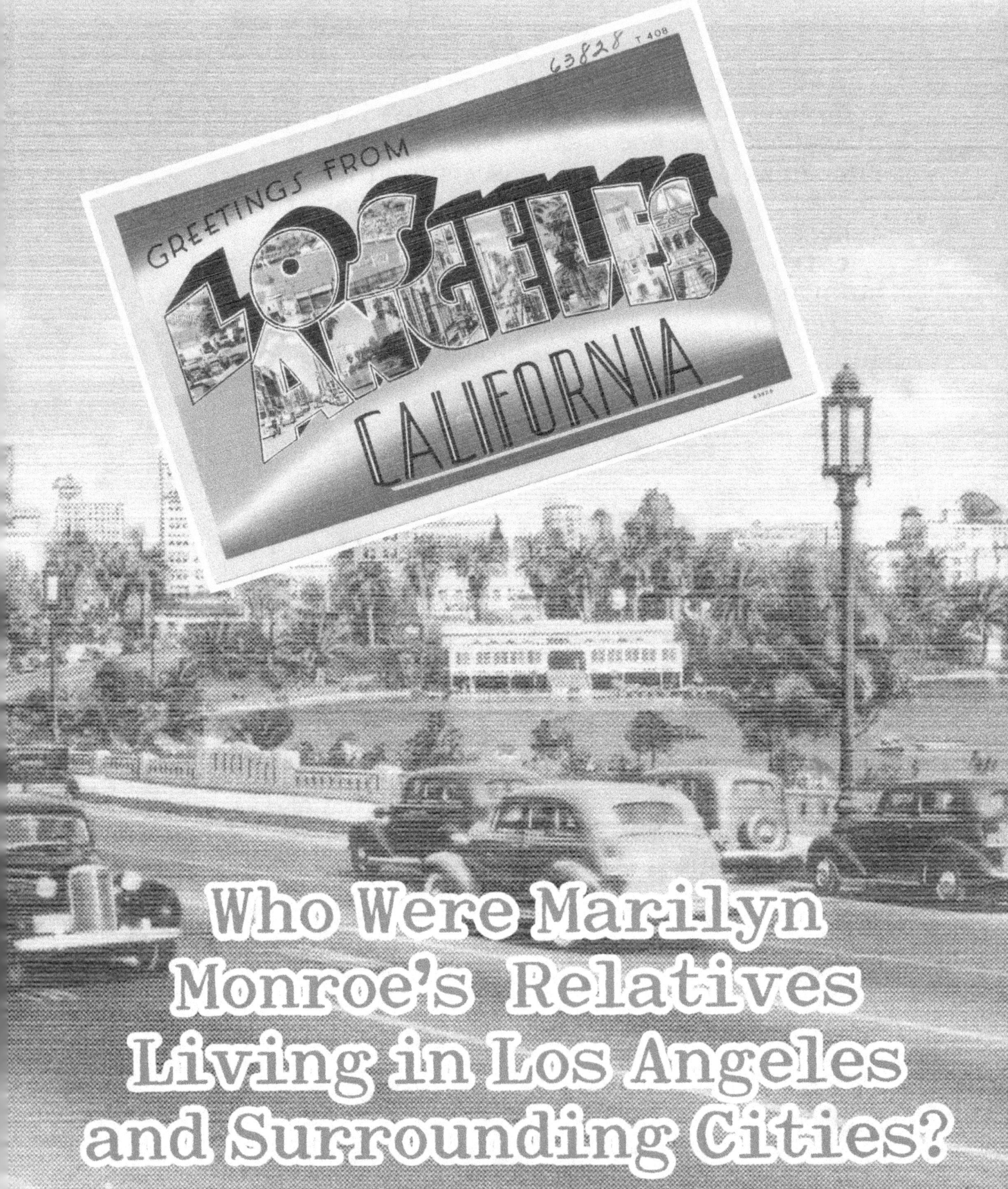

Who Were Marilyn Monroe's Relatives Living in Los Angeles and Surrounding Cities?

Marilyn Monroe Unveiled | A Family History

Marilyn Monroe's
Family Members' Vocations

Martin Edward Mortensen – Father – Meterman

Gladys Pearl Monroe Mortensen – Mother – Film Cutter

Della Mae Hogan Monroe Grainger – Grandmother (deceased 1927) – Housekeeper

Charles Grainger – Step-Grandfather – Oil Driller

Tilford Marion Hogan – Great-Grandfather – Farmer, Property Owner, Municipal Judge, Investor, Politician.

Dora Hogan Graham – Great Aunt – House Mother at Children's Home Inc., Portland Oregon. She also performed humanitarian duties in her community.

Louis Milton Andros – Great Uncle – Wealthy – Legal Background, Orchardist, Business Owner

Georgie Andros Andrist Baer – First Cousin Once Removed – Her father Louis Milton Andros was wealthy, she lived with her father's sister in a mansion in Minnesota with her children – third husband, Homer Baer, was a bank president.

Milton Stores Andros – First Cousin Once Removed – Married to Naomi Ella Love Andros – lived in Los Angeles near Marilyn and Gladys. He was a Hollywood plaster artist in the film industry.

Myrtle Hogan Myers – Great Aunt – Housewife, took care of her grandson.

Lewis Arnotte Myers – Great Uncle – Kansas City Police Officer and later a house detective for the Ambassador Hotel.

William J Myers – First Cousin Once Removed – He was a Kansas City Police Department Ballistics Expert

William Marion Hogan – Great Uncle – US. Army and U.S. Navy Veteran and Carpenter.

Clara May Slough Hogan – Great Aunt – took care of the home including an adopted daughter younger than Norma Jeane. The Hogans lived in San Bernardino near Gladys and Norma Jeane.

James Berry Sellars aka Jimmy Hogan – Great Uncle – Government Auditor for the Bureau of Entomology and Plant Quarantine

Marion Monroe – Uncle – Mechanic and Lifeguard, Laborer for Union Storage and Transfer Company.

Olive Monroe – Aunt – Worked as a Dressmaker.

John Alva Monroe – Great Uncle – Retired – Farmer, Later Railroad Laborer

Thomas Allen Monroe – Great Uncle – Retired Santa Fe Railroad Conductor.

Percival Adam – Spouse of First Cousin Once Removed – Accountant in household storage industry, secretary for A.B.C. Fireproof Warehouse in Kansas City.

Lottie (Monroe) Adam – First Cousin Once Removed – Housewife, Active Member of Second Presbyterian Church in Kansas City and Red Cross Volunteer.

Dr. William Day Moore – Spouse of First Cousin Once Removed (Husband of Nellie Monroe Moore) – Physician, Private Practice and then employed with City of San Pedro in California as M.D. Health Officer through

1922. Later, he was with the Los Angeles Board of Education as its physician.

Cordelia Olivia (Anderson) Monroe – Spouse of First Cousin Once Removed (Ervin Monroe) – Employee, Ladies' Clothing Department, Glantz Brothers Department Store, Park Rapids, Minnesota.

Ervin Monroe – First Cousin Once Removed – Family Farming, Repairman for the Winthrop Canning Company in Winthrop, Minnesota. Machinist in Davenport Iowa.

Lloyd Monroe – First Cousin Once Removed – World War I Veteran, Mechanic, Telegrapher for the Rock Island Railroad, Owner of Monroe Cabins in Estherville Iowa.

Henriette Monroe – Former Spouse of First Cousin Once Removed (Lloyd Monroe) – Office Assistant, Doctor's Office.

Hilma Monroe – Second Wife of First Cousin Once Removed (Lloyd Monroe) – Co-owner of Monroe Cabins in Estherville Iowa.

Byron A. Moore – Second Cousin (son of Nellie Monroe Moore) – Accountant, Expeditor for Shell Chemical, Merchant Marine Junior Purser, Concrete Blocks Salesman.

Sydell A. Moore – Spouse of Second Cousin (Byron A. Moore) – Bookkeeper in Appliance Business.

William Day Moore, Jr.– Second Cousin (son of Nellie Monroe Moore) – U.S. Navy.

John Everett Monroe – Second Cousin (son of Lloyd Monroe) – U.S. Navy.

Sgt. William L Monroe – Second Cousin (son of Lloyd Monroe) – United States Army, 452 AAF Bomb Group, World War II – Killed in Action, 1945.

George Washington Hogan – First Cousin Twice Removed – Arkansas Farmer.

Otis Hogan – First Cousin Twice Removed – Mover in Muskogee Oklahoma.

Clarence L. Hogan – Second Cousin Once Removed – Railway Car Distributor in Montana.

Marilyn Monroe Unveiled | A Family History

One of <u>Tilford Marion Hogan's</u> brothers was <u>Newton Hogan</u>.

1870 Federal Census.

In the 1880 Federal Census, Newton Hogan is living with his family and a hired servant in Chariton County Missouri.

<u>Newton Hogan married Eliza Josephine Switzer.</u>

Miss Alice Hogan

By 1900 Newton Hogan, Tilford Marion Hogan's brother is living in Los Angeles California with another hired servant.

- Miss Alice Hogan
- Chester Hogan
- Ethel Hogan
- Mary Hogan-missing

314

By 1920 Newton Hogan, Tilford Marion Hogan's brother, is living on 911 W. 35th Street in Los Angeles. Who is also living around the block from Newton Hogan on 900 ½ West Jefferson Blvd? Marilyn fans will recognize none other that Edward Martin, Ida, John, and Olive. Marion Monroe, Marilyn Monroe's uncle married Olive Bruning in 1924. Edward Martin was her stepfather.

STATE OF CALIFORNIA   **COUNTY OF SAN DIEGO**

Marriage License and Certificate

These Presents are to authorize and license any Justice of the Supreme Court, Judge of the Superior Court, Justice of the Peace, Priest or Minister of the Gospel of any Denomination, to solemnize within said County the marriage of **Marion Monroe**, native of **California**, color **White**, aged **22** years, resident of **Salinas**, County of **Salinas**, State of California; and **Olyve Brunings**, native of **Oregon**, color **White**, aged **19** years, resident of **San Bernardino**, County of **San Bernardino**, State of California. Said parties being of sufficient age to be capable of contracting Marriage.

In Witness Whereof, I have hereunto set my hand and affixed the Seal of the Superior Court of said County this **20th** day of **September** A.D. 192**4**.

J. B. McLees
County Clerk and Ex-Officio Clerk of the Superior Court in and for the County of San Diego

By **T. Buckley** Deputy Clerk.

State of California, } ss.
County of San Diego,

I hereby Certify, That I believe the facts stated in the above License to be true, and that upon due inquiry there appears to be no legal impediment to the Marriage of said **Marion Monroe** and **Olyve Bruning**; that said parties were joined in marriage by me on the **20th** day of **September** A.D. 192**4**, in **San Diego** said County and State; That **Mrs. Ida Martin** a resident of **Sawtelle**, County of **Los Angeles**, State of **California** and **Beulah Whittington**, a resident of **Sawtelle**, County of **Los Angeles**, State of **California**, were present as witnesses of said Ceremony.

In Witness Whereof, I have hereunto set my hand this **20th** day of **September** A.D. 192**4**.

LeRoy W. Lowell
Free Methodist Minister

Recorded at request of **Rev. Lowell** **Sep. 24** 1924 at — min. past **9** o'clock **A.**m.
JOHN H. FERRY, County Recorder.
By **A. Fogelstrom** Deputy.

Fee $1.00

California State Board of Health
BUREAU OF VITAL STATISTICS
STANDARD CERTIFICATE OF MARRIAGE
PERSONAL AND STATISTICAL PARTICULARS

PLACE OF MARRIAGE: County of San Diego   State Index No. ____   Local Registered No. ____

	GROOM	BRIDE
FULL NAME	Marion Monroe	Olyve Brunings
RESIDENCE	Salinas, Calif.	San Bernardino
COLOR OR RACE	White	White
AGE AT LAST BIRTHDAY	22	19
SINGLE, WIDOWED OR DIVORCED	Single	Single
NUMBER OF MARRIAGE	First	First
BIRTHPLACE	Los Angeles, Cal.	Astoria, Ore.
OCCUPATION	Mechanic	none
NAME OF FATHER	C. E. Monroe	Jack Brunings
BIRTHPLACE OF FATHER	St. Louis Mo.	New Orleans, La.
MAIDEN NAME OF MOTHER	D. M. Hogan	Ida Henderson
BIRTHPLACE OF MOTHER	St. Louis Mo.	Los Angeles, Cal.

MAIDEN NAME OF BRIDE, IF SHE WAS PREVIOUSLY MARRIED: ____

WE, the groom and bride named in this Certificate, hereby certify that the information given therein is correct, to the best of our knowledge and belief.

Marion Monroe Groom   **Olyve Brunings** Bride

CERTIFICATE OF PERSON PERFORMING CEREMONY

I Hereby Certify that **Marion Monroe** and **Olyve Brunings** were joined in Marriage by me in accordance with the laws of the State of California, at **San Diego, Cal.** this **20th** day of **September** 192**4**.

Signature of Witness to the Marriage: **Mrs. Ida Martin**
Residence: **Sawtelle, Calif.**

Signature of person performing ceremony: **LeRoy W. Lowell**
Official position: **Free Meth. Minister**
Residence: **145 W. Beech St. San Diego, Cal.**

FILED **Sept. 24** 1924 **John H. Ferry** Registrar (County Recorder)
By **A. Fogelstrom** Deputy.

COMPARED: *Gertrude N. Abbe*

40429

(1928) LOS ANGELES DIRECTORY CO'S

Marion (Olive) life guard h1412a 23d (SM)

Newton Hogan, the brother of Tilford Marion Hogan, Marilyn Monroe's great-grandfather, lived right around the block from Olive Bruning and her family in 1920. Della Mae Hogan's son Marion would marry Olive Bruning by 1924. Both addresses are now a part of the University of Southern California campus.

1928 Map of Los Angeles, California.

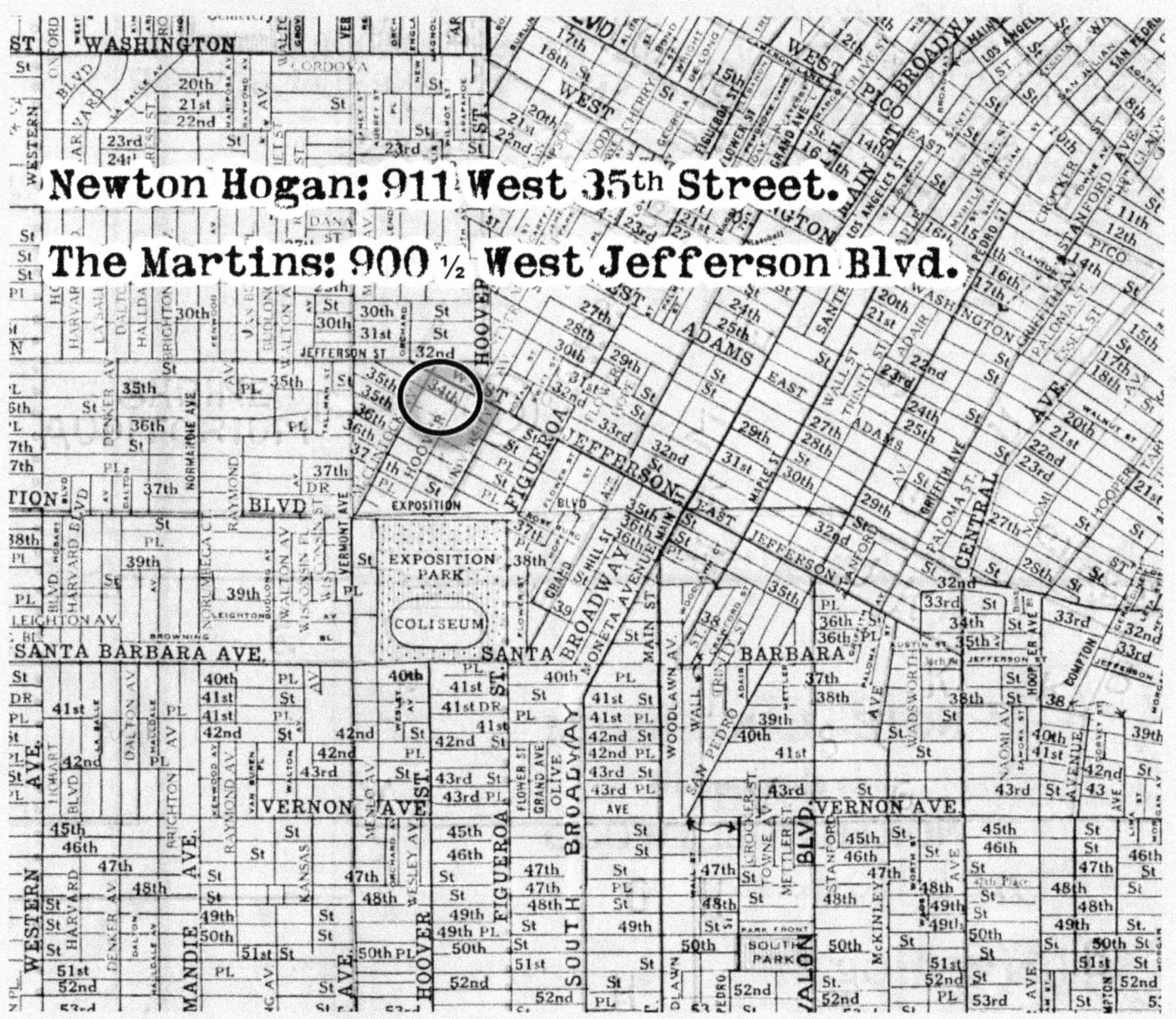

Newton Hogan: 911 West 35th Street.
The Martins: 900 ½ West Jefferson Blvd.

Newton Hogan

Tilford Marion Hogan's brother.

Newton Hogan was a prominent Carpenter and Contractor as documented on Federal Census Reports:

Los Angeles Herald, Number 47, 18 November 1902

avenues. Bids accepted as follows: Newton Hogan to improve Twenty-seventh street between Normandie and Halldale; F. O. Engstrum to improve Bixel street between Arnold and Sixth streets; proceedings were taken that, at expense of petitioners, city attorney was to repeal ordinance to open and widen San Pedro street; Hoover street to be opened from Seventh to Pico street to compare with Lone Star tract.

Los Angeles Herald, Number 33, 3 November 1903

James B. Lankershim to Newton Hogan and Eliza Josephine Hogan—Part lots 27 and 28, blk L, West L. A. $950

Los Angeles Herald, Volume 33, Number 337, 2 September 1906

MAKES NEW DORMITORY FOR UNIVERSITY BOYS

Numerous improvements which have been going on at the University of Southern California are nearing completion for the opening of the fall term September 17. The old college of music has been completely remodeled for use as a boys' dormitory, and will be known as Hodge hall. It will accommodate forty young men comfortably.

The large and handsomely furnished residence of Newton Hogan, adjoining the campus, has been leased by the university as a girls' dormitory and will add greatly to the comfort of the girls attending that institution.

A rather novel feature in college circles is to be undertaken by the ladies' auxiliary of the university during the coming year. The large and airy basement of the south wing of the college of liberal arts is to be floored and turned over to the ladies for use as a lunch room. This is expected to prove a great convenience to students who come each day from a distance. The prices will be calculated merely to make expenses. A similar scheme was tried with some measure of success at the state normal school last year and will be watched with interest by the friends of the university.

The college faculty has been strengthened by the addition of Miss R. W. Brown to the language department and Misses Macha Vance and Nancy K. Foster to the English department.

Newton Hogan's Children.

- Alice Hogan
- Chester Hogan
- Ethel Hogan
- Mary Hogan

Conclusive proof that Newton Hogan was tied directly to his brother Tilford Marion Hogan in Missouri comes from Newton's daughter Miss Alice Hogan. Alice was captured in two different publications visiting her uncle Tilford Marion Hogan (T.M. Hogan): The Laclede Blade of Linn County Missouri and the Los Angeles Herald.

THE LACLEDE BLADE.

A. J. CAYWOOD, Editor and Publisher.
A. J. BAUM Local Editor.

Entered at the Laclede postoffice for transmission through the mails as second class matter.

SATURDAY, AUGUST 27, 1904.

Miss Alice Hogan arrived Thursday to visit her uncle, T. M. Hogan, and her aunt, Mrs. Mary Williams.

THE LACLEDE BLADE.

A. J. CAYWOOD, Editor and Publisher.

Entered at the Laclede postoffice for transmission through the mails as second class matter.

SATURDAY, FEB. 4, 1905.

After spending several months with relatives here, Miss Alice Hogan returned to her home in Los Angeles, California, Thursday.

ALICE HOGAN VISITS UNCLE, T.M. HOGAN AND HER AUNT, MARY MAHURIN (Tilford Marion Hogan's sister).

LOS ANGELES HERALD: FRIDAY MORNING, FEBRUARY 10, 1905.

Social Notes

Miss Alice Hogan, daughter of Mr. and Mrs. Newton Hogan of 903 West Thirty-sixth street, is again at home, having returned recently from an eleven months' visit in Missouri and Illinois.

Birthday Celebration!

Mrs. C.M. Williams (Mary Mahurin)

and

Miss Allie (Alice) Hogan

Tilford Hogan's sister and niece.

LACLEDE, MISSOURI, SATURDAY, OCTOBER 8. 1904.

A Birthday Celebration.

There was a happy gathering of neighbors and friends at the hospitable home of Mr. and Mrs. Charles H. Parker, a mile south of town, last Monday, the occasion being Mr. Parker's 68th birthday anniversary. A good dinner and a pleasant visit made the day an enjoyable one to all present. Mr. and Mrs. Parker are among our best citizens and their host of friends wish they may live to enjoy many more such occasions.

Those present were J. A. Woollen, Wm. Burnett, W. A. Balcom and wife, H. Ehrich and wife, L. T. Rowland and wife, Levi Standly and wife, A. J. Leech and wife, G. W. Anderson and wife, L. Eichman and wife, J. H. Bagenstos and wife, Wm. Mahurin and wife, W. N. Harter and wife, H. H. Hawes and wife, W. O. Anderson and wife, Isaac Lawson and wife, Geo. Lloyd and wife, Mrs. E. J. Watson and daughters, Ellen and Zella, Mrs. C. M. Williams, Mrs. Alex. Welsh, Mrs. I. O. Webb and children, Grace, Marie and Myrtie, Mrs. Cecil Welsh, Mrs. J. G. Clinefelter, Mrs. Z. R. Kling, Mrs. Henry Woollen, Miss Allie Hogan, J. Q. Lewis, Misses Gusta Eichman, Rose Lloyd, Beatrice Harter, Ethel and Opal Leech, Ruth Bagenstos, Carrie and Rosa Lawson, Masters Kenneth Hoyt, Zina Anderson and Calvin Kling.

Los Angeles Herald, Number 144, 22 February 1911

Society

Miss Ethel Hogan, daughter of Mr. and Mrs. Newton Hogan, will become the bride of Dr. Joseph Pettee Copp, son of Mr. and Mrs. Andrew J. Copp, this evening at the home of her parents, 911 West Thirty-fifth street.

Ethel Josephine Hogan, Della Mae Monroe's first cousin married Dr. Joseph Pettee Copp. Dr. Copp was a Dentist. He was born in Los Angeles, California September 4, 1881. He was the son of Andrew James Copp Sr. and Carrie Pettee Bostwick. Andrew James Copp Sr. was a lawyer. Among his many accomplishments he was made chairman of the committee on the unemployed by the City Council of Los Angeles in 1893-1884. Refer to the OBITUARY RECORD OF GRADUATES OF YALE UNIVERSITY DECEASED DURING THE YEAR 1939-1940 for biographical information regarding Andrew James Copp Sr.

COPP Mr and Mrs. Joseph P. Boy. 308 South Union avenue. July 21

Ethel Hogan and Dr. Joseph P. Copp had three children:

Joseph P. Copp Jr., Andrew J. Copp, and Dr. Newton Hogan Copp.

Federal Title Building
HABS NO. CA-2153
page 3

1972 Order No. 4195, Superior Court, County
of Los Angeles, recorded July 7, 1972
(Case No. P. 572248)
Estate of Andrew J. Copp, Jr., to Atlantic
Savings and Loan, one-half interest

1972 Order No. 218, Superior Court, County of
Los Angeles, recorded June 23, 1972
(Case No. WE P-08356)
Estate of Joseph P. Copp to Atlantic
Savings and Loan, one-half interest

1972 Deed No. 219, recorded October 12, 1972,
Ethel Hogan Copp as Executrix of Will of
Joseph P. Copp, to Atlantic Savings
and Loan, one-half interest

1972 Deed No. 221, recorded October 12, 1972
Andrew J. Copp, III, and Jayne Feldman
Copp, Executor and Executrix of the Will
of Andrew J. Copp, Jr., to Atlantic Savings
and Loan, an undivided one-half interest

4. Builder: R. Milsap

5. Original Plans and Construction: Not located

6. Alterations and Additions: Minor alterations to the structure include the addition of modern aluminum frame doors and the filling-in of windows on the north side.

B. Historical Context: Construction of this building was part of the overall shift of business and commerce to the Pershing Square area in the late 1920's. The location next door to Subway Terminal Building must have seemed ideal and worth overcoming the disadvantages of the extra-narrow lot size. Federal Title is not represented in any other survey of historic buildings of Los Angeles and little is known of building tenants. The building is being refurbished in 1980, presumably to let for office uses. It is currently vacant.

LOS ANGELES HERALD: THURSDAY MORNING, FEBRUARY 23, 1911.

Society

MAID OF HONOR AT FOUR O'CLOCK HOME WEDDING YESTERDAY

Della Monroe's Uncle Newton Hogan and family were captured in a wedding announcement for Ethel Hogan February 23, 1911.

The marriage of Miss Ethel Hogan, daughter of Mr. and Mrs. Newton Hogan, to Dr. Joseph Pettee Copp, son of Mr. and Mrs. Andrew James Copp, was solemnized yesterday afternoon at 4 o'clock at the residence of the bride's parents, 911 West Thirty-fifth street. Dr. George Finley Bovard, president of the University of Southern California, read the double ring service in the presence of eighty relatives and friends. The house was beautifully decorated with a profusion of green, the living room where the ceremony was performed being converted into a veritable bower. The bridal party stood in front of the immense fireplace which was banked with palms and ropes of smilax formed a screen to the ceiling. Wide streamers of white tulle reached from the chandeliers to the four corners of the room and baskets of ferns and greens were hung everywhere. The bride, preceded by her only attendant, Miss Alice Hogan, descended the stairway alone and met the bridegroom and his best man, William W. Copp of Nevada, at the altar. She was attired in a becoming gown of white marquisette over messaline satin trimmed with chantilly lace and embroidered brocade. Her veil of tulle was held in place by a coronet of lilies of the valley and caught about the hem of her gown with sprays of the lilies and maidenhair ferns. Her only ornament was a string of exquisite pearls, the bridal gift of the bridegroom's mother, Mrs. Andrew James Copp. She carried a shower of bride's roses and white sweet peas. The maid of honor, Miss Alice Hogan, was attired in a gown of pale blue crepe de chine over pink silk and carried an arm bouquet of enchantress carnations with wide white tulle ribbons. An elaborate supper was served after the ceremony, the dining room being banked with greenery. In the bay window, which was hung with ropes of smilax, stood the bride's table and under a great bell the wedding cake was cut with a solid silver knife tied with butterfly bow of white tulle, which was the gift of the bride's brother. The chandeliers were wound with smilax and tied with yellow satin ribbons. Bowls of violets and maidenhair ferns decorated the tables. Dr. and Mrs. Copp left amid a shower of violets and rose petals, the bride attired in an oyster gray chiffon cloth with hat of wistaria straw trimmed with velvet in shades of the same. After a short wedding trip they will be at home to their friends at 410 Lucas street after March 15. Dr. Copp was graduated from the dental college of the University of Southern California and is a member of the Psi Omega fraternity. Miss Hogan was a student at the university for six years and is a member of the Entre Nous sorority of the U. S. C. and also of the Phi Gamma Upsilon, National sorority. Many affairs have been given in honor of the young couple since the announcement of their engagement a few weeks ago.

MISS ALICE HOGAN

also be a book shower and a program. The directors consist of Mrs. Fred Hooker Jones, Mrs. Russell Judson Waters, Mrs. William Warren Orcutt, Mrs. William Bowne Hunnewell and Miss Caroline M. Seymour.

Mrs. Emil Ostrom of 400 West Santa Barbara avenue entertained informally Thursday afternoon in honor of the eightieth birthday anniversary of Mrs. E. K. Rand. The dining room was decorated with ferns and smilax. Sprays of smilax, bowls of violets and sweet peas adorned the table, while in the center rested the cake, decorated with eighty candles. Among the guests were Mrs. E. K. Rand, Mrs. H. Bowen, Mrs. A. L. Blumberg, Mrs. V. Beckman, Mrs. A. D. Fraser, Mrs. H. H. Morrow, Mrs. F. E. McCollum, Mrs. James Q. Prentice and Miss Jessie McCollum.

The members of the Kappa Kappa Kappa sorority will be hostesses at a card party Saturday afternoon, March 4, at the home of Miss Dixie Osborn, 1732 Harvard boulevard. The hostesses will include Mrs. Irwin Barrett, Mrs. F. B. Mathews, Mrs. O. W. Cave, Miss Evelyn Tyler, Miss Edna Staples, Miss

ACADEMICS LOSE TO COLLEGIANS

BASKETBALL SEASON OPENS AT U. S. C.

Fast Work of Misses Hogan and Augur Result in Victory for Upper Class Team by Score of 24 to 14

Interest in basketball was reawakened at the University of Southern California yesterday afternoon by a hotly contested game between the college and academy girls.

The college girls won by a score of 24 to 14, due principally to the foot work of Misses Hogan and Augur at forward.

Hogan and Augur, forwards; Thornton, center, and Rush and Gerard, guards, represented the college. The academy team lined up with Oertly and Montgomery, forwards, Walters, center, and Speicher and Shartle, guards. Miss Griffin acted as referee and Miss Comstock umpired.

As this was the first game of basketball on the local courts for the present season there was a large crowd present to get a line on the sort of a team the varsity girls are going to put out.

Two years ago U. S. C. won the woman's basketball championship through splendid team work and the brilliant work of Ethel Hogan and Mabel Peyton at forward. Last year, with the loss of Miss Peyton, they put up a hard fight only to lose at the close of the season to L. A. high school after the most exciting game of woman's basketball ever seen on local courts.

This year the Methodist team will be an entirely unknown quantity, as only one of two years ago championship team will appear in the line-up. Lora Woodhead and Gladys Armstrong, the famous guards, are not in school, and Miss Hogan's parents forbid her further participation in the game.

Alta Thornton will be out for her old place at center, and the university has good new material in Miss Augur of L. A. high school, Miss Gerard of Ontario and Miss Butters of Long Beach. Miss Montgomery, a forward on last year's team, is also out for honors.

Coach Best says that with Thornton and Montgomery as a nucleus, he will endeavor to build a strong team out of the new material at his command.

Los Angeles Herald, Volume 34, Number 23, 24 October 1906

ETHEL HOGAN PLAYED BASKETBALL FOR THE U.S.C. TEAM AND WAS TEAM CAPTAIN AND LATER MANAGER. ETHEL WAS HEAVILY INVOLVED IN SORORITY AND OTHER SOCIAL ACTIVITIES WHILE IN COLLEGE.

Ethel Hogan is Marilyn Monroe's first cousin twice removed.

Ethel Hogan's basketball team playing a game in 1908. Credit U.S.C. Yearbook.

BASKET BALL

Girls' Basket Ball Team

Team

Anne Shepard	Center
Stella Knoles	Center
Ella Winstanley	Guard
Lora Woodhead	Guard
Ethel Hogan (Captain)	Forward
Katherine Asher	Forward

Games

U. S. C. 27	L. A. H. S.	3
U. S. C. 9	Collegiate	5
U. S. C. 28	Alhambra	7
U. S. C. 16	Alhambra	9
U. S. C. 33	Glendale	5

Men's Basket Ball

Team

Coloneus (Captain)	Center
Hall	Forward
Goode	Forward
Reed	Guard
Henderson	Guard

Substitutes

Selph	Deniston

Games

U. S. C. 23	Whittier	18
U. S. C. 44	Pasadena	14
U. S. C. 17	Whittier	47
U. S. C. 58	Huntington Beach	18
U. S. C. 19	Whittier	27

Ethel Hogan – USC Women's Basketball Pioneer and Champion

Ethel Hogan, Marilyn Monroe's first cousin twice removed, is revered as a pioneer in University of Southern California (USC) Women's Basketball.

In Hank Kraychir's book *USC Athletic Stories*, he introduces Ethel as a "forgotten star" and part of the Methodist Maidens team, which paved the way for the now powerful women's basketball legacy at USC.

Kraychir devoted an entire chapter to Ethel in his book and he explained that she was one of the youngest on the new team, which started playing against others circa 1904.

"During this foundation period," Kraychir wrote, "a now forgotten female basketball player arose to lead USC into prominence. Ethel Hogan became the Maidens' symbol of speed and grace, and in spite of resistance to women competing in sports, she pioneered women's basketball during her four years of play."

Ethel's team earned write-ups in the *Los Angeles Times* during 1904 for the championship game. She played left forward for the Methodist Maidens, then moved swiftly to the rank of team captain, because of "her inspiring method of playing basketball," Kraychir wrote.

"Hogan," Kraychir continued, "was unanimously chosen as the Maidens' team captain in 1905 because of her brilliant style of play, knowledge of the game, and for never giving up until the game was over, which was exemplified by her 1904 season."

Los Angeles Herald, Volume 32, Number 235, 24 May 1905

U. S. C. MAIDENS ARE TRIUMPHANT

WIN FROM THE HIGH SCHOOL BASKETBALL SQUAD
CAPTURE SENSATIONAL GAME

Deciding Match for League Championship Added to Methodist Ball Tossers' Laurels

ETHEL HOGAN

Los Angeles Herald, Volume 32, Number 213, 2 May 1905

For Basketball Girls

A merry little dinner at Hotel Lankershim last evening was that given by Dr. and Mrs. George F. Bovard in honor of the basketball team of the University of Southern California. The girls have done good work during the past season and the affair was in the nature of a celebration. College colors, gold and red, were used in an artistic table decoration, and covers were laid for the five members of the team, Misses Gladys Armstrong, Lora Woodhead, Mable Peyton, Alta Thornton, Ethel Hogan and the two young women who have helped to make the work of the team successful, Miss Beulah Wright and Miss Nellye Dickson, and Oliver Best.

University of Southern California, 15; Los Angeles high school, 12.

The fastest and most scientific exhibition of girls' basket ball that has been played in Los Angeles this season was the match between the crack U. S. C. team and the fast high school five for the championship of Southern California yesterday afternoon on the Marlborough school courts.

Although the blue and white finished on the short end the plucky little girls covered themselves with glory by their sportsmanlike manner of play. The girls from the school on the hill took their defeat gracefully and after the game they received the highest praise from the large crowd of enthusiasts that saw the struggle.

The game was wonderfully free from the wrangles and disputes that usually mar the game.

The team work of the U. S. C. five was as near perfection as is possible to drill into ordinary mortals. They did not fall to pieces when a play that they had figured out in practice was smashed up but had several new ones up their sleeve for such special occasions.

One of the clever plays came in the first half when Miss Peyton threw a sensational basket over her head. The high school forward tried for a basket but failed. Miss Woodhead, U. S. C.'s guard, got the ball and passed it across center court to the U. S. C. forward, who bounced it under the basket. Instead of trying for a goal she passed the ball to Miss Peyton, who was standing back near the center court. Miss Peyton advanced it along to the basket, but was guarded so closely that she could not get a clear throw, so she swung around and passed the ball over her head and into the basket with wonderful accuracy.

Following is the detailed score:

U. S. C.	F.G	F.G.	F.
Miss Hogan, f.	3	0	0
Miss Peyton, f.	2	5	4
Miss Thornton, c.	0	0	4
Miss Woodhead, g.	0	0	2
Miss Armstrong, g.	0	0	5
Totals	5	5	15
L. A. H. S.	F.G.	F.G.	F.
Miss Plummer	3	5	4
Miss Burke	0	1	0
Miss Griffin	0	0	2
Miss Hunter	0	0	7
Miss Augur	0	0	4
Totals	3	6	17

Officials—Miss Rust, Miss Furman and Miss Caswell.

In 1904 while playing against Occidental, it was Ethel's persistence that won over her teammates, in spite of the team taking a loss.

Ethel even continued to play during a match against Woodbury with a dislocated ankle, taking USC to victory in the final 10 minutes.

In those days, play was rough, and although USC was equipped with a new gymnasium, the Maidens often played outside, sometimes facing varied weather conditions.

Additionally, many women's teams did not play in the presence of men, with Occidental at USC and demanding at the start of their game that men be ousted from the audience, though one sly male USC student remained, under the safety of his sister's coat and sporting her hat.

Ethel gained notice in 1905 as part of a "southern team," combining with other schools of the region, versus northern schools like Berkeley and Stanford, taking the game 11-4.

On May 5, 1905, Ethel and fellow forward Mable Payton passed to each other, along with center Alta Thornton, during one notable game, the Maidens snagging a 27-11 win.

The *Los Angeles Times* reported on the impressive way that the USC Maidens took the cup on May 24, in only the second year as a team. They played against the Los Angeles High School "JUGS." The "JUGS" did what they could to stop the USC forwards Mable and Ethel, and a lively game ensued. USC was first in the lead, followed with an 11-11 tie, and then the "JUGS" took the lead 3-8. The "JUGS" broke into song, calling for baskets, which the Maidens upped the score instead 13-11. After a dispute among the game's timekeepers, an additional minute was tacked on and the Maidens finished in the lead, 15-12.

For her part in the victory, Ethel was honored with the team at the Lankershim Hotel, where the group was celebrated with a banquet. The festivities were in honor of the championship win and undefeated season.

"In a time when women's competitive sport was highly discouraged," wrote Kraychir, "Hogan displayed courage not only by playing basketball but also by leading her team to a first ever conference championship for USC."

Kraychir stated that Ethel was one of the best players in her day at USC "when competitive women's sport was young."

"Ethel Hogan," he concluded, "is certainly a worthy role model for women today. In the archives of USC hides a symbol of pioneering greatness, and her name is simply Ethel Hogan, who is another lost USC athlete who needs to be honored."

Young Women's Christian Association

Officers

Jennie M. Dick	President
Alta E. Thornton	Vice-President
Evelyn Davman	Secretary
Isabelle M. Bowers	Treasurer
Nellie L. Vale	Resident Secretary

Chairmen of Committees

Membership	Alta E. Thornton
Missionary	M. Elaine Anderson
Finance	Isabelle M. Bowers
Bible Study	Ethel J. Hogan
Religious Meetings	Zula F. Brown
Intercollegiate	C. Mauneena McMillan
Social	Pearl A. Russell
Capitola	Flora Robinson
Extension	Sarah K. Miller

Advisory Committee

Mrs. G. F. Bovard   Mrs. D. M. Welch   Miss Elsie Vanderpool
Miss Margaret Borthwick   Mrs. W. F. Cronemiller
Miss Stella Morgan

Faculty Committee

Miss Margaret Borthwick   Miss Elsie Vanderpool
Mrs. Lucy Best   Miss Ruth Brown
Miss Stella Morgan

...GIRLS' BASKET BALL...

Basketball is an enthusiastic sport among the women interested in athletics. Conditions for outdoor exercise at the University are admirable—the climate, to be sure, but also the surroundings. Beautiful pepper trees, their leaves filtering the sometimes intense rays of the sun, a court of careful and intelligent workmanship, the able supervision of trained coaches, all are conducive to eager interest in the game. The benefits to be derived from outdoor activity of this kind are invaluable, and the sport lacks the generally irksome routine of indoor gymnastics. President Bovard maintains that basketball is one of the finest sports for women, and has heartily supported the game.

The season of 1908 extending from January to May proved very successful, both on account of the result of the games played and of the interest displayed. Out of thirteen games played the 'varsity team lost but one contest, which was the championship struggle of the Women's League, and was won by Long Beach by the score of 13—6.

On December 11, 1907, a preliminary practice game was played with L. A. High School, and the score stood 18—4. Early in February of 1908 came the selection of the 'Varsity team. Miss Katherine Asher was chosen captain, with the following team: Miss Ella Winstanley, Miss Lora Woodhead, guards; Miss Anne Shepherd, Miss Ethel Hart, centers; Miss Ethel Hogan, Miss Katherine Asher, forwards. Substitutes were Miss Stella Knoles, Miss Florence Woodhead. Miss Ethel Hogan was elected manager of the team. By defeating Alhambra High School the 'Varsity won the championship of the Southern California Interscholastic League, which membered last season many of the strongest teams of the south. In a series of post-season games the 'Varsity defeated both the Selma and Madera High School teams, undoubtedly the strongest aggregations of Central California.

In February, 1909, the 'Varsity team for this season was chosen. Miss Ella Winstanley and Miss Katherine Asher were the only players of the 1908 'Varsity available for the squad, and the new 'Varsity was built up largely of new material. Miss Agnes Yoch quickly developed into the most consistent and unerring basket-thrower in the team and largely through her excellent individual playing the 'Varsity defeated Pomona in an exciting contest by the score of 17—13. Later the 'Varsity lost the Women's League honors to the veteran Long Beach team, by the score of 19 to 11.

Joseph Copp Jr.

Son of Ethel Hogan. Second cousin once removed of Marilyn Monroe.

CHINO CHAMPION, Chino, California

Friday, April 14, 1950

JOSEPH COPP JR. of 222 El Molino avenue entertained his parents, Dr. and Mrs. Joseph P. Copp sr. of Los Angeles, and his aunt, Miss Alice Hogan, also of Los Angeles, as his Easter Sunday dinner guests.

Descriptive Summary

Restrictions on Use and Reproduction

Property rights to the physical object belong to the UCLA Library, Department of Special Collections. Literary rights, including copyright, are retained by the creators and their heirs. It is the responsibility of the researcher to determine who holds the copyright and pursue the copyright owner or his or her heir for permission to publish where The UC Regents do not hold the copyright.

Restrictions on Access

COLLECTION STORED OFF-SITE AT SRLF: Advance notice required for access.

Additional Physical Form Available

A copy of the original version of this online finding aid is available at the UCLA Department of Special Collections for in-house consultation and may be obtained for a fee. Please contact:

Provenance/Source of Acquisition

Gift of Joseph Copp, Jr., 1979.

Preferred Citation

[Identification of item], Joseph Copp Papers (Collection 1230). Department of Special Collections, Charles E. Young Research Library, University of California, Los Angeles.

Biography

Joseph Copp was raised in Los Angeles, California; he opened his first landscape architecture business in 1937, and he eventually became a landscape architect for various political and professional people in the U.S.

California, Death Index, 1940-1997

Name: Alice Lenora Hogan
Gender: Female
Birth Date: 10 May 1875
Birth Place: Missouri
Death Date: 8 Feb 1955
Death Place: Los Angeles
Mother's Maiden Name: Switzer
Father's Surname: Hogan

Historical Newspapers, Birth, Marriage, & Death Announcements, 1851-2003

Miss Alice Hogan

Funeral services will be conducted at 11 a.m. tomorrow in Pierce Bros. Beverly Hills chapel for Miss Alice Hogan, 79, of 219½ Catalina St., who died yesterday. A former employee of the California State Employment Service, she had lived in California 70 years. Interment will be in Inglewood Park Cemetery. She leaves a brother, Chester Hogan; a sister, Mrs. Joseph P. Copp and three nephews.

Chester Hogan

Marilyn Monroe's first cousin twice removed indicated on his draft card in 1942 that he lived with his wife at 6342 Mulholland Drive (often referenced as Mulholland Highway). This photo is the home as it was newly constructed in the 1920s. Construction was finished in Marilyn's birth year, 1926. This home has had a famous history. It was first owned by oil magnate Patrick Longdon, and called "Longdon's Castle." Famous architect John De Lario was the designer. Known later as "Castillo Del Lago," or "Castle of the Lake," it was reportedly mobster Bugsy Siegel's home during the 1940s. Madonna purchased the home for $5 million in the 1990s, painting the mansion and its walls in orange striped tones. Since Madonna sold it with a list price over more than $14 million, it has been returned to its original white.

REGISTRATION CARD—(Men born on or after April 28, 1877 and on or before February 16, 1897) 242

SERIAL NUMBER	1. NAME (Print)	ORDER NUMBER
U 3122	Chester Leland Hogan	

2. PLACE OF RESIDENCE (Print): 6342 Mulholland Dr - Los Angeles - Los Angeles - Calif

[THE PLACE OF RESIDENCE GIVEN ON THE LINE ABOVE WILL DETERMINE LOCAL BOARD JURISDICTION; LINE 2 OF REGISTRATION CERTIFICATE WILL BE IDENTICAL]

3. MAILING ADDRESS: SAME

4. TELEPHONE: HE. 0603
5. AGE IN YEARS: 56 — DATE OF BIRTH: June 29 1885
6. PLACE OF BIRTH: Tulare County, California

7. NAME AND ADDRESS OF PERSON WHO WILL ALWAYS KNOW YOUR ADDRESS: Mrs. Dixie M. Hogan - 6342 Mulholland Dr - Los Angeles

8. EMPLOYER'S NAME AND ADDRESS: The Farmers & Merchants Nat'l Bank - 401 S. Main - Los Angeles, Calif.

9. PLACE OF EMPLOYMENT OR BUSINESS: 401 S. Main St. Los Angeles - Los Angeles - Calif

I AFFIRM THAT I HAVE VERIFIED ABOVE ANSWERS AND THAT THEY ARE TRUE.

C L Hogan (Registrant's signature)

D.S.S. Form 1 (Revised 4-1-42)   16—21630-2

Marilyn Monroe Unveiled | A Family History

On Sunday June 17, 1945, William Leonard Hogan, son of William Marion Hogan (Sellars/Nance) came home on military leave.

CITY SECTION
The Sun
Sun., June 17, 1945

WELCOME HOME

Following are the names of servicemen and women from San Bernardino and adjoining communities who are at home on leaves and furloughs, together with addresses and telephone numbers:

William D. Turnbull, aviation radioman 3/c, Navy, son of Mr. and Mrs. R. B. Turnbull, 1260 Canyon road, telephone 322-91. (On 10-day leave after service at Norfolk, Va., and Brazil; reports to Memphis, Tenn., for reassignment.)

Arthur F. Brown, yeoman 1/c, Navy, son of Mr. and Mrs. R. O. Brown, 870 Sixth street, telephone 394-18; wife and son reside at 673 Crescent avenue. (On 30-day leave after 17 months with Naval Air unit in Pacific.)

W. L. Hogan, boatswain's mate 2/c, Navy, son of Mr. and Mrs. W. M. Hogan, 375 Tippecanoe avenue. (Thirty-day leave after Pacific duty.)

Pharmacist Harry F. Wifenand, son of Mrs. Florence Botts

In 1937 Milton Stores Andros, his wife Naomi Love and their son Lee Milton Andros (U.S. NAVY) resided at 1736 HAUSER BLVD in Los Angeles.

Andros Corinne Mrs r839 S St Andrews pl
" Geo (Koula) h2924½ Malta
" Geo cook r230 S Flower
" Hilda E sten Canada Life Assurance Co r Glendale
" Lee M USN r1736 Hauser blvd
" Milton S (Naomi) studiowkr h1736 Hauesr blvd

Milton S. Andros STUDIOWORKER

Marilyn Monroe Unveiled | A Family History

William Marion Hogan (Sellars/Nance)

William, his wife Clara and children lived in Hawthorne near Gladys, Norma Jeane, and Marion and other relatives. He then moved to Los Angeles, and finally purchased a home at 375 Tippecanoe in San Bernardino California.

NAME		
Myrtle Myers	daughter	Kansas City, Missouri
Dora O. Schulties	daughter	Riverwood Route #8 Portland, Ore.
James B. Sellars	son	Vienna, Va.
Marion E. Monroe	Grand son	Hawthorne, California
Gladys P. Baker	Grand daughter	Hawthorne, California
William Nance	son	Hawthorne, California
Marion E. Monroe and Gladys P. Baker are children of Della Monroe, a deceased daughter		

Sun., Sept., 16, 1945 SAN BERNARDINO DAILY SUN

30 For Rent, Furnished Houses

WILL rent my completely furnished home at 4th & Tippecanoe, 1 block from Army Air Depot for one month or will sell you the whole works, lock, stock, barrel & all. Wm. M. Hogan, 375 Tippecanoe.

Marie Transue (Hogan), Gladys Monroe's first cousin and Marilyn Monroe's first cousin once removed. She was the daughter of William Marion Hogan (Sellars/Nance) Marie was an award winning Poet. In 1930 she was 14 years old and lived with her parents at W. Ave 31 in Los Angeles California. They lived approximately 19 miles away from Gladys, Norma Jeane and Ida Bolender.

Local poet wins Silver Award

Local poet Marie Transue has been recognized by the World of Poetry, a worldwide poetry association, who has honored her with a Silver Award, one of the highest honors bestowed upon a poet by that organization.

Transue will be traveling to Orlando, Fla., August 28-Sept. 1, where she will be presented her Silver Award at the Marriotts Orlando World Center.

"Indian Summer Love," written by Transue in the Fall of 1982, seems not only to be special to the judges who chose the poem for a Silver Award, it was also one of her husband's favorites.

"Poetry has been a part of my life ever since I could rhyme dog and cat," quipped Transue. But for the past 20 years she has concentrated her thoughts more on paper and has been quite successful. Transue gives much credit to Bess Foster-Smith, an accomplished and well-known local poet and her fellow writing friends, Viola Joseph and Betty Derig who both encourage and critique her work.

"Poetry is just a way to express myself and my feelings," commented Transue.

Bess Foster Smith said of Transue's poetry: "Like an artist who can portray a feeling with a quick stroke of the brush - Marie is an artist with words. Her poetry stimulates the imagination in its search for beauty - and sends you back for a second look."

Transue has had her work printed in many publications and she has had three books of her poetry printed which have been very successful.

Her first poetry book, "Wafers and Wine" was published in 1968. The second, "Cantus" was published in 1971. The third "Surf, Turf and Sky" was published in 1980 and includes sketches by the author.

In addition to encouraging Transue to write her poetry, her friends have also encouraged her to express her artistic abilities. She enjoys painting in oil and acrylics and just recently finished a watercolor course through Boise State University.

Transue spends much of the summer months at her cabin in Donnelly. She is a member of the Weiser Senior Citizens as well as the McCall Senior Citizens.

Born in Texas, Transue was only nine months old when her family moved to Colorado and then she moved to California. She was attending University of California at Los Angeles (UCLA), studying aeronautical engineering, when she met her husband, a serviceman. While on a short leave they were married and when World War II ended in 1945 they came to Notus, Idaho, where her husband, James, was from. He worked for the railroad for many years.

Transue has three children and one stepson. David Transue lives in Parma, Janet White in Council, Toni Salgado, Ontario and Jimmy Jr. in Salt Lake City, Utah.

Transue is an active member of the local Writers League and in addition to receiving several awards for her work, she has had poems published or won awards from the following: Ben Travato, Idaho Writer's League, Contest in Gem Writer's Newsletter, Idaho Historical Society, Creative Review, Writer's Gem Freedom Contest, Fellowship in Prayer, Nutmegger, Angel Hour, Pannmann Magazine and The Angels.

In addition Transue wrote a column for the Signal-American which she said included observations and local gossip and has had articles printed in The Statesman.

As a Silver Award winner from the World of Poetry, Transue and her fellow award winners from throughout the world will enter poems in the grand prize contest to win from several $500, $1,000 and the big $10,000 award to be presented at the convention in Florida.

Indian Summer Love

There was a boy born.
An "Indian Summer" child.
Before the winter solstice
Ice-locked alluvian streams.

There was a boy born.
Bright eyes dark and dreaming.
An Idaho child.
Thirsting after "Nature's secrets."

There was a boy born.
Earthy, wild as a panther.
Heart-soft as a cloud.
And I loved him.

—Marie Transue

Marie Transue

Marilyn Monroe Unveiled | A Family History

Rebecca Esther Hogan (Becky Hogan) took part in the 4-H Clothing Club at the San Bernardino-Colton Junior Academy in 1941. Esther Palhegyi and Twyla/Quyla Weilage, who acted as Pallbearer at Carol Ann Hogan's funeral(See Chapter 13), were elected president and vice-president respectively of the club.

SAN BERNARDINO DAILY SUN, FRIDAY, OCTOBER 24, 1941

4-H Club Girls Form Unit to Make Clothes

A new 4-H clothing club was organized Tuesday evening by 14 girls who met at the San Bernardino-Colton Junior academy. The group, known as the Sew-Sew Girls, is under the leadership of Miss Helen C. MacGregor and Mrs. R. M. Gardner.

Officers elected at the first meeting were Twyla Weilage, president; Esther Palhegyi, vice-president; Mary Keehnel, secretary-treasurer; Priscilla Obst, reporter. In addition to the officers the following girls were present: Alice Martinell, June Martinell, Arlene Fowler, Colleen Keehnel, Barbara Richards, Madge Dunson, Becky Hogan, Marguerite Scott, Audrey Hart, Evelyn Robertson.

Mrs. Sara Mott, home demonstration agent of the University of California agricultural extension service, supervises all home economics groups of the county 4-H clubs.

Clara Mae Hogan- William Marion Hogan's wife of 35 years.

—THE DAILY SUN Tuesday, June 26, 1956

CLARA M. HOGAN

Clara Mae Hogan, 65, 1022 E. Union St., San Bernardino, died Sunday in a San Bernardino hospital. A native of Missouri, she had been a resident of San Bernardino 19 years and of California 35 years. She was a member of the Seventh-day Adventist Church.

Survivors include four daughters, Mrs. Violet Lindsey and Mrs. Rebecca Fritz, both of San Bernardino, Mrs. Naomi Fowler, Arlington, and Mrs. Marie Transue, Weiser, Idaho; two sons, Robert L., Port Orchard, Wash., and William, Malone, Wash.; a sister, Mrs. Katie Templeton, St. Louis, Mo.; 15 grandchildren, and numerous nieces and nephews.

Services will be held Monday, July 2, at 2 p.m., at the Mark B. Shaw Chapel. Friends may call after 7 p.m. Saturday.

Interment will be at Montecito Memorial Park.

—THE DAILY SUN Tuesday, July 3, 1956

CLARA M. HOGAN

Services for Clara Mae Hogan were held at 2 p.m. Monday at Mark B. Shaw Chapel, with Elder John Elick of the Seventh-day Adventist Church, La Sierra, officiating.

Organ selections by Seward Brush were "The Old Rugged Cross" and "Nearer My God to Thee." Pallbearers were Arnold Palhegyi, Alex Palhegyi, John Palhegyi and Arthur Fowler. Interment was at Montecito Memorial Park.

Naomi Ruth Hogan, daughter of William Marion Hogan and Gladys Monroe's first cousin married Milo R. Fowler in 1942 (San Bernardino, California).

SAN BERNARDINO DAILY SUN. TUESDAY, FEBRUARY 10, 1942

VITAL RECORDS

FOWLER-HOGAN—Milo R. Fowler, 21, Minnesota, and Naomi R. Hogan, 17, California, both residents of San Bernardino.

Born September 1946 in San Bernardino California, Norman Eugene Fowler. His grandfather was William Marion Hogan. His mother Naomi Ruth Hogan (Gladys Monroe's first cousin) was proud of Norma Jeane's early modeling success and named him after her. He took the male version of Norma Jeane.

Name: Norman Eugene Fowler
Birth Date: 7 Sep 1946
Gender: Male
Mother's Maiden Name: Hogan
Birth County: San Bernardino
Birthdate: 7 Sep 1946; Birth County: San Bernardino

California Birth Index, 1905-1995

Marilyn Monroe Unveiled | A Family History

CHAPTER TWENTY

QUESTIONS HAVE ARISEN regarding the potential ancestral relationship between Marilyn Monroe and Anna Nicole Smith because of their Hogan relatives. So far, no direct connections have been found between the two entertainers at present, though some of their relatives' paths may have crossed in Muskogee, Oklahoma.

Anna Nicole Smith was a longtime Marilyn Monroe admirer. She even lived at Marilyn's home as a tenant for a period of time at 12305 Fifth Helena Drive in Brentwood, many years following Marilyn's death. Anna Nicole even slept in the bedroom that Marilyn had died in, posters of Marilyn having adorned her walls.

On February 8, 2007, Anna Nicole Smith was found dead at the Seminole Hard Rock Hotel near Hollywood, Florida. As an eerie coincidence, the autopsy report, which reflected a full battery of tests showed that Vickie Lynn Marshall, her then legal name, at age 39, was bombarded with drug intoxication in her system, with the most lethal drugs found running through her blood, Chloral Hydrate. Other drugs were: Diphenhydramine, Conazepam, Diazepam, Nordiazepam, Temazepam, Oxazepam and Lorazepam. Other drugs considered "non-contributory" were: Atropine, Topiramate, Ciprofloxacin, and Acetaminophen.

Many have questioned the autopsy's validity and due diligence for Marilyn Monroe, of which the report was drawn up on August 6, 1962, the day after her body was found in her Brentwood home. Although there were other medications, some with black box/lethal warnings attached to them that were found on her nightstand, the only two drug tests called for on the report were Chloral Hydrate and Pentobarbital. Like Anna Nicole's test, a dose of Chloral Hydrate, at eight milligrams percent was reportedly in Marilyn's blood and in her liver, 13 milligrams percent of Pentobarbital.

Eerily, as Marilyn's psychiatrist Dr. Ralph Greenson had a relationship with Marilyn Monroe that violated ethics, so did Anna Nicole Smith with her psychiatrist Dr. Khristine Eroshevich. While Dr. Greenson received no penalties, unfortunately, because he had friends who were a part of the "Psychiatric Investigative Team," the judge and jury of Marilyn's character after her death, Dr. Eroshevich received five years probation with the state licensing agency in 2012, as well as a 90-day suspension of her license to practice for misconduct, and the wrongful prescription of opiates to Anna Nicole.

Dr. Eroshevich was with Anna Nicole in Florida when she died and about 600 pills (of which 450 were muscle relaxants) were found missing at the hotel, while the prescriptions were not even six-weeks.

Dr. Eroshevich faced two felony charges initially, and the one was reduced to a misdemeanor charge. In 2015, Los Angeles County Prosecutors were still seeking jail time for Dr. Eroshevich, as well as Howard K. Stern, another professional in Anna Nicole's life who had an inappropriate relationship, as her attorney and lover. There were originally conspiracy charges filed against the two, with prescriptions written out for Anna Nicole via Howard K. Stern, with he and the doctor using pseudonyms to overprescribe her medications. Dr. Eroshevich's charge was a misdemeanor conspiracy and she was never given any jail time, but received a $100 fine and a one-year probation sentence from Judge Robert J. Perry. Judge Perry ruled in favor of Howard K. Stern too, dismissing two felony charges against him in July 2015, the judge stating that the "case reeks of unfairness," and the prosecutor was overzealous in convicting Stern, which the judge stated ran the Los Angeles taxpayers about $500,000 for the trial that lasted 50 days. Those in the District Attorney's Office stated that Judge Perry ambushed the prosecutors with criticism.

Dr. Sandeep Kapoor, another doctor who was Anna Nicole's friend and internist was acquitted of all charges, though his diary reflected that he, as her primary physician, may have forged medical records, hid her records in his closet at home, and was often spotted partying with her. One night, he wrote in his diary, the doctor and Anna Nicole were "making out" after he had given her prescriptions of Methadone and Valium, and penned in his thoughts, "Can she ruin me?"

In terms of the Hogan ancestry, Marilyn's did not begin until her maternal grandmother, Della Mae (Hogan) Monroe. For Anna Nicole Smith, born Vickie Lynn Hogan on November 28, 1967 in Houston, her Hogan ancestry began at birth. Her mother, still living, is Virginia Mae "Virgie" (Tabers) Arthur though a 2015 article has claimed that she has been pleading to see her granddaughter, Dannielynn, a little girl born of a relationship between Anna Nicole and Larry Birkhead. Virgie Arthur was estranged from her daughter.

Anna Nicole's mother and father divorced in November 1969, and he remarried. When her mother remarried to Donald Hart, Anna Nicole's name was Nikki Hart for some time.

After Donald Hogan passed away on September 19, 2009, his obituary revealed that he had other children through his wife, Cindy, Donna, Amy, and Missy.

Donald was born on July 12, 1947 to Clarence Eugene Hogan and his wife Helen. Clarence was born in Harris County Texas on February 17, 1922 and died August 2, 1971. Anna Nicole's grandfather was a welder and died early one morning in a pickup and tractor trailer truck collision on Highway 59 in Splendora, Texas. He suffered from a fractured skull, crushed chest and severe laceration to his arms and legs.

Clarence's father was Walter Hogan and his mother Vivian Cones. Walter, Anna Nicole's great-grandfather was born in Oklahoma on June 22, 1884. He died when Clarence was only four-years- old on March 11, 1926. Walter, who worked as a painter died very tragically himself and was murdered near Huston, with "pistol shot wounds" noted on his death certificate. Though "D.K." or "Don't Know" was annotated on the death certificate for his mother, his father was listed as "L.A. Hogan," and born in Oklahoma.

A 1900 U.S. Federal Census shows Lewis E. Hogan living with Annie B. Hogan and sons Lewis C and Walter J Hogan, ages five and 14. Louis E. Hogan was accordingly born in Missouri per the census and Annie in Arkansas.

Walter Hogan had several children with Vivian before he passed away including Luther (born 1917), Lucille (born 1919), Clarence (Anna Nicole's grandfather, born 1922) and Edna Louise (born 1925). What confuses many on the Anna Nicole Smith Genealogy Trail is the 1930 Federal Census for her grandfather in the Houston City neighborhood where the family resided at 626 West 87th Street in Houston. Some complexities exist in her family documents. Once one moves past those and realizes there is an anomaly, one is able to track back through Anna Nicole's family tree. That is because of the father listed in Clarence's family on that census, who is Luther Hogan.

With Luther Hogan listed as the father of the above children and the spouse of Vivian Hogan, one would think this is a different family. However, at this point, Walter Hogan was dead nearly four years.

But it is the records for the children that show Luther, who told the census taker he was a garage mechanic born in Missouri, as were both his parents was not the father of these children. Other details do not make sense such as his age at 41 (birth circa 1889), and the age at his first marriage, 29. In that case, young Luther would have been 12, though the census shows he was 13. Another glitch is that the children, though they are referred to as his children, show that both of their parents were born in Texas. Vivian's state of birth is also listed as Texas. Of course though, Walter Hogan was born in Oklahoma.

One of the difficulties with census records could be the inaccuracies from the record taker, the details being conveyed from someone in the household, or both.

Marilyn Monroe Unveiled | A Family History

Young Luther Hogan's death certificate reflects that Walter Hogan was his father, as does Clarence Hogan's. Edna Louise (called "Louise") shows that she was born to W.J. Hogan. However, interestingly enough, though W.J. Hogan was Edna's father's name (who was listed as a "Paper Hanger" for his occupation, and residing at the same address as her mother, their mother then was using the name "Vivian Bateman." Her full maiden name was "Marie V. Cones."

It is uncertain at this time who the person Luther Hogan was that was said to be the husband of Anna Nicole's great-grandmother on the census report, but based on the documentation that the authors have found, as well as the census report, it can be disputed that he is the father of the children.

The 1900 Federal Census shows the father of the children, Walter J. Hogan, Anna Nicole Smith's great-grandfather, living with his parents in "Indian Territory" in Tulsa, Oklahoma. His father was shown as born in Missouri and his mother in Kansas. Her name was Annabelle "Anna" (Surber) Hogan. Louis E., born in 1856, told the census taker that his mother was born in New York and his father Germany. With the German ancestry, that would negate the search for relatives connected to Marilyn Monroe's Hogan line, since the Hogans in her family did not hail from Germany. Lewis was listed as a liveryman in the 1900 census.

There was one child born in 1900 named Jennings, who died in 1937, and is buried in Idaho with his mother, who died 1948. Lewis predeceased her in 1927. In 1930, Anna, Anna Nicole Smith's second great-grandmother lived with son Lewis C. in Emmett City, Idaho, as well as a daughter named Clara, who was born around 1909. Lewis C. and his sister both worked for the phone company as a section patrolman, and his sister as an operator. When Lewis, Anna Nicole's second great-uncle died suddenly on June 8, 1952, his obituary revealed that he had three daughters that had outlived him, and two sisters, Clara (now Williams living in Cloverdale, California) and Lottie (Hogan) Bussman from Tulsa.

In 1910 the census shows that L.E. Hogan was living and he was a widower. This is uncertain why since his spouse is hown to have outlived him. A four-year-old son named Eugene was also on the report. A lodger named James, as well as a servant named Catherine, plus his brother-in-law reportedly lived with him. His career was that of a "Retail Merchant" in groceries.

There are some documents that can connect Anna Nicole's to Marilyn's indirectly, and it is through the community of Muskogee, Oklahoma.

In 1901, the *Muskogee Daily Phoenix* reported that L.E. Hogan, then of Tulsa, had arrived in the city on September 29.

However, like Marilyn's ancestors, Anna Nicole's would later be reported in the paper as illustrious, especially L.E. Hogan. Only a decade prior to his vocation as a retail grocer, L.E. Hogan was a Deputy Marshall in Tulsa being reported in the Muskogee Phoenix as hauling in those charged with crime to jail, including those charged with larceny and rape. The district he reported to was referred to as the Northern Judicial District, according to the listing of the U.S. Deputy Marshals for the Indian Territory and Oklahoma Territory from 1893 through 1896. Another article in the *Muskogee Phoenix* showed that he was also part of an arrest of horse thieves in 1901.

In other words, the same area where Anna Nicole Smith's second great-grandfather was a Deputy U.S. Marshal, some of Marilyn's Hogan relatives also resided.

By 1910, it is known at least one of Marilyn's relatives was living in Muskogee, Oklahoma, around the same territory where Anna Nicole's second-great grandfather had been a Deputy Marshal and was later a grocer.

Marilyn's first cousin twice removed, Otis Hogan, resided in Muskogee during this time frame. He worked in the moving industry, and lived with his wife, Rosa then, his second wife since spouse Ellen passed away in 1896. He and his second wife Rosa had a son named Frank, then nine-years-old. His sons from his previous marriage were Clarence and Houston, then 16 and 15. Some genealogists have confused Marilyn's second cousin once removed Clarence Lester, born in 1893, as related to Anna Nicole's grandfather Clarence, born in 1922 and even the same. However, their only commonality was their ancestry in the Muskogee area.

Marilyn Monroe Unveiled | A Family History

In 1920, also during Lewis E. Hogan's (Anna Nicole's second great-grandfather's) lifetime, Otis, along with Rosie, Huston and Frank still lived in Muskogee. Otis and Huston worked as movers, while Frank worked in a garage.

Later, but far surpassing the death of Anna Nicole Smith's second great-grandfather, Lewis E. Hogan, Marilyn's second cousin once removed, Huston Henry Hogan, became the owner of the Hogan Chick Hatchery, an industry that surely would have crossed paths with L.E. Hogan's work in retail grocery. However, in 1927, the same year that Anna Nicole's second great-grandfather L.E. Hogan died, Marilyn second cousin once removed, Huston, was still employed in the moving industry.

CHAPTER TWENTY-ONE

IN 1974, A book was released entitled *My Story*, claiming to have been the exclusive words of Marilyn Monroe herself.

Marilyn had already passed away twelve years earlier, and this revelation from the great beyond of her words wowed many.

However, there were some that were not fooled then, and are still not swayed by the smoke and mirrors, though it has been pushed down the throats of many Marilyn fans as the "Monroe Doctrine," so to speak, of Marilyn's life.

It turned out to be a collaboration, as the 1974 edition pointed out in the front cover, between "Miss Monroe's confidant and business partner Milton Greene, who with the executors of the star's estate, decided that the time had come for the world to know what Marilyn Monroe herself had to say."

That is suspect enough, considering how Marilyn's wills were drawn up, and how she was pushed into creating them because of undue influence. In fact, she was manipulated overall to create her business with Milton Greene, who then delivered her into the hands of Lee Strasberg. Marilyn had no business advice or counsel that she asked for their opinion representing her, although she had plenty of advisors in Hollywood. She was told to turn her back, something that would turn out to be a deadly mistake. Later, not only would these parties steal her money, they would later claim to have her voice with this work of fiction.

There are some major issues with this manuscript that go well beyond the "orphan stories" that Marilyn and Grace McKee Goddard fabricated. It makes one question its legitimacy as words coming entirely from the mouth of Marilyn Monroe. And certainly, with the new information presented in this book, *Marilyn Monroe Unveiled: A Family History*, the legitimacy of the entire manuscript fails as a truthful account of Marilyn's life story.

The female author of this book recalls tracking down *My Story* in the 1980s. Attempting to learn as much as possible as a young girl about Marilyn Monroe, she discovered this book in the bibliography section of another one of her Marilyn biographies, and believed it a "must have." It actually was out of print at the time, but the local bookstore indicated it could be ordered from a book warehouse. However, the book price was not just its retail price then of $1.75, it was actually six times the amount of the cover price when ordered (close to $10 for the paperback).

However, the words of Marilyn Monroe, right? It is something special, right?

That was what the female author believed as a young woman who held it in her hands for the first time. The pink cover reading "*My Story*, by Marilyn Monroe" on it was convincing enough. And then, not to mention the words within, which for a youngster adoring this icon, was influencing enough. "This was her life, these were her words," the teen believed.

Or so everyone thought.

But then if one also deeply explores the many events and details of her life, it becomes easier to separate fact from fiction. And *My Story* comes out rather than an autobiography or biography, but instead a work of fiction.

But having the opportunity to really learn about Marilyn's personality as the authors have, every fan should be infuriated about this book's existence. Unless they enjoy reading fiction. That is because it was never written by Marilyn. And these, in essence, were truly not her words, though it was portrayed that she had been seated at a typewriter, and typed it herself in the 1974 edition, and later, Ben Hecht was given credit as the writer.

It is time to air some background into this book, which was one way that the legacy of Marilyn Monroe has been snatched over the years.

Challenging "Marilyn's Autobiography"

The authors are not the first to challenge this topic, and certainly will not be the last. Plus, the female author of the team already challenged the topic to a degree in her book, *Marilyn Monroe & Joe DiMaggio – Love in Japan, Korea & Beyond*.

The novel *My Story* has been contested since its 1974 publication, to the threat of multimillion-dollar lawsuits from the one who generated it first – Milton Greene and his then publisher at Stein and Day.

First, one must backtrack to 1953. This was the year that Marilyn was catapulting to fame. She met Milton Greene that year and he photographed her for *LOOK* magazine, with her beautiful face landing the front cover. She demurely cradled a cigarette between her index and middle finger, her hand gently rested on her cheek, while she elegantly gazed into his camera lens, for a cover that was dated on November 17.

On The Archives LLC website, the site for the photos that Milton Greene took of Marilyn, there are two books also for sale. One is *Milton's Marilyn* and the other *My Story*. According to Greene's son Joshua on the site, Marilyn met Milton for the first time at mogul Joseph Schenck's home for the first photographic session. The account claims that there were several days that Marilyn and Milton took photos, and that screenwriter Ben Hecht, also joined them. "While the three of them were said to have spent their time together, Hecht interviewed Marilyn and got her to tell her life story. *My Story* is Marilyn's autobiography penned by Ben Hecht, based on stories told to him by Marilyn over a period of several days."

In the 2007 edition, which the text was copyrighted by Joshua Greene with Milton still holding the earlier edition, he has added photographs of his father's that the 1974 edition does not contain (there is one cover photo of Milton's), Joshua Greene penned the book's foreword. The story is slightly changed as to how the process took place with Marilyn's memoirs, and Milton's hand in them.

In Sarah Churchwell fashion, the authors of this book will compare the website, to the book account from 2007, which states that Marilyn and Milton met in 1953 and developed a rapport. But then the following year, they met at Schenck's home "with whom Marilyn was involved at the time." Joshua Greene stated that Ben Hecht was also present. The four of them (Marilyn, Milton, Hecht and Schenck) apparently discussed Marilyn's life story "the result of which is the book in your hands," readers are told. From there, Joshua Greene claimed that Marilyn and Hecht ended up engaging in a series of interviews to work on her "biography" (no longer considered an "autobiography" as in other accounts) and before she departed to New York and to live with the Greenes in early 1955, Hecht and Marilyn composed the manuscript. There is no mention of the legal dispute or much else.

However, the photos that ended up in the first *LOOK* magazine were not from Joseph Schenck's home, but photos of Marilyn with the same cable knit sweater and holding a mandolin. This was later part of what is called "The Mandolin Sitting," which was credited as the first sitting they did. The other was "The Nude Sweater Sitting," or "Beautiful in Black," also in the magazine.

Some of the photos from the time at Joseph Schenck's made it into the May 29, 1956 edition of *LOOK*, which offered a range of photos of Greene's. It is in an article entitled, "The New Marilyn," yet the article claims that the photos of Marilyn were taken by Milton Greene "during her furlough from Hollywood." That furlough occurred when she left to stay with the Greene's in 1955. However, the photos from Schenck's have been attributed to 1953 in all other locations. Marilyn's hairstyle is also evidenced in these photos as how she typically wore it in 1953.

Yet, the 2007 book is incorrect if there is an assumption that Marilyn was "involved" with Joseph Schenck in 1953. She was actually heavily involved with Joe DiMaggio, a fact that was known, with the couple tying the knot only several months after her session with Greene. There are also no photos of Marilyn that have publicly surfaced from that day at Schenck's home with Schenck or Hecht pictured with Marilyn. Though Marilyn was the subject of photos, one would envision perhaps there would be pictures of any of them together if that was the place of the rendez-vous and interviews for Marilyn's biography project.

The fact, however, that the tales of how *My Story* allegedly emerged, as told on the website and in the book differ, which is bothersome enough and should raise alarm.

Ben Hecht's Involvement

Actually the first biography cranked out about Marilyn was *The Marilyn Monroe Story*, a compendium of fan magazine copy stitched together, by Joe Franklin and Laurie Palmer. Today, this rare softcover book can fetch up to $1,500 for a copy.

Marilyn and Ben Hecht's paths crossed before Milton's and Marilyn's did, as he was the screenwriter for the 1952 Fox vehicle *Monkey Business* that Marilyn starred in with Cary Grant, Ginger Rogers and Charles Coburn.

Louella Parsons tipped off her readers in a March 13, 1954 column, following Marilyn's return from her second honeymoon with Joe DiMaggio in Japan and Korea that Ben Hecht was writing the story about Marilyn. Parsons reported many of the interviews were done before the trip to Korea, and it would be published in a Doubleday book, following its appearance in a top magazine. At that time, Hecht was "gathering additional material from her [Marilyn's] friends," wrote Parsons.

Parsons also indicated that Hecht did some of the interviewing before her suspension from Fox for not appearing in the film *The Girl in Pink Tights*, which the papers coined "*Pink Tights*" as its name in many articles. Marilyn was suspended on January 5, 1954, for being a no-show to the set, disappearing altogether. Joe was fighting in her corner with the studio and her agent, Charles Feldman, who was angry that she was standing up to the studio, for her lack of appearance would jeopardize his commission. Joe was a savvy businessman, and assisted her with a range of negotiations, including her purchase of the novel, *Horns For The Devil*, which eventually between the two of them, she had enough leverage and sold it to the studio for $150,000.

Yet with *Pink Tights*, Marilyn felt the film was unbecoming to her, and she wished to have approval over her script. She was intended to co-star with Frank Sinatra, who was slated to receive $5,000 weekly for the picture, while Marilyn was stuck at $1,250 weekly.

After her attorney, Loyd Wright, Jr. presented a statement to the press on Marilyn's behalf that "she has read the script and does not care to do the picture," she received her second suspension only about 12 days following her January 14 marriage to Joe. She had been given extra time after her nuptials and did not make a showing on the set.

Though Sheree North was later tested for the role, including Marilyn's wardrobe for it, she also did not make the picture, with controversy that she had been in an erotic film when she was an unknown that had surfaced.

While Fox claimed in a January 26 news blurb that there was a "tremendous investment" in Marilyn for the film, it ended up on the wayside. However, it made a brief appearance on Broadway for 115 performances, from March 5 through June 12 of that year.

The *Pink Tights* topic even made an appearance in the 1974 and later version of the *My Story* books, with Marilyn allegedly giving her view of the story.

On March 16, 1954 Marilyn Monroe and Ben Hecht drew up a contract between themselves, long before Marilyn's partnership was official with Milton Greene. In it, the two agreed that Hecht would write Marilyn's life story only for magazine publication only. Marilyn and Hecht agreed that either of them would be the author, and nothing would be published without Marilyn's approval. It was understood that Hecht would receive compensation for the story. The article was meant only for publication in the *Ladies' Home Journal*.

"It is expressly understood and agreed that the material to be written by you pursuant to this agreement and written by you from the facts concerning my life, which I have heretofore given to you, and will hereafter give you, shall not be put into book form by you and you shall have no right to the use of the material for anything except one magazine article to be published in the *Ladies' Home Journal* Magazine."

According to published reports, including from Nanette Barber, Hecht's secretary, who was present during their meetings she was a witness to Marilyn sitting in front of a picture window during one of the interviews in San Francisco. When asked where Joe may have been that day, Marilyn would look out towards the city, and quiped, "Out there."

Interestingly enough, Barber in an interview with the *Northbrook Star*, relayed a story that Marilyn reportedly told her about Gladys dry cleaning her laundry at home, placing the clothes on the lawn. Berniece in her memoirs wrote about Gladys cleaning her clothes with that method. Yet, that anecdote, though Marilyn confessed how she used to massage the grass as she sat with Gladys as she did laundry, and may have been the reason why she enjoyed the feel of her mink coats, did not appear in the 1974 or 2007 versions of *My Story*. That appears suspect that this may have been from Marilyn's sessions with Hecht that a story of such an interesting caliber, did not make the cut in her memories discussed about her mother. However, at the same time, a positive memory about Gladys would not fit the Cinderella theme of any of her life stories.

According to a 2001 article about Hecht, he did not express an interest in receiving credit as the writer of Marilyn's memoirs. Other writers had ghosted Marilyn's memoirs for magazine publication previously, adding her name as the author based on their interviews with her.

Marilyn's schedule became tight after her marriage to Joe, according to Hecht's correspondences with Doubleday early that spring. A month following his note to Doubleday's Ken McCormack, he sent off 168 pages to his agent, Jacques Chambrun. He asked Chambrun to pitch it to the *Ladies' Home Journal*, with 40 more pages to come. On those pages, he advised Chambrun, would be details about a few of Marilyn's recent films including *Gentlemen Prefer Blondes*, the passing of Grace Goddard, and her wishes to have children, and several other of the latest topics in her life. He would also supply photos from Marilyn's personal collection.

Hecht's correspondence with his agent reflected that Marilyn shed tears of joy over the story he had written.

One of the main points of the story, later expressed in third husband Arthur Miller's memoirs, *Timebends*, was that Hecht asked Marilyn about something interesting that had occurred in her life. She told him about the orphanage, another tale that Marilyn, Grace, and the studios had also bulked up to stir up sympathy from the public. The orphan topic was something that Hecht also honed in on, beefing it up to, once again, stay aligned with the myth.

In the process of working with Marilyn, Hecht had received an advance from Doubleday of $5,000 and asked his agent to seek a 50 percent advance from the *Ladies' Home Journal*.

Hecht advised Loyd Wright, Jr. in a May 19 correspondence that Collier's purchased the manuscript, yet the final approval was up to Marilyn's final edits. Wright had scolded Hecht for circulating it prior to publication, yet Hecht explained, "it would be rather impossible to sell it without showing it and since you agreed on my selling it and having it published after Marilyn's editing, I had it submitted under those conditions."

Hecht told Wright that Marilyn's participation in the process would yield her credit as an author, and precipitate "serious literary attention from the entire press and magazine world. It would bring her a high and wide-spread type of publicity superior to any she has received."

However, on June 1, the day that Marilyn turned 28, Hecht's correspondence reflected he had to deflect his involvement in a publication of *My Story* that appeared in the *London Empire News*, sending a cable to Chambrun, who he then suspected had sold the story behind his back, stating, "I denied that such a sale had been made because I couldn't imagine it being done without my knowledge and consent."

It was on that day that a stern cease and desist letter arrived to both Hecht and Chambrun from Wright, demanding that they return all materials, and that the contract from March 16 was broken, giving Marilyn editorial approval before the manuscript was to be disseminated.

Wright ordered that the duo immediately "notify said British newspapers or newspaper that they have no right to publish any further material concerning Miss Monroe written by Mr. Hecht or supplied by Mr. Chambrun, and that you send us copies of all correspondence with them concerning this matter."

Wright also demanded that all other offers, including a supposed one to Random House, be withdrawn.

"It is shocking that men will break their word as well as their written contract in a manner such as has been evidenced by the publication of this material," Wright continued. "The material is not accurate. Much of it is not true and does not represent a factual portrayal of Miss Monroe's life. Miss Monroe has given no one approval of any part of the material."

Though by some accounts Hecht fired Chambrun shortly after, Hecht scholar Florice Whyte Kovan, who wrote the 2001 article, vouched that Chambrun's termination did not occur until near Hecht's death in 1964, when Hecht reportedly entrapped Chambrun in a way that confirmed he was selling manuscripts behind Hecht's back. Whyte Kovan believed that Hecht may have felt indebted to Chambrun, in spite of his upset, because of his placement of Hecht's article about Nazi genocide in Reader's Digest during World War II.

Hecht returned his Doubleday advance, and neither he nor Marilyn made a penny on their collaboration, abandoning it altogether as the series progressed weekly through the *Empire News*. He ordered Chambrun to cease the publication with that tabloid newspaper, and back out of the Collier's deal.

In fact, Hecht's correspondence not only showed he lambasted his agent for breaking Hecht's word to Marilyn on his behalf, he also asked Chambrun to "destroy the entire Monroe copy. Your action has put me personally into the sort of hole I have never been in before. That of breaking my word."

Chambrun reportedly received about $50,000 that Hecht never saw a dime of, and also reworked what was in the *Empire News*.

On July 18, 1954, Hollywood Correspondent Erskine Johnson reported that Fox had attempted to quash the series, crediting it to Hecht, yet it was continuing in the Empire News, at that point about eight installments strong. Upcoming, according to Johnson, was the section about Marilyn's debacle with Joan Crawford.

On August 19, Erskine Johnson followed the topic once again, reporting that it was Hecht who allegedly received "$50,000 for British rights to the eyeball-popping wordage."

However, an August 1 report notes that the series was sold to the *Empire News* "without my knowledge or consent." Hecht allegedly turned the rights to the piece to Marilyn. Marilyn declined to comment when asked if she would continue with the series in book form.

On September 8, Erskine Johnson published that Marilyn's tale of the feud with Joan Crawford had aired in the *Empire News*.

The quotes that Erskine cited are identical to what appears in the 1974 and 2007 versions of the book, *My Story*. In it, again still credited to Hecht, Joan Crawford allegedly chided Marilyn for sporting a knit dress to Joseph Schenck's home for a dinner, and offered to assist Marilyn if she supplied Joan with a list of her wardrobe.

Later, Joan Crawford was appalled by the reaction Marilyn received at the Photoplay awards when she showed in her gold lamé gown. This was a William Travilla design that Marilyn was seen in from the rear (because the front was so low-cut) during a dancing scene with Charles Coburn in *Gentlemen Prefer Blondes*. She wore it as well for some photo sessions. Other stars appeared in copies of the dress, like Jeanne Crain, Jayne Mansfield, and Betty Grable after Marilyn wore the gown.

Though she believed to be off the record with Bob Thomas, Crawford attacked Marilyn's appearance, describing it as a "burlesque show." Yet, Crawford had her own brushes early in her career in adult films. This was something Thomas also pointed out in his report, that Crawford had qualifications to comment because of her "pretty racy buildup" in the flapper days. Many believed that Crawford was simply jealous over her young competitor.

According to Thomas, Marilyn declined comment when she was told about Crawford's fury, according to his March 27, 1953 report.

Again, another flaw can be pointed out with *My Story*, both the 1974 and 2007 editions. The focus on the feud with Crawford, according to the testimony from "Marilyn," focuses on Marilyn's appearance at the Academy Awards. While the news reports from 1954 about the *Empire News* story do not discuss the award ceremony, but to address Crawford's fury that Marilyn rebuffed her advances to assist with wardrobe advice, because she never supplied her clothing list.

Word for word, in both *My Story* and the news report of what appeared in the *Empire News*, it is written that "Marilyn" said, "For some reason, I couldn't tell Miss Crawford that she had seen my wardrobe in full."

My Story, precedes the statement with a small copy difference, with the word "But" at the start of its sentence.

The same pattern with the other sentence that the press reported appeared in *Empire*, where "Marilyn" stated, "Maybe she was just annoyed because I had never brought her a wardrobe list for her to approve," though the *My Story* version varied slightly with the statement reading, "Or maybe she was just annoyed because I had never brought her a list of my wardrobe."

It is well documented in 1953 that Marilyn and Crawford experienced their war in the press. Yet *My Story* elucidates about Joan Crawford's upset that Marilyn behaved vulgarly at the Academy as an award presenter, in a gown reportedly skin tight, when she was holding the sacred Oscar.

However, there was not a mention of a war between the women as a result of the Oscars. In fact, the only blurb was Marilyn's appearance as a presenter that night, March 29, 1951. The only mention of Joan Crawford that year in connection to the Oscars related to her 1940 acceptance when she was home ill and received her coveted statue in a blue nightgown with a modest and beautiful nightgown over it. Crawford held up her award while propped up in bed, her face dressed to the nines with makeup, appearing elegant and well in spite of her reported illness.

The fatal defect to the *My Story* testimony about the supposed post-Oscar war is the elegance of which Marilyn was attired that evening. Her gown was a far cry from being skin tight, crude, or anything less than elegant. While the gold dress accented her curves as if it was painted on, the Oscar gown, with its many sheer layers, was sexy, yet still reserved. Though some minor décolleté showed, it was by no means an inappropriately plunging neckline. Marilyn radiated Hollywood classic elegance instead, her hair groomed in a sleek style with a few curls, and the ball gown with a fuller skirt and floor length. The gown was on loan from the studio since its appearance in *The House on Telegraph Hill* when Valentina Cortese wore it.

The other deadly error was any reporting of the women arguing about Marilyn's appearance in 1951. In fact, there is no current newspaper report of Joan Crawford having even been in attendance in 1951 at the ceremonies.

On September 2, a report was published that Loyd Wright, Jr. was planning to file a lawsuit against Hecht, unless Hecht could furnish proof that Chambrun sold the manuscript behind his back.

Erskine Johnson faithfully reported to his readers on September 14, 1954 that Marilyn stated Hecht and Chambrun were "not in a good legal position," because the articles were reportedly stopped after the third run in the *Empire News*.

It was during this time period that Marilyn's relationship with Milton Greene was apparently strengthening, while her relationship with Joe was disintegrating. On September 20, Leonard Lyons reported that he sat down with Marilyn, actor David Wayne and Milton in New York's Sardi's, where Sidney Kingsley later joined them. Sam Shaw reportedly took their photos. Afterward, the ensemble, the columnist stated, headed to Little Club for dinner, with a stop along the way at Milton's studio to pick up her brown loafers, with Marilyn still attired in a mink coat, and Wayne placing the loafers on her feet for her.

An October 15, 1954 report noted Marilyn's split from Joe, and that Marilyn "will fly to N.Y. as soon as her movie is done and recuperate with friends in Connecticut." Naturally, that was Greene's residence.

The report also aired that "DiMaggio's departure leaves no further obstacles to the book Ben Hecht has written about Marilyn Monroe."

Marilyn Monroe Unveiled | A Family History

On November 1, it was obvious that Wright and Chambrun were still circling around the topic of the book. Chambrun, in his correspondence, was attempting to peddle the book idea with Marilyn and Hecht splitting the profits.

"This is simply a matter of money, and nothing else," Chambrun wrote, stating that Hecht had already invested time into the project. "It is exceptional indeed for an author like Ben Hecht to give a release of his rights in a manuscript he has written; but he will do so in this instance, provided again that his financial interests are safeguarded."

Chambrun suggested a "release and assignment," which he said would guarantee Hecht's financial position, stating that he doubted Marilyn would renege on the idea of compensating him, knowing that she was "a highly paid artist herself."

Little did any of them know, and Hecht did not want to admit, the greedy Chambrun had already taken his share, and was now seeking more.

Erskine Johnson was back on the story on November 4, 1954, stirring the pot and proposing that since Marilyn was now "available for dates again," if her "spicy life story as told to Ben Hecht now will be published in the U.S." Johnson gossiped that Marilyn forbade its publication in the United States after her marriage to Joe.

On Hecht's end, there was little mention of his attachment to his involvement in Marilyn's biographical work in the press again until 1956. Leonard Lyons alleged, "Ben Hecht's still-unpublished ghostwritten autobiography of Marilyn Monroe, completed a few years ago, contains the statement that her greatest thrill was experienced at a party – when her hand accidentally touched Arthur Miller's ankle."

Sidney Skolsky – Biographer and Marilyn Liaison

While there is no mention of Sidney Skolsky's involvement in Marilyn's autobiography process, including with the article that Nanette Barber was interviewed for, biographer Donald Spoto attested that Skolsky, a close friend of Marilyn's at that time, was there.

Skolsky cranked out his own version of a Marilyn biography in magazine form, simply entitled, *Marilyn*, which was released in June of 1954, as the *Empire News* controversy was beginning to crest. His account was an upbeat write-up about Marilyn, her career, and her personal life, including her marital bliss with Joe DiMaggio.

The preface explained that it was Skolsky who helped write about Marilyn, freeing her from obscurity. "…his story is based on an 'interview' that has been going on for years."

The editors additionally described it as a "artisan biography and Mr. Skolsky and the editors are proud of the fact. You see, we love Marilyn too."

Even on the topic of Joan Crawford, Skolsky noted that Marilyn took the high road, and that she is "devoid of venom or jealousy."

According to Skolsky's word, Marilyn did not retaliate though she did not comprehend why Joan Crawford had attacked her. Yet the *My Story* account painted Marilyn spilling all of her beans about it. And since it borrowed from the Empire News heavily, it was Wright's letter that attested those articles were false, thus, one can conclude what has been written in *My Story* to also be mostly bogus.

One of the other flaws about *My Story* was a teeny but significant detail about the venue where Marilyn and Joe met for the first time. The 1974 and 2007 versions noted it was Chasen's. Yet it is a well-known fact that Marilyn and Joe met on a blind date in 1952 at Villa Nova. How Marilyn would then screw up two monumental life events, first the story with Joan Crawford and the statement the feud occurred as a result of the 1951 Oscars, and then to not correctly name the restaurant where the pair dined for their first date? These are well-known Marilyn facts by most scholars, makes the 1974 and 2007 editions more dubious.

One notation in the Skolsky book was Marilyn's confession that she had met Arthur Miller from Elia Kazan and "liked Miller from the time she read his novel, Focus and then liked him personally."

Marilyn Monroe Unveiled | A Family History

Arthur Miller is not mentioned in *My Story*, yet in the 2007 edition, is strangely pictured in the chapter about acting coach Michael Chekhov.

While *My Story* airs all of the Oliver Twist type of tales, Skolsky's tale does not focus on that as much, though like all of them, they spotlight the orphan topic. He does not delve into many of the dark details, though he did mention that Marilyn was in 11 foster homes. At the same time, Sydney Skolsky aired a bit of truthful insight.

"I recall Marilyn's mentioning two foster mothers: Grace Goddard and Ana Lower. From her references to them, I would say they were her favorites."

That is because they were truly two of the people that Marilyn stayed with after Gladys's illness took hold. The many imagined foster homes was just that...a spin of the Hollywood yarn.

Skolsky did state that Marilyn at that time had received some childhood photos, although she claimed she did not remember the name of one boy she was pictured with, and stated she could not remember the names of the people in the photographs. Based on the statements, including a party dress and the boy, it was likely from her stay with Ida Bolender. How she could forget Ida is not a truth, because Ida was someone whose name she mentioned later, and in fact, Gladys stayed with Ida for a period after her release from the hospital and Marilyn had already become famous.

Yet, as Marilyn's life story was being aired, including her triumphant love story with Joe DiMaggio and recent marriage, a dark shadow was lurking in the wings.

Apparently, Milton Greene had not forgotten the passing conversations with Marilyn about starting her own production company. According to Carl Rollyson's book, *Marilyn Monroe: Day by Day, A Timeline of People, Places, and Events*, and Barbara Leaming's account *Marilyn Monroe*, Milton and Amy Greene met with Marilyn that May, with Milton attempting to sway her to start her own production company with him. She began challenging her legal counsel that she wished to have more control, as she commenced filming *There's No Business Like Show Business*. This was also when Marilyn's relationship with Joe started to further deteriorate.

Though a compromise was reached between the studio, Marilyn did not show to her meeting with her attorney on July 8. Wright assured the studio he would have her signature.

Yet, as Leaming's biography put it, "The moment Marilyn signed her new studio contract, his [Greene's] dream would be short-circuited."

The plan, according to Leaming's story, as well as Rollyson's timeline, was to circumvent Joe DiMaggio. On July 19, Marilyn told Fox she would sign her contract at the end of the week. In the meantime, she was allegedly making plans with Milton Greene. Greene avoided Joe because it was known Joe would pick up on the shady stench Greene carried with him in the deal. According to Leaming's account, the plan was a production of Jean Harlow's life story, with Skolsky producing, though Greene was seeking funds to make it a reality. Greene allegedly touched base with Skolsky, using Skolsky to set up a conference call with Marilyn. Joe reportedly felt that the studio had reached a fair compromise, and suggested Marilyn sign off on her paperwork. Greene challenged her to do otherwise.

As Barbara Leaming wrote, "DiMaggio, as was his nature, would be deeply suspicious of what Greene wanted."

Marilyn's negotiations behind her business savvy husband's back was a tragic error on her part, and showed her true lack of business competence. She could not, as the expression goes, "see the forest through the trees." Greene was an opportunist seeking to use her as a monetary vehicle. Joe would have picked up on that immediately. Instead at that point, he stayed out, and they learned to navigate around him, because of the fault that had started to widen between he and Marilyn.

Only two days later after her phone conference with Milton Greene, Marilyn verbally chastised Wright, and refused to sign the contract. Wright reached out to Charles Feldman, and Feldman suggested dinner at his home with Joe, Marilyn and Wright. Marilyn declined the invitation.

The contract topic remained status quo, in spite of the contract not having been properly addressed. It was then that Paula Strasberg visited Marilyn on the set of *There's No Business Like Show Business*, and soon *The Seven Year Itch* would be filmed.

Milton Greene still had an opening in the window.

Marilyn Monroe Unveiled | A Family History

Marilyn and Joe's relationship disintegrated more and the couple filed for divorce. In November, Marilyn arrived at Charles Feldman's office to discuss her contract. It is known that Fox did exploit her, however, worse exploitation was coming up the pike in two words – Milton Greene. Later, there would be other names who would manipulate her including Strasberg, Miller, Rosten and others.

Marilyn was on a mission to gather intel and showed to Fox legal counsel Frank Ferguson's office on November 22. While she previously led Feldman on and pretended she would remain his client, accepting a copy of *The Sleeping Prince* from him, which Marilyn would star later in as *The Prince and the Showgirl* with Milton Greene on board in the only Marilyn Monroe Productions film in 1957.

She dropped in to ask Ferguson for copies of all of her Fox contracts, though she had not signed anew with them. Ferguson was sidelined with the visit, and asked why Marilyn did not seek the contracts from Feldman or Wright. She explained that her contracts were in storage since the divorce, and neither of her lawyer nor her agent really understood the full situation.

Ferguson handed her the documents and tipped off Wright. He waited for word from Marilyn and none came. He telephoned Feldman. It was too late. Marilyn outfoxed the Fox crew and delivered the contracts to Greene for his attorney, Frank Delaney. In this case, Marilyn was outfoxed, and Greene and Delaney were waving the pen in front of Marilyn's face to sign. An undated letter was among the documents, informing Feldman that he would no longer be her agent.

Though Sidney Skolsky could have benefited from the Harlow transaction, he did not fully buy that Milton Greene had as much pull as Feldman. All along, Skolsky was playing both Feldman and Greene to see which one was more legitimate, and leaked of Marilyn's plans to purchase the Jean Harlow story. Feldman was shocked and said that *Horns For the Devil* had not fully resolved since she had not signed her new contract, and that she would not be able to take on another purchase. Feldman allegedly told Skolsky for Marilyn to seek independent counsel. She did no such thing. And though Feldman asked Skolsky to meet with him in December, and he canceled twice, blaming illness. Instead, Marilyn met with him at lunch and the two had a pleasant time, speaking about the future.

On December 2, Loyd Wright, Jr. informed Inez Melson, her business manager, in a correspondence that he was dining at Chasen's "when in walks Mr. Sidney Skolsky, Marilyn Monroe and another real little short guy whom I was informed was a *LOOK* photographer doing a series of pictures on Marilyn."

That photographer was none other than Milton Greene. It was through Skolsky that the Greenes were facilitating contacts to Marilyn. In fact, a card that had been sent to Marilyn in November 1954 from Amy Greene was first sent to Skolsky, with instructions to deliver it to Marilyn on her behalf. The card to Sidney Skolsky, as well as to Marilyn were both sold in a 2014 Julien's Auction, and each ripped in half. These two pieces of correspondence were found in Marilyn's "lost archive," and the deliberate tear down the middle an obvious indicator of Marilyn's later sentiments about the Greenes.

Wright reported after seeing Marilyn at Chasen's that Marilyn was "inscrutable," though friendly, and Sidney was extremely talkative, while he spent time talking about Marilyn.

Little did Wright know, Skolsky was grooming him for Marilyn's departure, as Skolsky "talked at great length to me about Marilyn, told me how Marilyn was up one minute and down the next emotionally, that she should get away etc."

He enclosed Marilyn's agency contract with Famous Artists and the amendments, a recording contract with R.C.A., the royalty contract with vocal coach Hal Schaefer, and a May 2, 1950 Fox contract.

"What is going to happen I still don't know," Wright signed off.

But soon, Marilyn was headed to New York on a plane under the alias of Zelda Zonk. Marilyn was spellbound with her new "friends," something that those who knew her from Hollywood immediately noted.

Marilyn Monroe Productions Is Born – Marilyn Monroe's Life Is Hijacked

Soon, both Wright and Feldman learned they were fired, and if the studio wished to reach her, they could speak to her new attorney, Delaney. He presided over the first board meeting for Marilyn Monroe Productions. Like Delaney, Milton Greene's accountant Joe Carr, also joined on the team. Attorney Irving Stein set up the company's documentation and drafted Marilyn's will in 1956. He crafted it in order for Marilyn's residence to be in Connecticut at Greene's address, so that the studio could not pursue her.

Though she kept on Inez Melson, Inez became a figure in the distance that she would correspond with, who spent time with Gladys as her guardian. She kept Inez's duties compartmentalized from then on.

This was how Marilyn allowed business to be conducted for most of her life's remainder. The vultures delved in, banking on the platinum cash cow salability, while those who were more advocates and sensible, such as Loyd Wright, Jr. were cut out.

Names like Strasberg, Rosten, and Miller ended up on her will when they barely knew her and Arthur Miller was not even divorced from his first wife.

Though Delaney assisted Marilyn with settling with the studio by 1956, in which she would receive $100,000 per picture, she was still grossly underpaid compared to her contemporaries. And then, she was portioning out her income to the likes of Milton Greene, and the Strasbergs in the process.

While Marilyn was a pioneer in women-owned businesses, she was being controlled by the decisions of men mostly, and was not wise in her transactions. It was Greene's advisors and Greene who cornered her to start the business. It was also Greene's Freudian psychiatrist Dr. Margaret Hohenberg, who began unethically sharing information about her appointments with Marilyn with Greene, and treating both of them at once.

While Greene was her partner and some blame their dissolution on her third husband Arthur Miller since he was another opportunist, it was Arthur, one predator, who detected the actions of another in Greene. Miller would later write to Marilyn on May 25, 1956 shortly before their wedding that Greene looked to her as a commodity rather than a human being, and that Arthur viewed that Greene held a proprietary attitude over her. He expressed that Milton Greene was about moneymaking and would try to marshal his allies "in the hope of forcing you back in the cage that he found you in."

Though Arthur had the same agenda, and although he claimed he had no interest in her business, later he and his advisors were advising her, in addition to his psychiatrist. History was repeating itself.

Arthur never had Marilyn's interests in mind, but his own, and the cash register "ca-chinged." Marilyn wrote before their marriage in her "Surgeon Story" account, "Arthur is the only one waiting in the outer room worrying and hoping operation is successful. For many reasons. For myself. For his play and for himself indirectly."

Though Marilyn claimed she had no Svengali, she was now allowing several to control her at varying times. Even columnist Dorothy Kilgallen noted on July 6, 1955 that Lee Strasberg was replacing Milton Greene. In a usual pattern, as she stayed at the Greene's, she was spending an inordinate amount of time with the Strasbergs, between the Actor's Studio, the Strasbergs' New York apartment, and their home in Fire Island. She also integrated deeply into the Rosten family.

"Marilyn listens to everything Strasberg has to say the way she used to listen to everything Milton has to say," Kilgallen wrote. "Milton isn't too happy about the situation."

With Arthur's influence over Marilyn Monroe Productions and Marilyn, she jumped from the fire to the frying pan. Less than four years later, the Miller marriage itself ended. However, Arthur Miller still had reach into Marilyn's life through her secretary May Reis, who was Arthur's long-term secretary before Marilyn. Her brother was Hollywood Director Irving Reis did the screen adaptation of Arthur Miller's play, All My Sons in 1948.

In 1957, the party between Marilyn and Milton broke up. Marilyn accused Milton Greene of mismanaging her company. Those who support Greene today will say how good he was to and for her and still defend him. They claim Marilyn was being controlled by others and not Greene. No one wants to look at the facts that Greene was another one who took advantage of Marilyn. If Marilyn had felt differently, she would not have allowed such blatant articles to make the front pages, such as on the fold of *The Bridgeport Telegraph* on April 12, 1957, with the headline on the AP article, "Marilyn Monroe Splits With Milton Greene, Accuses Him of Mismanaging Her Company."

In the article, it aired how Greene held 49.6 percent of Marilyn's earnings.

Later, Marilyn would reportedly pay about $100,000 to have all of the Marilyn Monroe Productions stock retained in her name. Though there were claims producers Ray Stark and Eliot Hyman had made an offer to buy 43 percent of Milton's stock in 1957 that did not occur, and that year the duo formed Seven Arts Production instead. Marilyn would still use the name, paying the IRS with a Marilyn Monroe Productions check in 1961, and even sending a letter to Fox advising them on March 29, 1962, months before her death, that they were permitted to send salary and expense checks to Cherie Redmond.

Greene told reporters, "It seems Marilyn doesn't want to go ahead with the program we planned, I'm getting lawyers to represent me...I don't want to do anything now to hurt her career...but I did devote about a year and a half exclusively to her. I practically gave up photography."

Greene claims he "practically gave up photography," however, Milton Greene's future photography career was greatly enhanced by his collection and ownership of Marilyn Monroe photographs. How did Milton Greene end up owning 100 percent of Marilyn's pictures while under the umbrella of her company name? While many argue that as a photographer, he likely had a release from her, at this time Marilyn was a meteoric star and these photos were filmed with a company that held her name – a company that she seized back from an unethical partner. Marilyn should have had controlling interest in her own photographs, she was, after all in partners with him and she was the asset, not him. However, Marilyn owned nothing of those photographic assets as purported over the years. And even with the right of publicity fight that occurred in the mid-2000s with Lee Strasberg's widow, Anna asserting she owned rights to the photography with her claim that she owned Marilyn's right of publicity (an idea a court judge quashed later), she could not wrestle away the photographs from Milton Greene's heirs, though they were taken when Marilyn had the reigning share of the company with Milton. However, Anna was able to seize other items through court orders from others with ease, including documents that were in the care of Marilyn's business partner Inez Melson's nephew.

In 1955 Marilyn documented in the "Surgeon Story" after her mind-numbing session, "Milton call's from big office with lots of room and everything in good taste and is conducting business in a new way, with style, and music is playing and he is relaxed and enjoying himself even if he is very worried at the same time. There's a camera on his desk but he doesn't take pictures anymore except of great paintings."

The reason Milton practically gave up on photography is because he knew he could after associating himself with Marilyn Monroe. Milton Greene remained low-key with his association with Marilyn until after her death, when the photos began to be published regularly again.

According to the article from April 12, 1957, Greene asked to be given the "executive producer" title in *The Prince and The Showgirl*.

Marilyn stated in the article, "He knows perfectly well that we have been at odds for a year and a half and he knows why. My company has been completely mismanaged by Mr. Greene. He made secret commitments for the company without informing me. He has misinformed me of what certain contracts contained."

She stated further, "As president of the corporation and its only source of income, I was never informed that he had elected himself to the position of executive producer of *The Prince and the Showgirl* and secretly signed contracts to that effect."

Marilyn further complained that her company was not in business to "provide false credits" and she was not consenting to it. She also said, "The company was not set up merely to parcel out 49.6 percent of all my earnings to Mr. Greene for seven years. My company was formed because I wanted to make better pictures, improve my work, secure my income and help others to make good pictures. Instead, have had to defend my aims, my interests and conditions of work against the demands of Mr. Greene himself."

Marilyn Monroe Unveiled | A Family History

In 1958, a quick news blurb claimed that Milton would produce a Broadway play, but nothing further was written about that topic.

Though Greene would later claim Marilyn spoke to him again just before she died, the partnership was long over at her death. Yet suddenly, 12 years later he came forth with a manuscript claiming to be Marilyn's words themselves.

Anomalies in Some Marilyn Biographies

One of the problems with manuscripts that did not have Marilyn's hands in them is the spelling of her name. This small detail should not be taken lightly. Some have spelled Marilyn's name "Norma Jean." The correct spelling of her name was "Norma Jeane." Even though Sidney Skolsky's book uses the spelling "Norma Jean" her marriage certificate to Joe DiMaggio is featured there, showing her signature using her birth name spelled correctly.

Those who have typically created the stories about Marilyn have spelled her name incorrectly a number of times. Her name was spelled "Norma Jeane." Just a look for example at both of her marriage certificates to her first two husbands Jim Dougherty and later Joe DiMaggio show the theme. On both instances she signed her name "Norma Jeane." (on her certificate however to Dougherty, her name is spelled "Mortensen," which is how her legal father spelled his name, though on Marilyn's birth certificate it is spelled "Mortenson" for her name). On her certificate with DiMaggio, she also spelled and signed her name "Norma Jeane." On her certificate with Joe, it is listed on the line maiden name, "Norma Jean Mortenson," while the rest of the document lists her as "Norma Jeane" and she signed it "Norma Jeane Dougherty."

It was at this stage she was not legally even known as Marilyn Monroe. It was in 1956 when she legally changed her name to Marilyn Monroe, after using the name professionally for nearly a decade.

Then why in the so called manuscript furnished by Milton Greene that are supposed to be the words of Marilyn herself, is she calling herself "Norma Jean?"

In letters before she became famous, including ones to Grace Goddard, she always signed her name "Norma Jeane." Even on her employee records with Radioplane, she lists herself as "Norma Jeane Dougherty."

That is because *My Story*, which has been listed as an autobiography by Marilyn Monroe, was not something that was ever written by her. Yet this book has become an "authoritative" source of Marilyn's own voice.

Maybe there were quotes from Marilyn in there, but this was not penned in her own hand has it has been believed for years.

Why first off, would Marilyn list herself as "Norma Jean," when she never signed her name like this on personal and legal correspondences?

My Story – The "New Marilyn Monroe Voice" Introduced to the World

Though in the beginning at its first publication in 1974, it was credited to Marilyn, Ben Hecht is now listed as the author, which apparently Hecht was associated with it in 2000. The authors suspect this was a decision that would have highly been displeasing to Hecht, based on his disdain for the *Empire News* series, which it resembles greatly.

However, even Hecht's widow Rose claimed the copy that has been floating around from Stein and Day and later The Cooper Square Press, was not something her husband was involved in, stating her husband's manuscript differed from that of what was published.

As *My Story* surfaced it additionally was supposed to be Marilyn's words for the first time, now revealed in 1974. Yet even in 1974 people were dubious of the manuscript having been transcribed from Marilyn's mouth.

It was explained in one newspaper that Marilyn's "typographical" errors remained, and the royalties were to be divided between the estate (Strasbergs) and Milton Greene.

Marilyn Monroe Unveiled | A Family History

Digby Diehl, who was the book editor for the *Los Angeles Times* in 1974 when Judith Martin wrote an article in the Washington Post published on May 25, 1974, stated that outside of a few copy changes, the manuscript in *My Story* resembled the London Empire News publication. Martin erroneously stated that Marilyn was with Greene in London at the time the article series ran, though that was a misstatement.

Greene was quoted as stating he "never heard of it," referring to the *Empire* series.

Greene also stated at that time Marilyn handed him the manuscript, with his purported claim that she told him to "do the right thing with it."

He smoothly alleged he "put it away and forgot about it," until about a decade prior when he was moving his studio and stumbled on it, thinking he could "do something with it." He claimed there was little interest, until Norman Mailer's book came out.

The authors of this book question, as Marilyn ended negotiations with Milton Greene why he would not return paperwork that he claimed Marilyn had given him, even though their business relationship fell apart.

Greene copyrighted the text, and was given a $25,000 advance from the publisher.

Sol Stein said that the writing sounded, "like her to people who knew her," and took the manuscript's validity on face value, though he would not tell Martin who those people were.

But as Diehl correctly stated, if it was a copy of the *Empire News* manuscript, it was copyedited. One must flash back to 1960 and a publication Marilyn Monroe by Maurice Zolotow, written while she was still living.

Marilyn's blind date with second husband Joe DiMaggio at Villa Nova, a well-known detail that the two met there for the first time, is discussed. In the 1960 book, many details are discussed about that evening. Marilyn and Joe, both shy, barely speaking to one another, and then she driving him home. Later, their follow up date is discussed, with the two hitting the highway for burgers and coffee off of the Pacific Coast Highway one evening.

On page 139 of the 1960 book, Marilyn and Joe reportedly discussed his photographs and a dialogue between the two. As it was written:

"'The best I ever got was Ethel Barrymore and General MacArthur.' He smiled. 'You're much prettier.' Marilyn wrote, 'This admission' – that she was prettier than Douglas MacArthur or Ethel Barrymore – 'had an odd effect on me. I had read reams and reams of writing on my good looks, and scores of men had told me I was beautiful. But this was the first time my heart had jumped to hear it.'"

However, in 1974 supposedly for the first time, Marilyn's words come out. There is the recount of the dinner; with "Marilyn" claiming it was at Chasen's, not at all true. By "Marilyn's" account instead of turning in as reported in the Zolotow book and meeting for a second date, the two drove around. Then the discussion came up in the 1974 book about photographs, "for the first time," with Marilyn posing to Joe about his publicity photos.

On page 129 of *My Story* it was written: "'I imagine you must have had your picture taken doing publicity stunts like that a thousand times,' I said.

'Not quite,' Mr. DiMaggio answered. 'The best I ever got was Ethel Barrymore or General MacArthur. You're prettier.'

'That admission had an odd effect on me. I had read reams of writing about my good looks, and scores of men had told me I was beautiful. But this was the first time my heart had jumped to hear it.'"

The only commonality between Ben Hecht and Maurice Zolotow is they had both interviewed Marilyn Monroe, though author Carl Rollyson claimed the two writers were friends. However, Zolotow never thanked Hecht in his acknowledgements. But he did acknowledge the 13 articles from the *Empire News*; he said which were run from May 9 through August 1, 1954.

"Most of the direct quotations from Monroe are drawn from my conversations with her," explained Zolotow. "Quotations identified by the phrase 'she wrote are generally taken from one of the three autobiographical pieces to which she has put her name."

Zolotow cited "The Truth About Me," that Liza Wilson helped to collaborate, "Wolves I Have Known," which Florabel Muir was the "as told to" author and the Hecht pieces, and "that autobiography has never been published except in this fragmentary form."

The New York Post knocked on Rose Hecht's door one day in 1974 to discuss *My Story* as a publication that long embraced Hecht's work. They asked her if she offered a release over the materials, which she told the reporter she gave a verbal go-ahead, but refused to sign the two quitclaim forms shoved her way that would finalize the transfer of rights.

Rose Hecht heavily debated the provenance of the book. She shared her husband's copy of the manuscript, and she was upset about her deceased spouse's reputation. She was terribly upset with a passage about suicide, which she said that her husband did not write.

Even Digby claimed this differed from the *Empire News*, but was the main point, as it was not featured in the 1954 *Empire* series. The statement alleged that Marilyn told her that she was the type of girl "found dead in a hall bedroom with an empty bottle of sleeping pills in my hand."

Stein and Day did not take accusations questioning the manuscript's legitimacy lightly.

"If someone calls this a hoax," Sol Stein stated in the Judith Martin article, "they can expect a suit in the neighborhood of $2 million. A hoax is a crime, and we're not guilty."

According to Florice Whyte Kovan's article, Rose Hecht was tossed that suit from the publisher's legal department too. Whyte Kovan also claimed that Irving Stein, who helped to form Marilyn Monroe Productions and took over as Marilyn's legal counsel when Greene was her partner, vouched the book's authenticity (Delaney claimed in a letter to Inez Melson in 1965 that he no longer represented Marilyn after December 31, 1955 after the Fox contract was renegotiated. In that letter, he admitted that the only people who truly cared for Marilyn were Inez and Joe). Whyte Kovan stated that when Milton Greene learned of Rose Hecht's commentary, he was surprised and told those who advised him that he had thought Rose Hecht had died.

Not wishing to be involved in a legal tangle and rock the boat, Rose Hecht backed away.

And so there was a new voice that was claimed to be Marilyn's in the book, but authentically was not, and muscled itself into the eyes and heads of the believing public.

A June 26, 1974 story aired that the book was in fact, Ben Hecht's ghostwritten word, and that Sol Stein admitted so. Rose Hecht acquiesced after the warning of a lawsuit against her, and the news blurb noted she "apparently had a change of heart and told a newsman last week that the manuscript was that of her late husband."

Like the controversy with *TIME*, however, this book perpetuates the untrue orphan tales that Marilyn and Grace started, as well as other tawdry messes, of her days as an unloved child, incorrect details of her Joan Crawford war, inaccuracies about the first date with her beloved second husband, the death of her precious Tippy (*My Story* states Marilyn's dog Tippy was split in half by an angry neighbor with a garden hoe, though the rest of the accounts stated that the neighbor shot Tippy) and more.

Donald Spoto's Take on *My Story*

On October 5, 1991, a Liz Smith column would note that a biography was in the works by Donald Spoto that had "already accumulated $900,000 in foreign rights." Smith noted the high price was because of Spoto's cooperation with the Milton Greene estate. Greene had passed away in 1985, and Spoto was said to have access to diaries, poems, supposed suicide notes, and more then 26,000 more pages of boxes that had not seen the public light, including documents that were said to be part of "Marilyn's unwritten autobiography."

Though Smith's article inferred that Spoto would be collaborating with Greene's heirs, in the case of *My Story*, Spoto's account was not in favor of Greene's materials. Spoto described the history as "tangled," with a shift of writers between Hecht, Skolsky and a writer or writers working with Greene.

But Spoto did not note this in his commentary about Greene's potentially enlisted writers, it is also known that Amy Greene was *Glamour's* beauty editor, as well as the author of the book, *The Successful Face*, about skincare and makeup application, first published in 1985. Amy Greene was versed in makeup application, and ran her business "Beauty Checkers" in Henri Bendel's salon. She co-authored *The Successful Face* with Molly Pomerance, plus co-authored the book, *But That's Another Story: A Photographic Retrospective of Milton H. Greene*, with son Joshua Greene. Joshua Greene's biography notes that he has written 15 books before on topics including gardening, food, and home furnishings, with his contributions in photography. Mary Emmerling's *American County Cottages* is one. *Milton's Marilyn* was another book under his name in a co-author capacity.

Spoto's examination of the book noted that the first 66 pages were not composed by Hecht, and "the vocabulary and diction of *My Story* in these sections [paperwork in folder 12 at the Newberry Library in Chicago, including Rose Hecht's notes] bear scant resemblance to anything ever written by Ben Hecht." Spoto also said that other manuscripts made their way into the Hecht papers, including those from Chambrun's provenance, which presented him with a full picture to assess the differences between Hecht's drafts and the finished *My Story* project. He felt it was a collaboration started by Hecht, with additions from Skolsky, and finished off by the Greene team.

Sarah Churchwell's Study

The author who delved greatly into this topic was Sarah Churchwell in *The Many Lives of Marilyn Monroe*. She aired the cause about the 1954 version of *My Story*, with the sections that Chambrun pirated. She noted that Maurice Zolotow also borrowed from the *Empire News* story.

In Churchwell's account, she evaluated many of the biographies about Marilyn Monroe, noting plenty of them regurgitated materials, or interviewed those who had never met Marilyn but "would hitch their wagons to her star."

In analyzing *My Story*'s 1974 version, Churchwell stated that both Hecht and Skolsky were deceased after its release, with Greene, not Marilyn or her heirs as the copyright holder. She stated that the book does not indicate what Greene's connection is to Marilyn's autobiography, or who he is. However, the inner cover of the 1976 softcover offers a review from the *Cleveland Plain Dealer* describing him as "Miss Monroe's confidant and business partner."

Churchwell discussed that the vignettes in the book concluded prior to Marilyn's relationship with Greene truly commencing, ending with her Korea trip. Though Marilyn had met him briefly in the latter part of 1953, there was a minimal connection until Greene began marketing the idea of starting a company together in mid-1954.

The last line of the book reads, "This is where Marilyn's manuscript ended when she gave it to me," and was signed Milton H. Greene.

"...he is never mentioned in the text; any reader unfamiliar with the specifics of Monroe's life could be forgiven for finding Greene's relationship to Monroe – and thus to her autobiography – obscure," Churchwell iterated.

Churchwell also, like Spoto, suggested, "he [Greene] probably revised the manuscript, perhaps with the help of other writers."

Churchwell wove in author Ernest Cunningham's analysis of *My Story*, in which Cunningham stated that Greene "threatened legal action against anyone who questioned the book's authenticity. Additions have been made to the 1954 version, to make it sound tragically prophetic," referring to the statement from "Marilyn" about the bottle of the pills in her hand.

In her account, Churchwell noted without reading Spoto, it would be difficult for anyone to doubt that Marilyn did not write the *My Story* that Milton Greene and later Joshua Greene copyrighted. She said other authors have accepted *My Story* as gospel. Among them were Gloria Steinem and Anthony Summers, though Summers only followed the *My Story* train though he considered the stories doubtful, it was then a source of information about her youth.

It was Norman Mailer who challenged Hecht and Marilyn the most as fairy tellers, but as Churchwell aptly noted, Mailer has been challenged for his misstatements about Marilyn in his book. Later, Mailer would also pen a book with Greene, *Of Women and Their Elegance*, and heavily used Greene's photos in his book Marilyn.

Following the publication of Churchwell's book, Lois Banner admitted in her book *Marilyn: The Passion and the Paradox*, that among her sources she had used "Marilyn's autobiography, published in 1974 as *My Story*."

Churchwell best sums up *My Story* as "likely composed of omissions and half-truths, created through dictation, collaboration, ghostwriting, ventriloquizing, and invisible editing, a narrative in which fact and fiction are often indistinguishable; and it is interpreted very differently through the lenses of varying sexual and textual attitudes. It is undoubtedly a fictionalized account."

Yet, Churchwell does correctly see through the looking glass that Marilyn's story in *My Story* was a tale recycled and aggrandized over time, like the game of telephone when myths continue to snowball as they make their way down the line, into the point of becoming something so skewed from the authentic truth.

These are the mistruths that have driven Marilyn's story, and kept the myth of the unwanted orphan alive for nearly seven decades. It is these fallacies as well that have carried on the saga that she died with a bottle of sleeping pills in her hand, or was assassinated by a sinister government force, with people coming out of the woodwork that they were Marilyn's confidants or executioners, cashing in on her legacy for money or fame, with the ideas that they knew who was responsible for her death or that they were the ones who murdered her.

Churchwell wrote, "This tendency to repeat what we already believe, to deny what we don't want to accept, will characterize the myth of Marilyn Monroe from beginning to end."

CONCLUSION

MARILYN MONROE'S STORY is the substance that Hollywood dreams are made of. A young woman who triumphed her way to the top, challenging obstacles along the way to become not only the star of the 20th Century but someone who has become revered in the 21st Century. Many young people have modeled themselves after her, believing they could achieve the type of heights that she did, as an unwanted and unloved orphan child who became a goddess of Hollywood success. Some of them have actually been thrilled that they had rough beginnings themselves in life, feeling that their lives paralleled Marilyn's, thinking that they experienced the same as Marilyn did in childhood, and shared a kinship with her.

But like Hollywood, the story is a figment of one's imagination. Her legend was built on the backs of those family members and friends that the press spun as abusers, while the true emotional abusers meaning her psychiatrists and acting coach and photographer, ran off with her entire fortune. Her family and close friends were demonized using the full extent of a Hollywood media propaganda machine.

And as those individuals did in life to Marilyn, the likes of Lee Strasberg and her Freudian doctors took advantage of her in death as well. Lee Strasberg hijacked her right of publicity. As Marilyn's will was tied up in probate for many years, his widow Anna Strasberg, continued to claim ownership following Lee's death. Marilyn's estate was willed exclusively to Anna by Lee. Anna Strasberg maximized the marketing of Marilyn Monroe, reigniting, what was already being done while Marilyn was alive: selling her name and image as a commodity. However, this round had Anna Strasberg charging extravagant licensing fees to vendors although she was not legally entitled to do so. Since 2007, Anna Strasberg has been judicially estopped several times in courts of law for her overzealous claims that she owns the right to Marilyn's name.

Anna Strasberg even sold a percentage of Marilyn's right of publicity to Authentic Brands Group and they are using trademark law to continue the deception. At times they attempted to have Facebook tribute pages created by Marilyn fans deleted. And they continue to promote that they own Marilyn's right of publicity on their website to intimidate others who try to exercise the fact that Marilyn died WITHOUT the right of publicity.

For Lee Strasberg, while he was living, he had a superstar actress to claim he created to further his theater and acting theorist ambitions; and in this case, he claimed to literally "own" Marilyn Monroe – her name, voice, image, and legacy.

And behind-the-scenes, the Anna Freud Center continues to pursue its permanent psychiatric cure using Marilyn's money.

They all continue to use Marilyn's name to promote their own financial success.

While we believe there should be a return of all of Marilyn's assets to her half-sister and niece, the truth of the matter is Marilyn's name does not belong to anyone. In fact, legally she is in the public domain, so in essence, she left this earth belonging to no one. Unfortunately, she is such a commodity to that company and those associated with her financial extortion and murder, that they continue to aggressively claim legality over her legacy. Today, the heirs of those that took her life and legacy still continue to benefit from that legacy and the loss of her life by the hand of Dr. Ralph (Romi) Greenson.

Marilyn Monroe Unveiled | A Family History

Marilyn's family and genuine friends from her past were hurt by the accusations that were made about them. Grace Goddard was one of the manufacturers in charge of the Marilyn fable, as she understood its necessity of some of the exaggerations to help rocket Marilyn to fame.

But people were emotionally injured and family and friends over the years upset by the tales as they became worse.

The reporting of Marilyn's ancestry was figuratively schizophrenic because it strays so far from the truth, and the reality is Marilyn's family was no different than any other American family. There were wealthy members, there were impoverished members, and there were those in between. However, the details of her childhood were heavily exaggerated and dramatized as bleak for effect. The darkness only intensified the strength of the "Cinderella Story."

While Marilyn was trying to become the next "baby star," and Hollywood was literally creating Cinderellas, her story likely would not have held the same power to attract the fan base if she told the public that her great-grandfather Tilford Marion Hogan was a prominent businessman, community leader, and farmer in Laclede Missouri. Or that, Tilford's uncle and cousins (The Honorable O.P. Hogan and Dr. O.P. Hogan Jr. and brothers) were prominent judges, lawyers, and politicians in Kentucky. Or that, her cousin Ethel Hogan was a pioneer in USC basketball. She also was a star who was known to the public. Or that, her cousin Milton Stores Andros worked many years in the film industry as a set designer and plaster artist. Or that, her great aunt Dora Graham fought a highly dramatized and public child abduction case before she was born. And that her cousin Georgie Andros lived with her father's sister in the Anson-Brooks Mansion while growing up. Or that, her cousin Marie Transue attended UCLA at the same time she was just starting out as a pinup model in Hollywood. Or that, her cousin Dr. Newton Hogan Copp MD practiced Medicine right in Hollywood on Beverly Hills Boulevard at the same time she was at the height of her fame.

All of these relatives and much more were alive and well living in Los Angeles, and other areas out of state while Marilyn was a child and while she making her own headlines in Hollywood. And they all had robust families.

In fact, Marilyn could never claim that she did not know about any of her relatives. She went to Aunt Dora Graham's (aka Dora Hogan, Dora Andros, Dora Bruce, Dora Schulties) house in Portland Oregon in 1945 with photographer Andre De Dienes while her mother was living there with Dora. And of course, Dora knew all of the relatives. She certainly knew about her father Tilford. She knew about her father's brother Newton (which was her uncle) and children living in Los Angeles for many years. She knew about her brother William Marion Hogan living in Los Angeles and then moving to San Bernardino. There is no doubt that her mother Gladys knew, as did, Grace McKee Goddard, who was Gladys's close friend since at least 1923 or earlier. Remember also that Marilyn's great-grandmother Virginia Nance passed away in 1927 in Los Angeles just months after her daughter Della passed away. Her son William Marion Nance (Hogan) was also living in Hawthorne, as were Gladys and Marion. And they all were certainly family. In fact, it can be concluded that the reason Virginia was in Los Angeles was because her daughter Della was ill.

All of these relatives definitely paint a different picture than what has been reported by over fifty years of so called biographers writing fantasy to fit an orphan story.

In other words, Marilyn Monroe's story would certainly have lost appeal as the little orphan lamb lost in the woods if she had told the public that she had doctors, lawyers, politicians, building contractors, and wealthy relatives in her family tree, though the publicity about them would completely ruin a handcrafted story of a little girl's rise from rags to riches.

Norma Jeane was never an orphan and she would have never been adopted as a child. While we do not know every detail of her life in Los Angeles and living with Grace McKee Goddard, the evidence is overwhelming that Norma Jeane's formative years in Los Angeles, as reported in the fable of the "Little Orphan Annie in Hollywood Story," were nothing more than gross exaggerations and outright lies by Marilyn herself, the fan magazines (including *Time* magazine) and many so called biographers who continued to support that fable for their own profit. Ezra Goodman knew Marilyn Monroe was exaggerating her life story with less than two months of research in 1956.

Marilyn Monroe Unveiled | A Family History

Some readers may ask why Marilyn spent time in an orphanage with all of these prominent relatives around. Most pointedly, many family members and some of Gladys's friends offered to take Norma Jeane when they knew Gladys was going through difficulties. Gladys refused their offers. While she was hospitalized, it is known that friends expressed to Grace Goddard the desire to take Norma Jeane. Again, Gladys also turned down these suggestions. All along, even when she was adjudged "insane" by the court system, Gladys NEVER lost or gave up her parental rights. That – is a critical point in understanding the entire situation. Norma Jeane was required to spend time in the orphanage as part of the "holding pattern" for transferring guardianship, regardless if a relative took her or not. That was a requirement by the state of California. But another issue was that Grace lied and told the courts no relatives were in the Los Angeles area in order to further Gladys's wishes. Yet relatives were everywhere in that area, including the man who was legally Marilyn's father. Both Grace McKee Goddard and Gladys Monroe took responsibility of Norma Jeane's care as a child. And they both never shirked that responsibility; Norma Jeane was always well cared for as a child.

Earlier in this book we stated that, "in the following chapters it is hoped that the reader will understand that Marilyn Monroe's family story checks out better than Marilyn's orphan stories." And if, "Marilyn Monroe's family story does not fit the "Little Orphan Annie in Hollywood" story, then it is time for the public to stand behind MarilynMonroeFamily.com and help us take back Marilyn Monroe's history and legacy from the sycophants and suckerfish who murdered her and financially extorted her estate."

Have we made our case?

As exposed by Douglas Kirsner PhD, a Professor at Deakin University in Australia, Anna Freud and Dr. Ralph (Romi) Greenson admitted that they were manipulating patients for money and abusing psychological transferences with those patients.

Lee Strasberg and his family bragged that he was working directly with psychotherapists as part of his Method acting.

Milton Greene, Lee Strasberg, and Arthur Miller were publically caught protecting themselves from the implication that they all were unduly influencing Marilyn in an article that was designed to counter rumors that were undoubtedly true.

Dr. Ralph Greenson and Dr. Margaret Hohenberg both admitted that they both were actively "treating" Marilyn in the months before her death and, in fact, collected monies from Marilyn's Estate after her death. Dr. Ralph Greenson saw Marilyn twenty-two days in the month of July, 1962, which had thirty-one days in total for that month. He then saw her every day of early August 1962 until the day of her death which was officially recorded on the 5th.

There was no one to ensure that Dr. Greenson was treating Marilyn ethically. Dr. Robert E. Litman, who led the original psychological investigating team into Marilyn's death was a colleague of Dr. Greenson, which was a major conflict of interest. Those involved in that team gave Dr. Greenson a complete pass and did nothing to question his techniques which went against his own standards, which he wrote about in his own book on the subject. Dr. Greenson was not treating Marilyn, he was manipulating her to make her more dependent on him and his family. In fact, on August 7, 1962, the *Pottstown Mercury* newpaper in Pennsylvania reported that Litman's team would assess Marilyn's troubled childhood, her broken marriages, her history of mental illness in the family, including her mother and maternal grandparents. Why? The parties were interested in the fable because it supported their agenda. All the while, Paula Strasberg, her daughter Susan Strasberg, and Lee Strasberg all knew about Ezra Goodman's research in 1956. And seven years of so called therapy did nothing but create mental problems where there were none. Lee Strasberg could not even inform the public that Marilyn's relatives were sitting in front of him as he read the eulogy he wrote when she died in 1962. Strasberg and the Freudians had their agenda and that agenda was to own Marilyn Monroe and separate her from family and relatives. And they did exactly that...

They manipulated the public's perceptions from day one, and not even Marilyn's closest relatives seriously caught on to that manipulation until right after Marilyn died. Today the estate holders continue to deny that Marilyn had any relatives while they continue to market Marilyn to the world.

Marilyn Monroe Unveiled | A Family History

Soon after Marilyn's death, Dr. Ralph Greenson reported to Dr. Marianne Kris by letter that he had an argument with Marilyn the very night she died. He also reported to Dr. Marianne Kris by letter, that he asked Eunice Murray to stay that night (a night which she did not normally stay). Additionally, he knew Eunice was going on vacation to Europe on Monday the 6th.

Dr. Ralph Greenson also told a reporter that he could not tell the entire story of what happened to Marilyn the night she died in a tape recorded confession over the phone. This confession countered the official Los Angeles County Police report. Yet, the Los Angeles Police Department failed to investigate when that recording became public.

The newspapers and Milton Greene himself boldly bragged that he was going to profit from his "new" Marilyn idea. He did just that by owning 100 percent of the pictures he took while under the umbrella of Marilyn's company. Legally he should have owned only 49.6 percent. Furthermore, Arthur Miller never challenged the ownership of those pictures that Milton Greene ended up having in his possesion after the break-up of Marilyn Monroe Productions, even though his personal lawyers were acting as Marilyn's legal counsel. All the while, newspapers reported as early as 1955 that Marilyn's pictures were a goldmine. Why would Marilyn give up 50.4 percent of those pictures?

Lee Strasberg, Dr. Margaret Hohenberg, Arthur Miller, and Milton Greene told Marilyn Monroe what they wanted from her in 1955 while under duress. Marilyn wrote it down and described in layman's terms what they did to her. They got exactly what they wanted! Not in one will, but in two different wills that would oddly be slanted in their favor while Marilyn's sister Berniece and her niece received nothing or relatively nothing in both wills. Milton Greene's wife Amy Greene admitted that they <u>cocooned</u> Marilyn Monroe.

Lee Strasberg wanted his theater and Dr. Margaret Hohenberg, Dr. Marianne Kris, Dr. Ralph Greenson, and Anna Freud all wanted a permanent psychiatric cure. Marilyn died and they all got what they wanted.

MarilynMonroeFamily.com is calling for the immediate cease and desist of all relations with Marilyn Monroe by The Anna Freud Centre, The Lee Strasberg Theatre and Film Institute, and Archives, LLC. We are calling for the unequivocal release of "Marilyn Monroe's estate" including all copyrights, trademarks, and all photographs taken of Marilyn by Milton Greene (while under the umbrella of Marilyn Monroe Productions), and all assets to be returned to Marilyn's rightful heirs — Berniece and Mona Miracle. We accuse the Anna Freud Centre, Lee Strasberg, and Archives, LLC of major ethical and criminal violations.

We want justice for Norma Jeane!

It is time for Norma Jeane to come home...

The character Marilyn Monroe was a Hollywood creation. Although talented and beautiful, her persona of the little girl who propelled her way to success from the ashes, would not have been possible without the Cinderella story in place. Norma Jeane Mortenson had a few points in her life that those who exploited her blew out of proportion to make her life tale even more compelling. In the process, Norma Jeane Mortensen became lost within Marilyn Monroe. However, one would see occasional glimmers of her hiding behind the glitz and glamour, as well as the private Marilyn that the public did not and still does not see. But the character that Marilyn created of herself turned out to be legendary, and talked about more than a half a century after her death.

Help us bring Marilyn back to life. Help us bring Marilyn home. We want to have her death certificate changed to murder. And we want to challenge the parties whose founders clearly broke their own ethical creeds. We want history to acknowledge that Norma Jeane Mortenson had many relatives that still care today.

We love you Norma Jeane! Wink, Wink!

<u>Marilyn Monroe Unveiled | A Family History</u>
Photo Sources and Acknowledgments

- Page: 100

Description: English: *Gentlemen Prefer Blondes*, the 1953 20th Century Fox movie is a musical comedy/romance directed by Howard Hawks starring Jane Russell and Marilyn Monroe, with Charles Coburn, Elliott Reid, Tommy Noonan, Taylor Holmes, and Norma Varden. This image shows Monroe in a pink dress surrounded by men in formal attire, 1953, Source: This is a screenshot from a trailer from 20th Century Fox. This work is in the public domain because it was published in the United States between 1923 and 1977 and without a copyright notice.

- Page: 139

Latest methods in man's ancient occupation -- ploughing on a prairie farm, Illinois, by Underwood & Underwood Original source: Robert N. Dennis collection of stereoscopic views. / United States. / States / Illinois. Stereoscopic views of western Illinois. (Approx. 72,000 stereoscopic views : 10 x 18 cm. or smaller.) This image is in the public domain because it is a mere mechanical scan or photocopy of a public domain original, or – from the available evidence – is so similar to such a scan or photocopy that no copyright protection can be expected to arise. The original itself is in public domain for the following reason: This media file is in the public domain in the United States. This applies to U.S. works where the copyright has expired, often because its first publication occurred prior to January 1, 1923.

- Page: 145

Description: Photo of Marilyn Monroe-appears to have been one of her first modeling jobs in the film industry, June 11, 1947, Photo by Dave Cicero-International News Service, Permission (Reusing this file), Pre-1978, no mark.

- Page: 159

The Miriam and Ira D. Wallach Division of Art, Prints and Photographs: Print Collection, The New York Public Library. "Escape of Rev. Thomas Andros, from the old Jersey prison ship, during the Revolutionary War" The New York Public Library Digital Collections. http://digitalcollections.nypl.org/items/510d47da-26e9-a3d9-e040-e00a18064a99

- Page 190

Randen Pederson: Field of Fire, Taken on July 8, 2014. No changes made. Free to use. https://www.flickr.com/photos/chefranden/15094030373/

- Page: 304

Description: Marilyn Monroe, 1962
Source: http://i895.photobucket.com/albums/ac154/inspiremehappy2/100117am6.jpg
AuthorGeorge Barris, This work is in the public domain because it was published in the United States between 1923 and 1963 and although there may or may not have been a copyright notice, the copyright was not renewed.

- Page: 309

Boston Public Library Follow Wilshire Blvd., looking though Westlake Park, Los Angeles, California. File name: 06_10_009727, Title: Wilshire Blvd., looking though Westlake Park, Los Angeles, Calif. Date issued: 1930 - 1945 (approximate), Physical description: 1 print (postcard) : linen texture, color

Marilyn Monroe Unveiled | A Family History

; 3 1/2 x 5 1/2 in., Genre: Postcards, Subject: Parks; Cities & towns, Notes: Title from item.Collection: The Tichnor Brothers Collection
Location: Boston Public Library, Print Department, Rights: No known restrictions
https://www.flickr.com/photos/boston_public_library/7631097872

- Page: 310

Greetings from Los Angeles, California. File name: 06_10_009688, Title: Greetings from Los Angeles, California, Date issued: 1930 - 1945 (approximate), Physical description: 1 print (postcard) : linen texture, color ; 3 1/2 x 5 1/2 in., Genre: Postcards, Notes: Title from item., Collection: The Tichnor Brothers Collection, Location: Boston Public Library, Print Department, Rights: No known restrictions, https://www.flickr.com/photos/boston_public_library/7631088240/

- Page: 323

Description: U.S. army - June 26, 1945 *YANK* magazine photo (colorized version) of Marilyn Monroe as Norma Jeane Dougherty, 1945-06-26, Source: *Yank, the Army Weekly*, Author   U.S.   army photographer David Conover's shot: This image is a work of a U.S. Army soldier or employee, taken or made as part of that person's official duties. As a work of the U.S. federal government, the image is in the public domain.

- Page: 346

Description: Marilyn Monroe in 1961, May 1961, Source *TV-Radio Mirror* page 25, Author Macfadden Publications page 1, Permission (Reusing this file), Copyright not renewed.

- Page: Various

Description: Photo of Marilyn Monroe in *The Asphalt Jungle* from the May 1961 issue of *TV-Radio Mirror*,
May 1961, Source: page 20, Author Macfadden Publications New York, publisher of *TV-Radio Mirror* Permission (Reusing this file), Copyright not renewed.

- Cover Photo: Taken on February 4, 200 Konstantin Kleine-Niermann, negative texture
for texture layer use, texture was altered, free to: Share — copy and redistribute the material in any medium or format. Adapt — remix, transform, and build upon the material for any purpose, even commercially. The licensor cannot revoke these freedoms as long as you follow the license terms.
http://farm3.static.flickr.com/2303/2242484856_b3cbdf94fc_o.jpg

- We are grateful for family photos and documents that relatives provided for this book.

Marilyn Monroe Unveiled | A Family History

Author Biographies

Photo taken August 4, 2012 in Canter's, Los Angeles, one of Marilyn's favorite restaurants. The authors met around the 50th Anniversary of Marilyn's death (she died August 4, 1962) and began working together online in 2012.

They were married in July 2015.

Jason Edward Kennedy

Jason Edward Kennedy is Marilyn Monroe's second cousin once removed (his grandmother Rebecca Esther (Hogan) Fritz was Gladys Monroe's first cousin). Getting the word out about Marilyn and investigating into the Cinderella myths holds a great importance to him because the cast of characters (and descendents of theirs) in Marilyn's financial extortion and murder continue to perpetuate the myths that keep Marilyn's legacy in their corner for their own profit.

Jason was featured in the November 3, 2014 issue of **CLOSER Weekly** Magazine:

"Marilyn's Hidden Diary Reveals: It Wasn't Suicide
EXCLUSIVE: Marilyn Monroe's Friends and Family Talk About Her Mysterious and Tragic Death"

Jason also served honorably for four years in the United States Navy as an Aircraft Electrician and Helicopter Plane Captain. He holds a Bachelor's Degree in Cultural Anthropology from the University of California, Santa Barbara. He also graduated from the Prehospital Care program at the David Geffen School of Medicine at UCLA - Emergency Medical Technician.

Jennifer Jean Miller

Jennifer Jean Miller has held a love of writing since childhood and turned it into her career almost a decade ago, starting off as a content writer. She is an investigative reporter, known for her compelling, in-depth and objective features, with a quest to not leave stones unturned. Jennifer was awarded the Media and Entertainment Award from the New Jersey Governor's Council for Mental Health Stigma in 2010 for objective and sensitive reporting on mental health issues. Jennifer runs the news site InsideScene.com and has worked for news outlets including Straus News and Reuters (with Reuters she was the State Director for New Jersey for the Reuters/Ipsos Election Reporting Program). As an Investigative Reporter, she was interviewed for an Oxygen Network episode of *Snapped: Killer Couples*. Jennifer has been also interviewed about Marilyn Monroe, appearing on segment on German TV, and also for the upcoming documentary *What Ever Happened to Norma Jeane?* She has already penned two books, *Marilyn Monroe & Joe DiMaggio – Love In Japan, Korea & Beyond*, as well as Arcadia Publishing's Images of America Book, *Stanhope and Byram*. As a lifetime admirer of Marilyn Monroe's, sharing the truth about her life and death have both been paramount to her.

Jennifer holds a Bachelor's Degree from the State University of New York at Cortland in French Secondary Education with a minor in Political Science. She also studied at the University of Neuchâtel in Switzerland.

Other Publications Coming Soon From Jason Edward Kennedy And Jennifer Jean Miller

Marilyn Monroe Unveiled: A Family History Companion Guide

Surgeon Story: Means, Motive, Murder

www.MarilynMonroeFamily.com